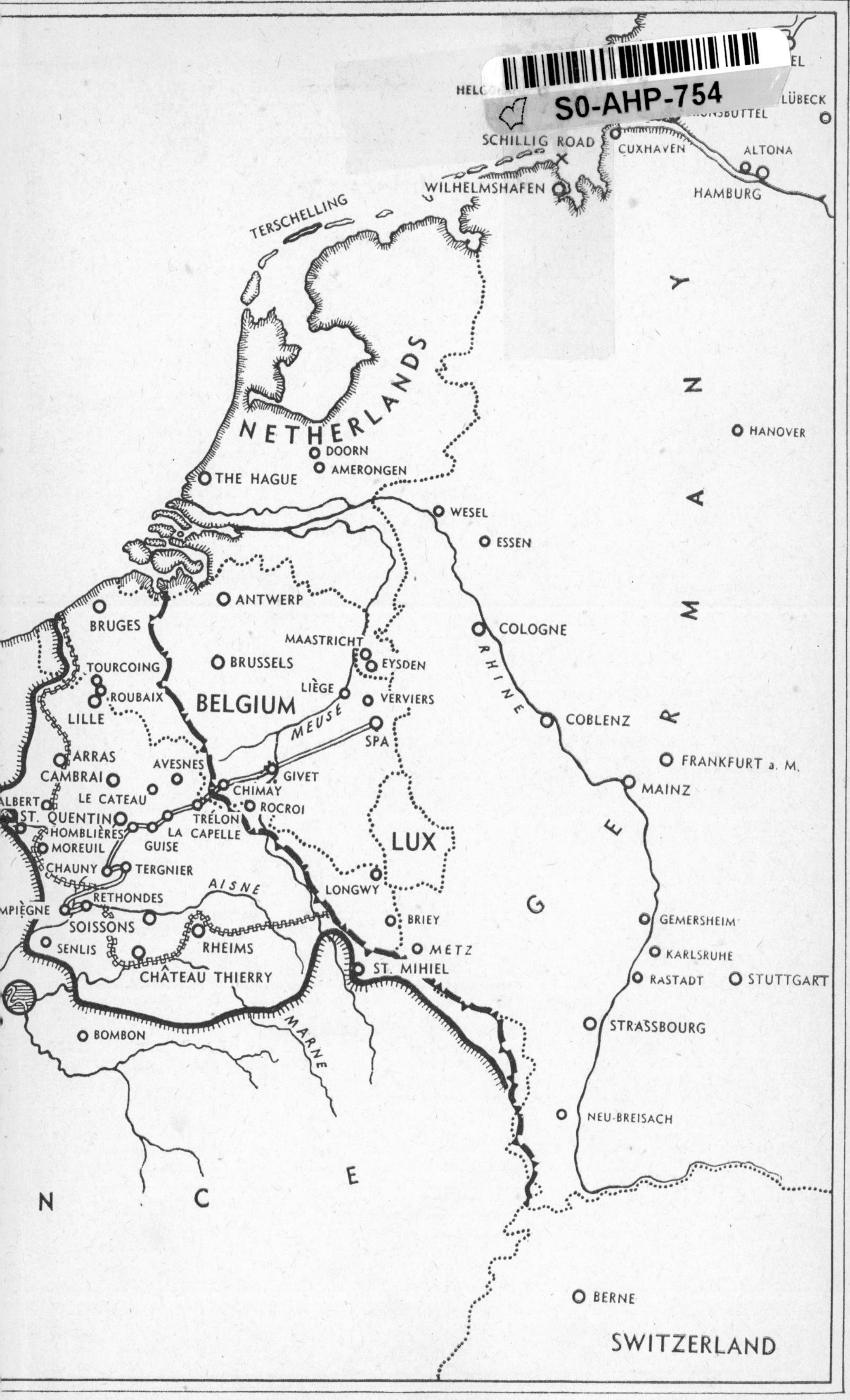

LÜBECK
SCHILLIG ROAD
CUXHAVEN
ALTONA
WILHELMSHAFEN
HAMBURG
TERSCHELLING
NETHERLANDS
DOORN
AMERONGEN
THE HAGUE
WESEL
ESSEN
HANOVER
G E R M A N Y
ANTWERP
BRUGES
COLOGNE
MAASTRICHT
EYSDEN
BRUSSELS
TOURCOING
ROUBAIX
LIÈGE
VERVIERS
BELGIUM
LILLE
MEUSE
SPA
RHINE
COBLENZ
FRANKFURT a. M.
ARRAS
AVESNES
CAMBRAI
GIVET
MAINZ
LE CATEAU
CHIMAY
ALBERT
ST. QUENTIN
TRÉLON
ROCROI
HOMBLIÈRES
LA CAPELLE
MOREUIL
GUISE
LUX
CHAUNY
TERGNIER
LONGWY
AISNE
RETHONDES
SOISSONS
BRIEY
GEMERSHEIM
SENLIS
RHEIMS
METZ
KARLSRUHE
ST. MIHIEL
CHÂTEAU THIERRY
RASTADT
STUTTGART
STRASSBOURG
BOMBON
MARNE
NEU-BREISACH
N C E
BERNE
SWITZERLAND

ARMISTICE 1918

BY

HARRY R. RUDIN

ASSOCIATE PROFESSOR OF HISTORY
AND FELLOW OF PIERSON COLLEGE
IN YALE UNIVERSITY

NEW HAVEN
YALE UNIVERSITY PRESS
1944

Printed in the United States of America

TO

ANDY
HARRY
ANN

Foreword

THIS book is what the title suggests—the story of the armistice signed by the Entente Powers and Germany in 1918. It seeks to tell why the Germans wanted an armistice, how the Allies went about drafting one, and how the two armistice delegations came to final agreement in the forest of Compiègne. The story touches on many controversial questions, with biased sources making it difficult to discover what actually took place. I do not regard this study as putting an end to controversy. I hope, however, that I have thrown some light on the "stab-in-the-back" legend; that I have shown that no person was more responsible than Ludendorff for stabbing the Army in the back; that the appointment of the Armistice Commission was a civilian affair; that the revolution was not a front for the Army Command or the Kaiser; that those who came into power in Germany in October, 1918, sincerely desired a peace based on the Fourteen Points; that Wilson's program saved the Germans from an unconditional surrender and had the effect of speeding the end of the war and of giving a provisional German Government a platform to stand on in a difficult transition period; that coöperation between allies is always a matter of profound difficulty; that democracies face hazards peculiar to their structure in the diplomacy necessary for the conduct and the conclusion of war. I have purposely avoided discussing what might or should have been done in the place of what was done.

Controversy was not the only factor making it hard to tell this story. The quantities of material are enormous—books, memoirs, newspapers, magazines, documents, etc. I wish to express my gratitude to those who have assisted me in the Sterling Memorial Library at Yale, the New York Public Library, the Library of Congress, the John Crerar Library, and the University of Chicago Library.

I should like to express my gratitude to the following publishers for permission granted to reprint material taken from their copyrighted books:

Doubleday, Doran & Company, Inc., for material from R. S. Baker, *Woodrow Wilson*, Volume VIII (New York, 1939), and from D. F. Houston, *Eight Years with Wilson's Cabinet* (copyright, 1926, by Doubleday, Page & Company).

J. B. Lippincott Company, and General John J. Pershing for material reprinted from Pershing, *My Experiences in the World War*, Volume II (New York, 1931).

J. B. Lippincott Company, and the Estate of Edward N. Hurley, for an extensive quotation from E. N. Hurley, *The Bridge to France* (Philadelphia, 1927).

Oxford University Press, for passages from Colonel T. Bentley Mott, *Twenty Years as Military Attaché* (New York, 1937).

Houghton Mifflin Company, for material from Charles Seymour, *The Intimate Papers of Colonel House*, Volume IV (Boston, 1928), and from *The Letters of Franklin K. Lane* (Boston, 1922).

Stanford University Press, for material from Ralph H. Lutz, *Fall of the German Empire* (two volumes, 1932).

Charles Scribner's Sons, for material from the *Memoirs of the Crown Prince of Germany* (New York, 1922); from *Selections from the Correspondence of Theodore Roosevelt and Henry Cabot Lodge, 1884–1918* (two volumes, New York, 1925); from Major-General Sir C. E. Callwell, *Field-Marshal Sir Henry Wilson* (two volumes, New York, 1927).

Dodd, Mead & Company, Inc., for material from two books by Frederick Palmer, *Bliss, Peacemaker* (New York, 1934) and *Newton D. Baker* (New York, 1932).

The Publishers of the *American Journal of International Law* for material from General Tasker H. Bliss, "The Armistices," Volume XVI (1922).

I wish it were possible for me to list by name all those who have assisted in the preparation of this study—from the one who first suggested a book on the Armistice of 1918 to those who have helped me with criticism, proofreading, and indexing. There are some whose assistance I would gratefully acknowledge: two former students, Antony Barker, Yale '40, for help in the collection of materials, and Anthony C. Davidonis, Yale '38, for informing me of Memorandum No. 65 in Appendix F; Professor Leonard W. Labaree, Chairman of the History Department of Yale, for enabling me to get some relief from teaching that I might hasten the collection of materials; Professor Samuel F. Bemis for helpful criticism of the manuscript and for other friendly assistance; Professor Arnold Wolfers of Pierson College for reading and criticizing this study in manuscript; President Charles Seymour of

Yale University for friendly interest, helpful criticism, and permission to use the papers in the Yale House Collection; Mr. Henry S. Kelly for the map. Members of the Yale University Press staff deserve special mention: Miss Ella Holliday, and Eugene Davidson, and particularly Miss Roberta Yerkes for her painstaking and constructive editing of the manuscript in both style and content.

Yale University, 1944. H. R. R.

Contents

I

Ludendorff Finds Victory Doubtful

IT had been the original plan of the German General Staff in 1914 to defeat France quickly in the west while holding off the Russians in the east. But it did not turn out that way. The fighting in the west ended in the indecisive stalemate of trench warfare. Victory here had to be postponed to a more favorable occasion while attention turned to the eastern front, where the prospects of ultimate victory in the war brightened considerably for the Germans after the overthrow of the Tsarist regime in March, 1917. The complete elimination of Russia did not come, however, until Lenin and his Bolshevist supporters achieved power in November, 1917, by their promises of bread and peace to the war-weary Russians. Lenin had been in Switzerland, where he had issued pronunciamentos against the imperialist war and against the Socialists who had violated the resolutions of the International Socialist congresses and thus brought about the collapse of the Second International. He saw in the war an opportunity for the proletariat to triumph over bourgeois capitalism; but he could not participate in that ultimate struggle until Ludendorff cynically permitted him to cross Germany into Russia. There he achieved by revolutionary tactics what the Germans had not been able to accomplish by military strategy. Having come to power in Russia, Lenin discovered the secret treaties that the Entente Powers had made during the course of the war, which confirmed his doctrinaire views about the imperialist nature of the war. He called on Russia's allies to state other war aims if Russia were to stay in the war. His demand was ignored; so he proceeded to arrange an armistice with Germany and to initiate negotiations for a separate peace at Brest-Litovsk.

Partly to prevent this separate agreement between Germany and Russia, President Wilson proclaimed to the world on January 8, 1918, his Fourteen Points, a program that went far to meet the demands of war-weary peoples everywhere for a peace of reconciliation and understanding, a peace that would bar unreasonable indemnities and extensive annexations, that would put an end to secret diplomacy and give the world an organization for the peaceful adjudication of differences between nations. The program was not an *ad hoc* device invented for the sole purpose of preventing the separate peace negotiations between Russia and Germany; in the mind of the American President it was a positive and constructive solution to many of Europe's age-old problems. In so far as it did not prevent the conclusion of the ruthless peace of Brest-Litovsk, Wilson's program was a failure; it was destined, however, for a larger role, that of bringing the war to an end on all fronts and of serving as the foundation of the world's future peace. Although the proclamation of the Fourteen Points was timed to save Russia and her allies from the consequences of a German victory, their historic importance was to be that of saving Germany from the consequences of unconditional surrender to those very allies.

With the eastern front more or less quiet after the Treaty of Brest-Litovsk, Germany was free to devote her attention to the defeat of France in the west, the unfinished business of 1914. But conditions in 1918 were far different from those at the beginning of the war. The Germans had had enough of war, and so had the English and the French; but American troops by hundreds of thousands were taking their place in the line and steadily adding to the strength of the Allied Armies in the west. To throw everything against the western front and to defeat the English and French before American help became decisive was Germany's only military policy. It was a gamble, with some Germans saying that it could not be done. But soldiers have to gamble. Despite the difficulties in the way, the decision was made; and on March 21 the German war machine was set in motion against Allied defenses in the west. The war of position had become once more a war of movement. Great gains were made as place after place was taken. Hopes rose high and many Germans began to feel that the chief difficulties of the war were almost over.[1]

This optimism was not shared by members of the German High Command. For them the military progress had been too costly and too slow. At the beginning of May Colonel Haeften, who represented Army Headquarters at the Foreign Office in Berlin, discussed the general political, military, and economic situation with members of the Foreign Office. It was his view that diplomacy would have to come to the aid of the military to bring the war to an end. He suggested that the Foreign Secretary, von Kühlmann,

1. *Die Ursachen des Deutschen Zusammenbruches im Jahre 1918* [Das Werk des Untersuchungsausschusses der Deutschen Verfassunggebenden Nationalversammlung und des Deutschen Reichstages, 1919–1929. Vierte Reihe. 12 vol., Berlin, 1925–1930.] II, 185. Referred to hereafter as *Ursachen.*

get in touch with the First Quartermaster General, von Ludendorff, to see what diplomatic moves should be attempted. The Foreign Secretary's attitude was decidedly cool; he referred to past personal differences with Ludendorff and said that talk of peace with the General would be a waste of time, particularly if the High Command continued in its refusal to give any assurances regarding Belgium's future independence. The answer displeased Haeften; Ludendorff, he said, would not block any energetic move for peace. In that case, countered the Foreign Secretary, Ludendorff should come directly to him. And there the matter was to stand, for Ludendorff never appeared.[2]

The military situation failed to improve. In the middle of May Ludendorff informed Haeften at Army Headquarters that only the addition of two hundred thousand good men to the Army could bring about a victory. He said he had informed both the Imperial Chancellor, Hertling, and the Minister of War of the grave situation. Haeften was deeply moved. "These utterances of General Ludendorff," he wrote, "made me see clearly the pressing need for ending the war as soon as possible; it was certain that the war could no longer be decided by military measures alone; political and diplomatic support was also needed." [3]

These pessimistic views had their confirmation elsewhere. On the first day of June Rupprecht, Crown Prince of Bavaria, Commander of the German Armies in Belgium, wrote a strong letter to Chancellor Hertling, saying that the German Armies could give the enemy only a powerful blow or two before bogging down again in a war of position. With the increasing aid from America becoming effective, the manpower factor favored the enemy. He said that Ludendorff knew that a decisive victory was no longer to be won but was unreasonably relying on one of the Western Powers collapsing as Russia had. Although he had favored Belgium's annexation to Germany in the past, Rupprecht said he was now convinced "that the only way to bring peace is to declare our desire to maintain the independence of Belgium inviolate." The prospect of prolonging the war troubled him. "If we have to fight through another winter the effect will be damaging on the morale of the troops, who in general hope that the war will be over in the fall. I should not have written this, did I not believe that haste is necessary and that every week is costly. . . ." [4]

2. *Ibid.*, p. 188.
3. *Ibid.*, p. 189.
4. Hertling, *Ein Jahr in der Reichskanzlei* (Freiburg, 1919), pp. 140–141; *Ursachen*, II, 191–192.

Rupprecht wanted to confer with Chancellor Hertling on the matter at Brussels. The Chancellor replied on June 5, postponing any serious consideration of the proposal by saying he would talk the matter over in July. Actually he was still hopeful as to the military outcome of the war. "A succession of blows destroying the military might of France and of England," he wrote, "would finally result in a powerful popular movement directed against those Governments, a movement that, taken together with the existing and increasing pacifist tendencies in both countries, would lead to the opening of peace negotiations, particularly when it was fully realized that hopes built on the promise of American help were not to be fulfilled very soon." He promised, nonetheless, to seize the opportune time for serious peace negotiations.[5]

Thus neither the Chancellor nor the Foreign Secretary saw any reason for acting diplomatically to end the war.

Colonel Haeften was impressed by the situation even if the civilians in the Government were not. After some study and consultation he drafted on June 3 a scheme for a diplomatic offensive that might assist the military in achieving victory. The move was not to be a request for peace; that would weaken morale at home. It was meant to weaken the enemy's will to fight. Under the Government's well-concealed sponsorship peace demonstrations were to be encouraged in Germany to create abroad the impression that the Germans were sick of the war. Talks, interviews, newspaper articles, pamphlets, and demonstrations would make the rest of the world think that powerful German groups were working for a peace of understanding, that at Brest-Litovsk Germany had sought the independence of border states and the protection of peoples and of moral values threatened by Bolshevism, that German war aims included such high goals as freedom of the seas and the protection of the laboring man in all countries, that Belgium's future would be such as to reassure peace-loving people in Great Britain and elsewhere without, of course, committing Germany officially to anything specific. This popular movement toward a humanitarian peace in Germany was to be made known to the world just when German Armies were about to begin a powerful offensive. Haeften cherished the fantastic notion that these demonstrations would prove so convincing to war-weary and pacifist groups in England, and later in France, that they would oppose their Governments to the point of civil war if there were

5. *Ursachen,* II, 192–193.

no other way of forcing those in power to accept Germany's reasonable terms for peace. While Germany's enemies were thus occupied with civil strife at home, the German Armies would make a sudden military thrust whose success would discredit those wishing to continue the war and bring in new Governments eager to negotiate peace.[6]

This incredibly naïve plan was submitted to Ludendorff at Spa on June 8 and approved by him. He wrote the Chancellor that "diplomatic action must accompany the military," and that Haeften's scheme was practicable and deserved support. Even Ludendorff at this point was admitting openly that arms alone were incapable of bringing the war to a successful end for Germany.[7]

Colonel Haeften now returned to Berlin to discuss the proposed diplomatic move with members of the Government, including Chancellor Hertling, Foreign Secretary Kühlmann, Vice-Chancellor von Payer, and others. Both the Chancellor and the Foreign Secretary expressed misgivings, particularly because the Imperial Government and the Army Command could not agree on the future of Belgium. Haeften said that he believed an agreement on that ticklish point was now possible since Ludendorff in a recent interview had expressed rather mild views on the question. Deutelmoser, Hertling's Chief of Press, warned that unless the Army and the Reichstag coöperated with one another and with the press the gesture might meet with as little success as had the Reichstag peace resolution of July, 1917.[8] To get the Reichstag behind the present move Deutelmoser urged that the Army use its influence toward achieving electoral reform in Prussia by the abolition of the three-class system of voting established by the constitution of 1850.[9]

These dark views of Germany's military prospects and this plan for psychological war in support of the military were matters of the greatest secrecy. The public generally was thinking of victory; the series of military successes in the west could lead to no other result. The prevailing optimism received a terrific shock

6. *Ibid.*, pp. 193, 339–344; Ludendorff, *Urkunden der Obersten Heeresleitung* (Berlin, 1920), 478–486. Hereafter, Ludendorff, *Urkunden.*

7. *Ursachen,* II, 195–196.

8. By this resolution the Reichstag majority voted for a peace of understanding and lasting reconciliation, a peace without territorial annexations and other forms of violence, a peace that would create international organizations to settle disputes, that would remove restrictions on the freedom of trade and the freedom of the seas. Johannes Hohlfeld, *Deutsche Reichsgeschichte in Dokumenten, 1849–1934* (Leipzig, 1934), II, 590–591.

9. *Ursachen,* II, 196–199.

when Kühlmann raised the question on June 24 in the Reichstag of whether the war would come to an early end or not, pointing out that recent German victories had produced no readiness for peace in the enemy. He let it be known that Germany was willing to enter into an exchange of views on terms of peace. "An absolute end [to the war]," he declared, "can hardly be expected through purely military decisions alone, unaccompanied by diplomatic negotiations." A military victory for either side was impossible.[10]

Although Kühlmann had every justification for saying that the military could not win the war and was merely repeating what was being said within the High Command, his speech had the effect of a bomb in Germany, particularly in Army Headquarters at Spa.[11] To keep the speech from having a harmful effect on the public, the Army Command gave out through the press that it had been painfully surprised by what had happened. It became impossible, of course, to proceed with Haeften's proposed peace offensive, and orders were issued for its abandonment. Hindenburg sent a telegram to Chancellor Hertling telling of the depressing influence of the Reichstag talk on the Army.[12] Both the Chancellor and the Foreign Secretary were well aware of the violent criticism that broke out and sought to calm people by reassuring words in the Reichstag on June 25, but they spoke in vain.

The reaction of the Army Command came quickly, for Ludendorff and Hindenburg had an opportunity to talk with Hertling when he came to Spa to take the waters. In vain the Chancellor defended his Foreign Secretary. Hindenburg declared himself bitterly opposed to Kühlmann, said he had never had any confidence in him and could no longer work with him. Ludendorff was equally critical. "In view of the serious danger to the nation's morale through Kühlmann's speech," he wrote afterward, "speedy action was required if the press was to be reassured at once and kept from coming to false conclusions about our military situation." [13]

The next day Hertling had an interview with the Kaiser, who repeated that it was impossible for the Army Command to work

10. *Reichstagsverhandlungen,* June 24, 1918, pp. 5610, 5612.

11. Hertling, *Ein Jahr,* p. 118. Ludendorff merely refers to the incident. Ludendorff, *Meine Kriegserinnerungen* (6th ed. Berlin, 1920), pp. 525–526.

12. *Ursachen,* II, 202–203; Hertling, *Ein Jahr,* p. 118.

13. Ludendorff, *Urkunden,* pp. 491–492; Friedrich Payer, *Von Bethmann Hollweg bis Ebert* (Frankfurt a.M., 1923), pp. 43–54. Referred to later as Payer, *Von Bethmann Hollweg.*

with Kühlmann. But he had several reasons for not wishing to appoint a new Foreign Secretary until fall.[14]

The unfortunate Kühlmann was now summoned to Spa. He came thinking that the Emperor wished to consult with him about filling the post in Russia recently made vacant by the assassination of the German Ambassador—a post for which he had already suggested von Hintze, who was Minister to Norway. Actually von Hintze was being considered as his own successor in the Foreign Office. On July 7 the Kaiser requested Kühlmann to remain at his post until fall when von Hintze could be named to succeed him. During the night, however, the Emperor changed his mind and the next day curtly informed the Foreign Secretary that he was through. Responsibility for this decision must undoubtedly rest with the Army High Command.[15]

On July 9 von Hintze was named to the Foreign Office. He had no real desire for the post; he would have preferred the assignment to Russia, where he had once served as Naval Attaché. But at the Kaiser's request he accepted the unexpected appointment. He did not take over his new duties immediately; something like a democratic procedure had to be observed to keep people from thinking that the Army Command could dismiss Cabinet ministers at will. The Reichstag should be informed, at least for form's sake. Vice-Chancellor von Payer suggested that the new Foreign Secretary come to Berlin to meet with party leaders and that the Chancellor explain the change.

For some time critics of the Government had been saying that Germany's destiny was completely in the hands of the military, that civilians had little to do with policy. On June 25, before Kühlmann was dismissed, the Independent Socialist Haase asserted in the Reichstag that the military party ruled Germany, a naked autocracy that could not be made respectable by such fig leaves as Hertling, von Payer, and Kühlmann.[16] On the 26th Noske of the Social Democrats said that the important question was no longer who was responsible for beginning the war but who was responsible for its continuation.[17] The most stubborn and consistent opponent of the Army was Noske's party colleague,

14. *Ursachen,* II, 204.

15. *Ibid.,* pp. 206–207. Commenting on Kühlmann's removal from office, Ludendorff blamed him for permitting Bolshevist propaganda in Germany. Ludendorff, *Kriegserinnerungen,* p. 526.

16. *Reichstagsverhandlungen,* June 25, 1918, p. 5661.

17. *Ibid.,* June 26, 1918, p. 5690.

Scheidemann. "Where is the civilian," he asked in the Reichstag on July 3, "who has the necessary authority to tell the gentlemen in Army Headquarters: 'You deceive yourselves if you believe you are able with your instruments to bring about peace; you can, perhaps, take Paris; you can, perhaps, drive Englishmen out of France; you can, perhaps, although it is not likely, force our opponents to accept a peace dictated by Germany. But world peace, which the German people desire and want to get as soon as possible, that you will never be able to obtain. It cannot be brought by the sword alone. It is possible only through a revolution in the minds of men, through some great political act.' " He described Germany's existing political system as "nothing more than a military absolutism, rendered somewhat mild through fear of parliamentary scandal." He declared that the people desired an end to the war, an end that would injure neither Germany's honor nor her vital interests. As a preliminary step he demanded that Germany declare Belgium's unconditional right to independence. He attacked Hertling's Government for its meek submission to the Supreme Army Command. Ledebour, Independent Socialist, went even further in attacking the military group. He criticized the court and military cliques as reactionary groups seeking to annex territory, and urged a general strike or even a proletarian revolution against the Government.[18] Von Payer, the Vice-Chancellor, endeavored to defend the Army by saying that peace would come only when the enemy's determination to destroy Germany by war had been finally broken.

Opposition to the Government became more intense after the dismissal of Kühlmann and his replacement by von Hintze. Some critics said that the appointment of the latter was a triumph for Pan-German interests. The *Frankfurter Zeitung* pointed out that the change of ministers would be interpreted by the enemy as signifying that Germany did not desire peace; that foreign opinion would say Kühlmann had been removed because he displeased the Army and the Pan-Germans and desired an end to the war. As a matter of fact the Paris *Temps* placed precisely that interpretation on the retirement of the Foreign Secretary in its issue of July 11. The fact that Kühlmann had enjoyed wide support in the Reichstag and that his successor had been named without prior consultation with the legislative body led to demands for an explanation by the Chancellor. People were asking many embarrassing questions: Who had named von Hintze? Who had dis-

18. *Ibid.*, July 3, 1918, p. 5713.

missed Kühlmann? Where does the Chancellor stand? Is the Cabinet under the strict control of the military? Does the appointment of von Hintze indicate a change in foreign policy? Was he properly qualified to accept a ministerial post in a party government? The *Berliner Tageblatt* charged that Hertling had forgotten during his stay in Army Headquarters that there was a German Reichstag. Kühlmann's retirement was taken as proof that the Government was being run not by the Reichstag majority but by forces outside that body. *Vorwärts* expressed the Socialists' view that the procedure of the Supreme Army Command toward Kühlmann went far beyond the limits of what could be tolerated.

The Chancellor replied to some of these questions when he introduced von Hintze to the Main Committee of the Reichstag on July 10. He did not tell his critics what he had written to von Payer at the time; namely, that the Army would not tolerate Kühlmann and that it was impossible to change the Army's point of view.[19] Instead, he said that the appointment of the new Foreign Secretary was not to be taken as indicating any change of policy. He made it clear that neither the German Government nor the German Army would reject any serious peace proposals made by the enemy. He reminded his hearers, however, that so long as Wilson and his allies were fighting a war to annihilate Germany, the latter would have to fight on.

Touching on the delicate point of Belgium's future, which had become for many critics of the regime the very touchstone of Germany's sincere interest in peace, the Chancellor said that the Government had no intention of holding on to the country permanently: Belgium would be held only as its possession would safeguard Germany's position and strengthen her hands in the peace negotiations. Hertling did not inform the Main Committee that the Belgian question had already been decided by the High Command at Spa in a conference on July 2 and 3; Belgium was never again to come under the influence of England and France, to serve them as a convenient base for military operations against

19. *Ursachen*, II, 206–207; Hertling, *Ein Jahr*, p. 131. The *Vorwärts* account of Hertling's meeting with the Main Committee of the Reichstag is given in Lutz, *Fall of the German Empire, 1914–1918* (Stanford University, 1932), II, 356–358. A Socialist view of the Kühlmann crisis is given *ibid.*, 354–356. The *Kölnische Zeitung* report of the meeting of the Chancellor and the Main Committee is given in a despatch from Garrett to Lansing, July 12, 1918, *Papers Relating to the Foreign Relations of the United States, 1918, Supplement I, The World War* (Washington, D.C., 1933), I, 284–285. This volume will be referred to later as *Foreign Relations, 1918, Supplement I*, I.

Germany. Flemings and Walloons were to be two states united only by a personal union. The Belgium of the future would be bound to Germany by special tariff and railway arrangements; in the meantime it could have no army of its own and would be occupied by German troops.[20]

After this brief visit to Berlin Hertling returned to Spa, where he reported to the Kaiser that the *affaire* Kühlmann had been settled peacefully. To soothe the feelings of the departing Foreign Secretary the Emperor conferred on him the Order of the Red Eagle, First Class. Happy over this fortunate ending of a serious political crisis, the Kaiser went to the front to pay his troops a visit before the big attack to be made at Rheims on July 15.

Von Hintze was apparently much more concerned about the opinion of the High Command than of the political leaders. He had no desire to repeat the mistake that had deprived his predecessor of office. It was the most responsible position he had ever held and he knew perfectly well that what he could achieve depended in very large measure on the success of the German Armies. Discretion made him realize that it was necessary to know and to abide by the mind of Ludendorff, now for two years Germany's virtual dictator. "At Avesnes [advanced German Army headquarters] in the middle of July, before I took over the post of Secretary of State," writes von Hintze in a memorandum, "I put to General Ludendorff the formal and carefully framed question whether he was certain of final and definitive victory over the enemy in the offensive that was going on. General Ludendorff repeated my question and then replied: 'That I can answer with a decided Yes.' "[21] The Quartermaster General's confidence in ultimate military victory, thus expressed before the renewal of Germany's offensive near Rheims, impressed von Hintze and made him more hopeful about his own future as Foreign Secretary. Thus assured, he returned to Christiania (Oslo) to wind up his affairs as Minister to Norway before taking up his new work in Berlin on July 20.[22]

Had von Hintze talked the situation over with Crown Prince Rupprecht of Bavaria he might have come closer to the truth. Prince Rupprecht told Hertling early in July at Brussels that

20. *Ursachen,* II, 204, 346–347.

21. Document 2, *Amtliche Urkunden zur Vorgeschichte des Waffenstillstandes 1918* (2d and enlarged ed. Berlin, 1924). Hereafter referred to as *Amtliche Urkunden.*

22. *Ursachen,* II, 207–209, 347.

the dark outlook for Germany made an early opening of peace negotiations necessary. As we have already seen, Ludendorff was professing an optimism that he did not really feel. He had already let people in his entourage know that victory was not to be gained by fighting only. The difficulty was that he suffered from the very nature of his profession as a soldier: he could not admit defeat openly, even when he knew victory was no longer possible. In Ludendorff's dilemma lay a much wider tragedy; there could be no peace until one person, Ludendorff, made up his mind that fighting could not issue in victory. As long as the First Quartermaster General refused to admit that he was beaten, men had to fight and die, women and children to weep and starve, and revolution prepare to strike.

If Chancellor Hertling and the Foreign Secretary believed that the crisis was ended, the opponents of the regime did not. Newspapers and political leaders continued to criticize the Government heatedly. They credited Pan-Germans and annexationists with having won a victory in getting rid of Kühlmann; said that peace was further off than ever; and blamed the Army for continuing the struggle. In the Reichstag the most violent attack was made on July 13 by Geyer, a member of the Independent Socialist party. "The war," he asserted, "was never a war of self-defense. It was and still is a war of conquest and of imperialist goals. The Government conceals the activity of the annexationists and really favors them. The change in the Foreign Office confirms again the fact that the will of the military party determines the course of official policy. A brutal peace was imposed upon Russia and Rumania. Unaffected by these peace treaties the war is still being waged in Russia and in Rumania, even after peace has been concluded. People who had been promised their emancipation with fine words are being oppressed and exploited. The right of self-determination is merely ridiculed. Occupied regions are being robbed of their natural resources, of stocks of food, of machinery. By its military intervention in Finland, going to the extent of a bloody suppression of the workers and peasants, the German Government has shown itself to be the protector of counterrevolution. The same is true of the activity in the Ukraine. Respect for the German Empire, faith in the reliability of promises made by the Government is everywhere being destroyed. The majority parties of the Reichstag, who support the Government, bear the complete responsibility for the policies being pursued by the Government." Geyer attacked the policy toward Belgium and the censorship in Germany. He attacked the war credits that were being debated and charged that those who approve them "support capitalism and militarism and help to prolong the war. . . . Imperialist governments and ruling classes are unable to discover any way out of this chaos and horrible misery. To free people from complete destruction it is more than necessary that all nations free themselves first from capitalistic rule and exploitation and from the oppressive rule of militarism. Only then can permanent peace be assured. Whoever sincerely desires peace will not vote for these war credits. . . . We vote against [them] and recognize our unity with the masses of people in all countries in the cry 'Proletariat of all nations, Unite! Down with the War!' "[23]

Germany's prospects for victory depended on more than the military front. The home front should have caused von Hintze to ask questions; there were many reasons why the German people longed for peace. In early July the Spanish influenza was spreading rapidly, affecting civilians and soldiers alike. On July 1 *Vorwärts* reported that the disease had come to Berlin from Bavaria and that large numbers of children in the capital city, 80,000 by a later report, had been stricken. By July 4 the epidemic had reached Hamburg. Shortages of food and of clothing made bad conditions infinitely worse. The failure of the potato crop had resulted in a cut in the potato ration. Pigs and cattle competed with human beings for the little food that was available, and many had to be butchered. The cows that were allowed to live did not get sufficient food to produce milk and butter of the quantity and quality desired. Near the exhaustion of all food supplies, Vienna became desperate in the first week of July and begged the Kaiser for help. The railroads were so occupied with military traffic that it was impossible to think of transporting food from Rumania and the Ukraine in sufficient quantities to meet human needs. On July 6 Food Administrator Waldow informed the Reichstag that the Government was being forced to cut the bread ration. Such news was particularly hard in view of the fact that the daily flour ration had been already reduced from 200 grams to 160 grams in June.[24] People were warned that meatless weeks were soon to be introduced. There was little comfort in official assurances that additional quantities of sugar and other foods would be distributed to make good the cut in flour, that Rumania and the Ukraine

23. *Reichstagsverhandlungen,* July 13, 1918, pp. 6145–6146.
24. Lutz, *Fall of the German Empire,* II, 197.

might solve the food shortage. On the last day of July the *Frankfurter Zeitung* reported that beginning August 19 the ration of flour would be restored to 200 grams. Unadulterated flour, however, could not be used in the manufacture of bread.

There were other serious shortages in the country. At the end of June the price of coal was raised three marks a ton, and the higher price was reflected in higher prices for iron and steel. Coal prices had been going up all the year. People were urged to save coal in the summer in order to prevent a shortage in the coming winter. A shortage of metals caused the Government to melt down some of the monuments in Berlin and even to confiscate metals from private homes in the city.

In July, 1918, the shortage of cloth became appalling. Many people were without underclothing; hospitals were without bed linen. Drastic measures had to be adopted to meet these needs. Early in the month the Government confiscated table linen from hotels and restaurants to get materials for underwear. There was even some talk of compelling people to surrender underclothing for the use of workers in essential industries. Communities were authorized by the Central Clothing Bureau to force the surrender of unused clothing by those owning more than they needed; a sensitive regard for the rights of private property, however, kept the Government from adopting a policy of general confiscation. But curtains, table coverings, and the like—anything that was merely decorative—could be taken from private homes and public buildings and made over into clothing for the poor and needy. People were required to report what clothing they had. Discarded garments had to be handed over to the Government under threat of a year's imprisonment or a thousand marks' fine. At the end of July a newspaper report stated that one million suits of outer clothing were needed for workers on farms, in factories, in mines, and on the railways. The authorities hoped that these could be secured by voluntary action; but they were evidently ready to search private houses and to impose fines if necessary.

Prevailing high prices for consumer goods led to much talk against profiteers, who were at times compared with cannibals. Taxes imposed on war profits, it was charged, were simply shifted to the workers in higher prices and rents, which rose more rapidly than wages. The cry was being heard more frequently and loudly that the real enemy of the German people was capitalism.

Verbal criticism was not the only form taken by the opposition to the Government. Strikes were increasing in number as workers protested against reductions in wages and increases in the hours of labor. French and English newspapers always commented on such outbreaks. The food shortages and rising prices made conditions intolerable for many. Although street-car fares in Berlin were reduced, fewer people than usual could afford them. Workers throughout the country became sullen and uneasy when it was reported that troops with gas masks and machine guns fought strikers near Nürnberg in early July.

But how could the masses of people make their desire for peace known? The peace resolution of the Reichstag on July 19, 1917, had produced no results. So long as the Army and the Conservatives disregarded the wishes of the Reichstag and of the people, there was little that could be done. The defeat of electoral reform in Prussia on July 10, 1918, showed how conservative interests could thwart the desires of large numbers of people and even of the Kaiser, who had promised reform a year before.

Austria also was losing heart for the war in the summer of 1918. According to the *Frankfurter Zeitung* of July 20 Count Czernin, who had resigned as Foreign Minister in April, gave expression in the *Herrenhaus* to the doubts of his nation. "In the final analysis," he said, "the war is a duel between Germany and England. Only when England and Germany reach an agreement can the war be ended. We have no direct quarrel with England and are in general less disliked than our big brother on the Spree. We are weaker and less dangerous. Besides, we are modest in our claims and fairly free of longings for more land." He expressed the fervent hope that Germany was still fighting a defensive war only, and had no annexationist aims. "The peoples of Austria," he said, "would never understand why this horrible war should be prolonged for the imperialistic aims of a foreign power. Such a demand would threaten the alliance." As for the enemy, he felt it essential that they abandon Utopian schemes for conquest. "The German Chancellor as well as Lloyd George and our own Foreign Minister [Count Burian] are, by their own statements, ready to examine proposals. But nobody will make any. There would still be a way out of this dilemma if each of the two hostile groups would communicate its peace proposals in writing to a neutral that could compare them and see whether an agreement is possible or not. If there were the slightest prospect of such an understanding, the attempt should be made. Whether the time for that step has come or not can be determined by authorized parties." These were dangerous thoughts for an ally.

Von Hintze tried to counteract this defeatist spirit in Austria-Hungary. His first official act on taking office July 20 was to send a telegram to Count Burian. His language was rather that of a Ludendorff eager to continue the war than that of a man eager to bring about an early peace by other means. "I should regard it," he wrote, "as the happiest good fortune if it should be possible with God's gracious help in a not-too-distant future to crown the successes of our loyally maintained alliance by a victorious, honorable peace." Significantly, Count Burian's answer omitted any reference to military victory as a means of achieving the peace that the peoples of the Dual Monarchy were longing for.[25]

It is surprising that these alarming signs did not take from Ludendorff and von Hintze every hope of ultimate victory. One wonders what might have happened if von Hintze had waited but three or four days longer before asking Ludendorff his question about the likelihood of military success. He would have received an answer quite different from the one he actually got; for by July 20, when he began his work in the Foreign Office, Ludendorff had already seen the failure of his offensive at Rheims. The original plans had called for the attack to begin on July 12, but it had been put off until the 15th. If one can put any trust in an incident referred to by Ludendorff, the significance of the coming battle was fully appreciated on both sides. On that day, at Army Headquarters, Ludendorff told Lersner, Foreign Office Representative, "If my blow at Rheims succeeds now, we have won the war." Lersner repeated this story later to Loucheur, who remembered that on that very day he was in Foch's Headquarters and heard the Generalissimo say, "If the German attack at Rheims succeeds, we have lost the war." [26]

Ludendorff's plan of attack was known to the enemy, who was ready when the blow fell. The attack was accompanied by the long-distance firing of Germany's Big Berthas on Paris. The German troops succeeded in crossing the Marne, but there they were stopped on July 16. On the 17th they had to recross the river. Abandoning the defensive, Foch counterattacked in the early morning of July 18, at a moment when Ludendorff was visiting Crown Prince Rupprecht of Bavaria. The resulting battle, between the Marne and the Aisne, proved to be the turning point of the war. Aided by American troops, the French attacked on a 45-

25. Both telegrams in *Frankfurter Zeitung,* July 22, 1918, No. 201.
26. For Lersner's account of the event, see Ludendorff, *Urkunden,* p. 498.

kilometer front and took the Germans completely by surprise. Without the customary artillery preparation, the French sent hundreds of small and speedy tanks against the Germans between Soissons and Rheims. A furious thunderstorm in the night had cut down visibility to 50 yards; so the Germans knew nothing until the tanks were upon them, and they had to yield ground.[27]

With this battle the German Army lost the initiative; it was the end of the costly effort to defeat the enemy before the arrival of American aid. The real answer to von Hintze's mid-July question was not the confident one given by Ludendorff at Avesnes; it is what he has written in his memoirs: "The attempt by a German victory to make the people of the Entente desirous of peace before the arrival of American reinforcements was wrecked. The Army's striking power was not adequate to give the enemy a decisive blow before the Americans had arrived with considerable force. I was now quite aware that thereby our whole situation had become serious." [28]

Gradually and unwillingly staff officers began to realize that this retreat was the beginning of the end. But Ludendorff would not admit defeat. On July 30 both Hindenburg and Ludendorff assured newspapermen that "there was no ground to judge the situation with less confidence than formerly." They did admit, however, that their plan of attack had failed. But, added Hindenburg, with that professional optimism of his that had a way of overlooking obvious facts, "If we yield territory to the enemy we do it according to plan. . . . We have shifted the battle to a favorable terrain. . . . We all long for peace, but it must be peace with honor. . . ." In his memoirs Ludendorff takes a somewhat more realistic view; he writes that "at the beginning of August we stood on the defensive on the whole front, we had given up the offensive." The change that had come over him is apparent in the "defensive order" he issued at the beginning of the fifth year of the war. He reminded the Army that it was in an excellent defensive position and warned against surprise attacks. The last paragraph is significant. "Officers and men should be animated with the indomitable will to conquer on the defensive as well as on the offensive. This fact will not be lost sight of during training. In the present situation we should not, therefore, devote our attention too exclusively to the offensive and neglect a coördinated defensive, which is generally more difficult. It is the latter, in fact,

27. Ludendorff, *Kriegserinnerungen,* pp. 534–540; *Ursachen,* II, 80.
28. Ludendorff, *Kriegserinnerungen,* p. 545.

which frequently more severely tries the morale of the troops." [29]

The situation was judged more darkly and more profoundly by people outside the Army Command. The most disturbing report on the military situation was written by Major Alfred Niemann on July 20, immediately after the failure of the Rheims offensive.[30] Niemann had served on numerous military fronts and was selected, a few days after writing this report, as a General Staff officer to serve the Kaiser. His report, which Ludendorff read and approved, took the view that after the Rheims offensive the German military situation had changed greatly. Its conclusion was that there was no longer any prospect "by attacks on land to compel the enemy to [sue for] peace." Germany was sure to become weaker as the war went on, there being no possible way to replenish the diminishing reserves of men and of materials. Unable to win a victory, the Army could do nothing better than to exert pressure in support of a German diplomatic move to end the war. Niemann tried to show how Germany, by abandoning her Navy and her dreams of an overseas empire, could offer the Entente generous terms that would out-Wilson Wilson and would yet enable Germany in the future to establish a great continental empire. How all this was to happen is outlined in a nine-point program:

1. Neutral states must acquire an economic interest in the maintenance of a strong German Empire. They should be freely assured of economic advantages in the future.

2. Among our opponents Japan is the one great power with whom we have the least friction, a power for whom in the future a powerful Germany is of vital significance. We must win Japan, we must promise Japan our economic and cultural support for the future, we must let Japan become the opponent of [our] annihilation in the circle of the Entente Powers.

3. England should be given to understand that we see our future—that is, our military and political orientation—not on the seas but on land. By means of a large-scale continental policy we must lay the foundation of Germany's future position as a world power. It is not by trying to maintain impossible coaling stations and *points d'appui* in all oceans that we shall attain a balance of power against

29. Quoted in Lutz, *Fall of the German Empire,* I, 660–661. See also the report made August 1 by Radowitz on the High Command's optimism in *Ursachen,* II, 213, 281–282.

30. *Ursachen,* II, 214–217.

English imperialism but rather by developing our power in Asia Minor. A Turkey with well-developed communications with several railways through the Balkans will bring us in one generation to the very heart [*Lebensnerv*] of the British Empire.

England will certainly take a bite on the reasonable bait of our surrender of sea power, a surrender forced upon Germany by her geographic position in Central Europe.

4. Our colonial development should be along new lines. Give up Morocco to the French; let England have German East Africa and Southwest Africa. Germany should establish a colonial zone for herself in Central Africa, including the Congo.

5. Accept Wilson's idea of a league of nations through the mediation of a neutral state, not for the purpose of realizing this Utopian scheme but in order to begin negotiations. The slogan that an end must be made to the massacre of peoples possessing highly valued cultures appeals most to nations. Wilson's cant must become the means of entrapping him.

6. Consideration should be given also to the matter of approaching the nations of the Entente directly with proposals of world-wide significance. Experience shows that Reichstag demonstrations, ministers' speeches, and newspaper opinions have only a negative effect.

In my opinion we are unreasonable if we expect the Entente to approach us with proposals. We should not forget that the whole world is opposed to us, that the mountain did not come to Mahomet but that Mahomet went to the mountain.

7. The diplomatic offensive must harmonize with the military offensive. In the beginning every attempt at a diplomatic offensive will be interpreted as weakness. Military successes must be the evidence that we are strong. Only in such wise will a victory of our arms serve as a means of exerting pressure.

8. Definitive settlement of the question of territories attached to us (*Angliederungsfragen*) in the west and in the east will give the impression of our strong determination. We must confront our opponents with accomplished facts. Delay on our part in solving the question of Alsace-Lorraine will be interpreted outside Germany as meaning that we are not certain of our possession of the land and that, without admitting it, we regard that territory as *Kompensationsobjekt*.

In defining relationships in the east we must create rivalry between Russia and the future Polish kingdom. A Polish *irredenta* in Russia would be the best means.

9. It is becoming clearer that we must organize our press and our propaganda on a solid basis. A united people must stand behind the successes of our arms. That unanimity does not exist; it depends upon the lead taken by the press. It is still possible to fight against the world of lies and calumny. For this struggle the whole press of Germany must be welded together. Up to the present we have dealt with the press in a negative fashion. Instead of forcing the press into the opposition by censorship and by prohibitions, let us supply the newspapers with the material.

That Ludendorff approved this document and that Major Niemann was soon thereafter assigned to the Kaiser's staff as representative of the Army Command are facts giving this document a very great significance.[31]

Responsible people in the Government were likewise beginning to lose faith in the possibility of an ultimate military victory for Germany. Conferences held at Spa and at Avesnes at the end of July with the Kaiser, Ludendorff, and Hindenburg made von Hintze very gloomy.[32] But the Kaiser and the High Command remained more or less optimistic until August 8, when the enemy repeated the surprise tactics of July 18 and attacked in the early morning on a 20-mile front, east of Amiens between Albert and Moreuil. English and French Armies had joined forces during the night without being observed by the Germans. Again omitting preliminary artillery bombardment, the Allies sent ahead 360 heavy tanks and 96 whippet tanks, mechanical monsters that were invisible in the fog and smoke-screen. The Germans fell back and did not stop retreating until four days later, in the entanglements and trenches of the old Somme battlefield.

Ludendorff did not long remain under serious illusions concerning the significance of the defeat he had suffered on August 8,

31. Colonel Bauer made some comments on the report. He, too, accepted the fact that Germany's military situation would become worse as the war went on. He, too, was ready to admit that Germany could not construct and maintain a fleet. "Germany's fleet has cost men and money and has gained nothing." Instead of limiting Germany in the future to the economic exploitation of Turkey, Bauer suggested the exploitation of the Ukraine, Caucasia, Russia, and Turkestan. He warned against the dangers inherent in the league of nations as proposed; it would mean the loss of Alsace-Lorraine, the restoration of Poland, and the dissolution of Austria-Hungary. *Ursachen,* II, 215–219. Niemann's proposal is remarkable. It would be difficult to find a paper that anticipates Hitler's *Ostpolitik* in clearer fashion. Compare, for example, some of Hitler's thoughts in *Mein Kampf* (New York, 1941), pp. 182–184, 855–967 *passim.*

32. *Ursachen,* II, 212–214.

"the black day of the German Army in the history of this war." "Success was easy for the enemy," he writes; "their radios and correspondence reported that the spirit of the German Army was no longer what it had been. The enemy also acquired a good deal of highly valuable documentary material. The Entente must have got a clear understanding of our replacement difficulties, another good reason for them to continue their attacks without tiring." [33] He summoned officers to Avesnes to report on the situation after he learned what had happened. "I heard of deeds of glorious valor, but also of behavior which, I must frankly confess, I should not have thought possible in the German Army; whole bodies of men had surrendered to single troopers or to tanks. Retiring troops, meeting a fresh division going bravely into action, shouted out things like 'strike-breaker' and 'You're prolonging the war' —expressions that were to be heard again later. The officers in many places were without any influence and allowed themselves to be swept along with the rest. . . . A battle commander from the front, who had come just before August 8 with reserves from home, blamed these conditions on the lack of discipline among the people and on the spirit which our soldiers brought with them. All that I had feared, all that I had endlessly and repeatedly warned against, had here at one place become actuality. Our fighting machine was no longer of real value. Our capacity for war had suffered harm even if the far greater majority of our divisions fought bravely. August 8 marked the decline of our military power and took from me the hope, with the replacement situation that existed, of discovering some strategic expedient that should restore the situation in our favor. On the contrary, I became convinced that the measures of the Supreme Command, which, so far as this was possible, I had been able to establish on a firm base, were now deprived of that foundation. The conduct of the war thereafter took on, as I expressed it at the time, the character of an irresponsible gamble, one that I always looked upon as dangerous. The fate of the German people was too valuable for that game. The war had to be ended." [34]

This was not the Ludendorff who had said to Chancellor Hertling shortly after this event, "In the course of the war I have been compelled five times before to withdraw troops but only in the end

33. Ludendorff, *Kriegserinnerungen,* pp. 547–550.
34. *Ibid.,* pp. 550–551.

to beat the enemy. Why should I not succeed in doing that a sixth time?" [35]

"As soon as I had obtained a grasp of the whole situation brought about by the events of August 8," writes Ludendorff, "I decided to arrange conferences as soon as possible with the Imperial Chancellor and the Secretary of State for Foreign Affairs. These took place on August 13 and 14 at Spa." The game was about up. Ludendorff even thought that events after July 15 might have shaken the confidence of the Kaiser and of the Field Marshal in him. He suggested that someone be appointed to take his place, but neither the Emperor nor Hindenburg would comply.[36]

The Emperor had been deeply affected by the news of August 8. He hurried to Avesnes, where Ludendorff admitted that Germany had suffered a serious defeat. When Ludendorff spoke of the lack of discipline in the Army, the Kaiser expressed the belief that too much had been required of the troops, a view that the Crown Prince also held. Niemann likewise thought that Ludendorff had given too little consideration to the physical and personal needs of the fighting men. According to the Kaiser, "General Ludendorff had declared that he could no longer guarantee a military victory." And so the Emperor came to the painful conclusion: "I see that I must balance accounts. We are at the end of our ability to do anything. The war must be ended. . . . I am expecting the gentlemen at Spa within the next few days." [37]

The mood of the fighting men was changing. The long years of war had made the German soldiers susceptible to the propaganda that was being dropped from airplanes or floated across the lines in balloons. On August 12 an order was issued by the Fifteenth Infantry Division: "Everyone will be strictly warned that all tracts, whether loose leaves, or packets tied up with a string, dropped by hostile airplanes or found, will be immediately turned over to Headquarters with a statement of the place where they were picked up. It should be explained to the men . . . how much damage they may cause by thoughtlessly distributing these

35. Quoted in Hertling, *Ein Jahr,* p. 146; *Ursachen,* II, 222.
36. Ludendorff, *Kriegserinnerungen,* pp. 551–552.
37. Niemann, *Kaiser und Revolution* (Berlin, 1922), p. 43; *Ursachen,* II, 222–223. According to Scheidemann, Ludendorff informed Haeften in Army Headquarters on August 12 that "there is no more hope for an offensive, the command having lost the ground under its very feet." Scheidemann, *Memoiren eines Sozialdemokraten* (Dresden, 1928), II, 175.

tracts, and that they are liable to severe punishment. Every man in whose hands such a tract has been placed is in duty bound to ascertain the name and unit of the distributor and to report it." [38]

The news from Austria-Hungary brought no cheer whatever to the Germans. Shortly after getting from Ludendorff his despairing account regarding the western front, the Kaiser received a telegram saying that Austria was near the limits of her strength. Her food virtually gone, Germany's ally was facing starvation. On August 9 and 10 Italian planes flew over the once gay city of Vienna, dropping propaganda instead of bombs, warning the people that their Government was feeding them lies instead of food, and telling them that they had sunk very low in the eyes of the world by donning the Prussian uniform.[39] On August 10 Germany learned that "Emperor Karl had categorically declared that peace must be concluded during the course of the year 1918, and that, if no general peace were negotiated, he would have to conclude a separate peace." [40]

Morale in Germany was breaking down rapidly as the war entered its fifth year. French newspapers commented almost daily on the shortage of housing, of coal and gas, of food for the Army as well as for civilians, the spreading influenza, the strikes, the futile attempts to represent German defeats as victories, the growing despair, the relaxing discipline in the Army, the effect of meatless weeks, the signs of growing disunity among the German states, the rising prices for bread and milk in Berlin, the increasing political strife within the country, the dawning disillusionment about the entire war—all signs of great significance. *Vorwärts* saw the situation as it really was. On August 10 it pointed out that the people knew very well that it was impossible to succeed in a war of many years' duration against a coalition of the entire world. It was time to abolish the military dictatorship in Germany and to let the world see Germany's better side so that the war could be brought to a happy end.

Even the military dictatorship could read the signs of the times. Just before the fateful conference that opened at Spa on August 13, Foreign Secretary von Hintze spoke privately with General Ludendorff. "He took me aside," reports von Hintze, "and admitted to me that although he had told me in July he had

38. Cited in Lutz, *Fall of the German Empire,* I, 161.
39. *Frankfurter Zeitung,* August 10, 1918, No. 220.
40. Document 4, *Amtliche Urkunden.*

been certain of breaking the enemy's fighting mettle and of compelling him to accept peace by the offensive that was then in progress, he was no longer sure of it." The Foreign Secretary then asked Ludendorff what he "thought of the further conduct of the war." The reply was "we should be able through a strategic defensive to weaken the enemy's spirit and gradually to bring him to terms." [41]

Ludendorff was still too optimistic.

41. *Ibid.*, document 2.

II

Ludendorff Demands an Immediate Armistice

At ten o'clock on the morning of August 13 the first of two conferences opened at Spa, in the Field Marshal's room in the Hotel Britannique. The Army leaders said that, although the future strategy would have to be largely defensive, they still were convinced of their ability to break the enemy's will to war and to compel him to sue for peace. The first part of the conference was devoted to a consideration of the nation's morale, the weakness of the Government, the lack of coöperation, of food, and of reserves. In Ludendorff's mind morale was a matter of the first importance; he was particularly concerned with the harm caused by the mysterious publication of a pamphlet written by Germany's former Ambassador in London, Prince Lichnowsky, in criticism of his Government's prewar policies, and wanted it counteracted by some effective propaganda at home to educate public opinion. Hindenburg was more optimistic than Ludendorff. He said nothing about the state of feeling within Germany and reminded those present that, although the military situation was serious, they were "still standing deep in the enemy's country." Von Hintze brought up the questions of Poland and Belgium in order to have everything clearly understood whenever diplomatic steps toward peace should become necessary. In the discussion that followed the Foreign Secretary did not get the impression that Germany's war aims had been lowered or that it was necessary to send out peace feelers through a neutral country. This session ran smoothly without arousing any high feelings. Convinced of their ability to force the enemy to sue for peace, the High Command thought that von Hintze took too dark a view of the situation when he discussed the prospects of Austria-Hungary and the tendency of Turkey to go her own way.[1]

After this conference and before the meeting of the Crown Council on the following morning, von Hintze told Chancellor Hertling that he found it impossible to share the High Command's optimism and believed it would be necessary to take diplomatic steps leading toward peace. He asked the Chancellor to

1. *Ursachen,* I, 136; II, 223–226; Ludendorff, *Kriegserinnerungen,* p. 552.

support him in his request of the Crown Council for authorization to take action for peace; he also informed the Chancellor "that in case he failed to get such power from the Crown Council he would hand in his resignation." [2]

On August 14 at 10 o'clock the Crown Council met.[3] Those present were the Kaiser, the Crown Prince, the Chancellor, Hindenburg, Ludendorff, von Hintze, Adjutant General von Plessen, the Chief of the Civil Cabinet, von Berg, and the Chief of the Military Cabinet, Baron von Marschall. The Chancellor spoke on the internal situation: the people's war-weariness, the lack of food, the greater lack of clothing, and the need for electoral reform. Ludendorff spoke of the need for greater discipline, for more energetic action by the Government, for closer coöperation between civilian and military authorities, a more rigid selection of recruits, and for the punishment of Prince Lichnowsky.

Von Hintze spoke on the external situation. "The enemy," he said, "is more confident of victory and more willing to fight than ever." Their reserves of men, their raw material and manufactured goods made the Entente feel that "time is working in their favor," whereas Germany's resources were steadily diminishing. Neutral powers were reported to be "sympathetic with the enemy . . . heartily sick of the war," and eager "to see the war come to an end, regardless of what sort." Austria-Hungary had "come to the end of her rope" and could hardly be expected to carry through another winter; Bulgaria was too weak to accomplish anything; Turkey was going her independent and insolently Oriental way "into a war of booty and butchery in the Caucasus." On every side the situation for Germany was becoming increasingly critical. The generals have admitted, the Foreign Minister went on, the impossibility of breaking the enemy's resistance by military measures and have said "that the goal of future strategy must be the gradual weakening of the enemy by defensive tactics." From this verdict of "the greatest military commanders that the war has produced" the conclusion to be drawn is that foreign policy must take this critical war situation into its reckoning. These views met with general acceptance. "We must be on watch," said the Kaiser, "for the opportune moment at which to arrive at an understanding with the enemy." He thought that either the Queen of Holland or the King of Spain could properly

2. *Ursachen,* II, 227.

3. For protocol of this meeting see document 1, *Amtliche Urkunden;* also *Ursachen,* II, 227–234.

mediate at such a time. There was no dissent when the Chancellor summarized the situation with the words that "on the diplomatic front beginnings must be made for reaching an understanding with the enemy at the proper moment. Such a time would come after the next successes in the west." [4]

The protocol of the meeting, which Ludendorff and Hindenburg approved while the details were still fresh in mind,[5] is evidence of the great confidence of the Army Command in its ability to make the enemy seek peace. Nobody came away from the conference feeling that the situation was so serious as to call for immediate diplomatic measures to end the war. The Chancellor and the Foreign Secretary were justified in assuming that the Foreign Office must wait for a psychological moment before acting, the moment to be determined by military successes.[6] In his later eagerness to shift responsibility for the armistice from his own to others' shoulders, Ludendorff has endeavored to get a number of compurgators to substantiate his thesis that the Foreign Office was instructed by this council to initiate such diplomatic steps.[7] Thus von Hintze has been blamed by the Army Command for failing to do what his predecessor in office had been dismissed for advocating; namely, ending the war by diplomacy. Although not present at this conference, Niemann, who was intimately associated with the Kaiser, has written that "the report made on the military situation apparently did not convince Secretary von Hintze that a critical point had come, making it necessary for Germany to enter negotiations with the enemy." [8]

The conference had stressed the need for a real propaganda, of which, no doubt, the official communiqué on this meeting could serve as an example. The public was informed only that generals

4. When he spoke of this session of the Crown Council to the Prussian State Ministry on September 3, Hertling repeated the statement that preparations were to be made for an understanding with the enemy when the proper time came. He added that the Kaiser wished to have detailed peace conditions worked out. Document 3, *Amtliche Urkunden.*

5. It is worth noting that Ludendorff suggested only one change. Where Hindenburg had said he *hoped* to remain on French soil and to force Germany's will on the foe, Ludendorff strengthened the wording to read that Hindenburg *was certain* he could remain on French territory and make the enemy yield. See note on protocol, document 1, *ibid.;* also *Ursachen,* II, 229–230.

6. Hertling, *Ein Jahr,* pp. 149–150.

7. Cf. Ludendorff, *Urkunden,* pp. 499–516; Ludendorff, *Das Scheitern der neutralen Friedensvermittelung* (Berlin, 1919), pp. 1–38 *passim.* It is interesting to see that Ludendorff's supporters cite several *private* conversations rather than anything else as evidence.

8. Niemann, *Kaiser und Revolution,* p. 58.

and statesmen had "a thorough and fruitful conference" and that the meeting had shown their complete agreement on political and economic policies.[9]

It was unfortunate that the German Government was so completely dependent on Ludendorff for its estimate of the military situation. Less optimistic views of the future were held by others. On the afternoon of August 14 Emperor Karl of Austria-Hungary arrived at Spa, accompanied by his Foreign Secretary, Count Burian, and his Chief of Staff, General von Arz. The delegation wanted diplomatic steps taken immediately to end the war, with the move taking the form of a direct appeal to all belligerents. Doubts were expressed whether the Austrian Army could endure another winter of fighting. Ludendorff argued against any peace move until "the favorable moment" had come, when the Germans were "firmly established on a new line or until some military success should cause a reaction among our enemies." The Germans objected to the proposal that an appeal should be made to all belligerents, preferring the mediation of neutral states instead. The Austrians were not convinced. But they went away somewhat cheered over the outlook after having exchanged some of their doubts for a bit of the German Army Command's excessive optimism.[10]

Unfortunately Crown Prince Rupprecht of Bavaria was not present at the session of the Crown Council on August 14, to repeat the views he gave in a letter of August 15 to Prince Max of Baden, at the time President of the Upper Chamber in the Baden Diet, that ". . . our military situation has deteriorated so rapidly that I no longer believe we can hold out over the winter; it is even possible that a catastrophe will come earlier." It was his opinion that bad handling of military reports caused people at home and in the Army to lose confidence in the Supreme Command. The exhaustion of the German soldiers, the effect of Allied propaganda, and the growing numbers of Americans arriving in France accounted for his gloomy outlook. "What we must, therefore, do, if we are to avoid a military catastrophe which will destroy our whole future as a nation, is to make haste and approach our enemies, especially England, with peace offers, and peace offers which both can and, in view of the temper of the English people, must be accepted." He suggested the complete

9. *Berliner Tageblatt,* August 16, 1918, No. 416.
10. *Ursachen,* II, 234–235; document 4, *Amtliche Urkunden.*

restoration and indemnification of Belgium and the cession of the French-speaking areas in German Lorraine in exchange for the return and rounding-off of Germany's African colonies. "Top speed is indicated," he wrote; "all-important decisions must be taken and sacrifices must be made in order to ward off what is far worse." [11]

After the middle of August von Hintze began serious work on diplomatic moves in the direction of peace. He made it clear that Germany was not going to make the enemy a formal offer of peace; rather, she was going to make her position known while she sought to discover the war aims of the Entente. The Foreign Secretary wanted to be ready when the military situation made it possible for the Foreign Office to initiate diplomatic action; he also hoped to block separate peace moves on the part of Austria-Hungary. He ran into difficulties with the German High Command, who still believed it possible for Germany to win the kind of peace she wanted. So long as this state of mind existed in Army Headquarters at Spa, it was impossible for von Hintze and von Payer to get support for a statement that would assure the Entente Powers about Belgium's future independence. Without such assurances it was believed that diplomatic negotiations could never be initiated. All that the civilian Government could get was a promise that Belgium would recover her complete independence at the end of the war provided no other country received [from her] a preference over Germany in political, military, and economic respects. Even that qualified principle could not be made public in a formal declaration; it had to await the occasion of von Payer's speech in Stuttgart on September 10.[12]

While the Foreign Secretary was making these preparations for an eventual peace move, he was shocked to learn on August 21 that Austria-Hungary was ready to invite all the belligerents to send representatives to some neutral country for the purpose of discussing the fundamentals of peace without making any specific commitments. It now became a matter of the utmost importance to restrain her from making this fatal move. It was learned on the 26th that Count Burian, Foreign Minister for the Dual Monarchy, by the simple trick of saying that Germany had approved the proposal, had secured the support of both Turkey

11. Max von Baden, *Erinnerungen und Dokumente* (Berlin, 1927), pp. 288–289. Hereafter, Max, *Erinnerungen.*

12. *Infra,* p. 38. For an account of the preparations for the peace move see *Ursachen,* II, 236–238, 382–383.

and Bulgaria for his scheme. For Austria-Hungary thus to reach an agreement with her other allies before consulting Germany was contrary to the understanding the two powers had. A warning to Burian on August 27 had no effect; the Austrian Foreign Minister believed that an immediate and direct appeal to the fighting nations to confer on peace terms was better than the German proposal to ask a neutral state to mediate when the appropriate time should come. Germany even sought the aid of Turkish statesmen to hold Austria back. The Austrian step appeared particularly dangerous just at this time because the military situation seemed rather favorable. Only after repeated warnings was Austria persuaded not to proceed with her peace effort. The driving force behind the step, according to the German Ambassador in Vienna, Count Wedel, was the Emperor himself; only with great difficulty had Count Burian got him to agree to a brief delay.[13]

On September 3 von Hintze hurried off to Vienna. After he had convinced Count Burian that mediation by a neutral state was the best procedure to follow, the Austrian Foreign Minister insisted that the Queen of the Netherlands be sounded out immediately. Von Hintze objected. At the outside, he argued, it would be necessary to wait only two weeks; by that time the German retreat would have been completed and the Army would be in a position to guarantee more or less prolonged resistance to attack. Burian was persuaded, but not for very long. On September 5 he was again urging an immediate appeal for peace talks. "For us it is absolutely the end," he said. But two days later Emperor Karl yielded again to German pressure, largely because of the intervention of General von Cramon, German Military Representative in Vienna. Good use had very likely been made of von Hintze's assurance that Germany would be ready with her peace move in about two weeks. But it was made clear that no delay beyond that time would be tolerated; every postponement was thought of advantage only to the enemy, who was thus enabled to strengthen his position. On September 7 the Austrian Emperor telegraphed Hindenburg in an attempt to bind the Germans to specific pledges. He wished to know on what line the German Army intended to make its defense, when that line would be reached, and when the German Government would initiate its peace move.[14]

13. Document 4, *Amtliche Urkunden; Ursachen,* II, 237–240.

14. Document 4, *Amtliche Urkunden; Ursachen,* II, 242–243, 352–356.

To representatives of the German press in Vienna Count Burian explained on September 9 what Austria wanted. After making it clear that the alliance with Germany was not regarded as "simply a paper document," he said it was "unthinkable that even the most confident hope in ultimate victory is justification for the enemy always to refuse to consider whether they can continue to justify the enormous efforts and sacrifices to achieve principles of which they have no monopoly or to regulate the internal affairs of other peoples who are well able to do that for themselves." An honest study of war aims "would cause many on the other side to see that they are in large measure fighting for imaginary things." What was desired was only an opportunity to discuss these war aims, not actual peace negotiations; there was a possibility that such a conference would render further fighting unnecessary and might bring the rivals nearer together.[15]

On September 10 Burian told Ambassador Wedel of his determination to send out his peace note; it was impossible to delay longer. Wedel urged the Foreign Secretary "to wait at least until the result of the pending and imminent consultation of the Secretary of State [von Hintze] with the Supreme Army Command has been made known." But he doubted the possibility of preventing the despatch of the note.

Von Hintze was successful in his efforts of September 10 to persuade Hindenburg to do something in this critical matter. The Field Marshal regarded the proposed Austrian peace note "harmful for our armies and our peoples." But he declared his "agreement with the mediation of a neutral power for bringing about a conference *without delay*." It was the most significant step thus far taken by the German Army Command toward peace. It was done not because the military situation, dark as it appeared to many disturbed people, troubled the General Staff; it was done in a final desperate effort to forestall the proposed Austrian note.

On September 11 von Hintze instructed the Foreign Office to inform German missions in Austria-Hungary, Bulgaria, and Turkey that German officials had reached an agreement "on the immediate initiation of a peace *démarche* by some neutral power." On the same day the Germans learned of the reason for Austria's proposed move. Wedel reported from Vienna that the Emperor's opposition to the German plan for neutral mediation came from

15. *Berliner Tageblatt,* September 10, 1918, No. 463; *Frankfurter Zeitung,* September 11, 1918, No. 252.

a desire to be himself a peacemaker because he saw "in that role the promise of the restoration of the lost confidence in the Crown, which, in view of the dread of revolution, is looked upon as the principal object to be attained."

The Germans became desperate. On September 12 Wedel received instructions to warn Count Burian against the peace move "and to express to him once more that the impression will be gained in Germany that Austria-Hungary is betraying us." He was to point out that if the German proposal for neutral mediation failed, other procedures were still open; if Burian's move should fail, no way remained, least of all, that of calling upon neutrals to mediate. Burian would, in that case, have to bear all responsibility for blocking the way to neutral mediation. Burian answered that he could "dissipate any doubt as to fidelity to the alliance" with Germany, although he begged the German Government to influence the press so that bad feeling would not arise after the despatch of the note on September 14. He pleaded with the Germans "to accede as soon as possible to the note so it would be utterly impossible at the very beginning for our opponents to misinterpret the *démarche* as meaning a separate step by Austria-Hungary."

German pressure on Austria continued on September 13. Burian would not yield. "The die is cast," he said; he assumed "full and complete responsibility for the act" and promised to do everything he could to show that Austria was still faithful to her alliance with Germany. Once again he asked Germany to consent to the step "in order to avoid even the appearance of dissension." General von Cramon saw Emperor Karl, but his urgings were hopeless. Protesting his loyalty to Germany, the Emperor said he was "firmly convinced that the note going out on the 14th would make a favorable impression on all the belligerent powers." He sent a telegram to the Kaiser asking his consent to the Austrian move. The answering telegram, asking that the proposed step be abandoned, arrived too late; the Austrian "appeal to the nations" had already been despatched.[16]

Burian's peace note of September 14 was long and discursive.[17] Despite the fact that people in all countries long for a speedy end to the war, it began, no success has been achieved in formulating the preliminary conditions for peace negotiations. Since

16. These efforts to restrain Austria are recounted in document 4, *Amtliche Urkunden;* see also *Ursachen,* II, 245.

17. The note is document 5, *Amtliche Urkunden.*

the road to peace is long and costly if one of the parties insists on a victory over the other, it is a duty to open negotiations to permit the belligerents to exchange views without interrupting the war itself. The advantages of such discussions were stressed. "The Imperial and Royal Government therefore comes again to the Governments of all the belligerent states with a proposal to send to a neutral country, upon a previous agreement as to the date and place, delegates who would open confidential, nonbinding conversations over the fundamental principles of a peace treaty. The delegates would be instructed to communicate to one another the views of their respective Governments on those principles and very freely and frankly to exchange information on every point that needs clarification."

The publication of the note in Berlin papers on September 15 had the effect of a bolt out of the blue, the more so because during the days preceding very bad news had been coming from the battle front.

For some time staff officers at Headquarters had taken a very grave view of military prospects. Returning from leave on September 1, a Colonel von Mertz received from Ludendorff himself a picture so dark that he inquired whether the Foreign Office had been informed. Ludendorff replied that it was impossible to let people there know the truth of the situation; they were so nervous that a catastrophe would be sure to follow. This want of trust between the Foreign Office and the High Command disturbed von Mertz considerably.[18]

Ludendorff's view of the situation had almost immediate confirmation. On September 2 the Germans suffered a severe defeat and found themselves forced to withdraw on the Arras-Cambrai line from the Scarpe to the Vesle. The Kaiser, then attending the Kaiserin during a somewhat prolonged illness, was so upset by the defeat that it was feared he might suffer a "moral and physical collapse." The Chancellor was deeply alarmed; on September 3 he wrote to Army Headquarters to find out how the Generals viewed the military prospects for the immediate future. Although Ludendorff gave the impression to some that he was not affected by this defeat, he was reported to be suffering so much under the strain that the Kaiser arranged to have Colonel Heye sent to Army Headquarters to relieve the General of some work so that he could devote more time to military operations. Rumors were abroad that Ludendorff would soon resign; they were reported to

18. *Ursachen,* II, 249.

Berlin by the Political Division of Army Headquarters with a request that the Chancellor issue a statement on his unshaken confidence in the leadership of Hindenburg and Ludendorff in order to prevent any popular unrest.[19] Albert Ballin, the Hamburg shipping magnate, visited the Kaiser on September 5 and came away with the feeling that the Emperor had been so misinformed about conditions that he even looked upon the failure of the spring offensive against France as something of a success.[20]

The Chancellor received no answer to his inquiry of September 3 as to the military outlook. He then decided to send von Hintze and Colonel von Winterfeldt to Spa on the 8th, giving the former a list of questions to which he desired answers and the latter special instructions to investigate conditions at the fighting front. After two days von Hintze reported that, although there were difficulties with replacements and food, the High Command thought it could maintain its present line. Writing later, the Foreign Secretary said that at Army Headquarters there was "no word of doubt, no warning, no fear. Only confidence."[21] Von Winterfeldt reported to the Chancellor that the spirit of the troops at the front was good and that the situation was not thought to be critical. As a consequence of these two reports Hertling concluded that the time had not yet come for any peace move, feeling that hasty action in this respect would be to Germany's disadvantage.

Then on September 12 came the loss of St. Mihiel, a section held by the Germans for four years and now reconquered by the Americans in thirty hours. Major Niemann saw General Ludendorff on this day and found the Quartermaster General so affected by what had happened that a calm and exhaustive conference with him was impossible. "On this day," he writes, "I was overwhelmed by the certainty that the nerves of 'The Tireless One' [i.e., Ludendorff] had been strained too far."[22]

In various other ways Ludendorff gave indications of his anxiety. Instead of following the advice of officers who recommended speedy retirement to shorten the line, to rest their men, and to

19. *Ibid.,* II, 241, 243–244.

20. Niemann, *Kaiser und Revolution,* pp. 75–76.

21. *Ursachen,* II, 244, 396. An account of von Hintze's mission is given in Hertling, *Ein Jahr,* pp. 164–167. Von Hintze's very dogmatic report on his findings is hard to reconcile with his telling Hertling that the Army Command was disturbed and begged the Government to bring about peace as soon as possible. *Ibid.,* p. 164.

22. Quoted in *Ursachen,* II, 247.

spare their few reserves, the High Command said that it was better to hold advanced positions as long as possible and to retreat only when it became absolutely necessary. On September 11 Ludendorff said that the infantry lost territory when they lacked officers; and he appealed for the release of as many officers as possible from staff duty.[23]

Although men closely associated with Ludendorff noted how deeply affected he was by these setbacks, the General was apparently determined to make no admission of the fact, either publicly or privately. It is possible to assume that he was aware of impending defeat but did not want anybody to know it. How else can one explain the optimism of the confidential military report dated September 15? The defeats near Arras on September 2 and at St. Mihiel on September 12 merely resulted in the shortening of the German line, which had its advantages. The withdrawal at St. Mihiel was described as done according to plan.[24] Conditions in England and in France were said to be unfavorable although morale had risen with recent victories. Both countries were said to regard the Americans coming to France with satisfaction qualified by a desire to see the role of the United States minimized in European affairs after the war had been won. England was said to be troubled by a growing demand for peace; while in France dissatisfaction had come with the calling up of the military class of 1920 despite the victories won and the increasing help from America.[25]

Morale on the military and on the home fronts was not improved by the publication of the Austrian peace note on September 15. For some time the Army Command had been concerned with the nation's morale and had been urging that something be done to improve it. So far as the Army was concerned, steps could be taken to check the spread of enemy propaganda by warning men against reading and distributing the leaflets that the enemy was showering down on the soldiers in increasingly large quantities.[26] There was little, however, that could be accomplished toward checking propaganda among civilians. Hindenburg said that some Germans were guilty of weakening the

23. *Ibid.*, pp. 253–254.

24. The *Berliner Tageblatt* for September 17 asserted that the Germans had planned since 1916 to surrender the salient and that the order to evacuate had been issued on September 8. That order hardly tallies with German losses of 13,520 men and 460 guns!

25. Document 10c, *Amtliche Urkunden.*

26. Cf. Lutz, *Fall of the German Empire,* II, 162–163, 163–166.

morale of the nation. "It is our strength, as well as our weakness," he wrote, "that even in time of war we permit the free expression of public opinion." He mentioned specifically that enemy military reports were printed in the German newspapers as well as the speeches of enemy statesmen—all of it propaganda containing poison for the German people.[27]

There were many reasons for bad morale on the domestic front. The internal situation was becoming steadily worse as the summer came to a close and the war entered its fifth year. The food shortage continued. Every third week was a meatless one and was to be until the end of January. Prices of butter and milk were rising; people protested, and addressed vain appeals for help to the Kaiser and the Chancellor. It was charged that workers were not getting enough food whereas well-to-do people could get along fairly well despite rising prices. Workers' complaints were increasing; there were demands for a reduction in the long working hours in some industries. Reports of strikes became more numerous. The shortage of cotton for both clothing and munitions was getting to be more and more serious. The confiscation of cloth hangings in private homes was being more rigidly enforced. On September 17 it was officially reported that existing supplies of tobacco would be exhausted by the end of the year. Tuberculosis and grippe were spreading; and seven cases of Asiatic cholera were reported in Berlin.

Opposition to the Government was increasing, an opposition that fed on many grievances. There were those, especially the Social Democrats, who wanted the war ended as soon as possible in a peace of understanding and reconciliation, who knew from the speeches of the American President that Germany must first become a parliamentary state in which the will of the people was supreme before any offer of peace would be seriously considered by the Entente. Hertling was criticized for his want of faith in parliamentary rule and for doing nothing to end the war. The critics attacked Germany's real rulers on many counts: for the invasion of Belgium that brought England into the war, for the failure to bind the Government to Belgium's unqualified independence after the war, for the submarine that brought America into the war and could not stop the transport of American troops to France, for interference with civil liberties, for martial law, for censorship, for the annexationists who looked to the acquisition of territory, for the militarism that operated cruelly against

27. *Frankfurter Zeitung*, September 5, 1918, No. 246.

the people in the Ukraine and in the Baltic States, for the failure to check the profiteering that made a few rich and many hungry. If Germany should actually be invaded by armies that the High Command could not hold back, it would be impossible, these critics said, for the existing Government to rally the nation for a last-ditch fight.

The failure of the Imperial Government to get rid of the three-class system of voting in Prussia became a symbol of the political grievances felt by critics of the regime. The Socialist *Vorwärts* said on September 2 that the question of Prussian electoral reform was no longer a Prussian or even a German question; it had become a matter of great international significance, for there was no other way of getting rid of Prussian militarism, which "must go before all Germany, not Prussia alone, is ruined by its influence." The Kaiser had urged that reform; and when discussion of the bill was in committee in early September, Chancellor Hertling urged its passage on the ground that, since all parties and all classes had fought in the war, there should be no discriminatory treatment of a political nature after the war. He also brought forth the novel argument that, in his opinion, "the question is one bearing on the protection and maintenance of the Royal Crown and dynasty." [28] The argument should have hastened action on the part of conservative Prussians, but failed to do so. *Vorwärts* said that Hertling was interested in electoral reform only because the Kaiser wanted it, not because he was convinced of its intrinsic desirability. The debate continued for weeks.

Significant efforts were made to improve morale. Speaking at Karlsruhe on August 22, on the occasion of the one hundredth anniversary of Baden's constitution, Prince Max von Baden asked the nation to put aside religious, political, and regional differences and to unite in national coöperation toward peace.[29] On September 10 the Kaiser told the Krupp munition workers at Essen that Germany had several times declared her readiness to make peace, only to have her offers rejected by the enemy. "Thus we are confronted with our enemies' absolute will to destruction," he said, "and against the absolute will to destruction we must oppose the absolute will to preserve our existence. . . . Everything now depends on our final exertions. All is at stake. . . ."

28. Quoted in *Frankfurter Zeitung,* September 5, 1918, No. 246; also in *Vorwärts,* September 5, 1918, No. 244.

29. *Berliner Tageblatt,* August 23, 1918, No. 429.

After a reference to the great achievements of Germany during the war he said, "only in the west do we still fight, and is it to be thought that the good God will abandon us at the last moment?" He asked those who "intend to fight and hold out to the last" to shout, "Yes!" Although the assembled workers shouted, "Yes!" Major Niemann, who was present as aide to the Kaiser, felt immediately that the speech was a failure.[30]

The most significant speech during these critical days was that of Vice-Chancellor von Payer at Stuttgart on September 12.[31] He considered a number of matters depressing popular opinion and showed why people should take heart. It was true, he admitted, that the submarine war had not succeeded as Germany had hoped; yet it had destroyed considerable enemy shipping. It was also true that territory had been surrendered in the west; but it was territory that the Germans had conquered from the enemy. The war had been fought on enemy soil for four years; it was still being fought there; and the military problem was to keep it there. He regretted the postponement of electoral reform in Prussia, but prophesied that opponents could not prevent ultimate passage of the measure.

Von Payer had most to say about the coming peace. He doubted that it would take the traditional form of getting all booty possible, although he admitted that some Germans cherished notions of that sort. The war's sacrifices had prepared the people for a different kind of peace; it would be a good peace, for people would not be satisfied with an armistice lasting only a decade or two. "The coming peace will be concluded, not by Governments alone, but by Governments working in close coöperation with the whole people. For them the chief concern is not any gain in population, land, property, or honor; their concern is, at least in these days, first of all to have a lasting peace. The people will avoid everything that will start a new war and will welcome measures to prevent it. For that reason there will be no war of conquest. For our enemies, who have made our destruction and that of our allies and the ruin of our Government their war aim, that will signify a renunciation amounting to a confession of defeat. But not for Germany, which despite all temptation during the whole war has been faithful to the solemn assurances of the Kaiser that no desire for conquest urges us on and by that fact has made

30. Niemann, *Kaiser und Revolution,* pp. 80–81.

31. *Frankfurter Zeitung,* September 13, 1918, No. 254; Lutz, *Fall of the German Empire,* II, 365–374.

known that its policy in this matter is not merely a just one but also a far-seeing one. If conquest is opposed by both belligerents, it obviously becomes necessary to restore territories as they were before the war." That did not mean that Russia, whose Government had collapsed because it had failed to grant autonomy to its many peoples, should recover Poland, Finland, or the Baltic States. Germany's treaties with Russia, Rumania, and the Ukraine were not to be submitted to the enemy for approval. "Elsewhere," continued von Payer, "territorial possessions can be restored as before the war. The preliminary condition for us and for our allies must be that all will be returned, all that we had on August 1, 1914. Germany must consequently in the first place get back her colonies, a procedure in which the thought of some kind of exchange, where practical grounds suggest it, need not be excluded."

As soon as peace was concluded Germany could evacuate occupied territories. "We can even evacuate Belgium just as soon as we get to it. Just as soon as we and our allies recover what belonged to us and as soon as we are sure that no other state is more favored in Belgium than we are, then Belgium—I believe I can say it—will be restored without any incumbrance or reservation." He added that Belgium should realize that her economic interests run parallel with those of Germany, her natural economic hinterland.

"We are convinced," he went on, "that as the innocent party that was attacked we have a right to claim indemnity." But knowing that the enemy would not pay such an indemnity, Germany would not ask for it. He spoke in favor of a league of nations based on equality, just treatment, and disarmament fair to all parties. He demanded freedom of the seas, the open door in all overseas possessions, the protection of private property at sea, and the protection of small nations and all minorities. He warned that "impossible conditions attached to our participation in peace negotiations must not be made." It was his belief that hope for a peace of understanding without annexations and indemnities was spreading among the German people. "Responsibility for the blood yet to be spilled," he concluded, "lies with the enemy."

In some respects the speech was a bold one. The *Berliner Tageblatt* praised it because it gave Germany a clear program.[32] The liberals were pleased that it declared war on the conservatives

32. *Berliner Tageblatt,* September 13, 1918, No. 468.

and the Pan-Germans, and was a step forward on the way to peace. Pan-Germans and other imperialists, naturally, held opposite views. *Tägliche Rundschau*[33] called von Payer a pacifist and his speech a "national scandal" as well as a "diplomatic and political catastrophe."

The rising tide of opposition to the Government was too elemental to heed mere words. By the middle of September a serious political crisis was developing, one that could not be wished away. For some time newspapers had been referring to it. On September 10 the *Berliner Tageblatt* carried an article based on reports said to have originated in Vienna that Hertling was to be replaced by Dr. Solf, former Colonial Secretary, and that Erzberger of the Centrist party and Scheidemann of the Social Democratic party would join the new Government as representatives of their respective political parties. Very clearly a "Hertling crisis" was in the air. The Paris *Temps* carried reports on September 11 and 12 of coming political changes in Germany, of a Cabinet crisis, even of a possible military dictatorship.

The crisis came into the open on September 11, when the Executive Committee of the Social Democratic party issued a proclamation to the members of the party. "Our brothers are engaged," it stated,

> in the most terrible struggle which they have had to endure since the beginning of the World War. At home in the meantime the Prussian Herrenhaus plays a dishonorable game with the nation's rights. . . . How long shall the laboring people of Prussia and Germany stand and look on at this unworthy game? If the Government, in incomprehensible misunderstanding of the demands created by necessity, delays again and again the fulfilment of its duty, then the people must give it an emphatic reminder. . . . The overwhelming majority of our fellowmen went into this war with the conviction that they were to fight not for the preservation of Germany as was the case before the war, *but for a better and freer Germany.* They were strengthened in this conviction by numerous ministerial speeches and finally by the suffrage reform message of July 11.[34] . . . The refusers of rights in the Prussian Chamber have by their irresponsible action greatly harmed the nation which fights for its very existence. No pettifogging will free them from the charge of having

33. Quoted *ibid.,* September 13, 1918, No. 469.

34. This is a reference to the Kaiser's appeal of July 11, 1917, for electoral reform in Prussia. Cf. Lutz, *Fall of the German Empire,* II, 425.

placed in an hour of historical responsibility their circumscribed class interest above the vital necessities of the whole. . . . In the name of millions which stand behind us and which today cannot exert their influence upon the decision of the Government, we protest most emphatically against the continuation of the suffrage-right comedy in the Herrenhaus and we demand the

IMMEDIATE DISSOLUTION OF THE CHAMBER OF DEPUTIES.

Away with the Three-Class Parliament, away with the Herrenhaus! Give us universal, equal, direct, and secret suffrage! Long live democracy and peace![35]

Important political events now succeeded one another rapidly. On September 12 leaders of the majority parties in the Reichstag met to consider the general political situation. The Independent Socialists voted to ask for the immediate calling of the Reichstag.

With Ludendorff beginning to have doubts about Germany's military prospects, with political leaders pressing the Government hard for reform, with the Balkan offensive just begun against a collapsing Bulgaria, it is understandable that the *Berliner Tageblatt* and the *Frankfurter Zeitung* should question the timing of the Austrian peace note of September 14, while sympathizing with its motives and hoping for its success. The German Government could not repudiate the move however much it disagreed with it. Rejection of the proposal might have alienated Germany's best ally; it certainly would have embittered Germans eager to have some steps taken toward ending the war. Even the publication of the note had such an effect on morale that Hindenburg had to remind the Army and the nation that Burian had not called for a cessation of the fighting; the war must continue until the enemy was ready for peace.[36]

To satisfy opinion at home and an ally abroad, the German Government endeavored to "engraft" on the Austrian proposal the original plan for mediation by the Dutch. Von Hintze sought to persuade the Government of the Netherlands to propose The Hague as the place for the conference the Austrians desired. If he succeeded, Holland would have the presidency of the proposed

35. *Ibid.*, II, 70–71.
36. *Frankfurter Zeitung*, September 20, 1918, No. 261.

congress. On September 24 Austria-Hungary and Bulgaria declared their acceptance of von Hintze's suggestion; and on September 28 the Dutch Queen officially placed her residence at the disposal of the powers for the conference sessions.[37]

Austria's allies declared their willingness to participate in the proposed conference of all belligerents, although, curiously, their acceptances came after England, France, and the United States had rejected the suggestion. The *New York Times* thought that the offer could be honorably accepted. "Reason and humanity demand," read the leading editorial on September 16, "that the Austrian invitation be accepted. . . . We cannot imagine that it will be declined." But the *Times* was in a minority. Great hostility to the note was generally expressed in political and newspaper circles in the United States. The American Government received the Austrian note from the Swedish Minister officially at 6.20 P.M.; the rejection was announced twenty-five minutes later. "The Government of the United States," said Wilson in his reply, "feels that there is only one reply which it can make to the suggestion of the Imperial Austro-Hungarian Government. It has repeatedly and with entire candor stated the terms upon which the United States would consider peace and can and will entertain no proposal for a conference upon a matter concerning which it has made its position and purpose so plain." [38] Senator Borah said that Wilson's "reply suits me exactly," and Senator Lodge spoke at great length in the Senate against enemy peace propaganda.

The *Daily Chronicle* of London[39] believed that "the note deserves and will receive careful and courteous attention." But Foreign Minister Balfour said, "It is incredible that anything can come of this proposal," which he described as a cynical effort designed to divide the Allies. Clemenceau said in the French Senate on September 17 that the Allies would fight until the enemy recognized that right cannot negotiate with crime. A copy of the *Journal Officiel* containing his speech was sent to Austria as France's official answer to the note of September 15.[40] A differ-

37. *Ursachen,* II, 246; Hertling, *Ein Jahr,* pp. 166–167; see document 4, *Amtliche Urkunden* and note, p. 19.

38. *New York Times,* September 17, 1918; Lansing to Ekengren, September 17, 1918, *Foreign Relations, 1918,* Supplement I, I, 309–310. Wilson's Fourteen Points and other principles are given in Appendix A.

39. Quoted in the *New York Times,* September 17, 1918.

40. Mordacq, *Le Ministère Clemenceau* (Paris, 1930), II, 231–232.

ent answer from France would have been most unlikely after the five hour air raid made on Paris the night of September 15–16.

In a discussion of his peace move with a representative of the *Berliner Tageblatt* on September 21 Burian said he was not surprised at the note's reception. Even if the Entente did not enter into negotiations, it was necessary now and then to do something to make the situation clear; nothing should be omitted that would bring peace nearer. From Wilson's formal reply he made the interesting deduction that the American President desired to become *arbiter mundi* and feared that France and England might get ahead of him.[41]

The Austrian note intensified the political crisis in Germany. Although it was a Sunday when the appeal was made public in the Berlin newspapers, party leaders insisted upon an immediate interview with the Chancellor. They wished to know what lay behind Austria's proposal. Hertling reassured his visitors by promising to summon the Main Committee of the Reichstag to hear a full report on the situation. Von Winterfeldt spoke for the Army and said that the High Command stood behind the Government.[42] On September 17 it was reported that the Main Committee would meet on the 24th.

The political excitement produced by the note is evident from opinions aired in the newspapers. Scheidemann wrote in *Vorwärts* on the 19th that people wished to know more about what was going on and to have a say in determining their own destinies. He attacked the blindness of the Prussian leaders who refused to pass the reform bill. The peace move, according to *Vossische Zeitung*,[43] raised the question whether Hertling had a working majority of the Reichstag with him. Germany needed a strong, unified leadership,[44] but where was there a man fit for the post, one in whom the people could have implicit faith and to whom they could give dictatorial powers? Hertling was not the man, and they regretted the support given to him by the Centrists. The *Frankfurter Zeitung*[45] wondered whether Hertling would remain in office and whether the Socialists would be given a share in the Government.

On September 23 the Social Democratic representatives in the Reichstag and the Executive Committee of the party defined the

41. *Berliner Tageblatt,* September 23, 1918, No. 486.
42. Hertling, *Ein Jahr,* pp. 167–168; *Ursachen,* II, 245–246.
43. September 16, No. 473.
44. *Vossische Zeitung,* September 22, No. 485.
45. September 23, No. 265.

conditions under which party members would enter the new government that might be formed:

1. The unqualified acceptance of the resolution of the Reichstag of July 19, 1917, and a willingness to enter a league of nations that is based on the principle of a peaceful settlement of all disputes and on universal disarmament.

2. An absolutely unconditional declaration on the Belgian question, the restoration of Belgium, an agreement on compensation, and also the restoration of Serbia and Montenegro.

3. The peace treaties of Brest-Litovsk and Bucharest to be no obstacle to universal peace; the introduction immediately of a civil administration in all occupied regions; all occupied lands to be set free when peace is concluded, and democratic representation to be established at the same time.

4. Autonomy for Alsace-Lorraine; universal, equal, secret, and direct franchise for all German States; the Prussian Landtag to be dissolved unless the equal franchise is the result of discussions in the Committee of the Herrenhaus.

5. Unity of government for Germany; the removal of irresponsible "by-governments" [*Nebenregierungen*]; the appointment of members of the government from the parliamentary majority or from people who support the policy of the majority; the nullification of Article IX of the Imperial Constitution;[46] the political communiqués of the Crown and of the military authorities are to be communicated to the Imperial Chancellor before publication.

6. The immediate annulment of regulations limiting freedom of assembly and of the press; censorship to be applied only for purely military matters (questions of strategy and tactics, the movement of troops, the production of war material); the creation of a political control to supervise the measures decreed because of the existence of a state of siege; the removal of all military institutions that serve to influence politics.[47]

On September 24 the Main Committee of the Reichstag opened

46. "Each member of the Bundesrat shall have the right to appear in the Reichstag, and must be heard there at any time he shall so request, in order to represent the views of his Government, even when such views shall not have been adopted by the majority of the Bundesrat. No one shall at any time be a member of the Bundesrat and of the Reichstag."

47. From *Berliner Tageblatt,* September 24, 1918, No. 489. For another translation see Lutz, *Fall of the German Empire,* II, 375.

a three-day session.[48] Ebert, the Social Democratic leader, presided. The Chancellor told the Committee it had been summoned to receive information about the crisis that was developing. He was disturbed to see many Germans seized by dissatisfaction because of the mere fact that the High Command had found it necessary to shorten the line. Touching on war aims, he said he approved Wilson's Fourteen Points and the four principles in the American President's speech of February 27; he was drawn particularly to a league of nations, to disarmament, and to freedom of the seas. General von Wrisberg, Minister of War, admitted that Germany had failed in the great spring offensive and that the enemy had successfully counterattacked, but he asked that military reports from the enemy be read with caution since the Entente had an interest in breaking down German morale. His report was considered inadequate by the Centrist leader, Gröber, who deplored the lack of coöperation between civilian and military authorities. Von Hintze, speaking on foreign affairs, said that Germany was ready for peace but made it clear that he had disagreed with Austria about the timing of the peace move, although he had accepted it after it was made.

The boldest and frankest criticism came from Scheidemann, who said that the Chancellor had been "unable to prevent what we do not want and could not achieve what we desired." He felt the military situation to be critical. "The war must be ended to keep us from being smashed." The militarists' ideal of a victory was not his, he said; and he attacked the treaty of Brest-Litovsk as an obstacle to world peace. He criticized the Army, the police, the censorship. "Our military," he said, "is becoming more and more lordly, but our Government is getting weaker and weaker." Hertling admitted there was some justification for complaints made about censorship and interference with public gatherings. As a result of the sessions, Hertling got very little support, even from his own Centrist party.

Foreign Secretary von Hintze had the most difficult task during the sessions of the Main Committee, for on September 27 he had to report the shocking news that Bulgaria was seeking a separate peace. As we have already noted, the Bulgarian crisis had been developing for some time. On September 26 news came from Austria that "Bulgaria was going to conclude a separate peace immediately." On the 27th the *Frankfurter Zeitung* re-

48. *Ursachen,* II, 248–249; *Frankfurter Zeitung,* September 25–28, 1918, Nos. 266, 267, 268.

ported that the Bulgarian Premier Malinow had offered an armistice to the Entente Army in the Balkans on the 25th. The German Army Command was at last persuaded to send reinforcements to Bulgaria and asked Austria-Hungary to do so too. The troops arrived at Sofia on September 28, but it was too late. President Wilson received a message on the 27th asking him to terminate the fighting in the southern theater of the war with an armistice. The reply stated that he would be "willing to urge an armistice upon the Entente if the Bulgarian Government will authorize him to say that the conditions of the armistice are left to him for decision and that the Bulgarian Government will accept the conditions which he imposes." Otherwise, he was not hopeful of accomplishing anything.[49] The armies of the Allies continued their advance against Bulgaria, and the latter soon felt compelled to turn to their commanding general for terms.

There was other bad news for von Hintze during the sessions of the Main Committee. On the 26th a telegram from the Foreign Office Representative at Army Headquarters, von Lersner, urged him to come as soon as possible to Spa. Since September 15 Lersner was being educated by Colonel Mertz into a knowledge of Germany's very serious military plight. The process of learning was slow, but at last Lersner was convinced that a catastrophe was impending. Von Hintze also was aware of the approach of a crisis and mentioned his forebodings to the Chancellor. He suggested that the Government be organized on a broader basis, with parties of the Left invited to participate. The suggestion was not to Hertling's liking, for he was in principle opposed to anything like the democratization of the Government. "Do you really want to admit Social Democrats into your Ministry?" he bluntly asked von Hintze. The Foreign Secretary replied that the time had come for either a dictatorship or a government resting on a broad political basis; as for the Social Democrats, they would recognize the necessities of the moment. As the sense of catastrophe grew on him during the last week of September, von Hintze repeatedly expressed his fears to the Chancellor, only to be told that he was a pessimist. He did nothing about the situation, he says, because the Army Command had not confirmed his views; but he made up his mind to visit Headquarters as soon as he could to discover what the situation really was.[50]

49. Lansing to Bliss, September 27, 1918, *Foreign Relations, 1918,* Supplement I, I, 324.

50. *Ursachen,* II, 249–251.

Before his departure for Spa, the Secretary held preliminary conferences with experts in the Foreign Office to get light on the conditions necessary for any peace move. Three members of the staff, von Rosenberg, von Stumm, and von Bergen, had studied the general question and had arrived at conclusions which they embodied in the following memorandum of September 28:

The most important prerequisite for the coming of peace is the formation, on the free initiative of His Majesty the Emperor, of a new Government on a broad national base. To this end it would be desirable that there should arrive in Berlin by tomorrow evening a telegram announcing the acceptance of Count Hertling's resignation as requested by him, and ordering Vice-Chancellor von Payer to make immediate suggestions to the Emperor for the new Chancellor and for the composition of the new government. The new Cabinet should unite all the forces of the people on the broadest national foundation, and make them available for the defense of the Fatherland. To make sure that this object is attained, the Vice-Chancellor, upon the express wish of the Emperor, should consult with the President of the Reichstag and with party leaders and should work out his proposals with the closest coöperation of those who represent the people.

The new Government formed in this way should approach President Wilson at the opportune moment with the request "to undertake the restoration of peace and for this purpose to propose to all belligerents that plenipotentiaries be sent to Washington."

If it be the wish of our military authorities, it should be suggested to the President that he invite the belligerents, possibly at the same time, to conclude an armistice. Our request to Mr. Wilson should be accompanied by the declaration that Germany, and, possibly the Quadruple Alliance also, is ready to base peace negotiations on the President's familiar Fourteen Points.

It might be advisable to forward our communication to Mr. Wilson in the most direct way, and thus leave to his judgment the question of open or secret negotiations. For this purpose it might be the most suitable course for one of the Imperial Ministers at some neutral capital to be instructed to turn over the communication in writing to his American colleague. The choice of such a neutral country should depend upon the fitness of the local American representative concerned. A confidential inquiry in this connection is being sent out today to the various Imperial Ministers.[51]

51. *Ibid.*, p. 251; the memorandum is document 12, *Amtliche Urkunden*.

It is important to note that the three Foreign Office experts were not advocating an immediate end to the war. Their haste had for its primary goal the speedy transformation of the Government for the nation's defense. So far as peace went, the new Government was to approach Wilson "at the opportune moment"; whether an armistice should bring hostilities to an end while the proposed conference of belligerents went on was dependent on the "wish of our military authorities." [52]

The suggestion to approach Wilson has some history behind it. On September 10 Albert Ballin had written to Berg, Conservative member of the Cabinet, that he opposed the intention "after a return to the Hindenburg Line, to send an offer of peace to England or to France through the Queen of the Netherlands. . . . The key to the temple of peace lies no longer there but in Washington. . . . We can even yet count upon having in Wilson the kind of person who wants to end the war ideologically. . . . I cannot believe that Wilson can be won by a royal mediation for peace. It is my opinion that it is necessary for such an offer to come from the head of the Reichstag or the Committee of the Reichstag under the initiative of the Kaiser." [53] Von Hintze had given thought to the matter for some time. So had the Army Command, for on September 21 Lersner informed the Foreign Secretary that Ludendorff had inquired whether he was thinking of approaching America for peace negotiations through the German representative in Berne.[54] Von Hintze's reply of September 24 was that the preliminaries for such an approach had already been made.[55]

The timing of the peace move depended on the military situation, which only the High Command could evaluate. On September 27 von Hintze suggested that Hertling go himself to Spa to find out. The Chancellor refused. The next morning the Foreign Secretary decided that he would go to Spa "to get an unequivocal and definite statement on the military situation from the Army High Command and to propose measures that might appear

52. It should be remembered that this memorandum was not occasioned by President Wilson's speech of September 27 in the Metropolitan Opera House. That address was not yet available in Germany. See *infra,* p. 80, *n* 73.

53. Stubmann, *Ballin: Leben und Werk eines deutschen Reeders* (Berlin, 1926), 272–273. On September 16 Ballin wrote again "that the way to peace can be found only in a direct offer to Wilson." *Ibid.,* p. 274.

54. Document 11, *Amtliche Urkunden; Ursachen,* II, 252.

55. Document 11a, *Amtliche Urkunden.*

necessary on the basis of that statement." Later in the day the Chancellor also decided to go, moved by a report that the Army Command wanted the Government reorganized on a broad political basis.[56] It is possible that the Chancellor was reacting to public criticism of his policies. On September 23 the political editor of the *Vossische Zeitung* suggested that the Reichstag should come to a decision on policy to end the war. On the 26th the *Frankfurter Zeitung*, after condemning the Government's defense before the Main Committee, said that "people desire to know what the real situation is and by what means the Government is thinking of bringing the war to a happy end." The *Berliner Tageblatt* demanded the Chancellor's resignation because he had not been strong enough to keep military leaders from indulging in politics. On the 27th *Vossische Zeitung* referred to the prevalent belief that a stronger man than Hertling was needed, a personality able to organize the different political parties for concerted action. The *Frankfurter Zeitung* called for the formation of a new Government by the three majority parties in the Reichstag, the Centrists, the Social Democrats, and the Volkspartei. There was a rumor that Hertling had been informed on September 28 that not only the Social Democrats but the Inter-Party Committee had doubts about his remaining longer in office. The demand of the major parties for action became stronger when the impending collapse of Bulgaria and of Austria made it clear that Germany might soon be fighting alone; in such an extreme contingency there should be at the helm of Government a man in whom people could have complete confidence.

A sense of catastrophe was developing also at Spa. In late September Allied attacks began again in great strength: the British on the front near St. Quentin, the French and Americans in the Meuse-Argonne. It was known that Bulgaria was about to give in to the Entente armies in the Balkans. German troops were weary and surrendered to the enemy in large numbers. The continuous withdrawal of the troops had produced poor morale among the officers. Still Ludendorff would not admit that the situation was beyond hope. But a more or less casual remark showing that he based his hope for victory on health conditions in the French Armies opened the eyes of officers in the Operations Bureau, and they immediately persuaded Lersner to send the

56. *Ursachen,* II, 252–253. A note on page 253 throws some doubt on this being the Chancellor's motive.

telegram of September 26 to von Hintze that caused the Foreign Secretary to set out for Spa.[57]

Before von Hintze arrived at Spa, the great decision was made. "At six o'clock on the afternoon of September 28," [58] writes Ludendorff, "I went down to the Field Marshal's room, which was on the floor below mine. I laid before him my views as to a peace offer and request for an armistice. The situation could only get worse, on account of the Balkan position, even if we held our ground in the west. Our task now was to act clearly and firmly, without delay. The Field Marshal listened to me with emotion. He answered that he had intended to say the same to me in the evening, that he also had considered the whole situation carefully and thought the step necessary. We were also agreed that the armistice conditions would have to permit the controlled and orderly evacuation of the occupied territory and the resumption of hostilities on our own borders. From the military point of view the first was a tremendous concession. We did not consider any abandonment of territory in the east. I believed that the Entente were aware of the danger threatening them as well as ourselves from Bolshevism." [59]

A problem was now created by the fact that the Army Command had decided on the need for an immediate armistice and peace at the moment when political leaders were forcing a change in the Government. This coincidence of events caused serious embarrassment. Taking the time to form a new government would mean postponing the move for peace, which Ludendorff wished to be made "without delay." That a new kind of government was a necessary preliminary to negotiations with Wilson did not enter into the considerations of the Army Command. "The Field Marshal and I," writes Ludendorff, "were not aware of the trend of opinion in Berlin when we decided upon the armistice and peace

57. *Ibid.*, pp. 248–249. Ludendorff's account stands in interesting contradiction to the one here given. "Since September 11," he writes, "General Headquarters had heard nothing of the peace proposals placed before the Queen of Holland. Since the middle of August time had passed without anything being achieved. Count Burian's note had vanished, traceless like an echo. Our diplomacy, in the face of the enemy's determination to destroy us, had a hopeless task. As these thoughts developed, not suddenly, but bit by bit in my mind from the beginning of August onward, and through difficult struggles within me, I called Secretary von Hintze to Spa on September 26." Ludendorff, *Kriegserinnerungen*, p. 580.

58. In his memorandum of October 31, 1918, Ludendorff gives the date as September 27 and the hour as four, both incorrect. See *Ursachen*, II, 256, 365.

59. Ludendorff, *Kriegserinnerungen*, pp. 582–583.

proposals in the evening of September 28." [60] Only the civilians had taken Wilson seriously when he had insisted again and again that a responsible government must supplant the military autocracy at war with the United States and the powers associated with her.

On Sunday, September 29, at 10 A.M., there was another important conference in the Hotel Britannique at Spa,[61] between Hindenburg, Ludendorff, Secretary von Hintze, and Colonel Heye, Chief of the Operations Bureau. The Foreign Secretary discussed the diplomatic situation: Bulgaria out of the fight, Austria-Hungary about to collapse, Turkey only a burden, no possible help from the outside, the growing confidence of the enemy, the increasing need within Germany. He referred to the steps taken to have Holland mediate and reported that the Dutch Queen had offered the use of her palace for peace negotiations.

After describing the military situation Ludendorff said that an immediate armistice was necessary. Von Hintze got the definite impression that a catastrophe confronted the Army if the armistice could not be arranged right away. Ludendorff has denied use of the word "catastrophe"; von Hintze, however, was certain that this word best described the situation, and it was on the assumption of an impending catastrophe that he acted from now on. He pictured the effect upon the people, the Army, the Empire, and the monarchy of the change from the prospect of victory to the threat of defeat. He wished to see the nation's entire strength coordinated for a final defensive struggle and recommended either a dictatorship, or a "revolution from above." To bring about an immediate armistice he recommended that a peace conference be called by the President of the United States on the basis of the principles he had proclaimed. A dictatorship, he believed, would have to win some military successes in the near future, however, if not a victory over the enemy; otherwise revolution and chaos would follow. In a "revolution from above" von Hintze had in mind a proposal made by the Supreme Command on September 28 for the admission of important parliamentary leaders into the Government. A change of that sort was necessary, he felt, to enable the nation to bear the sudden change from confidence in victory to the certainty of defeat.

Ludendorff objected to any dictatorship; furthermore, there

60. Ludendorff, *Urkunden*, p. 523; *Ursachen*, II, 365.

61. Described in *Ursachen*, II, 260–281. See also Ludendorff, *Das Friedens- und Waffenstillstandsangebot* (Berlin, 1919), pp. 1–23.

was no possible chance of winning the kind of victory it needed. He liked the idea of a "revolution from above" and an offer of peace carrying with it a plea for an armistice. To put an end to the fighting was his chief concern. When Hindenburg interrupted at this point to urge the Foreign Secretary to acquire Briey and Longwy for Germany in the peace terms, Ludendorff broke in curtly to say that this was no time for anything like that.

The discussion of the details of a peace and armistice that followed, von Hintze has written, was conducted on the principle that "every hour's delay is dangerous." "Ludendorff," he said, "talked like a man who had struggled through to a difficult conclusion and was prepared to accept the consequences." This was not the time, according to the Foreign Secretary, to ask the Army Command why it had not given a true picture of the actual situation earlier; the time called for action, not for questions. He had recommended "revolution from above" because he was convinced that a "revolution from below" would mean suicide. Only in this way would it be possible for the nation to present a united front, "prepared to die before it would accept dishonorable and unworthy conditions of peace." The Army's insistence upon an immediate armistice wrecked the plan he had before coming to Spa for the reorganization of the Government on a new basis and for approaching Wilson with a request for peace at an opportune time. That project assumed that the military situation would permit something like normal and orderly procedure. He had come to Army Headquarters hoping to find the High Command ready for peace; he never dreamed he would be confronted with a demand for an immediate armistice. To his mind that demand injured Germany's cause from the very start.

The Kaiser arrived at Spa on September 29. Since the last big conference there on September 14 he had visited soldiers at the front, and he had been inspecting naval activities at Kiel when news came of Bulgaria's collapse. During the automobile ride to Army Headquarters the Kaiser and Major Niemann discussed the military outlook in great detail; it never occurred to them that it might be necessary to ask the enemy for immediate peace and an armistice. They arrived at Spa in the morning. Calling at the Operations Bureau at nine o'clock, an hour before von Hintze and the High Command opened the conference just described, Niemann met General von Bartenwerffer, Chief of the Political Division in Army Headquarters, who told him of the decision in favor of peace and armistice. "Our situation is such," he explained, "that it can tolerate no further delay. The Field Marshal and General Ludendorff, independently of each other, have reached the decision. Not another hour must be lost." [62]

Between 11 and 12 o'clock there was a second conference, over which the Kaiser presided. Hindenburg, Ludendorff, and von Hintze were present. The Emperor listened without interruption while the Foreign Secretary described the diplomatic as well as the internal situation. Hindenburg was then asked to speak. He spoke much as Ludendorff had spoken in the earlier morning session and finally arrived at the conclusion that the Army needed an immediate armistice. Ludendorff confirmed the report and the recommendation. Asked for suggestions for dealing with this new situation, von Hintze mentioned the notion of a dictatorship, which the Kaiser rejected as "nonsense." The Foreign Secretary then spoke of the danger of a revolution from below and suggested it be avoided by one from above, by organizing the Government on a broader basis. He recommended that Wilson be asked to summon a peace conference on the basis of the Fourteen Points with self-determination of peoples and the rejection of the economic boycott; that, at the same time, in accordance with the wishes of the military, an immediate armistice be sought. According to von Hintze, the Kaiser listened calmly and then declared his approval of the program. The Foreign Secretary thereupon asked permission to resign, for the reason that his reputation as a reactionary might keep some people from putting faith in the new government and might make negotiations with the enemy more difficult. The Kaiser would not accept the resignation; and he declined it a second time when it was offered on the following day.

The conference now turned its attention to the first specific step to be taken. Von Hintze recommended that Vice-Chancellor von Payer be named successor to Chancellor Hertling in case the latter should withdraw. Von Payer was one of the most influential leaders of the Progressive party, had long participated in government, and knew what was going on. The Kaiser favored the recommendation and, for a time, regarded von Payer as future Imperial Chancellor.[63]

Chancellor Hertling, as we have seen, was not in favor of making Germany more democratic and had made up his mind to resign in anticipation of such a move. When he learned on Septem-

62. *Ursachen,* II, 264–265.
63. *Ibid.,* pp. 265–266.

ber 28 that the Army favored the kind of change he opposed, he went immediately to Spa, where he arrived in the afternoon of the 29th. He was accompanied by his son and several members of the Cabinet. During the journey there was no discussion whatsoever of the need for an armistice. Upon arrival at Army Headquarters he learned from von Hintze that the Army Command demanded an immediate cessation of the fighting. The news shocked him; and he admitted to his son that the Foreign Secretary had been right in his pessimistic views of late.[64]

In the afternoon conference the Kaiser accepted Hertling's resignation. Instead of von Payer he now looked upon Prince Max von Baden, Count Roedern, and Dr. Solf as possible successors. He told von Hintze he did not believe there was any danger of an immediate revolution. "We can afford, therefore," he said, "to postpone for a while the formation of a new government and the question of peace. They [presumably the officials with whom he had been conferring] want to remain at Spa quietly for about two weeks to consider the matter." The Foreign Secretary opposed any delay, because the matter was too urgent and the Army was in great haste. When Ludendorff had asked von Hintze for a date when the new government would be formed and the note would be sent to Wilson, the Minister had given Tuesday, October 1, a date which the Army accepted as final. Von Hintze reminded the Kaiser that a new government, one that the enemy could trust, had to be formed before offers of peace and of armistice could be made. The Emperor did not want to make up his mind and turned toward the door. On the table lay the draft of the decree providing for a change of government. "I followed His Majesty to the door," writes von Hintze, "and repeated that the formation of a new government is the necessary preliminary to an offer of peace and armistice. The Kaiser turned back, went to the table and signed the decree."[65]

This decree was published next day in Berlin, the same day that people learned of the defection of Bulgaria and the capture of Damascus by the British under General Allenby. The decree informed the nation that Chancellor Hertling had resigned but had promised to remain at his post until his successor could be found. And then came the rather revolutionary item: "I wish that the German people would coöperate more actively than hitherto in the determination of the fate of the Fatherland. It is, there-

64. Hertling, *Ein Jahr,* pp. 176–180.
65. *Ursachen,* II, 267–268.

fore, My will that men who have the confidence of the people should have a broad share in the rights and duties of government."[66] The *Frankfurter Zeitung* said the following day that for the first time the Imperial Government was a government of the people. "With the change of government . . . the political modernization of Germany is accomplished."

At 9.40 the evening of September 29, before he left Spa for Berlin, von Hintze instructed Undersecretary von Stumm of the Foreign Office by a confidential telegram to "inform Vienna and Constantinople that I propose to suggest peace to President Wilson on the basis of the Fourteen Points and to invite him to call a peace conference in Washington, at the same time asking for an immediate cessation of hostilities." Communication of the decision to Bulgaria was made dependent on the news to come from that ally the next day.[67] "If our allies agree," the telegram concluded, "the new Imperial Government now in process of formation will consider this proposal to be laid before President Wilson in such a way as to make it appear that the proposal originated with itself [that is, with the new Government]."[68] These instructions were carried out at 3 A.M., September 30.[69]

Now that Austria-Hungary and Turkey had been informed of the intended peace move, there was no retreat from the decision taken at Spa on the 29th. The civilian Government may be criticized for having committed two grave errors: first, letting itself be stampeded into the decision by Ludendorff and Hindenburg without questioning the judgment of the two Generals and without asking for any postponement of the decision in order to study the matter more thoroughly; and, second, letting it appear that the new Government was responsible for the decision and not the High Command that had so strongly insisted upon it. Thus it became established early in the minds of many Germans that the sole responsibility for this fateful decision lay with the civilians and not with the Army, where it belonged. What should have been made known was what Ludendorff told three officers about the

66. *Berliner Tageblatt,* September 30, 1918, No. 500.

67. It was actually about two hours later during the night of September 29 that the Bulgarians accepted the terms of the enemy and signed an armistice with the Commander-in-Chief of the Allied Armies in Macedonia, General Franchet d'Esperey. The terms of that armistice are given in Appendix B. Late in the evening of September 30 the German Minister at Sofia, Count Oberndorff, was informed in confidence of the decision to make a peace offer. Document 15, *Amtliche Urkunden.*

68. *Ibid.,* document 13.

69. *Ibid.,* document 14.

decision of September 29; namely, that the High Command assumed full responsibility for the matter.[70]

For the moment, at any rate, Ludendorff had definitely made up his mind.

70. Ludendorff, *Das Friedens- und Waffenstillstandsangebot,* p. 28; *Ursachen,* II, 284–285. The Kaiser's views are given in Ex-Kaiser William II, *My Memoirs* (London, 1922), pp. 268–269.

III

Ludendorff Forces Prince Max to Sue for Peace

LATE in the evening of September 29 von Hintze left on a special train for Berlin to speed the formation of the new Government and the despatch of the note to Wilson by October 1. With him were Count Roedern and Baron von dem Bussche, the latter under special instructions from the Army Command to inform Reichstag party leaders how serious the military situation was in order to hasten things on. Roedern's task was to prepare the way for the broadening of the Government's political base. Before his departure he had talked with Ludendorff and Hindenburg, who stressed the need of an immediate armistice to avoid a sacrifice of men that would be useless in view of the Entente's superiority. Not well informed as to the military situation, Roedern sought information during the night journey from Major Baron von dem Bussche, who said the crisis was so serious that it was a matter of gaining hours, not days, for the offer of peace and armistice. Another member of the party returning to Berlin was General von Gontard, who was to report on developments to the Kaiserin; it was his opinion, based on numerous talks he had had at Army Headquarters, that the enemy might break through the German defenses and push the Army far back; so he urged Roedern to make all possible speed.[1]

In Berlin the morning of September 30 von Hintze and Count Roedern got in touch with von Payer, who was overwhelmed by the request for an armistice. "That was the first time," he wrote in 1922, "that I learned of the conviction of the Army Command that the war could no longer be won by arms." Until that moment he had believed in Germany's ability to hold off the enemy in a defensive war if not to win an ultimate victory.[2] Unable to understand the High Command's decision, he thought that the commanding generals might have suffered a nervous collapse.[3] It was not an unreasonable explanation, for reports were current in

1. *Ursachen,* II, 268–271.
2. *Ibid.,* p. 282.
3. Payer, *Von Bethmann Hollweg,* pp. 87–88.

early September that Ludendorff's health had suffered greatly from the strain under which he had been working.[4]

The day of September 30, when the nation learned of Bulgaria's surrender and of the Kaiser's decision to form a government on a broader base, was spent in the difficult task of framing the new regime. Von Payer took a leading part in this work. Political parties held meetings during the day and drafted programs that resembled that already made public by the Social Democrats. Count Roedern informed Government officials who would be involved in the preparation of the peace negotiations, and participated in conferences to inform party leaders and a committee of the Prussian Upper House of the situation at the front.[5]

The Army Command found that a political machine does not respond to the orders of generals as promptly as does the military. And the Army Command was in a hurry. "Between ten and eleven o'clock in the morning of September 30," writes von Haeften, "General Ludendorff called me up on the telephone from Spa . . . and begged me . . . to do everything possible in Berlin to move the Government to swift and energetic action. *He insisted most expressly that he had no desire to rush them,* but that every day of delay and inaction might be fateful.

"He urged me to use my influence with Secretary of State von Hintze to make him stay at his post and initiate peace overtures. In the afternoon I spoke in that sense to the Secretary of State, but he adhered to his decision to resign his office. If the peace step were to succeed, he said, it must be taken by the new Government. I remarked that some time might elapse before the new Government was formed, and that action must be taken immediately. He interrupted my words with the reply: 'Oh, but the new Government will be formed by tomorrow afternoon at the latest and the peace offer can be issued tomorrow evening.' I took the liberty of expressing my doubts on that point.

"Late in the evening of September 30 I rang up General Ludendorff. I began with a report of the stage reached in the ministerial crisis, and expressed my unfeigned astonishment at the way in which the Crown was pushed aside in finding a solution. The Crown must now decide who was to be entrusted with the formation of the new Government and the negotiations with the politi-

4. Kronprinz Rupprecht von Bayern, *Mein Kriegstagebuch* (Munich, 1929), II, 442, 451.

5. *Ursachen,* II, 283–284.

cal parties. Meanwhile the political parties had been acting on their own authority and had offered the post of Imperial Chancellor to Vice-Chancellor von Payer, who refused the offer, so that at the moment the position was confused. And it was quite uncertain when the new Government would be formed. Proceedings in the matter of forming the Government, which so far had been without precedent even in countries with parliamentary rule, no longer meant *evolution,* but rather *revolution,* as the sovereignty of the majority parties was ousting the sovereignty of the Crown.

"In reply to my question as to who was responsible for all this and for the exclusion of the Kaiser, General Ludendorff replied that Secretary of State von Hintze had suggested it to His Majesty." [6]

Talking that evening with Colonel von Haeften, von Payer said that Prince Max von Baden was the only person able to command the support of a parliamentary majority in this crisis.[7] He suggested that Hindenburg and Ludendorff should first approve Prince Max's candidacy and urged von Haeften to get such approval by telephone. The generals were satisfied; but Ludendorff said that the opinion of the Chief of Cabinet, von Berg, should be sought, since he had opposed the naming of Prince Max in the Spa conference. Von Berg gave his approval and asked that Prince Max, who was with his sister in Dessau at the time, be summoned to Berlin.[8]

Germany was without a government on October 1, the day on which Ludendorff and von Hintze had agreed that the new Government was to despatch its peace offer. The Quartermaster General became impatient. He telephoned Major Baron von dem Bussche to end the delay in the formation of the Cabinet. "He ordered me," writes the Major, "to act on his instructions and put pressure on Vice-Chancellor von Payer, who was then in charge of affairs, to see that the offer of peace was made at once." Ludendorff added that "since the Supreme Army Command had finally made this difficult decision, it must insist that no time be lost." When the Major objected that time was necessary for the formation of a government, Ludendorff replied, "In that case we must insist that the gentlemen in Berlin make haste and come to an agreement."

6. Ludendorff, *Urkunden,* 527–528; *Ursachen,* II, 283, 372–373.

7. As early as September 7 Prince Max remarked that he was considering whether to accept the chancellorship. Haussmann, *Journal d'un Député au Reichstag* (Paris, 1928), p. 251.

8. *Ursachen,* II, 283, 372–373.

"I executed my instructions with regard to Vice-Chancellor von Payer," writes the Baron, "and he assured me that he was doing everything in his power. He again called my attention to the great difficulties involved in the fact that there was no one as yet to sign the offer of peace. He regarded his own signature as improper. The new Imperial Chancellor was not yet named; nor was he certain whether he could succeed in forming a Cabinet. I was requested to ask the Supreme Command whether the publication of our offer of peace could not be postponed." [9]

The question was sent to Spa and shortly after noon came the reply from Hindenburg. "If it is certain by seven or eight o'clock tonight," the Field Marshal's telegram read, "that Prince Max von Baden is forming a Ministry, I can agree to postponement until tomorrow morning. If, on the other hand, the formation of the Ministry is in any way doubtful, I regard the issue of our peace proposal to the foreign Governments as imperative." [10] At 2 P.M. von dem Bussche handed the telegram to von Payer.

"The reason for this message," said von dem Bussche, "was not —as report had it in Berlin immediately afterward—that we were faced with a collapse on the western front in the next few days. Its real purpose was to bring pressure on the ministers and parties to put their own and their party interests to one side and to subordinate everything to the prime interests of the Army and the Fatherland." Ever since these eventful days of 1918 Ludendorff has taken the position that he exerted no pressure for an immediate armistice. Given, however, all that preceded this telegram it was only natural for authorities in Berlin to regard the telegram as additional pressure from the High Command to get a speedy despatch of the request for an armistice.[11]

Pressure from the Army Command continued. In the middle of the afternoon a telegram arrived at the Foreign Office from its Representative at Army Headquarters, Lersner. He had talked

9. Ludendorff, *Urkunden,* pp. 528–529; *Ursachen,* II, 285. Cf. von Payer, *Von Bethmann Hollweg,* pp. 91–92.

10. Ludendorff, *Urkunden,* p. 529; document 22, *Amtliche Urkunden.*

11. Ludendorff, *Urkunden,* p. 529; *Ursachen,* II, 286. It seems clear that Ludendorff actually feared a break-through. He may have known of gaps in his lines where one could occur if the enemy discovered them. The fear of such discovery might well have occasioned his "loss of nerve" and his pressure for an immediate armistice. Ludendorff tried to make it appear that the pressure never came from him, but rather from others. Crown Prince Rupprecht was convinced at this time that Germany must have peace in order to avoid a catastrophe. He had been informed by Ludendorff on October 3 that the withdrawal of Bulgaria from the war signified that the war was lost for Germany. Rupprecht, *Mein Kriegstagebuch,* II, 452, 454–455, 460.

matters over with Ludendorff, who urged the immediate despatch of the peace offer, arguing that, although the troops were holding their own today, it was impossible to foresee what would happen the following day.[12] Grünau, Foreign Office Representative with the Kaiser, was present at the same conference with Ludendorff and also sent an appeal to the Foreign Office. He, too, wanted the note sent immediately, without waiting for the formation of a new government. Ludendorff had said that the enemy might break through the German lines at any moment, and such a time would be most unfavorable for a peace note. Grünau reported "the impression that they have completely lost their nerve here," but he did not want that idea to get abroad. "If things come to the worst," he suggested, "we can justify our action to the outside world by Bulgaria's behavior." [13] Von Payer was puzzled by the pressure coming from Army Headquarters. Why had the High Command given the nation a sense of security for so long and why must the peace note now be sent immediately? Although for a time he had thought that Ludendorff's nerves might be the reason, he soon came to think that the Army feared a great catastrophe.[14] The Kaiser was apparently in no such violent hurry as his generals. Grünau reported to the Foreign Office in the late afternoon that "His Majesty is of the opinion . . . that the step in question should be taken only by the new Government." [15]

Prince Max, his candidacy approved by the Army Command, had been asked on the morning of October 1 to come to Berlin. He was not very well known and the *Frankfurter Zeitung* wondered whether he would be a successful Chancellor. He was 51 years old, cousin to the Emperor, and heir presumptive to the Grand Ducal throne of Baden. For eleven years he had been President of the First Chamber of the Baden Diet. At the beginning of the war he was on the Headquarters Staff of the 14th Army Corps; but after a few months of service bad health had made it necessary for him to retire. Working for the Red Cross, he had done much to improve the condition of foreign prisoners in Germany and of German prisoners abroad. A certain reputation for liberalism had become attached to him, for he had spoken in behalf of a peace of understanding and had taken an open stand against the militarists. Information of this vague sort

12. Document 21, *Amtliche Urkunden.*
13. Document 23, *ibid.*
14. Payer, *Von Bethmann Hollweg,* p. 96.
15. Document 24, *Amtliche Urkunden.*

recommended him by making it appear that he was a person of some independence, one who might initiate peace moves for Germany.

Immediately upon his arrival in Berlin at 4 P.M. Tuesday, October 1, Prince Max was told by Colonel Haeften that the Army Command insisted upon an immediate armistice. The news upset his plans; for he had expected to have a completely free hand. He refused to believe that as grave a measure as an armistice request had become necessary.[16]

For the first time the demand of the Army for an immediate armistice was challenged by someone in authority; and the Army Command did not like it. "He came," writes Ludendorff, "into one of the most critical situations that a statesman could ever be called to. He had to change his manner of thinking entirely. He had believed that the world was ripe for reconciliation and understanding; he fought against taking brutal realities into his reckoning. Apparently he knew nothing of the events of September 29 and saw in everything, especially in the telegram [from Hindenburg] of October 1, 1.30 P.M., only the sudden pressure of the Army Command." [17]

Prince Max was warned by his close friend, the leading Jewish banker of Hamburg, Max Warburg, against making the peace move that the Army insisted upon. "If the military leaders have such a view of the situation," he said, "let them approach the enemy with the white flag." [18] Warburg believed that the Army should continue the fight even though it meant that his only son, just finishing his military training, would be sent to the trenches in four weeks. "I beg you," he concluded, "don't give up now." [19] The Grand Duke of Baden protested against the Prince's accepting the chancellorship, saying that the liquidation of a lost war would be fatal to him and to his house.[20]

Von Hintze, still Foreign Minister, was definitely on the side of the Army and did all he could to hurry things along without waiting for the formation of the new Government. He was ready

16. Payer, *Von Bethmann Hollweg,* pp. 97–99; *Ursachen,* II, 286–287. One may wonder whether Prince Max was affected by Haussmann's warning of September 7 of the need for independence from the Army and from the Kaiser. Haussmann, *Journal,* p. 251.

17. *Ursachen,* II, 286–287; Ludendorff, *Das Friedens- und Waffenstillstandsangebot,* p. 47; Ludendorff, *Kriegserinnerungen,* 528–544; Payer, *Von Bethmann Hollweg,* pp. 97–99. The telegram referred to is that given *supra,* p. 59.

18. Max, *Erinnerungen,* p. 344.

19. Niemann, *Revolution von Oben* (Berlin, 1927), p. 125.

20. Max, *Erinnerungen,* p. 343.

to remove every cause of delay. One of his problems was Austria-Hungary. After all that Germany had done to keep her ally from sending off a separate peace note on September 15, it was the more necessary to make it appear that the allies were in agreement on the present peace move. Early in the morning of September 30 Austria-Hungary was informed of Germany's decision to seek an end to the war. It was not until 6.20 P.M. that a reply came from Count Wedel, Germany's Ambassador in Vienna. The Austrian response was not completely satisfactory. "Count Burian asserted," said the Ambassador, "that in principle we could count on the acceptance of our proposal. He could not, however, give me a formal answer until evening, perhaps not before tomorrow, as he would have to get the consent of the Emperor and, as was demanded by the Constitution, that also of the Premiers [of Austria and Hungary]." Burian expressed some scruples over the proposal to hold the peace conference in Washington: the city was too far away and its atmosphere would be unfavorable to the Central Powers. These scruples were not outweighed, in his mind, by the compliment paid to Wilson in the suggestion. He thought The Hague a better place, and would agree to Washington only if it could not be avoided.[21]

The Foreign Office was not satisfied with mere agreement "in principle" and had no desire to become involved in debate over the place for negotiations. But a long telephone call from Berlin to Vienna in the late morning of October 1 brought no results. Count Burian refused to approve the step until he knew the details of the procedure to be followed. He believed that the new Government should bear the responsibility for the note; the old one would meet only with refusal.[22]

Von Hintze's effort to meet Austrian doubts shows how far he had gone toward working out the details of Germany's peace move. Without having sought Cabinet approval, he had made up his mind what should be done. Late on October 1 he sent the details of the procedure to Count Burian. This was to be the *modus operandi:*

As soon as the new Government is formed, presumably tomorrow or the day after, the Imperial Minister at Berne will receive the following instructions:

"Kindly transmit immediately to the Government where you are

21. Document 16, *Amtliche Urkunden.*
22. Document 19, *ibid.*

the following note: 'The Undersigned Imperial Minister is instructed and has the honor to request the Government of the Confederation to inform the President of the United States by cable that the Imperial Government requests President Wilson to undertake the restoration of peace, and for this purpose to invite plenipotentiaries of all the belligerent nations to Washington. The Imperial Government combines with this request the suggestion to propose to the belligerents the immediate conclusion of a general armistice on all fronts. It declares that it accepts as a basis for the peace negotiations the 14 Points laid down in the message of the President of January 8 and the 4 guiding principles announced in the message of February 11.

" 'Final determination of formalities is left to Your Excellency. Kindly wire at once text of the note submitted and use all possible means to induce the Swiss Government to act with greatest speed and to maintain a rigid discretion in the meantime. Wire report of submission and reception.' "

Count Burian was also told he would be promptly informed when Germany undertook her *démarche* so that Germany and Austria-Hungary could make their moves simultaneously.[23]

Von Hintze was acting with great confidence. At 7.20 in the evening of October 1, in reply to the telegrams that had come from Lersner and Grünau at Spa, he sent this message:

New Government will probably be formed tonight, October 1. So the proposal can also go out tonight. Military situation is strongest means of pressure on unreasonable and arrogant parties.[24]

At an evening conference attended by von Payer, von Hintze, Count Roedern, Major von dem Bussche, and others further pressure was put on Prince Max to send out the note.[25] "I said only a few words," von dem Bussche wrote afterwards. "The Prince said he knew everything. He asked me only whether the proposal for an armistice must be issued as soon as I said. I said 'Yes.' . . . The Prince wished to make an offer of peace

23. Document 20, *ibid.* Late in the afternoon of September 30 the German Foreign Office had already inquired of the German Minister in Berne what he thought of the advisability of asking the Swiss Government to transmit the official peace proposal to Wilson. Document 18, *ibid.*

24. Document 23, *ibid.*

25. Von dem Bussche's account of the conference is given in Ludendorff, *Urkunden*, p. 530. See also Payer, *Von Bethmann Hollweg*, pp. 99–100; *Ursachen*, II, 289–290.

only. His suggestions were given short shrift by the ministers present."

Von Payer says that von Hintze, as Foreign Minister, had prepared the draft of a note to Wilson for this conference to approve and despatch.[26] Prince Max refused to sign it. Both he and several ministers present thought that the responsibility of the new Government. A peace offer should precede a request for an armistice. Further, he wished to have more time to consider whether the note should be sent or not. Referring to this meeting in a session of the Cabinet on October 11, Prince Max said that "he was offered the post of Imperial Chancellor and simultaneously requested to seek at once the peace mediation of Wilson; he objected to this and wished to wait at least a week, in order to consolidate the new Government and not to create the impression that we are making our pleas for peace mediation under the pressure of military collapse." [27]

The Prince proposed to speak about a peace move in an address to the Reichstag, hoping thus to influence the world, particularly the neutrals and the people in enemy countries interested in peace. After such preparation, a request for an armistice could be made. Whether such a request should be made to Wilson was a matter deserving further consideration. Roedern and von Payer sympathized with the Prince's views and would have liked to proceed as he suggested; but they thought that, with a catastrophe near at hand, it would be impossible to delay that long. At the same time they opposed the Army proposal to have the outgoing Government send out the note if a new government could not soon be formed. Von Payer wanted no decision made until political conferences set for the following day had concluded their work and Hindenburg and the Kaiser had arrived in Berlin for consultation. If the Army continued to press for the immediate despatch of an armistice note, von Payer believed it should go out no matter who signed it. He proposed to inform party leaders next morning of the grave situation confronting the nation.

Continuing his account of the conference with Prince Max on the evening of October 1, von dem Bussche wrote: "At this time there always seemed a possibility that the peace note could be issued on October 2, if agreement were reached as to its contents. Then another obstacle appeared. The Grand Duke of Baden had not yet approved Prince Max's accepting the office of Imperial

26. Presumably that suggested for submission to Switzerland.
27. Cabinet protocol, document 42, *Amtliche Urkunden.*

Chancellor.[28] All the gentlemen thought it quite impossible to obtain his approval before the next morning. The question had to be sent through His Majesty the Kaiser. His Majesty was on his way from Spa to Berlin. I proposed that the matter should be settled by telephone. Spa took it in hand. The special train of His Majesty the Kaiser was stopped at Cologne, the castle of Karlsruhe notified, the telephone connections made, and the inquiry was put through without any difficulty in an hour and a half. At midnight the approval of the Grand Duke of Baden had been obtained. . . ." [29] When Army Headquarters informed von Payer of this, Ludendorff urged that Prince Max should sign the armistice note next morning at the latest.[30]

On Tuesday evening, October 1, particularly after hearing from von Hintze that it might be possible to send the armistice note out that night, Ludendorff proceeded on the theory that negotiations were soon to begin and appointed an armistice commission. Lersner reported at 9.45 P.M. on the wishes of the High Command:

General Ludendorff requests that you inform him as soon as possible of the text of our peace proposal, and when it will go to Wilson. He asks also that the peace proposal be communicated to the other enemy Powers. The Hague would suit him best as the place for peace negotiations.

The proposal must contain a demand that the enemy determine on a locality for the conduct of armistice negotiations at the front. [Here followed the names of the members appointed by Ludendorff to the German Armistice Commission, including representatives of Turkey and Austria-Hungary.]

Should the armistice negotiations commence at once, I should, assuming that Your Excellency agrees to this, go with them as the Representative of the Foreign Office, until Your Excellency has appointed a representative.

The Field Marshal will give the credentials to the military, the Imperial Chancellor presumably to the civilians.[31]

28. According to the law of Baden this approval was required. Payer, *Von Bethmann Hollweg,* pp. 100–101.

29. Ludendorff, *Urkunden,* pp. 530–531.

30. Payer, *Von Bethmann Hollweg,* pp. 100–101; *Ursachen,* II, 290–291. It may have been at this time that, according to Prince Max, Ludendorff telephoned "that if he, the Prince, were not Imperial Chancellor by ten o'clock the following morning, it would be better for Vice-Chancellor von Payer to send the note that very evening." Document 42, *Amtliche Urkunden.*

31. Document 26, *Amtliche Urkunden.*

At midnight there came a second message from Lersner:

> General Ludendorff told me that our proposal must be forwarded *immediately* from Berne to Washington. The Army could not wait forty-eight hours longer. He [missing word is probably "begged"] Your Excellency most urgently to make every effort to have the proposal issued in the quickest possible manner.
>
> I showed him plainly that notwithstanding the greatest possible haste the enemy would hardly make a reply in less than a week.
>
> The General insisted that everything depended on the proposal being in the hands of the Entente by Wednesday night or early Thursday morning at the latest, and begs Your Excellency to leave no stone unturned to that end. He thinks that, in the interest of speed, the note might be sent by the Swiss Government by wireless from Nauen in Swiss cipher to the persons addressed.[32]

This message from Lersner followed closely on Ludendorff's insistence by telephone that Colonel von Haeften get Prince Max to sign the note during the night. Von Haeften promised to do it early next morning, although he doubted the Prince would sign until he had concluded negotiations with party leaders for the formation of the new Government.[33] When he called on Prince Max the following day at 8 A.M. he received the refusal he expected.[34]

The Prince regarded it as his first duty to form a coalition Government and he spent October 2 on that task. The difficulties of getting an agreement among the various parties were many and great. Von Payer had worked all the day before, without success. Some people, particularly the Centrists, had wanted von Payer to accept the post of Chancellor, but he declined. Max had told the Vice-Chancellor that he would accept the post only if he had the complete confidence of the majority parties for his program. The Social Democrats had doubts about him because, as a matter of principle, they had long opposed members of ruling houses and future monarchs. And they wanted to know specifically where he stood on proposed changes in the German Constitution and the Prussian Suffrage Law.[35] Prince Max, for his part, refused to

32. Document 27, *ibid.*
33. *Ursachen,* II, 291.
34. *Ibid.*, p. 293; Ludendorff, *Urkunden,* p. 531.
35. On October 1 the Army Command had asked that equal suffrage be accepted by the Prussian Herrenhaus without delay because the political and the military situation demanded it. According to Payer, *Von Bethmann Hollweg,* p. 287.

take office as Chancellor unless the Social Democrats also entered the Cabinet.[36]

Because von Payer thought it expedient to have representatives of all political parties informed about the military situation before the meeting of the Reichstag and the publication of the peace note to Wilson, the Army Command had sent Major von dem Bussche to Berlin. The party leaders met on the morning of October 2, when the Vice-Chancellor felt reasonably sure that the note would soon be forwarded to the American President.[37]

This critical meeting was opened by von Payer: ". . . after a few introductory words I told them what the Army Command demanded and informed them of the approximate contents of the note we intended to send. They sat there shocked; only Count Westarp and Stresemann declared it impossible that we had come to such a desperate situation." [38] Then von dem Bussche spoke. Because his speech had been approved by Ludendorff, and because of the violent reaction it produced, it is given here in full:

> The military situation before the recent great events has been made known through General Wrisberg (Minister of War). In a few days it has changed fundamentally.
>
> The collapse of the Bulgarian front upset our arrangements completely. Communication with Constantinople was threatened, likewise transportation by way of the Danube so indispensable for our supplies. If we did not want to give the Entente a completely free hand in the Balkans and yield the Black Sea and Rumania, we were compelled to move in German divisions and some Austro-Hungarian divisions intended for the western front. The quickest decision was necessary. The first detachments of our troops have already arrived. There is good reason to hope that we shall restore our situation in the Balkans to the degree that is necessary for our interests; unfortunately, however, as I shall explain, not without causing serious harm to our position in general.[39]
>
> Almost at the same time as the Macedonian offensive, mighty attacks commenced in the west. They did not find us unprepared. All

36. Scheidemann, *Der Zusammenbruch* (Berlin, 1921), p. 174.

37. Payer, *Von Bethmann Hollweg*, p. 103; *Ursachen*, II, 293–296, 376. Prince Max says that he did not know about this meeting. Max, *Erinnerungen*, pp. 342–343.

38. Payer, *Von Bethmann Hollweg*, p. 103; *Ursachen*, II, 295–296.

39. Ludendorff had approved this part of the speech before he had learned that Bulgaria was completely lost and that Germany should evacuate her troops from that country. See von Hintze's telegram to Lersner, October 1, document 9a, *Amtliche Urkunden*.

means of blocking them were taken. Eastern divisions were on their way to relieve the much-tried divisions of the west. Unfortunately, part of them had to be diverted to the Balkans. Every last man capable of bearing arms was taken from the east. Calmly we waited for the decisive battle. The Entente was clever in keeping the places on the front secret where the attacks were to be made. Offensive preparations were apparent on the whole line from the sea as far as Switzerland, but the strongest ones were opposite Lorraine and the Sundgau. We were compelled to distribute our reserves and to keep the entire front more or less ready for defense. Considerable strength had to be prepared particularly in Lorraine and in the Sundgau to defend German soil.

After the execution of the necessary movements, there was complete confidence that we would hold out victoriously in the coming battles, and, by inflicting heavy losses, would break the determination of our enemies to destroy us.

In the end, we succeeded in checking the enemy wherever he penetrated our lines either by tanks, by surprise, or by superior strength, and in stopping the drive by bringing up reserves at the right time. The fighting of the last six days has turned out successfully despite losses in prisoners and material. In comparison with our successes in the spring offensives the enemy has achieved little success. At most places his attacks, carried through with unaccustomed stubbornness, were repelled. According to reports from our troops the enemy has suffered very great losses.

The larger part of our troops fought excellently and achieved superhuman results. The old spirit of heroism has not disappeared. The enemy's superiority in numbers did not frighten our soldiers. Officers and men vied with one another.

Despite all this the Army Command has had to reach the immensely difficult decision of acknowledging that, according to human calculation, there is no longer any prospect of forcing the enemy to seek peace.

Two facts above all others have been decisive for this conclusion. The tanks. The enemy threw them in in unexpectedly large numbers. Where they suddenly appeared after laying thick smokescreens about our positions, the courage of our soldiers was frequently no match for them. In such places the enemy broke through our forward positions, opened a way for their infantry, appeared in our rear, produced local panics, and wrecked our conduct of operations. As soon as we spotted the tanks our anti-tank defenses and our artillery dealt with them readily. But by that time the harm had been done; and it is simply by the success of the tanks that we explain the huge numbers of prisoners that cut our own strength so greatly and resulted in a more rapid than normal use of reserves.

We were not in a position to oppose the enemy with an equal number of German tanks. To produce them went beyond the power of our extremely strained industrial system; otherwise, we should have had to neglect other and more important things.

Finally decisive was the question of reserves. The Army entered the big battle with weak resources. In spite of all measures taken, the strength of our battalions sank from about 800 in April to about 400 in September. And even this figure was maintained only by breaking up 22 divisions (66 infantry regiments).

The Bulgarian defeat took 7 more divisions. There is no prospect of raising our strength to higher figures. Current replacements, the convalescent, the men carefully combed out of civil life—these will not amount even to the losses of a quiet winter campaign. The calling up of men from the class of 1900 will raise our battalion strength by only 100 men. After that our last reserve of man-power is exhausted.

Losses in the current battle were, as already pointed out, unexpectedly large, particularly in officers. That's a decisive matter. Whether they are to hold their ground or to attack, the troops demand more than ever a good example from their officers. The latter have had to go in and sacrifice themselves without a thought, and they have done so. Regimental commanders and higher officers fought with their men in the most advanced positions. To give but one example; in two days of fighting one division lost all its officers, dead or wounded, with three regimental commanders killed. The small supply of still available officers has shrunk even more. To build up the strength of the divisions coming from the great battle is hardly practicable. What is true of the commissioned officers is likewise true of the noncommissioned men. The enemy, by virtue of American help, is in a position to replace its losses. The American soldiers as such are of no particular value or in any way superior to ours. Despite their superior numbers they were turned back wherever they made initial gains by means of mass-attacks. It is of critical importance, however, that they were able to take over long stretches of the front and thus enable the English and the French to relieve their experienced divisions and to acquire almost inexhaustible reserves.

Up to now our reserves have been adequate to fill the gap. The railroads have brought them up at the right time. Violent attacks of unheard-of fury have been turned back. The fighting has been described as being far more serious than any hitherto experienced.

But now our reserves are coming to an end. If the enemy keeps on attacking, the situation might require our withdrawal on large sections of the front, fighting as we retire. In this fashion we can carry on the struggle for a considerable time, causing our opponent heavy losses, yielding devastated land; but we are no longer able to win in that fashion.

These events and this understanding of them have caused the General Field Marshal and General Ludendorff to resolve to propose to His Majesty the Kaiser that an effort be made to end the struggle in order to spare the German people and their allies further sacrifices.

Just as our great offensive of July 15 was halted when to continue it bore no relation to the sacrifices required, so now the decision has had to be made to abandon further prosecution of the war as hopeless. There is still time to accomplish this. The German Army is still strong enough to hold out against the enemy for months, to win local victories, and to require additional sacrifices of the Entente. But every day brings the enemy nearer his goal and will make him less inclined to conclude with us the kind of peace we shall find bearable.

For this reason no time should be lost. Every twenty-four hours can make the situation worse and give our enemy an opportunity to comprehend our present weakness.

That might have the most unhappy consequences both for the prospects of peace and for the military situation.

Neither the Army nor the home front should do anything to make our weakness known. On the contrary the nation and the Army must coöperate more closely than hitherto. When our peace offer is made, a united home front must arise to make it clear that there is an unyielding determination to continue the war if the enemy will grant us no peace or only a dishonorable one.

Should this latter possibility result, then the capacity of the Army to fight on will definitely depend on the firm will of the home front and on the spirit coming into the Army from the home front.[40]

These revelations shocked all who heard them, even von Payer, who had already been told what the military situation was. People left the meeting utterly crushed, their pale faces indicating that they had heard news that overwhelmed them. According to reports given later to Prince Max, "Ebert went as white as death and could not utter a word; Stresemann looked as if he had been

40. Document 28, *Amtliche Urkunden.*

struck; Count Westarp alone rose up in protest against the unreserved acceptance of the Fourteen Points. The Prussian Minister von Waldow is said to have left the room with the words: 'There is only one thing left now, and that is to put a bullet through one's head.' " Two parties hostile to the Government, the Polish and the Independent Socialist, were represented by Seyda and by Haase, respectively. It was said that Seyda came away from the meeting looking overjoyed and that Haase rushed up to Ledebour, a party colleague, with the words: "Now we have got them!" [41]

When von Payer informed the Bundesrat of the situation later that day there was the same reaction of shock and dismay.[42]

Now there was "panic in Berlin." ". . . up to this moment," writes Prince Max, "the home front had stood unbroken. . . . Now the spark leaped across to the people at home." [43]

The Army disavowed responsibility for the effect of these damaging revelations, finding others on whom to settle the blame. "The Chancellor," writes Ludendorff with typical disregard for fact, "never put these considerations before the representatives of the people, the Reichstag, although he was expressly requested by General Headquarters to do so. Indeed, all this must have been actually withheld from the Reichstag, just as was my view as to the military situation and the need for peace since August 8. Only thus can one understand the misconception of the whole position that existed in Berlin."

Ludendorff was all innocence. "I was so surprised by the effect of Major Baron von dem Bussche's speech that I repeatedly questioned him on his return as to whether he had said anything different from what we had discussed. He gave me the draft of his speech, to which he kept word for word. This draft lies before me now as I write. I do not know whether the manner in which the Major spoke, or the seriousness of his personality, heightened the effect of his words on his hearers, but such an explanation is humanly possible. The Major himself noticed the great effect his words produced." [44]

Von dem Bussche believed himself quite innocent of saying anything to cause such a reaction. That he and the Army Command understood that their revelations would shock people is apparent

41. Max, *Erinnerungen,* pp. 342–343.
42. Payer, *Von Bethmann Hollweg,* p. 104.
43. Max, *Erinnerungen,* p. 343.
44. Ludendorff, *Kriegserinnerungen,* p. 587.

in their desire to keep the information secret. "Before I began," the Major has explained, "on instructions from Main Headquarters, I asked those present most earnestly to observe strict secrecy as to the contents of my speech. I reminded them most solemnly of the excellent work done by the enemy intelligence service and the advantages which would accrue to the enemy if he clearly realized our position. Not one member of that conference raised any objection to my request. The consequences are well known. Within a few hours the most monstrous rumors were current on my authority." [45]

Somebody was responsible, reasoned the military men afterward, for letting the secret out. "It was highly regrettable," writes Ludendorff, "that the preceding Government did not inform the Major that there was a Pole among his hearers. It must have known that this individual would immediately publish at home and abroad everything that he heard." [46] This opinion receives some support from Haeften, although he was not present at the meeting at which von dem Bussche spoke. Von Haeften has said that he would have opposed the presence of Seyda, the Pole, and Haase, the Independent Socialist; the latter was said to have his connections with Moscow, and the former to have his with Paris by way of Stockholm. The two men were thought to have informed Russia and the Entente about Germany's military weakness, which the Army Command had desired to keep a secret.[47]

The Army Command feared also that the fighting forces would be demoralized if the impression got abroad that the end of the war was near.[48] On October 1 Headquarters asked the Foreign Office to approve the draft of an imperial decree to be issued to the Army and Navy at the time the peace note was sent to the enemy. The proposed draft, however, made Germany's situation appear so hopeless that it was abandoned and a less disturbing one was prepared. Germany, it declared, "had decided once again to offer peace to the enemy." Only an honorable peace would be acceptable, and there would be no cessation of fighting until that was achieved.[49]

It is surprising that the Army Command manifested virtually

45. Quoted in Ludendorff, *Urkunden,* pp. 538–539.

46. Ludendorff, *Kriegserinnerungen,* p. 587.

47. *Ursachen,* II, 293–295, 376.

48. On the afternoon of September 30 the Army Command asked "to be informed of all public announcements of our peace negotiations so that it can keep the Army posted at the proper time. Otherwise, there is danger that demoralization may result." Document 17, *Amtliche Urkunden.*

49. *Ursachen,* II, 296, 379–380.

no concern about the possible effect of a peace proposal on the home front. Although the public had been deceived about conditions on the fighting front, there were some facts that could not be concealed. Meatless weeks were being continued; the butter ration was further limited. Morale was not aided by complaints from trade-unions that some people could escape the effect of these drastic measures because they had means to do so with impunity. The grippe that had died down somewhat after its first appearance in June reappeared in October. Despite years of suffering people had to prepare themselves for the war's fifth dreary winter. They longed for the end of their miseries; they were ready to grasp at anything that promised release. The Army's failure to do anything to avert violent civilian reactions to the request for an armistice must be ascribed to the fact that public opinion was traditionally disregarded by the military.

Ludendorff's first concern was to have a note despatched to Wilson, a note worded as he wished it. That was the issue that arose immediately out of von dem Bussche's speech. The Conservative leader, Count Westarp, expressed approval of the Major's statement that Germany would not accept dishonorable peace terms. But he objected to the note it was proposed to send to Wilson because of its outright acceptance of Wilson's Fourteen Points. Von Payer angrily rejected that interpretation of the note. The debate that followed aroused the suspicions of von dem Bussche, and he promptly informed Army Headquarters that the Government's peace note could be interpreted to mean "that Germany would accept Wilson's demands [i.e., his Fourteen Points] without condition." [50]

Shortly after noon Ludendorff instructed von dem Bussche by telephone to inform von Payer that he agreed with the note in so far as it stipulated "that the Fourteen Points of Wilson's note [*sic*] should serve as the basis for the peace discussions, but should not be the actual conditions imposed by the enemy." The Quartermaster General requested that the note be communicated to him in full before being despatched "in order that I might know what view to take." [51] According to von Payer, the Army Command feared that the first wording of the note would commit Germany to such things as the loss of Prussian Poland and of Alsace-Lorraine.[52]

50. Payer, *Von Bethmann Hollweg,* p. 103; Ludendorff, *Urkunden,* p. 533.
51. Document 29, *Amtliche Urkunden.*
52. Payer, *Von Bethmann Hollweg,* p. 111.

Impatient of delay, Ludendorff a few hours later proposed to the Foreign Office that the following note be sent to Wilson:

> The German Government requests the President of the United States to take steps for the restoration of peace and to invite for this purpose plenipotentiaries of all the belligerents.
>
> It agrees that the points of the program laid down by the President of the United States in his message to Congress of January 8, 1918, and in his subsequent pronouncements, should serve as a basis for the peace negotiations.
>
> The German Government furthermore proposes the conclusion of an armistice on land, on sea, and in the air, and requests the President of the United States to bring about an armistice at once in order to avoid further bloodshed.

In explanation Ludendorff added that he assumed only the familiar Fourteen Points plus four other points were involved. He asked why Austria-Hungary and Turkey should not be asked to participate in this note. Comments of the Foreign Office on the note explain that these two allies were to make separate peace offers and that the General's assumptions regarding Wilson's points were correct.[53]

But before any note could be sent to Wilson a government had to be formed. On October 2 the Social Democrats had prolonged debates in several conferences over the question of participating in a government under Prince Max. Of the party leaders Scheidemann seemed strongest in opposition. "Why participate in a bankrupt enterprise?" he asked. Ebert, who had been profoundly stirred by von dem Bussche's military report in the morning and a talk with Prince Max, challenged this attitude. He argued that the party must coöperate; while he did not believe that the Social Democrats could save the situation, they should not expose themselves to taunts later of having done nothing if Germany should actually suffer a complete internal and external collapse. After prolonged debate it was decided by a considerable majority to take part in the new Government.[54] The National Liberals were also opposed at first to participating, but on October 4 changed their minds and became part of the parliamentary majority.

The afternoon of October 2 the Kaiser and Field Marshal von Hindenburg reached Berlin from Spa. The Kaiser wished to be

53. Document 30, *Amliche Urkunden.*
54. Scheidemann, *Der Zusammenbruch,* pp. 174–176.

near the capital while important decisions were being made. The Field Marshal has explained why he came: "I wanted to be near my Emperor, in case he should need me in these days. Nothing was farther from my thoughts than to wish to control political developments." [55] Ludendorff, who remained at Spa, wanted to have Hindenburg represent General Headquarters in the capital and "instructed Major von dem Bussche to coöperate with the Field Marshal in pressing urgently for the despatch of the note on October 1, or, at the latest, at noon on the 2d." [56]

At 3 P.M. Prince Max had his first conference with von Hindenburg in the Vice-Chancellor's office. There were present also von Hintze, Roedern, and von Berg, Chief of the Kaiser's Civil Cabinet. Prince Max asked that the new Government be given "time to present itself to the world and to Germany, to frame a home policy and to declare its war aims." He asked for a breathing space of 10, 8, or even 4 days before making his appeal to the enemy. Solf too urged a few days' delay.[57] But the only answer they could get from Hindenburg was "the gravity of the military situation permits no delay." In a private conversation Prince Max asked Hindenburg "whether the military situation actually made such precipitate action necessary." The Field Marshal said he expected a new mass attack within a week; the results might be "a catastrophe, or," he corrected himself, might "at least entail the most serious consequences." [58]

The Prince's conferences that day with political leaders proved fairly successful. He was now ready with his program, one that the Kaiser, under the Constitution, had to approve. At 6 P.M. an important conference under the Kaiser's presidency took place in the Imperial Chancellery, with Prince Max, von Hindenburg, von Payer, von Hintze, and a few others present.[59] The Kaiser was in a good mood, writes Prince Max, and opened the meeting with a comment on the "state of nerves Berlin is in."

Von Payer was optimistic as he told of his meetings with political leaders and discussed the new Government. The outlook, he thought, was favorable; the majority parties had already worked out their program and had been accustomed for some time to co-

55. Hindenburg, *Out of My Life* (London, 1920), p. 430.

56. Ludendorff, *Kriegserinnerungen,* p. 587. Ludendorff seems confused about his dates here.

57. Document 42, *Amtliche Urkunden.*

58. Max, *Erinnerungen,* p. 345; Payer, *Von Bethmann Hollweg,* p. 107.

59. Payer, *Von Bethmann Hollweg,* pp. 107–108; Max, *Erinnerungen,* p. 346; *Ursachen,* II, 298.

operate through their Inter-Party Committee. Prince Max was recommended as Chancellor and Dr. Solf as Foreign Secretary. The actual naming of Prince Max and the signing of the necessary papers could not take place, however, until the Social Democrats had definitely stated their willingness to enter the new Government, and that decision was confidently expected in the course of the evening.[60]

Prince Max declared his willingness and readiness to accept the chancellorship, but made it clear that he was opposed to asking for an armistice right away. When he sought the Kaiser's support for his views, the Emperor cut him short. "The Supreme Command considers it necessary," he said, with typical bluntness; "and you have not been brought here to make difficulties for the Supreme Command." [61]

Prince Max was not convinced by this outburst. He put through a telephone call to Ludendorff in an effort to have the matter postponed; but in vain.[62] Late into the night he discussed the matter with people in the Imperial Chancellery. With the exception of Dr. Solf, all the members of the old Government urged on him the necessity of sending off the note to Wilson. Despite the Kaiser's faith in the competence of the Army Command to decide the question, Prince Max had no desire to be responsible for an armistice request which was certain to harm Germany's military situation without first learning the precise military reasons for it. He was unwilling to become an Imperial Chancellor whose first and most important policy—a policy with which he strongly disagreed—was forced upon him by others.

At 9 A.M. on October 3 Prince Max conferred with Hindenburg, to whom he presented a list of objections to the proposed armistice request:

> An immediate armistice offer would be ineffective and dangerous.
>
> All over the world it would be regarded as an admission of German defeat.
>
> It would strengthen jingoism in enemy countries to such an extent that Wilson would be powerless against it.
>
> All the favorable effects the formation of a new government would have in furthering the cause of peace would be lost in the sensation which the armistice offer would make.

60. Haussmann, *Journal,* pp. 276–277.
61. Max, *Erinnerungen,* p. 346; *Ursachen,* II, 298.
62. Max, *Erinnerungen,* pp. 346-347.

As an alternative to despatching the note as the Army Command desired, Prince Max suggested that in his first Reichstag speech upon entering office he give a detailed program of war aims in "close, but not undignified correspondence" with Wilson's points and then to request all belligerent governments to negotiate on this basis. Such a speech by the new German Chancellor, he believed, would have a psychological influence quite different from that produced by a diplomatic note.

Hindenburg would not yield. Thereupon Prince Max promised his consent to the immediate despatch of a note, but "only on the condition that the Supreme Command states in writing—so that I may be in the position to communicate their statement to the Cabinet today, and eventually to publish it—that the military situation on the western front does not allow delaying the note till my speech is made—or rather till it reaches enemy countries on Saturday, October 5." Max warned Hindenburg that the Army Command was being asked to express its opinion on the military situation, not on whether the proposed speech would be a more or less effective method than the sending of a note.[63]

That the Army Command might know precisely what information he desired Prince Max telegraphed the five following questions to Hindenburg in the early afternoon of October 3:

1. How long can the Army hold the enemy on the other side of the German border?

2. Does the Supreme Army Command expect a military collapse, and, if such is the case, at what time? Would the collapse mean the end of our power to defend ourselves?

3. Is the military situation so critical that action for the purpose of bringing about an armistice and peace must be inaugurated at once?

4. In case Question No. 3 is answered in the affirmative, does the Supreme Army Command realize that the inauguration of a peace move under the pressure of a critical military situation might result in the loss of the German colonies and of German territory, such as Alsace-Lorraine and the purely Polish districts of the eastern provinces?

5. Does the Supreme Army Command agree to the enclosed draft of the note? [64]

63. Max, *Erinnerungen,* pp. 347–348; *Ursachen,* II, 298–300.

64. The draft of the proposed note to Wilson was not included. Its contents were discussed, however, in a later conference, but no final agreement was reached. Document 32, *Amtliche Urkunden.*

The Field Marshal sent the following telegram in partial reply:

The Supreme Army Command persists in its request of Sunday, September 29, of this year, urging the immediate despatch to our enemies of the peace proposal.

As a result of the collapse of the Macedonian front, entailing the weakening of our reserves in the west, and as a result of the impossibility of making good the very considerable losses sustained in the battles of the last few days, there exists, according to all human calculation, no further prospect of compelling the enemy to sue for peace.

Our opponents, for their part, can continuously bring new and fresh reserves into the battle.

The German Army is still firm and in good order, and is victoriously repulsing all attacks. But the situation is daily growing more acute, and may force the Supreme Army Command to very serious decisions.

Under these circumstances it is imperative to bring the struggle to an end in order to spare the German people and their allies useless sacrifice. Every day's delay costs the lives of thousands of brave soldiers.[65]

Answers to the other questions were given orally in the conference that met later in the afternoon to discuss the proposed note to Wilson.[66] Here Hindenburg explicitly declared that the Fourteen Points "should serve only as the basis for the negotiations" for peace. Germany, he said, must continue to fight before surrendering any considerable amount of German territory; better to be defeated than to lose honor. The Field Marshal believed it possible to request both peace and an armistice without going into more detail regarding the basis of negotiations. Count Roedern wanted something more explicit, reminding those present that half-way measures would be rejected, like Austria's recent peace proposal. Prince Max still objected to sending any note until he had addressed the Reichstag. Solf's proposal that the note should be addressed to England and France as well as to the United States was rejected on a motion of von Hintze's.

65. Max, *Erinnerungen,* pp. 348–349; document 33, *Amtliche Urkunden.* It is believed that Hindenburg consulted Ludendorff about this telegram as well as about the answers he made later to Prince Max's five questions. *Ursachen,* II, 300.

66. Document 32, *Amtliche Urkunden;* Ludendorff, *Das Friedens- und Waffenstillstandsangebot,* p. 61; *Ursachen,* II, 200, 301–302, 425. Cf. Payer, *Von Bethmann Hollweg,* p. 109.

Hindenburg was now inclined to agree with Prince Max's plea for delay. But he ran into the opposition of von Hintze, who had clung to the Army Command's decision of September 29 to press for an immediate armistice. Berlin officials had been made to feel that anyone who delayed the despatch of the note would be held responsible for whatever military catastrophe or loss of life might result.

Acting for Prince Max, Colonel Haeften tried by telephone to persuade Ludendorff to agree to the sending of a peace note without an express demand for an armistice. He said that Hindenburg's picture of the military situation was not so dark as that painted by von dem Bussche. Ludendorff's answer could leave no doubt concerning his position. "The Field Marshal is doubtless right in his estimate of the situation," he said, "but all the same I must insist on the armistice offer and its *speediest possible* despatch. Even if the situation is not at the moment threatening, still a repetition of the Entente's mass attacks on the whole front is certainly to be expected before long. And in that case—in two or three weeks' time—it might be decisive whether the German Army got its much-needed respite twenty-four hours sooner or later." [67]

In the late afternoon of October 3 there was a second and final conference over the wording of the note to Wilson. Its final form was fixed although it was agreed that the note was not to be sent until the formation of the new Government had been formally completed. The differences between this draft and that sent to Berlin by Ludendorff the day before were slight. The chief one was that, whereas Ludendorff wanted the Government to declare that Wilson's Fourteen Points should "serve" as the basis for peace negotiations, the new text declared that the German Government "accepted" the President's program as a basis for negotiations.[68] This note, like all but the last one addressed to Wilson, was discussed without the Kaiser's being informed.[69]

The task of forming the new Government proceeded on October 3 and the new Cabinet held its first session that evening.[70]

67. *Ursachen,* II, 302–304, 378; Max, *Erinnerungen,* p. 351.

68. *Ursachen,* II, 305 and note. Ludendorff makes much of the fact that his note did not ask for an "immediate" armistice. Although that word was not used, it is obvious that the wording he suggested could hardly be given a different interpretation, particularly when considered with all the other moves he made to procure an early end to the fighting. Ludendorff, *Urkunden,* p. 534.

69. William II, *My Memoirs,* p. 271.

70. Scheidemann, who was not pleased with being put into the Cabinet by his party, says that he was dining in a restaurant when he was told by telephone to

Here it was decided to send the note immediately. Prince Max had virtually to choose between resigning an office hardly yet taken over and signing the note.[71] Writing later of the events of the day, he said, "Toward evening the final form of the note was decided upon. I signed it and was appointed Chancellor the same day." [72]

That night the note was sent to Switzerland, and the German Minister, Romberg, was instructed "to request the Confederate Government to transmit the following telegram to the President of the United States of America":

The German Government requests the President of the United States of America to take steps for the restoration of peace, to notify all belligerents of this request, and to invite them to delegate plenipotentiaries for the purpose of taking up negotiations. The German Government accepts, as a basis for the peace negotiations, the program laid down by the President of the United States in his message to Congress of January 8, 1918, and his subsequent pronouncements, particularly in his address of September 27, 1918.[73]

In order to avoid further bloodshed the German Government requests the President to bring about the immediate conclusion of an armistice on land, on water, and in the air.

(Signed) Max, Prince of Baden,
Imperial Chancellor.[74]

"When I woke up on the morning of the 4th," the Chancellor wrote in his Memoirs, "I felt like a man who has been condemned to death, and has forgotten it in his sleep." News came that day that King Ferdinand of Bulgaria had abdicated in favor of his son Boris. From the front came reports of British Armies pushing hard on German defenses near Cambrai; they broke through the following day.[75]

The day was spent partly in completing the Government. The seventy-one-year-old von Payer was retained as Vice-Chancellor, a post of undefined functions recently created. Although von

appear at the meeting of the Cabinet. There to his great surprise he was greeted as a Secretary. Scheidemann, *Der Zusammenbruch,* p. 176.

71. Payer, *Von Bethmann Hollweg,* p. 110.

72. Max, *Erinnerungen,* p. 351.

73. This speech in the Metropolitan Opera House in New York had just been made public in Germany.

74. Document 34 and note, *Amtliche Urkunden;* Oederlin to President Wilson, October 6, 1918, *Foreign Relations, 1918,* Supplement I, I, 337–338.

75. Max, *Erinnerungen,* p. 353.

Hintze had his supporters, Dr. Solf was made head of the Foreign Office and given control of colonial affairs, a field in which he had already acquired a good reputation. Bauer, long in the trade-union movement and a Social Democratic member of the Reichstag since 1912, was put in charge of labor. He was President of the Ministry that, in 1919, accepted the Treaty of Versailles. Scheidemann was appointed Secretary of State (that is, member of the Cabinet) without portfolio. The Centrist leader, Matthias Erzberger, a member of the Reichstag since 1909, entered the Cabinet over the Kaiser's protest as head of the propaganda department.

The other new Cabinet members were Trimborn, Interior; Scheüch, who was made head of the Department of War on October 9; Haussmann, appointed Secretary of State on October 14. The following members of Hertling's Cabinet continued to hold the same positions in that of Prince Max: von Krause, Justice; Roedern, Treasury; Rüdlein, Post Office; von Stein, Economics; von Waldow, Food; von Mann, Admiralty.

Asked for an opinion about the new Imperial Chancellor, the former American Ambassador to Germany, Gerard, said, "The Prince is a man who knows English perfectly and is one of the high Germans who seem to be able to think like an ordinary human being. . . . Putting forward a man of Prince Maximilian's personality and views in the position of Chancellor, to my mind, means a very definite attempt to seek peace and an abandonment of the Pan-German policy."[76]

The program of the majority parties composing the Government was published on October 4.[77] The new Government committed itself to the answer given by Germany to the Papal peace note of August 1, 1917, and accepted without qualification the Reichstag peace resolution of July 19, 1917. It was ready to enter a league of nations that would include all countries and was based upon the equality of all peoples; that would guarantee permanent peace and the independent existence and free economic development of nations; that would guarantee all member states the rights assured them by the league and exclude all special treaties running counter to its purposes; that was based on a comprehensive development of international law; that would impose on mem-

76. Quoted in the *New York Times,* October 4, 1918. *Le Temps* looked upon Prince Max as a person chosen to make peace before the Allies could defeat Germany and impose severe terms.

77. *Berliner Tageblatt,* October 5, 1918, No. 509.

ber states the reciprocal obligation to submit to peaceful negotiation every dispute that could not be solved by diplomacy; that would stand for the freedom of the seas; establish universal and simultaneous disarmament on land and on sea; guarantee the open door for economic relations without discrimination; and work for the development among the nations of social legislation and of workers' protection. The new Government declared its absolute commitment to the restoration of Belgium and its willingness to make an agreement regarding indemnification. It rejected the treaties made with Russia and Rumania, taking the position that they should not be allowed to obstruct the conclusion of universal peace. In the Baltic States, in Lithuania, and in Poland, it advocated the establishment of popular representation on a wide basis as soon as possible. The program favored making Alsace-Lorraine an independent state within the German Confederation, assuring the people of complete autonomy in accordance with the demand of their representatives. It demanded immediate electoral reform in Prussia and in other federal states. It called for a unified control of Germany's Government, by members to be chosen from Parliament. It demanded a strict maintenance of constitutional responsibilities and the removal of military establishments that might influence political developments. For the protection of personal freedom, the right of assembly, and freedom of the press, an immediate modification of martial law was demanded so that censorship would henceforth be confined to questions affecting relations with foreign governments, military strategy and tactics, troop movements, and the protection of war supplies. The creation of an agency for the supervision of the measures taken under martial law was also advocated.

On October 5 Prince Max made his first official appearance before the Reichstag as Imperial Chancellor. There was great public excitement over this meeting of the legislature: none had been expected until November 5 and there were rumors that the new Chancellor would say something about peace.

Great care was used in preparing the speech. Everything depended upon it. Rarely is a message of such significance the first act of a new government. During the evening of October 4 a number of intimate friends of Prince Max worked on the speech, which in its first draft contained a detailed analysis of Wilson's Fourteen Points, the basis of the peace that Germany desired. In that form the speech was read to the Cabinet, where the opposition was unanimous. This attempt to interpret Wilson's mind, it was argued, could only offend the American President and delay the conclusion of the war. The speech had to be rewritten and there was not much time left.[78] This may explain why the opening of the Reichstag was postponed from noon to 5 P.M.

While waiting for the session to open, Haase and Ledebour, both members of the Independent Socialist party, insisted upon the right to debate the new Chancellor's policies, and it was only after warm discussion that it was arranged to have no debate on the speech. At the last minute Prince Max had to be persuaded not to wear his customary military uniform; civilian garb was judged more suitable for the occasion.

At 5.15 President Fehrenbach called the Reichstag to order. The chamber was crowded. There were not seats enough on the tribune for all members of the new Government. Scheidemann, Gröber, Erzberger, and Bauer had to stand, at Prince Max's right, symbols of the Government's turn to the left. The excitement was intense, but subdued. Fehrenbach spoke somberly. "Since we separated on July 13," he said, "events have intervened to cause us anxiety. Our western Army after its mighty offensive has shifted to the defensive and to slow retreat."

Then came Prince Max. "The words I speak to you today," he said, referring to the political changes that had occurred, "I speak in the name of the German Empire." As he outlined the program of the new Government as determined by the majority parties, a program of reform and of peace, his hearers were astonished by its liberal, even radical character, though the terms were already familiar. The most exciting part of the address came last, its significance not destroyed by the Chancellor's clear but monotonous reading of the words:

More than four years of the bloodiest struggle against a world of numerically superior enemies lie behind us, years full of the hardest battles and most painful sacrifices. Everyone of us carries his scars, too many of us in fact have wounds still open—it may be in the depth of his soul or upon a body offered on the battlefield as a willing sacrifice for German freedom.

Nevertheless, we are of stout heart and full of confident faith in our strength, resolved to bear, if it cannot be otherwise, still heavier sacrifices for our honor and freedom and for the happiness of our

78. Haussmann, *Journal,* pp. 279–280. Prince Max later regretted that he let himself be persuaded to abandon a discussion of the Fourteen Points, which he thought might have procured Germany a better armistice, even if a later one. The speech he wanted to give is found in his *Erinnerungen,* pp. 359–370.

posterity. We remember with deep and warm gratitude our brave troops, who, under brilliant leadership during the whole war, have accomplished almost superhuman deeds and whose past deeds are a sure guaranty that the fate of all of us will in the future also be in good and dependable hands in their keeping.

For months a continuous, terrible, and murderous battle has been raging in the west. Thanks to the incomparable heroism of our Army, which will live as an immortal, glorious page in the history of the German people for all time, the front is unbroken. This proud consciousness permits us to look to the future with confidence.

But, just because we are inspired by this feeling and this conviction, it is also our duty to make certain that the murderous and bloody struggle be not protracted for a single day beyond the moment when a close of the war seems possible for us, a close that does not affect our honor. I have, therefore, not waited until today to take an active step to further the idea of peace. Supported by the consent of all duly authorized institutions of the Empire and by the consent of all our allies acting together with us, I sent on the night of October 4–5 [actually the night of October 3–4] through the mediation of Switzerland, a note to the President of the United States of America, in which I asked him to work for the restoration of peace and to communicate to this end with all the belligerent states. The note will reach Washington today or tomorrow.

It is directed to the President of the United States because he, in his message on January 8, 1918, and in his later proclamations and especially in his speech in New York on September 27, proposed a program for general peace which we can accept as a basis for negotiations.

I have taken this step toward the salvation not only of Germany and her allies but of all humanity, which has been suffering for years through the war, because the thoughts regarding the future well-being of the peoples which were proclaimed by Mr. Wilson are in accord with general ideas cherished by the new German Government and by the overwhelming majority of our nation.

So far as I am personally concerned, my earlier speeches to other audiences will testify that the conception which I hold of a future peace has undergone no change since I became entrusted with the direction of the nation's affairs.

What I want is an honorable, lasting peace for all mankind, for I believe that such a peace would at the same time be the strongest wall of defense for the future prosperity of our own Fatherland. I see, therefore, no distinction whatever between the national and international mandates of duty in respect to peace. For me the deciding factor is solely that all participants with equal honesty acknowledge these mandates as binding, and respect them, as I do and as do the other members of the new Government.

And so, with an inner calm, which my clear conscience as a man and as a servant of the people gives me, and which rests at the same time upon firm faith in this great and true people, this people capable of every devotion, and upon their glorious armed power, I await the outcome of the first action which I have taken as directing statesman of the Empire.

Whatever this outcome may be, I know it will find Germany firmly resolved and united, either for an upright peace which rejects every selfish violation of the rights of others, or for a final struggle for life and death to which our people would be forced through no fault of theirs, if the answer to our note by the Powers opposed to us should be dictated by a will to destroy us.

I do not despair over the thought that this second alternative will come. I know the measure of the mighty strength still possessed by our people, and I know that the incontrovertible conviction that they were fighting only for our life as a nation would double this strength. I hope, however, for the sake of all mankind that the President of the United States will receive our offer as we mean it. Then the door would be opened to a speedy, honorable peace of justice and reconciliation for us, as well as for our opponents.[79]

There was no debate on the Chancellor's program. A motion against discussion was made by Ebert, leader of the majority, and was carried, to the profound relief of the new Government, which felt that a crisis had been averted. Rightists and Leftists were overwhelmed to see how liberal Prince Max had become. At the conclusion of the session President Fehrenbach congratulated the Chancellor on the outcome, saying he had feared "a hysterical outburst" from the deputies. The Prince felt that his speech had kept a panic from developing into a catastrophe.

German liberal newspapers were well pleased with the new Government because it was Germany's first parliamentary experiment and because it was working for a peace of understanding. Speaking in the Reichstag on October 22, Ebert said, "October 5 is really regarded as the turning point in German history. It is the birthday of German democracy." In this mood of joy few realized

79. Document 34a, *Amtliche Urkunden.* Max, *Erinnerungen,* p. 370; Haussmann, *Journal,* pp. 282–283.

that Prince Max had been forced by the Army Command to make the peace move. At this time the Chancellor was as careful to keep that fact from becoming known as others were later to place the entire responsibility on him. For the moment it was enough for the people that "Max equals Pax."

The papers were almost unanimous in cautioning against thinking that the war was over. On October 5 the liberal *Vossische Zeitung* reminded the nation that "the fate of Germany is placed in the hands of President Wilson"; there was no reason to believe that peace was certain to follow from this first step. The Socialist *Vorwärts* was equally cautious on October 5 when it said that the peace to come would be no peace of victory for the Germans, yet not a hard peace if it corresponded with the five points of Wilson's speech of September 27, just now made public in Germany. If the peace move should succeed and Germany should become a member of a free league of nations, German Social Democrats could be proud of their work to this end. Pointing to Russia as an example of what happens when discipline breaks down, *Vorwärts* warned that a relaxation of discipline might assist the imperialism of Germany's enemies. The trade-unions issued a similar warning. The nation must still defend itself, for although it wanted a peace of understanding, it was not ready to accept peace at any price.[80] And the Conservative Count Westarp declared that "the German people, however, will not and need not surrender to insulting and annihilating peace terms." [81] The Pan-Germans were the people most thoroughly displeased by the peace move and Prince Max's speech.

The German Crown Prince had no idea that the Army Command at Spa had forced Prince Max into his peace gesture. "While my brave divisions, ragged and tattered as they were," he writes, "were retiring step by step and defending themselves as they went—Berlin despatched to the President of the North American Republic, via Switzerland, the offer which suggested a 'just peace' based in essence upon the principles put forward by Wilson—an offer which was coupled with a disastrous request for the granting of an armistice." [82]

Few German patriots could have been more shocked than Walther Rathenau, who criticized the peace offer in a newspaper

80. Quoted in *Vossische Zeitung,* October 7, 1918, No. 513.
81. *Ibid.,* October 7, 1918, No. 512.
82. *Memoirs of the Crown Prince of Germany* (New York, 1922), p. 263.

article entitled "A Dark Day."[83] He, too, was ignorant of the circumstances. To this loyal Jew the action appeared overhasty; the Government had let itself be swept into a policy to which it had given far too little thought. The proper time for peace negotiations, he argued, was not when troops were retreating but rather when the front held firmly. "Wilson should be asked what he means by the most insidious of his Fourteen Points, especially about Alsace-Lorraine, Poland, and the indemnification of the lands in the west. The premature request for an armistice was a mistake. The land is untouched, its means are not exhausted, its people are not worn out. We have fallen back, but we have not been broken. Wilson's answer will come and it will not be satisfactory; more than that, it will be scornful, humiliating, demanding. We should not be surprised if we are asked to evacuate the west, if not actually imperial territory. Point 8 will be interpreted to mean the surrender of Lorraine, presumably also of Alsace. Danzig may be the Polish harbor. The restoration of Belgium and of northern France can lead to a concealed demand for an indemnity amounting to fifty billions. Has this been overlooked? If anybody has lost his nerve, he should be replaced." Rathenau believed that Wilson's demands might be extended by interpretation because it could be assumed that Germany's will was broken. Fearing an unsatisfactory answer that would deprive Germany of her *Lebensraum*, he suggested that Germany prepare herself by a *levée en masse*. He also wanted a ministry of defense independent of existing authorities, composed of citizens and soldiers, and endowed with full powers. It should make an appeal to the nation to assist soldiers at the front; all soldiers on leave should be recalled; those doing guard duty throughout Germany should be called to the front. A strong Germany would get very different peace terms from a helpless Germany. "We desire not war, but peace; and not a peace of subjection."

Care was taken to keep the peace offer from having a harmful effect on the fighting men. On October 5 the Kaiser signed an appeal to the soldiers and sailors to be ready with all their power to withstand any strong attack that the enemy might make despite the fact that a peace note had been sent.[84]

83. *Vossische Zeitung*, October 7, 1918, No. 512. Also in Lutz, *Fall of the German Empire*, II, 464–465.

84. *Ursachen*, II, 380, footnote. Lutz, *Fall of the German Empire*, II, 166–167. Cf. *supra*, p. 72.

There was need for calling upon the German people to maintain discipline. The admission of defeat had come too suddenly, even for those who knew something of what had been taking place. People now awoke to the fact that for years they had been getting *Ersatz* for truth as for other consumer goods. Despair crept over them when they learned there was no hope of victory. It was impossible to rouse them to fight to the finish even against actual invasion. As censor-in-chief Ludendorff had been responsible for keeping the truth out of circulation; now he criticized the Government for failing to prepare the people for the impending catastrophe. The heads of the propaganda departments had long wanted the nation to know the bitter truth, but had always been checked by the assurance that the front would hold firm.

There were ominous signs. At the meeting of the Spartacus Bund in Gotha on October 7, the delegates demanded a dictatorial government by workers' and soldiers' councils after the manner of the Russian Bolsheviks. The meeting was thought by some to have a significance out of proportion to its size.[85]

Discussing the note to Wilson in a conference of ministers on Sunday, October 6, Prince Max could say what he had been unable to tell the Reichstag. "I fought against the note; first because I thought the time premature; second, because I wished to turn to the enemy in general." Now that it had been despatched, Germany "must quietly consider the consequences." Max's faith in Ludendorff was gone. "The situation at the front must be determined, and that through experienced officers." Solf pointed out the effect of such a proposal: "Haeften states that Ludendorff looks upon the establishment of a commission [of investigation] as a lack of confidence in himself, and says that, if it be done, he would hand in his resignation. That would entail the resignation of Hindenburg." Prince Max answered that nevertheless "the leaders of the Army must be heard." He hoped by a talk with the Emperor to find a way to do it. "It is necessary to find a way," said von Payer. "We must hear other people besides Ludendorff. Ludendorff's nerves are no longer reliable." And in this proposal for an inquiry the Vice-Chancellor was supported by both Solf and Erzberger.[86]

85. Eduard Bernstein, *Die Deutsche Revolution* (Berlin, 1921), p. 21.
86. Protocol of conference, document 35, *Amtliche Urkunden.*

IV

Wilson Disregards the Allies

THE German note to President Wilson was forwarded from Berne at 5.45 P.M. on October 4.[1] It reached Washington October 6 but was not formally presented to the Government by the Swiss Minister until the 7th.[2]

If the Germans had hoped, by addressing their request to Wilson, to gain an advantage over the Entente Powers, they were to be partly disappointed. The message was intercepted by the French Intelligence and decoded. Thus the French were able to start preparations as early as October 5 for the kind of armistice they desired.[3] The German appeal to Wilson filled the French with alarm. They did not know what to expect from a "man of principle" like President Wilson, being puzzled as were other continentals at the sight of an Anglo-Saxon moralist in politics. Like their European allies the French feared that Germany's request for an armistice was a trap set by the wily Germans for the unwary enemy. *Le Matin* looked on the change of Government under Prince Max as a mask, a veil to cover something fearful.[4] The Germans were suspected of trying to escape the consequences of certain defeat. The London *Times* on October 6 expressed the thought that prevailed generally in the minds of Germany's enemies. "Their one determination is that the defeat of those who made this war shall be complete and absolute, that the task which they have undertaken shall be performed to the very end, and that there shall be no peace until Germany has surrendered without conditions to the terms which will leave her not merely without

1. Note to document 34, *Amtliche Urkunden.*

2. Oederlin to Lansing, October 6, 1918. *Foreign Relations, 1918,* Supplement I, I, 337–338; R. S. Baker, *Wilson,* VIII, 447, 456. The Austrian plea for an armistice and for peace was presented to the American Government by the Swedish Minister on October 7. Lansing to President Wilson, October 7, 1918, *Foreign Relations of the United States. The Lansing Papers, 1914–1920* (Washington, D. C., 1940), II, 160. Hereafter referred to as *Lansing Papers.* The note itself is given in Ekengren to Lansing, October 7, 1918, *Foreign Relations, 1918,* Supplement I, I, 341.

3. Mordacq, *L'Armistice du 11 Novembre 1918* (Paris, 1937), p. 151; Mordacq, *La Vérité sur l'Armistice* (Paris, 1929), p. 68. Weygand, "Le Maréchal Foch et l'Armistice," *Revue des deux Mondes,* November, 1938, p. 8.

4. *Le Matin,* October 6 and 7, 1918.

the will, but without the power, to break it." The new German Government it referred to as "camouflage democracy."

It was in this mood of distrust and determination that people in France began work on armistice conditions. Clemenceau, who had no faith in the American President, on October 5 asked Foch to prepare a report on the question. The Marshal's report, which was ready by the 8th, read as follows:

There must be no question of halting hostilities in what concerns the armies operating in France and Belgium unless the following conditions are fulfilled:

(1) *Liberation of the countries* which, in violation of all law have been invaded, viz.: Belgium, France, Alsace-Lorraine, Luxembourg, with the return of their inhabitants.

Therefore, the enemy should evacuate these territories within fifteen days and repatriate their inhabitants immediately.

First condition of the Armistice.

(2) *Assure a suitable military base of departure* permitting us to carry on the war until the enemy's forces are destroyed in case peace negotiations fail.

For this we need two or three bridgeheads on the Rhine: Rastadt, Strasbourg, and Neu-Breisach. (A bridgehead would be a semicircle traced on the right bank, with a radius of 30 kilometers taking the edge of the right bank as a center). This also to be effected within fifteen days.

Second condition of the Armistice.

(3) *Take securities for reparations,* to be exacted for damage done in the Allied countries, the bill for which is to be presented at the time of the peace negotiations.

For this purpose the territory on the left bank of the Rhine must be evacuated by the enemy's troops in not more than thirty days; this territory will be occupied and administered by Allied troops in concert with the local authorities until such time as peace shall have been signed.

Third condition of the Armistice.

In addition, the following supplementary conditions should be exacted:

(4). All the war material and supplies of every kind that cannot be removed by the German armies within the time limit prescribed must be left on the spot; their destruction is forbidden.

(5). Troops which have not evacuated the territory specified within the time limits fixed shall be disarmed and made prisoners of war.

(6). All railway material, including track and operation equipment, must be left where it is, and none of it destroyed. All seized Belgian and French material (or its numerical equivalent) shall be immediately returned.

(7). Military establishments of all sorts intended for the use of troops—camps, barracks, ammunition dumps, arsenals—must be left intact, it being forbidden to take away or destroy anything therein.

(8). The same applies to industrial establishments and factories of all sorts.

(9). Hostilities will cease twenty-four hours from the day on which these conditions shall have been approved by the contracting parties.[5]

According to Mordacq, Clemenceau approved these recommendations on October 9.[6]

Like the French, the British had no intention of being unprepared for the armistice. To Field Marshal Sir Henry Wilson the matter seemed simple. He regarded the German appeal to President Wilson as a "pretty piece of impertinence" and thought there should be no negotiation with Germany until "the Boches get behind the Rhine."[7]

At 3 A.M. on October 6, before the German note had reached Washington, Admiral Hope telephoned to Admiral Wemyss, the First Sea Lord, asking him to draw up the naval terms to be sought in the armistice with Germany. To Wemyss the terms themselves presented no difficulty, because he had long before made up his mind what they ought to be. The chief problem was to get them agreed upon. That took many conferences. Beatty and the Grand Fleet held out for another Trafalgar. The Government, on the other hand, was eager for an early peace; the labor situation, the many strikes, including a police strike, and the discontent in the Navy made a speedy end to the war desirable, and harsh terms could not be allowed to delay reaching that objective.

5. Maréchal Foch, *Mémoires* (Paris, 1931), II, 270–272. Foch claims the initiative in this matter whereas General Mordacq ascribes it to Clemenceau. Mordacq, *Le Ministère Clemenceau* (Paris, 1930), II, 266.

6. Mordacq, *L'Armistice*, pp. 69–70.

7. Major-General Sir C. E. Callwell, *Field-Marshal Sir Henry Wilson* (New York, 1929), II, 133.

A compromise had to be effected between those who would yield nothing and those who might be ready to yield too much.[8]

The great fear in the Entente countries was that Wilson would negotiate with Germany without consulting them. Everything possible must be done to keep him from acting independently of the nations with whom the United States was associated in the war. In a private discussion Lloyd George "took the line that we pandered and bowed too much to President Wilson," a view that Field Marshal Sir Henry Wilson found to his liking. " [I] am certain," wrote the British General, "that a few good home truths would do the President good." But though Sir Henry and Lloyd George agreed about Wilson they were not in agreement on the policy toward Germany. The British Premier, and Bonar Law as well, thought the General's proposal for disarming the Germans and confining them back of the Rhine too severe. The blunt soldier, on the other hand, had no love of "nervous" politicians, and he could not see "what guarantee we shall get worth having unless we disarm the brutes." [9]

There was a meeting of the Prime Ministers of France, Great Britain, and Italy in Paris on October 5, ostensibly to arrive at an agreement about the situation in the Balkans, where it was feared a general collapse might come and find the European Powers in disagreement on the "general principles of adjustment." In the mind of General Tasker H. Bliss, the American Representative on the Supreme War Council, that meeting had another purpose, which was, "perhaps, the more important of the two." It was occasioned by the rumors that the German Government had appealed to the United States. If Germany should collapse, the European Powers should also have an understanding with one another about the matter. According to Bliss, "there were some who did not see how such an appeal could be made or entertained without the possibility of a separate peace or, at least, of such action as would reduce the Allies to playing second part in the making of a general peace." [10]

In Washington President Wilson was acting without consult-

8. Lady Wester Wemyss, *Life and Letters of Admiral of the Fleet Lord Wester Wemyss* (London, 1935), pp. 384–385.

9. Callwell, *Field-Marshal Sir Henry Wilson,* II, 134.

10. Report of General Bliss to Secretary Lansing, February 19, 1920, *Lansing Papers,* II, 289–290. See also "The Armistices" by General Bliss in *The American Journal of International Law,* Vol. XVI (1922), 509–522, and Callwell, *Field-Marshal Sir Henry Wilson,* II, 131–133.

ing his allies about the reply to be made to Germany, and in Paris the representatives of three of these allies conferred and reached an agreement on guiding principles and policies for an armistice with Germany without asking General Bliss to participate. On October 6 they concluded that Germany would have to accept the following conditions:

Paragraph 1 Total evacuation by the enemy, of France, Belgium, Luxembourg, and Italy:

Paragraph 2 The Germans to retire behind the Rhine into Germany:

Paragraph 3 Alsace-Lorraine to be evacuated by German troops without occupation by the Allies:

Paragraph 4 The same conditions to apply to the Trentino and Istria:

Paragraph 5 Servia and Montenegro to be evacuated by the enemy:

Paragraph 6 Evacuation of the Caucasus:

Paragraph 7 Immediate steps to be taken for the evacuation of all territory belonging to Russia and Roumania before the war:

Paragraph 8 Immediate cessation of submarine warfare. Unnumbered paragraph (It was also agreed that the Allied blockade should not be raised.) [11]

At a meeting on October 7 the three Powers decided "to refer to the Military Representatives at Versailles, with whom shall be associated Representatives of the American, British, French, and Italian Navies, the consideration of the terms of an armistice with Germany and Austria" on the basis of these enumerated points.

At 9 P.M. on October 7 General Bliss, the American Military Representative, was officially informed of the October 6 meeting

11. Report of General Bliss to Secretary Lansing, February 19, 1920, *Lansing Papers,* II, 289–290. Also, Bliss, "The Armistices," p. 513. Just why the last paragraph is unnumbered and in parentheses is puzzling. That the question of the blockade was debated is clearly implied in Lloyd George, *War Memoirs,* VI, 248–249. The British Premier gives the same document with the following sentence added to the unnumbered paragraph: "This decision seems harsh but we are anxious that the period of the armistice should not be utilized to reëquip Germany for a renewal of War." In a conversation with Frazier, the American Liaison Officer with the Supreme War Council, Lloyd George referred to an armistice with Germany and suggested that "Germany might for instance agree to abstain from submarine warfare if the blockade were removed; such points could be decided by the naval authorities." Frazier to Lansing, October 7, 1918, *Foreign Relations, 1918,* Supplement I, I, 344.

of the Prime Ministers and of the principles of armistice they had agreed upon. At the same time he was told that the whole question was being referred to the Representatives of the Allied Armies and Navies, who were to meet at 9:15 A.M., October 8. Having no specific instructions for such a conference, General Bliss "decided not to participate in the discussion and recommendation of armistice terms thus requested," although "it was commonly believed in every Allied capital in Europe that a German note on this subject was then pending before the Government at Washington."[12] He immediately cabled the "principles" of the proposed armistice to Washington. In his cablegram he called attention "to par. 2 of the note, under which, if not modified, the Germans could retire to a strong position behind the Rhine with their army, armament and supplies intact."

To make doubly sure that President Wilson would not forget the Powers associated with him, Lloyd George had a talk during the afternoon of October 7 with Frazier, whom he informed of the agreement made concerning the basis for an armistice and of the decision to have the Military Representatives work out the details. In Frazier's words Lloyd George seemed to be "exceedingly anxious to find out whether President Wilson had replied to the German peace proposal and earnestly hoped that the President would send Colonel House over at the earliest possible moment." The various ministers who had come to Paris, the Premier told him, planned to remain until October 9 in the hope that something might be heard from President Wilson.[13]

The fear that Wilson might act independently of the Allies was not confined to the major Powers alone. On October 7 Hymans, the Foreign Minister of Belgium, wanted the United States to know that his Government desired, in case an armistice was being considered, "to be heard as to the guarantees that it would deem indispensable to the safety of Belgium."[14]

Thus it was that Military and Naval Representatives of the Allies met during the morning of October 8 and arrived at important conclusions without any American participation. They agreed "that the first essential of an armistice is the disarmament of the enemy, under the control of the Allies." On the basis of that opinion and of the guiding principles established by the

12. Bliss, "The Armistices," p. 513.

13. Frazier to Lansing, October 7, 1918, *Foreign Relations, 1918*, Supplement I, I, 344–345. This despatch reached Washington October 8 at 1 P.M., just about the time Wilson had drafted his reply to Germany.

14. Whitlock to Lansing, October 7, 1918, *ibid.*, p. 344.

Entente ministers on October 6 they recommended the following specifications:

1. Total and immediate evacuation, by the enemy, of France, Belgium, Luxembourg, and Italy on the following conditions:

(a) Immediate re-occupation by Allied troops of the territories so evacuated;

(b) Immediate repatriation of the civil population of these regions interned in enemy country;

(c) No "sabotage," looting or fresh requisitions by enemy forces;

(d) Surrender of all arms and munitions of war and supplies between the present front and the left bank of the Rhine;

2. Germans to retire behind the Rhine into Germany.

3. Alsace-Lorraine to be evacuated by German troops without occupation by the Allies, with the exception stated in Clause 18 below. It is understood that the Allies will not evacuate the territory in their occupation.

4. The same conditions apply to the territory included between the Italian frontier and a line passing through the Upper Adige, the Pustherthal as far as Toblach, the Carnic Alps, the Tarvis and the meridian from Monte Nero, cutting the sea near the mouth of the Voloska (see Map of the Italian Military Geographical Institute 1 over 500,000).

5. Serbia, Montenegro and Albania to be evacuated by the enemy under similar conditions to those stated in Clause 1.

6. Evacuation of the Caucasus by the troops of Central Powers.

7. Immediate steps to be taken for the evacuation of all territory belonging to Russia and Roumania before the war.

8. Prisoners in enemy hands to be returned to Allied Armies without reciprocity in the shortest possible time. Prisoners taken from the Armies of the Central Powers to be employed for the reparation of the wilful damage done in the occupied areas by the enemy, and for the restoration of the areas.

9. All enemy surface ships (including Monitors, River craft, etc.), to withdraw to Naval Bases specified by the Allies and to remain there during the Armistice.

10. Submarine warfare to cease immediately on the signature of the Armistice. 60 submarines of types to be specified shall proceed at once to specified Allied Ports and stay there during the Armistice. Submarines operating in the North Sea and Atlantic shall not enter the Mediterranean.

11. Enemy Naval air forces to be concentrated in bases specified by the Allies and there remain during the Armistice.

12. Enemy to reveal position of all his mines outside territorial waters. Allies to have the right to sweep such mines at their own convenience.

13. Enemy to evacuate Belgium and Italian coast immediately, leaving behind all Naval war stores and equipment.

14. The Austro-Hungarian Navy to evacuate all ports in the Adriatic occupied by them outside national territory.

15. The Black Sea Ports to be immediately evacuated and warships and material seized in them by the enemy delivered to the allies.

16. No material destruction to be permitted before evacuation.

17. Present blockade conditions to remain unchanged. All enemy merchant ships found at sea remain subject to capture.

18. In stating their terms as above, the Allied Governments can not lose sight of the fact that the Government of Germany is in a position peculiar among the nations of Europe in that its word can not be believed, and that it denies any obligation of honor. It is necessary, therefore, to demand from Germany material guarantees on a scale which will serve the purpose aimed at by a signed agreement in cases amongst ordinary civilized nations. In those circumstances, the Allied Governments demand that within 48 hours:

> 1st. The fortresses of Metz, Thionville, Strassburg, Neu Breisach and the town and fortifications of Lille be surrendered to the Allied Commander-in-Chief.
>
> 2nd. The surrender of Heligoland to the Allied Naval Commander-in-Chief of the North Sea.

19. All the above measures, with the exception of those specially mentioned in paragraph 18, to be executed in the shortest possible time, which it would appear should not exceed three or four weeks.[15]

General Bliss cabled this document at once to Washington. The Military Representatives who had drafted it for submission to the Prime Ministers asked him to sign it for the United States; but that "he declined to do in the absence of instructions from his government." Bliss "had no criticism of the general tenor of the document and he, of course, accepted the establishment of the essential principles of disarmament and the fixing of guarantees." It was his belief "that one or both of only two reasons" explained the action of the Prime Ministers. "One is this: it was known that

15. Bliss, "The Armistices," pp. 513–514. Found also in *Lansing Papers,* II, 291–292.

the question was then pending in some form in Washington; it was not known what attitude towards it would be there taken; it was apprehended that some committal might be made adverse to Allied wishes or interests. If this were the reason, the Allies, who knew that this action would be immediately cabled in full to Washington, would also know that in this indirect way Washington would be made aware that they had views of their own on the subject of an armistice. The other reason may be that the Allies wished to be tentatively prepared by studies of their own in case notes should be addressed to them by Germany as had been done to the United States." [16]

This was not the only warning that Washington got from Paris. Early on October 8 Frazier reported to Secretary Lansing that the French Government favored "an uncompromising attitude toward the peace proposal of the Central Empires" and had instructed the French press accordingly. The opinion was general, he believed, that the Germans were working on a "suspicious maneuver, a device to enable the German Army to extricate itself from a difficult position and to placate public opinion at home." French feelings were said to be hurt because the Germans had not addressed their proposal to France instead of President Wilson.[17] Later in the day Frazier reported again that Allied leaders were waiting for President Wilson's response to the German peace proposal and that Lloyd George and other foreign representatives in Paris had decided to remain another night in the hope of receiving word from Mr. Wilson.[18]

The Germans, too, were waiting and speculating; but they also made use of the time. At 9 A.M. on the 7th the Armistice Commission that Ludendorff had already appointed held its first meeting. While the members expected the Allies to demand guarantees, it is clear that they desired to be prepared to resume fighting if they failed to get acceptable conditions. The Commission arrived at the following findings:

1. We must make concessions; they consist of evacuations.
   First stage: East of Bruges-Valenciennes-Le Cateau.
   Second stage: West of Antwerp-Alost-Meuse.

16. Bliss, "The Armistices," p. 515. In his later official report to Lansing, Bliss suggests that perhaps "one of its [the document's] main objects was accomplished by the one fact that I had cabled it in its entirety to Washington." *Lansing Papers,* II, 292.

17. Frazier to Lansing, October 8, 1918, *Foreign Relations, 1918,* Supplement I, I, 345–346.

18. Frazier to Lansing, October 8, 1918, *ibid.,* p. 346.

2. The evacuation must be executed in such a manner that we are always ready to fight. A question to be made clear, however, is whether, in the evacuation, the interests of a peace economy or of a war economy should prevail. Presumably there will be a compromise. A priority list will be prepared.

3. Time for the first stage of the evacuation, four to eight days; for the Fourth Army, eight to fourteen days.

The second stage is still incalculable. Time limits up to nine months are mentioned but are not to be considered. Evacuation to behind the Meuse, in some places to home territory, is being carried out to a limited degree.

4. Navy: the cessation of the submarine war must certainly be granted, but its resumption must be assured. Counterdemands in the matter of commerce should be made.

A neutral zone must be created, the submarines withdrawn.[19]

The German press manifested great anxiety about Wilson's reply. Importance was attached to any report on its possible character. The fact that no immediate answer was made inspired some cautious and hopeful people to say that Wilson was giving the proposed step most careful study. On October 7 the moderate *Vossische Zeitung* quoted French and English sources indicating the existence of a belief that Germany did not sincerely mean peace. The Social Democratic *Vorwärts* wrote on October 8 that the fate of the world depended on the reply to Germany's note. An unfavorable reply, it said, would be particularly felt in socialist circles throughout the world and socialist attacks on the privileged would become more vigorous. It felt that the democratization of the Reichstag should convince all foreign socialists, in whom the German Socialists had a blind faith, of the sincerity of the German peace movement. Foreigners were assured that there would be no repetition in Germany of what had happened in Russia. Here and there appeared warnings to the German people that the note from Wilson might be unfavorable, that his terms might be dishonorable for Germany to accept and that, in that case, they would have to prepare for a fight to the end.

The Government of Prince Max also had anxious moments of waiting. Reports from abroad were studied with care in an effort to anticipate what Wilson's answer might be. On October 7 the German Ambassador at The Hague reported:

19. Document 35a, *Amtliche Urkunden*.

A reliable confidential agent informs me that from his conversation of yesterday at the American Embassy, he has got the impression that Wilson will not reject the German peace proposal *a limine* but that he will submit it to discussion and will possibly demand the evacuation of Belgium and France. It is also the impression of the confidential agent that our estimate of American pride and Wilson's idealism has favorably impressed the Americans at The Hague. Solf's appointment was taken at the American Embassy as proof of the complete abandonment of secret annexationist plans and as an important factor for peace.[20]

During the evening of October 8 von dem Bussche transmitted this report to Army Headquarters.

The Chancellor did not wait for Wilson's reply before preparing to answer the expected note. The peace move was a matter of policy with which he strongly disagreed; he was disturbed by the possibility that conditions on the front were not quite so bad as pictured by the Army Command. He sensed early that the Army was trying to place the responsibility for the peace negotiations upon the civilians in the Government because of their professional distaste for anything like an admission of defeat. He had no desire to bear that responsibility, and he persisted in asking the Army for very definite information regarding the military outlook for Germany. On October 8 he wrote to Ludendorff, who had just arrived on summons to Berlin:

The reply of the President of the United States of America to our request for peace and for armistice will presumably consist neither in a plain acceptance nor a plain refusal, but will state conditions on which the President will make his procedure depend.

We must figure on the possibility that these conditions will be severe. We shall thus have to face the question whether our military situation will permit us to negotiate an amelioration of the conditions, with the dangerous prospect that several weeks will elapse during that process. Austria-Hungary and Turkey may desert us, and we may finally have to accept the President's conditions in their original form.

That he might "get a correct picture of our military situation" Prince Max then listed fifteen questions that covered a number of

20. Document 36a, *ibid.*

different contingencies: How long can the enemy be held outside Germany's borders? Will a military collapse come within the next few weeks or before spring? How long will the present critical situation last? What can and should Germany do to enable her to hold out until spring in case the peace move should fail? What can Germany do without any allies? There were other questions about reserves, the *levée en masse*, evacuation demands and answers, the possibility of German counterdemands, and so on.[21]

As soon as he received news of the German note on Sunday, October 6, President Wilson had the report telephoned to Colonel House in New York and asked him for advice. Cautioning the President against a "direct reply," House recommended that a statement be issued from the White House saying that "the President will at once confer with the Allies regarding the communication received from the German Government." He urged the President to send him to Paris to discuss matters with the Allies. He expressed the idea, a surprising one in view of what was taking place in Paris, that the Allies would "want to throw the burden" on the President; they should be made to accept their full responsibility. "If the Entente," House concluded, "permit this opportunity to go by and if the German resistance should stiffen, I am confident that there would be such a demand for peace this winter in those countries that their Governments would be compelled to give Germany better terms than could now be made."[22]

Writing the same day to President Wilson, Colonel House gave his reasons for delaying the reply. The Germans would be eager, he thought, to have "immediate action" whereas the Allies need be in no hurry. With Foch hammering away on the military front and with the President at work on the diplomatic front, it was possible "that the war may be over by the end of the year."[23]

On Monday, October 7, House received a telephone summons to Washington, where he arrived in the evening. The President had had a busy day. He had formally and officially received both the German and the Austro-Hungarian requests that steps be

21. Max's letter and its questions are in document 36, *Amtliche Urkunden.* The precise form of his questions will be given *infra*, pp. 111–114, when Ludendorff gives his oral answers. Written answers were also given. *Infra*, p. 118.

22. Charles Seymour, editor, *The Intimate Papers of Colonel House* (4 vols., Boston, 1926–28), IV, 75–76. Referred to later as Seymour, *House Papers.* See also Baker, *Wilson,* VIII, 454.

23. Seymour, *House Papers,* IV, 75–76.

taken to end the war. At 12.30 he had received Sir Eric Geddes, Chief Lord of the British Admiralty, and the British Naval Mission. Sir Eric had "pointedly asked the President for his interpretation of the term 'freedom of the seas.' . . ." and received no answer. Reporting this interview later to Lloyd George, Sir Eric said that "in talking of his Fourteen Points the President's views on the Freedom of the Seas appeared to be unformed." [24]

There were already signs that Wilson would find it difficult to deal with the enemy's request for peace.[25] As in France and in England, the German note was commonly thought to be a trap. There was no faith in the new regime that had been created by Imperial Decree; and no one believed that the proposed constitutional changes would transform Germany into a genuine democratic state. "No Peace with the Hohenzollern," said a *New York Times* editorial of October 7. "If Germany wants peace, let her do away with her irresponsible, braggart Kaiser and speak by a government of her own people."

The same day Porter James McCumber, Republican from North Dakota, introduced the following resolution in the Senate:

Be it resolved by the Senate of the United States, the House of Representatives concurring:

That there shall be no cessation of hostilities and no armistice until the Imperial German Government shall disband its armies and surrender its arms and munitions, together with its navy, to the United States and her allies [*sic*] in this war;

That before any armistice shall be considered the Imperial German Government shall unreservedly consent to the principles of reparation declared as terms of peace by our allies;

That it will pay in damages the cost of rebuilding and reconstructing all the cities and villages destroyed by its armies, and restore to fertility the lands devastated by it;

That it will repay every dollar and the value of all property exacted from the people of any territory invaded by it;

That it will make proper compensation and allowance for every crime committed by its armies contrary to the laws of warfare and humanity, whether on land or sea;

24. *War Memoirs of David Lloyd George,* VI, 260–261; also Baker, *Wilson,* VIII, 456.

25. How opposed the American people were in May, 1918, to peace with Germany on Wilsonian terms is made clear in *The Autobiography of Lincoln Steffens* (New York, 1931), pp. 773–777.

> That it will return to France Alsace and Lorraine and the indemnity exacted from her in 1870 [*sic*];
>
> And that it further accepts all the conditions laid down by the President in his address of January 8, 1918.[26]

And Senator Henry Cabot Lodge of Massachusetts, ranking Republican member of the Senate Committee on Foreign Relations, wrote to former President Theodore Roosevelt:

> I am living in constant anxiety now of a sudden plunge of the Administration for a negotiated peace. At this point, if we make an armistice we have lost the war and we shall leave Germany about where she started. I am sure that the American people want a complete victory and an unconditional surrender. They want to win this fight on German soil, and every man who comes here who has been fighting on the western front says the soldiers are determined to go to Germany and would resent it bitterly if they were to be held back.[27]

Colonel House has given an account of Wilson's difficulties in replying to the German note. "I arrived at the White House as the clock was striking nine o'clock [October 7]. . . . The President met me and we went into his study. He said he had asked Lansing to come over and he arrived within a few minutes. The President had prepared his reply to the German Chancellor . . . and read it to us. He seemed much disturbed, when I expressed a decided disapproval of it. I did not believe the country would approve of what he had written.[28] After arguing the matter some half hour or more, he said that I might be able to write something and embody what I had in mind, but he had to confess his inability to do so. . . .

26. *Congressional Record,* October 7, 1918, p. 11162.

27. *Selections from the Correspondence of Theodore Roosevelt and Henry Cabot Lodge, 1884–1918* (2 vols., New York, 1925), II, 539–540. On September 30 Senator Lodge wrote to Roosevelt of his desire "to make it difficult for Wilson to betray the United States and the Allies by negotiating a peace with Germany with a view to the German vote in this country." *Ibid.,* p. 536. Lodge wrote similar views to his colleague, Senator Poindexter, who expressed agreement with them. Seymour, *House Papers,* IV, 76.

28. In a memorandum in 1922 House wrote: "The President's first draft of a reply to Germany was mild in tone and did not emphasize the need of guarantees providing for thorough-going acceptance of Wilson's peace conditions." *Ibid.,* IV, 77n.

"After breakfast on Tuesday, Dr. Grayson came in with the expectation of playing golf with the President. When I had finished breakfast, the President appeared and announced that he had given up the idea of going out and asked me to go with him to his study. We read what the papers had to say; I called attention to what the French Socialists' Convention said upon the subject in Paris, and the comments of the Manchester *Guardian* and the London *Daily News*. He, on his part, read me the debate which took place in the Senate Monday.

"He then began to amend his draft and before he finished with it the next day, there was not much left of the original. He worked on it steadily until nearly one o'clock Monday night. I then suggested we leave it until morning. He replied that he had thought of playing golf, as he had had no exercise either on Sunday or Monday and was feeling the need of it. I advised him to go to the links, and disagreed with him as to the necessity for haste in giving an answer. He evidently wished to have it ready for the Tuesday morning papers if possible, and certainly not later than the editions Tuesday afternoon.

"I took this occasion to tell him I thought his answer to the last Austrian note was a mistake, not only in the celerity with which it was answered but also in the manner of it. He said 'What would you have done?' I replied that I would have answered it in some such way as his speech in New York, September 27. . . .

"I found the President's viewpoint had changed during the night. . . . He did not seem to realize before, the nearly unanimous sentiment in this country against anything but unconditional surrender. He did not realize how war-mad our people have become. This had to be taken into consideration, but not, of course, to the extent of meeting it where it was wrong.

"The President thought if such an offer had been made by a reputable government, it would be impossible to decline it. After he had gotten the note into its final form, he suggested sending for Tumulty to try it out on him. Tumulty had just written the President urging that he should not give in in any particular but make a decided refusal. Tumulty's letter and the note were not in harmony, but we were therefore anxious to see what he would think of it. Much to the surprise of both of us, Tumulty thought the country would accept the note favorably, not enthusiastically at first, but that it would appeal to the sober-minded and, later, to everyone.

"The President was not happy over this effort. . . . That it has taken with the public as well as it has, makes me content." [29]

Wilson gave his answer to the German note to the Swiss Legation in Washington on Tuesday, October 8. Lansing handed a copy to the newsmen at 4 P.M., making the interesting comment, "It is not a reply, but an inquiry." [30] The note read as follows:

Sir:

I have the honor to acknowledge, on behalf of the President, your note of October 6, enclosing a communication from the German Government to the President; and I am instructed by the President to request you to make the following communication to the Imperial German Chancellor:

> Before making reply to the request of the Imperial German Government, and in order that that reply shall be as candid and straightforward as the momentous interests involved require, the President of the United States deems it necessary to assure himself of the exact meaning of the note of the Imperial Chancellor. Does the Imperial Chancellor mean that the Imperial German Government accepts the terms laid down by the President in his address to the Congress of the United States on the 8th of January last and in subsequent addresses and that its object in entering into discussions would be only to agree upon the practical details of their application?
>
> The President feels bound to say with regard to the suggestion of an armistice that he would not feel at liberty to propose a cessation of arms to the Governments with which the Government of the United States is associated against the Central Powers so long as the armies of these powers are upon their soil. The good faith of any discussion would manifestly depend upon the consent of the Central Powers immediately to withdraw their forces everywhere from invaded territory.
>
> The President also feels that he is justified in asking whether the Imperial Chancellor is speaking merely for the constituted authorities of the Empire who have so far conducted the war. He deems the answers to these questions vital from every point of view.

ROBERT LANSING [31]

29. *Ibid.,* IV, 77–79.
30. Baker, *Wilson,* VIII, 463.
31. Lansing to Oederlin, October 8, 1918, *Foreign Relations, 1918,* Supplement I, I, 343. Cf. document 37, *Amtliche Urkunden,* for German translation of the note.

The note was published in German newspapers October 10. Expressing the views of the Social Democrats, *Vorwärts* thought that prospects for peace were favorable, and reflected that peace negotiations could not be hurried: "A war that has lasted four years and two months . . . cannot be ended within twenty-four hours." Walther Rathenau felt that Wilson's demand for evacuation meant "unconditional surrender" and would make it easier for the Allies to increase their demands on Germany.[32] Prince Max, on the other hand, was somewhat relieved by Wilson's answer, having feared an unhappy outcome of a step he had disapproved. He commented the same day:

> The note appeared to justify the optimists. It is true that the demand for evacuation was made, as had been feared, and that we were to accept the Fourteen Points as *conditions* and not as a mere *basis* for negotiations. Then, too, his question to the German Government: In whose name do you speak? was an interference of Wilson's in our internal affairs. But in spite of all that, the prevailing impression at the time was, that the note spoke in a different tone from the howl of rage to which the yellow press of the Allies had given vent. Wilson does not say 'No' and is ready to undertake mediation. . . .
>
> There are three possible answers to Wilson:
>
> 1. We could consent to the evacuation, but reject the unconditional acceptance of the Fourteen Points, coming forward with our interpretation of them.
> 2. We could reject the demand for evacuation only.
> 3. We could assent to both demands, adding in reply to his inquiry a short disquisition upon constitutional law.
>
> The first course was no longer open; our reservations should have been defined on October 5. To announce them after that time could give the President ground for suspecting the good faith of the German offer and thus for refusing or temporizing. At the time nobody knew whether Wilson was sufficiently strong-minded or well-disposed to maintain his principles in opposition to American public opinion. Perhaps he was only waiting for a pretext for a change of front, particularly as the elections for Congress were imminent.
>
> Only a report from the military could decide whether we were in a position to reject the demand for evacuation.[33]

32. From letter of Rathenau to Scheüch, cited in Niemann, *Revolution von Oben,* p. 144.

33. Max, *Erinnerungen,* pp. 388–389.

Wilson's reply met with a good deal of hostile criticism from his political opponents in America and from the Allies. Senator Lodge told the press that he was "keenly disappointed." "I believe," he explained, "in a dictated, not a negotiated peace." [34] In a letter to ex-President Roosevelt he said that Wilson's note was "disheartening" and seems "to open the door to endless discussion." [35] Roosevelt held similar views. "I fear," he said, "that the President's latest announcement will be treated as an invitation to further note-writing. . . . Personally, I believe that our sole aim should be to win the war and not to discuss peace terms with the enemy until the war has been won." He reiterated his demand for the unconditional surrender of Germany "and her vassal allies." [36] There was warm debate over the matter in the Senate, where critics of the White House read letters to show that many American citizens were demanding unconditional surrender.[37]

Frazier reported the reaction of the Allied leaders in Paris to Wilson's note. On the morning of October 9 he talked with Lloyd George and Bonar Law and "noted a tone of disappointment that the President had not left the terms of the armistice to the military men." The British Premier thought it regrettable that Wilson had not included a demand for the evacuation of Alsace-Lorraine and of the Trentino. He "intimated that M. Clemenceau was not entirely in accord with President Wilson's Fourteen Points and said that the British Government would like to have a definition of the meaning of the expression 'freedom of the seas.' " [38]

There was more criticism of the note during the afternoon of October 9, when representatives of the Allied Governments met at the Ministry of Foreign Affairs to hear Marshal Foch state his armistice terms. According to the Marshal's account, Lloyd George convinced those present, with the exception of Clemenceau, that a message should be sent to President Wilson calling attention to the inadequacy of his conditions. Those conditions, the British Prime Minister felt, would not prevent the Germans "from drawing such advantages from a cessation of hostilities as

34. *New York Times,* October 9, 1918.

35. Lodge to Roosevelt, October 9, 1918, *Selections from Correspondence of Roosevelt and Lodge,* II, 541.

36. *New York Times,* October 10, 1918.

37. *Congressional Record,* October 10, 1918, pp. 11169–11181.

38. Frazier to Lansing, October 9, 1918, *Foreign Relations, 1918,* Supplement I, I, 351–352. See also Callwell, *Field-Marshal Sir Henry Wilson,* II, 134.

to be in a better military situation at the expiration of an armistice not followed by peace than they were at the moment when fighting ceased. The opportunity would be given them to extricate themselves from a critical situation, save their war material, reform their units, shorten their front, and retreat without loss of men to new positions which they would have time to select and fortify." And he argued strongly that "the conditions of an armistice cannot be determined until after consultation of the military experts and in consideration of the military situation at the moment when negotiations are begun. . . ." Foch thought the position well taken.[39]

More details of this conference come from the diary of Field Marshal Sir Henry Wilson. Clemenceau and Pichon wanted to take no notice of the President's answer because they had not been consulted. "Lloyd George pressed," writes Wilson, "that an answer, not for publication, be sent, pointing out that if the Boches accepted the 14 points we should be in a difficult position, as we could not agree to Point 2, 'Freedom of the Seas,' and that therefore we should tell Wilson plainly that evacuation of occupied territory was a necessary preliminary to any exchange of views about an armistice, which would then be a matter for the Military to settle. Further, Bonar Law pressed my point that President Wilson should come over here, or send someone with full powers. In the end Lloyd George got his way about both these points." [40]

At eight that evening Frazier transmitted to Washington the following joint note from the Prime Ministers of Great Britain, France, and Italy:

The Allied Governments have taken cognizance of the reply addressed by President Wilson to the Chancellor of the German Empire, with the greatest interest.

They recognize the elevated sentiments which have inspired the reply. Limiting themselves to most urgent question, that of the armistice, they agree with the President of the United States that the preliminary condition of all discussion of this question is the evacuation of all invaded territory. But they think for the conclusion of an armistice itself this condition, while necessary, would not be sufficient. It would not prevent the enemy from profiting by a suspension of hostilities to install himself, after the expiration of an

39. Foch, *Mémoires,* II, 273.
40. Callwell, *Field-Marshal Sir Henry Wilson,* II, 135.

armistice not followed by peace, in a better military position than at the moment of the expiration of hostilities. He would be left the facility of retiring from a critical situation to save his war material, reconstitute his units, shorten his front and retire without loss of men to new positions which he would have the time to choose and fortify.

The conditions of an armistice cannot be fixed until after consultation with military experts and in accordance with the military situation at the moment of engaging in negotiations. These considerations have been forcibly exposed by the military experts of the Allied Powers and especially by Marshal Foch. They are of equal interest to the armies of the Governments associated in the battle against the Central Empires.

To these considerations the Allied Governments draw the entire attention of President Wilson.[41]

Later that night the three Prime Ministers, still mindful of Wilson's disregard of them, sent him a direct appeal. After pointing out "that the time has come when decisions of supreme importance in regard to the war may have to be taken at very short notice," the telegram stated that the Allied Governments "think it would be of very great assistance if an American representative possessing the full confidence of the United States Government could be sent to Europe to confer when occasion arose with the other Associated Governments so as to keep them accurately and fully informed of the point of view of the United States Government."[42]

The French Socialist party and the labor groups of France approved Wilson's note.[43] The Commission on Foreign Affairs in the Chamber of Deputies gave "its full approval" and "counts upon the Government to accept in the name of France no armistice which would fail to assure the satisfaction and the guarantees to which the victorious armies of the Entente have a right."[44] The French press, according to the American Ambassador, approved Wilson's reply, although some papers expressed the view "that the evacuation of Alsace-Lorraine should have been specifically mentioned in connection with the references to the evacuation of the invaded territories." Viviani, the former Premier,

41. Frazier to Lansing, October 9, 1918, *Foreign Relations, 1918,* Supplement I, I, 353.

42. Frazier to Lansing, October 9, 1918, *ibid.,* pp. 353–354.

43. Sharp to Lansing, October 14, 1918, *ibid.,* pp. 398–403.

44. Sharp to Lansing, October 11, 1918, *ibid.,* pp. 355–356.

said "that it was a document of the highest statesmanship, and would be sustained by the entire people of France." Mr. Sharp, the American Ambassador, warned, however, that the French were developing a "whetted appetite for demanding ever-increasing penalties from a hated foe." [45]

In Italy Ambassador Page reported that the note was regarded as a "complete response" to the Central Empires and "as perfect diplomacy." [46] A little earlier Page had reported the French Ambassador in Rome as expressing the hope that Wilson would answer immediately "to prevent spread of idea that armistice will be granted, of which [there is] great danger here." [47]

The London *Times* had been awaiting Wilson's response with anxiety. On October 9 the leader asserted that the big victory that day, when much ground was regained between Cambrai and St. Quentin, was the "best of all answers to the German note." Commenting next day on Wilson's reply, the paper was still worried, still sharing the fears of England's statesmen that Wilson would go his independent way: "Allied confidence in President Wilson cannot absolve the Allied Governments from the duty of establishing the closest practicable coöperation in diplomacy both between themselves and with their great associate in Washington."

45. Sharp to Lansing, October 10, 1918, *ibid.,* pp. 354–355.
46. Page to Lansing, October 11, 1918, *ibid.,* p. 355.
47. Page to Lansing, October 8, 1918, *ibid.,* p. 354.

V

The Submarine Threatens Negotiations

FOR the purpose of preparing an answer to Wilson's note, a conference had been called for October 9 in the office of the Imperial Chancellor. An essential preliminary to that discussion would be the consideration of the questions that Prince Max had addressed to Ludendorff the day before. Before the session actually opened, the Chancellor had an opportunity for a brief interview with the General. With current Berlin rumor in mind he noted that Ludendorff "did not give the impression of being in shaken health."

"I thought it necessary to remind him," writes Prince Max, "of the way in which the armistice offer had originated—I who was already being called the 'pacifist Prince' and being made responsible for the armistice request. I told the General that, to avoid disclosing our weakness still more, I was not in a position to lay bare the true state of affairs before the public—that I was obliged to cover the armistice offer with my name. The General replied: 'I thank Your Grand Ducal Highness in the name of the Supreme Command and in the name of the Army.' "[1] Time was to reveal the extent of the Quartermaster General's gratitude for this civilian protection.

This conference was to be one of the most significant held in Germany during the war. Ludendorff opened it with a description of the military situation, going back, in characteristic German fashion, to 1914. Then he spoke of the conditions on the western front in the spring of 1918, when Germany had a "superiority of twenty or twenty-five divisions." The great offensive then undertaken was deemed "necessary to hold our allies and to win a victory, if possible, in the west before the arrival of the American masses." That "hope remained unfulfilled" because of tanks, influenza, and the potato famine. Still, the military situation was favorable until August 8, a day which resulted in "six or seven divisions broken up in the fog, within two or three hours," and a "grievous break" in the line. The lack of fighting men in Germany and the tanks of the enemy constituted

1. Max, *Erinnerungen,* p. 389.

the great unsolved problems for the Army Command. "After August 8 the Supreme Army Command informed the Imperial Chancellor that it was no longer in a position to bring the war definitely to an end by a military blow that would make the enemy willing to make peace. At the beginning of September neutral mediation for peace [was] suggested by the Supreme Army Command. Then [came] the collapse of Bulgaria." [2]

After a few uncomplimentary remarks about Bulgarian political and military inefficiency Ludendorff painted a dark picture of the situation in the east. "Turkey will drop out. . . . We are not in a position to protect the Danube and Rumania. . . . If we want to hold Rumania, we must know how great the Bolshevist danger is to be estimated. We could bring a few divisions to Rumania from the Ukraine, but then we should not be able to give ourselves military protection against Bolshevism." As to the west, there "the lack of troops is decisive. . . . We have had to retire. The divisions are no longer capable of fighting. We prefer to retire rather than to be beaten."

The summary seems calm, even if slightly one-sided. It is worth noting that there was no pressing demand now for speed in bringing the war to an end. Had Ludendorff already recovered his nerve?

The General now came to the queries he had received the day before from Prince Max, remarking that "it is difficult to reply to such questions." [3] His answers and the accompanying discussion are given in a much abbreviated protocol of the meeting:

Question 1. [1. How long will our Army be able to hold the enemy on the other side of the German border, either by remaining in its present positions or by a gradual retirement?] The frontier being distant from the western front, we can protect it for a long time. Attacks in Lorraine possible, but I see no danger to the Lorraine frontier. There is no danger I can see from Holland, as such troops as might cross the border would be interned.

Question 2. [2. Is it true today that we must reckon on a military collapse before spring, and in case it is true, does this danger threaten us during the next three or four weeks?] There is always danger of a break-through. The English could have broken through in the first tank attack.

Question 3. [3. How long is the present critical state of affairs

2. Protocol of the meeting, document 38, *Amtliche Urkunden*.

3. Prince Max's questions are given in brackets. Document 36, *ibid*.

likely to last? Will the danger point be passed when the enemy finds himself compelled to cease from his big attacks, and when will this probably occur?] Yes, only big attacks are dangerous.

Question 4. [4. Can a consolidation of our front be counted on after the danger point has been passed, and by what means can it be accomplished?] If the attack is stopped, the danger is over.

Question 5. [5. What is the status of the reserve supplies of men and materials?] We lack 70,000 men [a month, according to Prince Max]. There is enough material.

Question 6. [6. Can we carry on the war alone until spring, despite the defection of one of the two allies yet remaining to us, in case of the failure of the present peace move?] We need a period of rest for the purpose; then we could consolidate.

Question 7. [7. Does the Supreme Army Command see any promise of a sufficient strengthening of the forces in the *levée en masse* recommended by Walther Rathenau in the *Vossische Zeitung?*] *No.* In spite of the lack of men, I can see no advantage in a *levée en masse.* We always wanted to increase the labor service. I cannot judge whether slackers can be got hold of. In the opinion of the Supreme Army Command the system of training men for garrison duty should stop; the garrison-man does not want to fight. We could get more men by taking more stringent measures at home. A *levée en masse* would cause more harm than we can stand.

Should other generals be heard also? Should be glad to be relieved of the responsibility, but am certain that other leaders think as I do. I have discussed the peace move with Kuhl, Lossberg, and Schulenburg.[4] They all agreed. It was hard for us to decide on it, but we recognized our duty and did not hesitate. Commission is unnecessary. The Supreme Army Command can also carry this responsibility alone.

COLONEL HEYE: I have belonged to the Supreme Army Command for the last four weeks. Believe that, with the reserve situation as it is, we can no longer count on carrying on the war successfully. It will be gambling with fate on the part of the Supreme Army Command, if it does not hurry on the peace move. We *may* be able to hold out until spring. But a turn for the worse may come any day. Yesterday the question of a break through our lines hung on a thread.

Earnestly beg that you do not talk about nervousness. Move for peace is absolutely necessary, still more one for an armistice. The

4. Respectively, Chiefs of Staff of the Army Groups under Rupprecht, von Boehn, and the Crown Prince.

troops no longer get any rest. It is impossible to foresee whether the troops will hold out or not. There are new surprises every day. I do not fear a catastrophe, but I want to save the Army, so that we can use it as a means of pressure during the peace negotiations.

The Army needs rest. If it gets it and receives fresh recruits, it will be able to show fresh achievements.

LUDENDORFF: Defense is more costly than attack. On May 27, we lost from 60,000 to 70,000 men in the offensive, but captured just as many prisoners. Enemy's other losses must be added to that. Thus the balance was in our favor.

[Prince Max had a number of questions to ask concerning the evacuation of territory by Germany. This part of his letter read: "According to the news that has already been received, it seems possible that President Wilson may demand the evacuation of Belgium and northern France as a preliminary condition of entering into negotiations; therefore the further questions arise:

1. (8) Would the Supreme Army Command advise that we accept such demands unconditionally, or that we reply to them with counterdemands? In case the military situation admits of a delay for the purpose of negotiations under the conditions referred to above, we might introduce the following counterconditions:

a. (9) The evacuation of the districts occupied by France and England (Upper Alsace, possibly the German colonies too).

b. (10) Guarantees to be given that the enemy would not pursue us. It might even be demanded that the French territory evacuated by us should be occupied by American troops only, and that Belgium should be entered only by Belgian troops, that its neutrality should be observed by all belligerents, and that Belgian territory should not again be turned into a theater of war.

c. (11) A declaration on our part that, in order to compensate for the injury to our strategic position in the west, we should have to recall our troops from the territories in the east occupied by us (the Baltic Provinces, Lithuania, Poland, and the Ukraine), which would expose these territories to Bolshevism."]

In regard to the question of evacuation: [8] We have an enormous mass of material in the occupied territories. Roughly, evacuation should take two or three months if men retire on foot (*longer* by transport). Army must be ready to fight. It can retire only in sections. If it takes a stand at the frontier, it can ward off every hostile attack. Only critical question would be danger to industrial areas from the air. [10] So we should try to arrange to have only Belgian troops follow into Belgium. The demand that we evacuate Metz would be contrary to our military honor.

IMPERIAL CHANCELLOR: Should negotiations with the Entente cease if French or English troops also follow into Belgium?

LUDENDORFF: No.

IMPERIAL CHANCELLOR: [9] How does the matter stand with reference to a demand that the enemy evacuate occupied *German* territory?

LUDENDORFF: Depends on the situation at the front.

IMPERIAL CHANCELLOR: No matter whether we get a formal armistice (*Waffenstillstand*) or a temporary suspension of hostilities (*Waffenruhe*)?

LUDENDORFF: Armistice (*Waffenstillstand*). Question concerning the Bolsheviki: [11] Good to exert that pressure.

Final question: [12. In what time could the evacuation of northern France and Belgium be carried out, if it should commence with the signing of the armistice?] Two to three months. [13. Would we be able to hold the Franco-German border with the troops we should still have at our disposal after the evacuation if in their further course the peace negotiations should fall through and our opponents should start a new attack?] We are in a position to hold the frontiers. [Prince Max had written: "President Wilson might demand the occupation of German fortresses on our western frontier, on the ground that he required security. (14) In view of the military situation, should we be compelled to comply with such a demand?] We cannot surrender German fortresses. [15. To what extent could the acceptance of conditions be made dependent on counterconditions?] We must make counterdemands.

Other questions were put to Ludendorff by those present at the conference. From the answers elicited we learn that the Quartermaster General feared another winter campaign less than he feared the exhaustion of his troops; that much material could be salvaged in the process of evacuating enemy territory, railway equipment in particular; that orders had already been issued that dwellings should not be destroyed, that mines should be dismantled not ruined. Admitting the enemy's superiority in tanks and motor trucks, he expressed the hope that Germany would have six hundred tanks by spring. Oil stocks were low, the Navy having a ten months' supply and the Army enough for its planes for only two months; the oil situation was sure to become worse if the Danube should be closed. Ludendorff was convinced that morale had improved since August 8; but new men would improve it further. The newly appointed Minister of War, Scheüch, believed that a more careful combing of the country for men was possible and he promised to investigate the possibilities.[5] The next day he informed Ludendorff that he thought he could get 600,000 men within a few months.[6]

Prince Max concluded from this conference that the Army wanted to have armistice negotiations continue, even at the price of evacuating occupied territory. Ludendorff "left no doubt of the fact that we had to withdraw to our borders, either driven there by pressure from the enemy or withdrawing under an agreement with them." On one point the Government and the Army Command agreed completely; namely, that "we would reject demands making it impossible for us to resume hostilities." [7]

Outside Government circles, however, there was pressure to have the negotiations broken off. Count Westarp of the Conservative party, Walther Rathenau, and Stresemann of the National Liberals opposed the peace move and the evacuation of territory. The Pan-Germans and papers of the Right clamored that pacifists were behind the peace offer. The liberal *Frankfurter Zeitung* printed the facts and gave, prophetically, the reason why the truth should be known. "It is necessary to oppose this view [of pacifist instigation] from the very beginning, *a view which could develop into a dangerous legend,* and it can be expressly confirmed that the Army Command has had no share in the construction of this legend." [8] It was not long, however, before the legend took root, with the Army Command greatly interested in its prevailing over other views.

The task of framing an answer to Wilson was still undone and conferences for that purpose had to be called. One at which Ludendorff was not present was held on October 10. His absence gave those present an opportunity to discuss him. Criticism of the generals was in the air; the previous day the Kaiser had issued a decree requiring commanding generals to consult civil authorities in nonmilitary questions, particularly in regard to

5. Document 38, *Amtliche Urkunden.* Also Max, *Erinnerungen,* pp. 389–392.
6. *Ibid.,* p. 392.
7. *Ibid.,* pp. 393, 395.
8. *Frankfurter Zeitung,* October 11, 1918, No. 282. Italics mine.

matters of censorship and the right of assembly.[9] In this conference of October 10 doubts were raised about Ludendorff's competence to judge the military situation. Vice-Chancellor von Payer said that his statements needed confirmation, "especially his questioning von Kuhl, Lossberg, and Schulenburg."[10] Erzberger pointed out that according to letters of General Hoffmann which were circulating in Berlin "the western front could be held." Some of those present believed that Hoffmann, who had been Chief of Staff at Tannenberg, had better judgment in such matters than Ludendorff and should be consulted. Solf and Roedern advised talking things over privately with Hoffmann; otherwise, Ludendorff might resign.

The conference now considered Wilson's note and how to reply to it. As Secretary of Foreign Affairs, Solf took the task in hand. He gave a three-part analysis of the note and suggested a general answer for each part:

A. [Does the Imperial Chancellor mean that the Imperial German Government accepts the terms laid down by the President in his address to the Congress of the United States on the 8th of January last and in subsequent addresses and that its object in entering into discussions would be only to agree upon the practical details of their application?] Yes.

B. [The good faith of any discussion would manifestly depend upon the consent of the Central Powers immediately to withdraw their forces everywhere from invaded territory.] We arrived at no conclusions yesterday. I asked Ludendorff, "Can you hold the front three months longer?" Ludendorff answered, "*No.*" We shall, therefore, have to agree in principle to evacuation.

C. [The president feels that he is justified in asking whether the Imperial Chancellor is speaking merely for the constituted authorities of the Empire who have so far conducted the war.] That matter will be easy to answer.

To the Chancellor's question whether "the Foreign Office takes the position that we evacuate without any counterdemands" Solf replied that he "desired to leave that to the negotiations."[11]

The Foreign Office had a draft of a reply to Wilson ready on October 11 and sent it in the middle of the afternoon to Baron

9. Payer, *Von Bethmann Hollweg,* p. 123.

10. Document 39, *Amtliche Urkunden;* Stresemann had raised the same question in a letter to Prince Max, *ibid.;* also Max, *Erinnerungen,* p. 395.

11. Document 39, *Amtliche Urkunden.*

von Berckheim, the representative at Army Headquarters,[12] requesting immediate approval by telephone and by telegraph of that part pledging the Central Powers to the evacuation of occupied territory. Prince Max was determined to have the High Command share the responsibility for policies made necessary by the appeal to Wilson for peace and armistice. The draft read as follows:

> The German Government has accepted all conditions laid down by President Wilson in his address of January 8 and in his subsequent addresses as the basis of a permanent peace of justice. After entering upon negotiations it will discuss only the details of their practical application.
>
> The German Government in accord with the Austro-Hungarian Government declares itself ready to evacuate immediately the territory of the Powers associated with the United States. Furthermore both Governments agree to withdraw their troops from other occupied territory at any time. The German Government leaves it to the President to bring about the meeting of a commission of the participating Powers whose function it would be to make the necessary arrangements for the evacuation.
>
> The present German Government which has undertaken the responsibility for this step toward peace has been formed after negotiations and agreement with the great majority of the Reichstag. The Chancellor is supported in all his actions by the will of the majority, and speaks in the name of the German people.

The note was discussed in the Cabinet on October 11. Dr. Solf read it while Prince Max read and explained Wilson's note. "The supreme Army Command," said the Chancellor, "has come out strongly in favor of action for peace; it wants us to give our consent to evacuation." Discussion of the note itself quickly veered in another direction when Solf said "that it is necessary for all the Secretaries of State to give their express consent." Baron von Stein, Minister of Economics, objected that he "could do that only after all the deliberations, particularly the declarations of the military authorities, were made known." The Minister of War, Scheüch, asked for his opinion of the military situation, replied that it was impossible for him to give it. Thus the discussion of the contents of the note became a discussion of its necessity, and particularly of the reasons for the first note to

12. Document 40, *Amtliche Urkunden.*

Wilson. The Chancellor, von Haeften, Deutelmoser, von Payer, and Dr. Solf all testified to how the Army Command had pressed for it. On the evening of October 1, Prince Max said, "The pressure exerted by the Supreme Army Command . . . had been intense." The others explained that the Army Command wanted the note sent even before the new Government was formed. Solf said that "he had also asked Field Marshal von Hindenburg if we could not wait a week or at least four days. The Field Marshal had replied that he could make no definite answer to that, and had closed his remarks with the words: 'Hurry up! Hurry up!'" Prince Max gave the impression that Army pressure had somewhat relaxed since early October. "In the note now to be drafted," he said, "the consequences of that first step have to be dealt with. Perhaps the Supreme Army Command is a little less disturbed at the present time, but it is nevertheless firmly insisting on the demand for an immediate armistice." [13]

"My colleagues," Prince Max wrote later, "were all at last convinced of the necessity of answering the note in such a way that Wilson could not very well break off." [14]

No message from Army Headquarters caused the Chancellor to change his mind about continuing negotiations, although the High Command had several opportunities that day to make its opposition known. Just before noon Prince Max had telegraphed that Ludendorff's written reply to his fifteen questions on the military situation should be in his hands by noon of the 12th. In the evening the reply came, but the answers were essentially the same as the earlier oral ones.[15] The evening also brought a telegram from Hindenburg, who suggested a differently worded note from that which it was proposed to send to Wilson; he accepted the latter, however, after a telephone call from the Foreign Office.[16]

13. Cabinet protocol, document 42, *ibid.*

14. Max, *Erinnerungen,* p. 396.

15. Prince Max's request is document 39b, *Amtliche Urkunden;* Ludendorff's reply is document 43, *ibid.*

16. Hindenburg's draft differed from that of the Foreign Office in several respects. He wanted to have peace negotiations "begin *immediately*" in order to avoid a surrender on Germany's borders. He particularly wanted the note to state that "the German Government assumes that the other participating Governments also take the position stated in Wilson's speeches and that the negotiations will commence without delay." On such assumptions, his draft went on, Germany and Austria-Hungary declared themselves prepared to evacuate the territory of the Powers associated with the United States. The fighting should stop when the evacuation began. To avoid misunderstandings it should be made

Before the final text of the note was agreed to on October 12, two matters arose to introduce complications into the Cabinet discussions. During the night Hindenburg changed his mind and telephoned Colonel von Haeften to have the draft amended to include the point "that the Allies of America also bind themselves to the Fourteen Points." The Field Marshal "saw in that condition a re-insurance against more far-reaching demands from the Entente." Von Haeften moved to amend the draft and found the change acceptable to all present.[17]

The second matter was to be far more serious. Early on October 12 a prophetic despatch marked "urgent" and "secret" arrived from the German Minister in Berne. He had been conferring with a "confidential agent" who expressed anxiety over what would happen in case after Germany had complied with Wilson's request, a German submarine should sink a steamer with American citizens aboard. It was suggested that submarine commanders should be instructed to spare all passenger ships. The agent believed it "also important that the reply to Wilson's note should have the approval of the Reichstag as soon as possible, an act that at the same time would constitute a vote of confidence in the new Government, an element that was missing at present." Solf noted on the margin of the despatch that "an effort will be made to prohibit the torpedoing of passenger steamers";[18] and the German Minister at Berne was informed "that the Imperial Government has already made the attempt to communicate an order to its naval forces to refrain from now on from sinking ships off the American coast." In view of the technical difficulties of communicating such an order, no guarantee could be given that it would reach the submarines. Solf told the Minister that "no publication

clear that evacuation would require weeks. He believed it impossible to evacuate Russian territory on account of conditions there, but thought evacuation could be carried out in accordance with the wishes of the peoples in the areas occupied. He saw no fundamental objection to German evacuation of Rumania. Document 41 and note, *ibid.*

17. Protocol of October 12, document 44, *ibid.*

18. Document 68 and note, *ibid.* The warning of the "confidential agent" was repeated soon afterward: the drowning of American citizens by a submarine at this time would have particularly serious consequences. "Given the bad luck that our Navy has had, such an eventuality does not appear impossible." Document 69, *ibid.* The former Ambassador to the United States, von Bernstorff, had already informed Prince Max "that it would be useless to appeal to him [Wilson] if we are not prepared at once to abandon the unrestricted U-Boat war, as he feels this measure as a personal offense." *Memoirs of Count Bernstorff* (New York, 1936), p. 240.

of this information can take place because of the danger of compromising our naval policy."[19]

This is the first indication that the new German Government was making a fundamental change in its submarine policy. The role of the submarine had come up for discussion earlier. When Ludendorff and Hindenburg came to their decision of September 29 that the war must end, the Naval Command was notified of the proposed step. Admiral Scheer at once asked whether the submarine construction program was to go on. Ludendorff replied in the affirmative, for he saw in that program an important means of pressure during the armistice negotiations. And should Germany fail to get proper conditions and have to continue the war, the submarine would still be necessary. The Kaiser held the same views. In conferences on October 1 Army and Navy officials, industrialists and representatives of submarine construction companies worked out plans to this end. It was after this meeting that Scheer received a telegram from Secretary von Hintze asking for the consent of the Naval Command to the abandonment of the submarine campaign during the armistice negotiations. Scheer was ready to agree if Germany acquired thereby the right to import food and raw materials. Ludendorff's attitude was that only such concessions should be made in the course of armistice negotiations as would permit the resumption of hostilities in the event the negotiations should fail.[20]

The question of abandoning use of the submarine now came up during the discussion of the reply to Wilson on October 12. Von Mann of the Admiralty deplored the proposal to give up a weapon that was costing the enemy 500,000 tons of shipping a month.[21]

Vice-Chancellor von Payer was not satisfied when the Cabinet had agreed on the final wording of the note. Made wise by recent experience, he inquired whether "the Supreme Army Command

19. Document 70, *Amtliche Urkunden.*

20. Hans Kutscher, *Admiralsrebellion oder Matrosenrevolte?* (Stuttgart, 1933), pp. 14–16.

21. This total tonnage destroyed is about double the amount given by the Entente Powers. Later in the day Secretary von Mann addressed a letter to Solf to explain his views. "We give the Entente," he concluded, "an enormous advantage by abandoning the submarine war in case peace negotiations should break off. It means for us giving up the sinking of 4 to 500,000 tons of shipping a month. Thus we destroy most certainly the one offensive weapon that we still possess and that would bring us to a happy peace." Document 45, *Amtliche Urkunden.*

also agrees" to the amended draft. Von Haeften said he believed so; but his caution suggested the advisability of making absolutely certain by telephoning Headquarters.[22] Before 3 P.M. Prince Max received from Ludendorff and Hindenburg a telegram stating their agreement with the wording as given over the telephone by Haeften.[23] But at 2.05 the note had been despatched to Wilson.

At the very time that von Mann protested the sheathing of Germany's only offensive weapon, that weapon had most inopportunely shown its deadly destructiveness. On October 12 the news went round the world that the *Leinster*, a passenger-carrying Irish mail steamer running between England and Ireland, had been torpedoed without warning the day before and had sunk in fifteen minutes with the loss of 450 lives, among them 135 women and children and some Americans. The submarine commander was a German boy of 22. "Not since the *Lusitania*," writes Prince Max, "had sorrow and anger been so great in England and in America. We had indeed recalled the submarines from the American coast, but unfortunately had neglected to anticipate such a catastrophe, which could have been taken into reckoning as things were." [24]

It was under the dark cloud of the *Leinster* disaster that the Germans addressed their second note to Wilson:

In reply to the question of the President of the United States of America the German Government hereby declares:

The German Government has accepted the terms laid down by President Wilson in his address of January 8 and in his subsequent addresses as the foundations of a permanent peace of justice. Consequently its object in entering into discussions would be only to agree upon practical details of the application of these terms.

The German Government believes that the Governments of the powers associated with the United States also accept the position taken by President Wilson in his addresses.

The German Government in accordance with the Austro-Hungarian Government for the purpose of bringing about an armistice declares itself ready to comply with the propositions of the President in regard to evacuation.

The German Government suggests that the President may oc-

22. Document 44, *ibid.;* Max, *Erinnerungen,* p. 396.
23. Document 46, *Amtliche Urkunden.*
24. Max, *Erinnerungen,* p. 404.

casion the meeting of a mixed commission for making the necessary arrangements concerning the evacuation.

The present German Government which has undertaken the responsibility for this step towards peace has been formed by conferences and in agreement with the great majority of the Reichstag. The Chancellor, supported in all of his actions by the will of this majority, speaks in the name of the German Government and of the German people.

SOLF[25]

When news of this note arrived in the United States, President Wilson was in New York City. The evening of Saturday, October 12, he spent with Colonel and Mrs. House.

"We dined with the President and Mrs. Wilson at the Waldorf Hotel," House wrote in his diary. "Just before dinner was announced, Tumulty came in with the news that Germany had accepted the President's terms. The Military Intelligence Bureau had telephoned it from Washington. We wondered whether the news was authentic but concluded from its construction that it was. When we went in to the table the President wrote me a little note in which he said 'Tell Mrs. W.' and signed it 'W. W.' . . .

"After dinner we went almost immediately to the Italian Fête at the Metropolitan Opera House. There was an enormous crowd which cheered the President with much enthusiasm. I was so stirred by the news that had come from Berlin that I could not listen to the programme. Tumulty and I went to the Directors' Room in the Opera House, called up Washington and received confirmation from Frank Polk [Counselor for the Department of State] and the Washington *Post.* Shortly after ten o'clock I returned home. . . . Frank Polk called over the telephone at 10.30 (over the private wire), and we had a long talk. It was decided that Joe Grew should keep in touch with the Swiss Legation and let us know the official text as soon as it came.

"I did not try to sleep for a long while, for it seemed to me that the war was finished, certainly finished if we have the judgment to garner victory." [26]

Sunday evening President Wilson returned to Washington. On Monday morning he and House began working on the answer

25. Oederlin to Lansing, October 14, 1918, *Foreign Relations, 1918,* Supplement I, I, 357–358. Also document 47, *Amtliche Urkunden.* The Swiss Chargé in Washington formally presented the note to the Secretary of State on October 14, but copies had arrived earlier.

26. Seymour, *House Papers,* IV, 81–82.

to the German note.[27] The day, says House in his diary, "was one of the most stirring days of my life. The President and I got together directly after breakfast. I never saw him more disturbed. He said he did not know where to make the entrance in order to reach the heart of the thing. He wanted to make his reply final so there would be no exchange of notes. It reminded him, he said, of a maze. If one went in at the right entrance, he reached the center, but if one took the wrong turning, it was necessary to go out again and do it over. He said that many times in making extemporaneous speeches he had gone into the wrong entrance and had to flounder out as best he could. . . .

"I thought he should make one condition to a discussion of armistice, and that was the immediate cessation of all atrocities both on land and sea. He agreed to this and it stands in the note.

"He went into the question of the German Government and decided to use what he said in his Fourth of July speech about autocracies. . . . We were anxious not to close the door, and yet desired to make the note as strong as the occasion required. He fell back time and again on the theory offered when the last note was written: that was, if Germany was beaten, she would accept any terms. If she was not beaten, he did not wish to make any terms with her. At the same time, neither the President nor I desired to make a vengeful peace. Neither did he desire to have the Allied Armies ravage Germany as Germany has ravaged the countries she has invaded. The President was especially insistent that no stain of this sort should rest upon the Allied arms. He is very fine in his feeling and I am sorry he is hampered in any way by the Allies and the vociferous outcry in this country. It is difficult to do the right thing in the right way with people clamoring for the undesirable and impossible.

"The President soon formulated the points which appear in the note. . . ."[28]

It was, indeed, "difficult to do the right thing in the right way." On October 12 in an editorial entitled "Ferocity Asks for Peace" the *New York Times* pointed out that submarines were sinking ships while the peace note was being considered. The sinking of the *Leinster* had impressed the world as it had Balfour, who called it "an act of barbarism." Senator Borah had his doubts about the new German Government; to his mind Prince Max

27. The same day Wilson received Turkey's request for an armistice. Baker, *Wilson,* VIII, 475, 477–478, 479.

28. Seymour, *House Papers,* IV, 82–83.

represented the Kaiser. "We must either insist," he said, "upon dealing with a Government responsible to the German people or go on with the war. . . ." [29]

In the *New York Times* for October 14 appeared a message to the American people dictated by Theodore Roosevelt:

I regret greatly that President Wilson has entered into these negotiations, and I trust that they will be stopped. . . . I earnestly hope that the President will instantly send back word that we demand an unconditional surrender and that we refuse to compound felony by discussing terms with the felons. . . . Moreover, I most earnestly hope that the Senate of the United States and all other persons competent to speak for the American people will emphatically repudiate the so-called fourteen points and the various similar utterances of the President. . . . These fourteen points are couched in such vague language that many of them may mean anything, or nothing and have a merely rhetorical value, while others are absolutely mischievous. To do as the President has done in this case . . . becomes dangerously near to being treacherous diplomacy.

Roosevelt attacked specifically the so-called "freedom of the seas." "Let us," he concluded, "adopt as our motto 'unconditional surrender.' " The *New York Times* adopted it in an editorial October 14. "Surrender," it said, "not an armistice, must be the condition precedent to any talk about peace." And in the Senate steps were actually taken to implement Roosevelt's views. The arrival of Germany's second note gave Republican Senator Poindexter of Washington an opportunity to speak his mind. "If the President," he said, "on the strength of this statement by the German Foreign Secretary, undertakes to induce our allies to grant an armistice and thus enable her to escape the military disaster which the allied forces, after heroic fighting and great sacrifices, are about to bring about, it would be a crime against civilization. . . . An armistice brought about by the efforts of President Wilson would be equivalent to German victory." [30] On October 14 Senator Lodge introduced the following resolution into the Senate: "Resolved: That it is the sense of the Senate that there should be no further communication with the German Govern-

29. Quoted in Baker, *Wilson,* VIII, 475.
30. *New York Times,* October 13, 1918.

ment upon the subject of an armistice or conditions of peace, except a demand for unconditional surrender." [31]

The President was getting a good deal of advice, sought and unsought, on the question of dealing with Germany. At one o'clock on Monday, October 14, Senator Ashurst arrived at the White House to discuss the Senate point of view on the German note. Lansing, Polk, House, and Tumulty came in at 2.30.[32] At the request of the British Chargé Secretary Lansing transmitted to the President three messages from Balfour to the British Embassy, all dated October 13. The English had definite ideas about the nature of the terms to be made with Germany. The first note said that Germany had no intention of giving up all the Polish areas or the whole of Alsace-Lorraine. The second urged that it be made clear to Germany that a cessation of hostilities would be agreed to only on terms that would "render any resumption of hostilities by the Central Powers impossible." The third note stated English objections to the Fourteen Points: (a) There had been no discussion by the Associated Powers of the "points at issue"; (b) to some interpretations of these points the British Government would object "most strongly"; (c) certain other terms to which the President had made no reference would probably have to be insisted upon. Care must be taken "to prevent the Allies from being deprived of the necessary freedom of action in the settlement of the final terms in the Peace Conference"; the doubtful points should be discussed by the chief Powers arrayed against Germany that they might come to "some agreement amongst themselves." [33]

How strongly opposed the English were to President Wilson's independent action is evident in Sir Henry Wilson's account of a meeting in England on October 13, when Lloyd George, Balfour, General Wilson, Bonar Law, Milner, Churchill, Reading, Admiral Wemyss, and others discussed the German acceptance of the Fourteen Points and the demand to evacuate territory. "It was a very interesting afternoon," says Sir Henry. "Everyone [was] angry and contemptuous of Wilson." It was agreed to cable the American President "that he must make it clear to the Boches that his 14 points (with which we do not agree) were not a basis for an armistice, which is what the Boches pretend they

31. *Congressional Record,* October 14, 1918, p. 11214.
32. Baker, *Wilson,* VIII, 476–477.
33. *Ibid.,* pp. 478–479.

are." Further, it was agreed to inform the press "that Wilson is acting on his own, that the war is *not* over, that the 14 Points are *not* an armistice, and that an armistice is *not* a peace." Field Marshal Wilson insisted on disarming the Germans and sending them back behind the Rhine unarmed, whereas Foch had merely wanted to tell the Germans to go behind the Rhine and had claimed three bridgeheads. "The meeting became all in favor of my plan," the General writes.[34]

In Italy Sonnino informed the American Ambassador that he would not be sorry if Wilson rejected the German proposal.[35]

Late in the afternoon of October 14 Wilson's answer to Germany's second note was given to the Swiss Chargé d'Affaires. And at about the same time the President sought to reassure a critical America by issuing the following statement:

> The Government will continue to send over 250,000 men with their supplies every month, and there will be no relaxation of any kind.[36]

Wilson saw more and more clearly that the fight for a decent peace would be arduous. He was already considering the composition of the American delegation to the peace conference, which he thought would meet very soon. After a White House meeting the afternoon of the 14th Colonel House told Lansing that the President was planning to name Lansing and himself as two of the American plenipotentiaries to the Peace Conference and that the President himself was thinking of going. The last bit of information troubled the Secretary of State.[37] Steps were taken to send Colonel House to Europe immediately and Lansing notified Italy, France, and Great Britain of that decision.[38] At a conference with the President in the evening House spoke of having arranged a secret code for their use during his mission in Europe. When he left Mr. Wilson said, "I have not given you any instructions because I feel you will know what to do." [39] On Thursday, October 17, House left for Europe and landed the 25th at Brest.

34. Callwell, *Field-Marshal Sir Henry Wilson,* II, 136.
35. Page to Lansing, October 14, 1918, *Foreign Relations, 1918,* Supplement I, I, 363.
36. *New York Times,* October 15, 1918.
37. Baker, *Wilson,* VIII, 477.
38. Lansing to Laughlin, October 14, 1918, *Foreign Relations, 1918,* Supplement I, I, 361.
39. Baker, *Wilson,* VIII, 477.

The German Government could not know what lay ahead. Fears were stronger than hopes as people considered the prospects. Always pessimistic, Crown Prince Rupprecht of Bavaria hoped that the German Army would not be defeated before Wilson's answer arrived.[40]

Political disunity came more and more into the open. The Pan-Germans demonstrated against the peace move, denounced the Government's apparent readiness to surrender Alsace-Lorraine, and proclaimed that the Army was defeated by the collapse of the home front. They called Max's reply to Wilson a "document of shame." Already some groups were appealing to people to fight in a last stand against the harsh terms of the Entente.[41] There was a counterdemonstration on October 16, when the German Armies began their great retreat from western Belgium. Some thousand workers gathered near the Reichstag to make known their desire for peace.[42]

While awaiting the answer to the second note, the German Government was confronted with insoluble problems at home. There was a real financial crisis, banks were failing, and industrial stocks were dropping. Poorer people were cashing their war certificates for whatever they could get, in spite of official assurances that they were covered by the resources of the Reichsbank. The paper shortage led to further restrictions on the size of newspapers and the space available for advertisers. On October 8 railway transportation was cut and people were cautioned not to travel unless it was necessary. On the same day it was reported that only twenty grams of butter a week would be available for people in Greater Berlin. The influenza continued to spread; 1,722 deaths from it alone occurred in Berlin on October 15.[43] On the 17th *Vorwärts* reported that 10,000 people were laid up with it. Many schools had to be closed as a result.

In the midst of all this trouble a political crisis developed that threatened to overthrow the parliamentary Government of Prince Max. Enemies of the Chancellor had had published, just about the time the second note went off to Wilson, a letter that the Prince had written on January 12 of that year to his cousin Prince Alexander zu Hohenlohe. It was critical of democracy and parliamentary institutions, in which the Prince saw nothing of ad-

40. Rupprecht, *Kriegstagebuch,* II, 460.
41. According to *Vossische Zeitung,* October 14, 1918, No. 525.
42. *Frankfurter Zeitung,* October 17, 1918, No. 288.
43. Max, *Erinnerungen,* p. 411.

vantage for Germany.[44] It was believed that Prince Max might have to surrender his office because liberal members of his Government would find it impossible to work with him. Vice-Chancellor von Payer feared that the Government would be unable to survive the crisis. Because the letter appeared first in Switzerland, the *Berliner Tageblatt* suggested that enemies of the Government in the Entente had had it published in order to embarrass the Chancellor in his negotiations for peace. For a while the Social Democrats in the Government thought of resigning, in order to force the appointment of a new Chancellor. Scheidemann and Bauer sent in their resignations on October 12 after failing to persuade Prince Max to resign. But Max explained his letter to the satisfaction of the Inter-Party Committee of the Reichstag, which decided on October 13 that it was no occasion for loss of confidence in him. On October 15 the Social Democrats decided to accept the explanation; so Scheidemann and Bauer remained in the Government.[45] The crisis was followed closely by the Paris *Temps*, which spoke on October 15 and 16 of the possibility that Dr. Solf might succeed Prince Max as Chancellor. According to *Vorwärts*, October 15, Max was ready to resign; he let it be known that he had no desire whatsoever to stand in the way of peace. In labor circles it was said that Haase and Ledebour, leaders of the Independent Socialists, might head a new Government.

Several concessions had to be made to the liberals by the new regime. On October 12 the Kaiser declared a general amnesty for persons arrested for political crimes, or for participating in strikes and street demonstrations or causing difficulties because of the shortage of food. More and more authority was taken from the military and given to the civilian administration. On October 15 the Kaiser issued a decree making it clear that the military authority was now completely subordinate to the political, that he as Emperor issued orders to the Army Command only after consultation with the Imperial Chancellor or the latter's representative. By this act the Supreme Command lost much of the authority it had possessed under special decree of July 31, 1914.

44. The letter is printed in full in *Vossische Zeitung,* October 15, 1918, No. 527. Scheidemann has an account of the crisis in *Der Zusammenbruch,* pp. 178–183; the Chancellor's account is found in Max, *Erinnerungen,* pp. 397–403. See also Haussmann, *Journal,* pp. 288–292.

45. Scheidemann, *Der Zusammenbruch,* pp. 181–184; Payer, *Von Bethmann Hollweg,* p. 131.

At least in law the civilian head of the Government was now the responsible authority.[46]

The prospects facing Germany's allies rendered them incapable of giving either aid or comfort in this hour of crisis. Austria-Hungary was on the verge of dissolution: the various races and nationalities—German-Austrians, Hungarians, Czechs, and Slovaks, southern Slavs and Poles—were determined to go their separate ways in the future. The effort to allay the surging nationalism by seeking a separate peace had achieved nothing. Leaders saw that only as a federal state could the Dual Monarchy exist in the future. On October 16 Emperor Karl issued a manifesto "To My Loyal Austrian Peoples" in a last desperate effort to check the inevitable. "We must now without fail undertake the rebuilding of the Fatherland on its natural and therefore sure basis. The wishes of the Austrian peoples must here be carefully harmonized and fulfilled. I have decided to undertake this work with the free collaboration of my peoples. . . . Following the desires of her peoples Austria must become a federated state in which every race will form its own state commonwealth in the districts inhabited by it. . . . Until this change shall have been executed constitutionally the existing institutions for the protection of general interests will remain unchanged. My Government has the task of preparing, without delay, all work necessary for the change in Austria. . . . So may our Fatherland, solidified by the harmony of the nations of which it is composed, come out of the storms of war as a federation of free peoples." [47] The move was a bold one for Austria-Hungary; but it came too late and failed to convince. As the new states struggled to birth, the process of dissolution continued for the old monarchy.

Turkey was likewise in need of peace. Entente victories in Syria and in Mesopotamia and the capitulation of Bulgaria had left her isolated. A change of Government took place the first week of October and toward the middle of the month the new administration asked Spain to present its appeal to Wilson to "take upon himself the task of the reëstablishment of peace" and urge its request that "steps be taken for the immediate conclusion of a general armistice on land, on sea, and in the air." [48] On October 17 news of Turkey's peace move reached Berlin.

46. Decree printed in *Vossische Zeitung,* October 16, 1918, No. 530.

47. Stovall to Lansing, October 18, 1918, *Foreign Relations, 1918,* Supplement I, I, 367–368. Cf. Nowak, *The Collapse of Central Europe,* pp. 348–349.

48. Riaño to Wilson, October 14, 1918, *Foreign Relations, 1918,* Supplement I, I, 359–360.

Wherever the Germans turned, they found nothing to give them cheer or hope. They were all the more concerned about the nature of the reply that Wilson would make to their second note. From a "dependable agent who has intimate connections with the American Legation" the German Minister at The Hague reported on October 14 that "the sinking of more passenger ships might be fateful for Wilson's influence"; the submarine was "like a red flag to public opinion in America." [49] The evening of October 15 he reported that a prominent Englishman about to return to England, but hesitating because of his fear of submarines, had described British policy to a "select group":

"Lloyd George wants two months more of war because, by that time, Germany would be so completely beaten that she must simply accept whatever terms would be imposed on her. For that reason he wants to impose conditions that Germany cannot accept. They were published in the Sunday morning papers: the occupation of Metz as well as of the bridgeheads of the Rhine; the dismantling of the Navy; the surrender of the submarines, etc. After the rejection of these terms he expects a *levée en masse* in Germany and a war to the knife. This final struggle would last only two weeks, and after that would come the collapse. By the abolition of autocracy people in England mean the abdication of the Kaiser." [50]

The same evening a report from "a reliable confidential agent in Holland" stated that "within the English Government there is increasing opposition to the conclusion of a peace with Germany, [that] instructions to the Army Command demanded energetic action on the front, . . . that the English Navy wants to strike its blow before peace is made." "The French Government," the report continued, "refuses to make peace with Germany on the basis of Wilson's program. Clemenceau visited Foch and has learned from him that Foch would resign immediately if the Government enters into the peace maneuver. Clemenceau agrees with Foch and has personally informed General Haig of his opinion." [51]

The German authorities were in a confused and despairing state of mind when Wilson's reply arrived in Berlin at 5.20 A.M. Wednesday, October 16. It read as follows:

49. Document 70a, *Amtliche Urkunden.*
50. Document 49, *ibid.*
51. Document 49b, *ibid.*

The unqualified acceptance by the present German Government and by a large majority of the German Reichstag of the terms laid down by the President of the United States of America in his address to the Congress of the United States on the 8th of January, 1918, and in his subsequent addresses, justifies the President in making a frank and direct statement of his decision with regard to the communications of the German Government of the 8th [*6th*] and 12th of October, 1918.

It must be clearly understood that the process of evacuation and the conditions of an armistice are matters which must be left to the judgment and advice of the military advisers of the Government of the United States and the Allied Governments, and the President feels it his duty to say that no arrangement can be accepted by the Government of the United States which does not provide absolutely satisfactory safeguards and guarantees of the maintenance of the present military supremacy of the armies of the United States and of the Allies in the field. He feels confident that he can safely assume that this will also be the judgment and decision of the Allied Governments.

The President feels that it is also his duty to add that neither the Government of the United States nor, he is quite sure, the Governments with which the Government of the United States is associated as a belligerent will consent to consider an armistice so long as the armed forces of Germany continue the illegal and inhumane practices which they still persist in. At the very time that the German Government approaches the Government of the United States with proposals of peace its submarines are engaged in sinking passenger ships at sea, and not the ships alone but the very boats in which their passengers and crews seek to make their way to safety; and in their present enforced withdrawal from Flanders and France the German armies are pursuing a course of wanton destruction which has always been regarded as in direct violation of the rules and practices of civilized warfare. Cities and villages, if not destroyed, are being stripped of all they contain not only but often of their very inhabitants. The nations associated against Germany cannot be expected to agree to a cessation of arms while acts of inhumanity, spoliation, and desolation are being continued which they justly look upon with horror and with burning hearts.

It is necessary, also, in order that there may be no possibility of misunderstanding, that the President should very solemnly call the attention of the Government of Germany to the language and plain intent of one of the terms of peace which the German Government has now accepted. It is contained in the address of the President delivered at Mount Vernon on the Fourth of July last. It is as follows: "The destruction of every arbitrary power anywhere that can separately, secretly, and of its single choice disturb the peace of the world; or, if it cannot be presently destroyed, at least its reduction to virtual impotency." The power which has hitherto controlled the German Nation is of the sort here described. It is within the choice of the German Nation to alter it. The President's words just quoted naturally constitute a condition precedent to peace, if peace is to come by the action of the German people themselves. The President feels bound to say that the whole process of peace will, in his judgment, depend upon the definiteness and the satisfactory character of the guarantees which can be given in this fundamental matter. It is indispensable that the Governments associated against Germany should know beyond a peradventure with whom they are dealing.

The President will make a separate reply to the Royal and Imperial Government of Austria-Hungary.[52]

52. Lansing to Oederlin, October 14, 1918, *Foreign Relations, 1918,* Supplement I, I, 358–359. Document 48, *Amtliche Urkunden.*

VI

Ludendorff Changes His Mind

WILSON'S second note produced shock and alarm in Germany. It brought home to the people for the first time how threatening the military situation was. And it was so worded as to suggest that Wilson was aiming at the Kaiser's abdication. So different was the tone of this note from the earlier one that it became a question whether the negotiations should continue or not. Some groups favored breaking off the correspondence and urged that the war be fought to its bitter end; others, anxious for peace, wished at all costs to avoid a break with Wilson. The struggle between the two groups was to make history.

The Kaiser was at Potsdam when the note arrived. He summoned his aide, Major Niemann, showed him the despatch and exclaimed, "Read it! It aims directly at the overthrow of my house, at the complete overthrow of monarchy." [1] To the Crown Prince it had an "arrogant and implacable" tone and was "interference in Germany's internal affairs." The "spirit of Foch" he thought was threatening to overpower Wilson.[2] Rupprecht of Bavaria found Wilson's attitude a hard one, but felt that Germany must accept the President's demands whatever they were; under no circumstances must enemy troops be allowed to invade the country.[3]

During the night of October 15 Prince Max, unable to sleep, wrote a letter to his cousin, the Grand Duke of Baden. He said that he had thought of resigning the post of Chancellor because "there was no longer any military power to support my policy." But now he was determined to stay on, to do what he could. "It was my belief," he wrote, "that I was coming at five minutes before twelve; actually I was summoned five minutes after twelve." He hoped he could save the Kaiser, and thought he could do it—admitting the irony of it—with the assistance of the Social Democrats. But "Germany today is no longer fighting for her Kaiser

1. Niemann, *Kaiser und Revolution,* p. 100; Niemann, *Revolution von Oben,* pp. 192–193.
2. *Memoirs of the Crown Prince,* p. 268.
3. Rupprecht, *Kriegstagebuch,* II, 461–462.

or for Alsace-Lorraine, if she can have peace without either. . . . Perhaps I can achieve a peace that leaves us our lives and a hope for the future."[4]

Wilson's note arrived only a few hours after the Chancellor had written these none-too-optimistic thoughts. He found it a "frightful document," of which "not a word . . . suggested the high office of arbitrator" that Wilson had professed even after entering the war. "First, his yielding to the Allied Commanders-in-Chief; then the aspersions against our Army and Navy; the demand for the termination of the intensified submarine war; and, at the end, in dark and equivocal words the appeal to the German people to take its destiny into its own hands and in that way only to fulfill the preliminary condition for the conclusion of peace." The note, he wrote, had changed the situation fundamentally. The passion for peace aroused by Germany's first note to the American President had kept the people together. "Now their disillusionment was like the bursting of a dam."[5]

This disappointment was universal. "The Caudine yoke of Mr. Wilson" was the way the nationalist *Tägliche Rundschau* described the note. The Pan-German *Lokal-Anzeiger* said Wilson seemed to have abandoned his idealism the first time it was put to the test; he who has the means of ending a war and does not is as guilty as he who began it.[6] The liberal *Frankfurter Zeitung* said that this note, in tone much harsher than the first, showed that the spirit of Clemenceau and of Lloyd George had been at work. The personal rule of the Kaiser, the paper pointed out, had already ended and the Bundesrat had approved measures taking the power of peace and war from the Emperor and placing it in the hands of the people.[7] The paper was far from optimistic, however; a day later it professed to see no hope for Germany and no prospect of peace.

While some in despair urged Prince Max to trust Wilson completely and throw himself on his mercy, others appealed to him to halt the peace negotiations, to sound the alarm, and summon the nation to its final struggle. Letters and telegrams signed by outstanding men in schools and universities and in government administration urged him to make a stand.[8] On October 16 the

4. Max, *Erinnerungen,* pp. 405–407.
5. *Ibid.,* pp. 408–409.
6. *Lokal-Anzeiger,* October 16, 1918, No. 529.
7. *Frankfurter Zeitung,* October 16, 1918, No. 287.
8. Max, *Erinnerungen,* p. 411; also *Vossische Zeitung,* October 16, 1918, No. 529.

Conservative party issued an appeal to the nation, saying that Wilson had left the people no choice but to continue the war to the end. Otherwise, "for generations to come every German citizen and peasant, every man of business and of property, and, above all, every employee and laborer would be the wage-slave of our enemies. . . . We shall not voluntarily let ourselves be deprived of our weapons. No enemy shall put foot on the soil of the Fatherland." [9]

On October 17 the Social Democrats issued a counterappeal, supported by the professors of the University of Berlin.[10] The party admitted that "Germany and the German people are in danger of becoming a sacrifice to the lust for conquest found in English and French chauvinists and imperialists . . . the German people will never agree to a peace of violence, of humiliation, and in violation of their vital interests." The party claimed to be at work in the Government to get a peace of understanding and conciliation, participating in the peaceful revolution that was transforming Germany into a democratic state. It urged people to oppose the activities of the Pan-German and Conservative groups interested in imperialistic conquest. "We are on the way to peace and democracy. All rebellious agitation blocks this way and serves the counter-revolution." [11]

The Social Democrats also watched the activity of the Communists with anxiety and through *Vorwärts* appealed to those who might be attracted to their propaganda. "First we Social Democrats desire peace and government by the people. Then we want to institute all the socialist reforms for which we have won the support of the people. Every intelligent Social Democrat must warn workers against following the mad counsels of irresponsible agitators. . . ." [12]

Ludendorff was highly critical of Wilson's note. "In his answer . . . Wilson gave us nothing; nor did he even tell us whether the Entente took its stand on the Fourteen Points. He demanded, however, the suspension of the submarine campaign, he stigmatized our conduct of the war in the west as contrary to international law, and once again in obscure phrases interfered with intimate questions of internal politics. . . . We now faced

9. *Frankfurter Zeitung,* October 17, 1918, No. 288. See also Max, *Erinnerungen,* pp. 411–413.

10. *Vossische Zeitung,* October 21, 1918, No. 538.

11. *Vossische Zeitung,* October 18, 1918, No. 534. This manifesto is translated in Lutz, *Fall of the German Empire,* II, document 473, pp. 400–403.

12. *Vorwärts,* October 17, 1918, No. 286.

the question clearly whether we were to place ourselves at the mercy of the Entente or whether the Government was to call on the people to fight a last fight of desperation. We had to reply to the note in a determined and dignified way and to emphasize once more that our desire for an armistice was sincere, but at the same time to come out strongly for the honor of our brave Army. We should not allow ourselves to be deprived of our submarine weapon; that would lead directly to capitulation." Ludendorff was convinced that the enemy was determined to destroy Germany.[13] He now began to see where Germany's appeal to Wilson was leading and was apparently thinking seriously of proceeding no further with negotiations for an armistice.

As early as October 14, before Wilson's note had arrived, Hindenburg had written to Prince Max to point out the dangers arising from the despondent attitude of the nation and from internal divisions, which served only to give the enemy "new strength for attack, and a new determination to raise their demands." The people should be aroused "to defend themselves to the limit against every humiliating condition." Only then will the Army be made stronger against the enemy, only then will those who negotiate peace have the needed support at the conference table. "I regard it therefore as absolutely necessary," Hindenburg went on, "that more than hitherto the terrible consequences of a peace at any price be made perfectly clear to every German in the entire press, in the gatherings of all parties, of all unions and professional associations, in the churches, schools, theaters, and moving picture houses. In public demonstrations of every kind expression should be given to the determination that for the German people there are only two ways open: an honorable peace or a fight to the end." He welcomed Erzberger's appeal through the press to the people "to stand together in united determination." [14] Two days later in an order to the Army, after referring to the political happenings of recent days, Hindenburg said that he supported the Government and agreed with the peace move.[15]

The Germans were quite right in believing that England and France lacked enthusiasm for Wilson's peace program. Frenchmen and Englishmen felt that, through the German appeal to

13. Ludendorff, *Kriegserinnerungen*, p. 604.
14. Document 49a, *Amtliche Urkunden.*
15. Document 50, *ibid.*

him, Wilson had acquired more authority to negotiate the conclusion of the war than American effort had earned for him. Americans abroad became aware of this attitude; in a letter to General March, the American Chief of Staff, General Bliss wrote on October 14 that France and Great Britain were indisposed to give Americans the help they had promised and, thinking they had the Germans on the run, "will attempt to minimize the American effort as much as possible." Bliss referred to an opinion he had heard "that the United States was building a bridge for the Allies to pass over; that the time for the United States to secure acquiescence in its wishes was while the bridge was building; that after the Allies crossed over the bridge they would have no further use for it or for its builders." Time, he thought, would show whether the opinion had any basis in fact.[16]

The great doubts of the Allies concerned the Fourteen Points. On October 15 the American Chargé in London reported that "grave doubts were expressed as to whether they adequately connote the demands which must be imposed upon Germany to obtain a satisfactory and lasting peace. It is felt even more strongly that some of the points are detrimental to the interests of certain of the Allies, especially Great Britain, and especially is this true of the second point, [calling for] the freedom of the seas. . . ." Points three and five were questioned; point twelve was thought to be in possible conflict with previous engagements of the Allies. Fear was expressed that President Wilson might go still further without consulting the Allies.[17]

It would appear that Wilson drafted his second note to Germany with an eye to its effect on critics abroad and at home. It is true that some of the doubts that existed in England vanished with the appearance of the second note, which found favor with many.[18] "We had set in England (there is no harm in saying) a very exacting standard for President Wilson's reply to the German request for an armistice and for peace," said the London *Times* editorially on October 16, "but he has satisfied it. It makes an end of all idea of a bargained peace, and that, after all, is the main test." This view was not that of the War Cabinet. According to Field Marshal Wilson, the second note was looked upon as "a complete usurpation of power of negotiation." The President was blamed for ignoring the British and the French—he was

16. Frederick Palmer, *Newton D. Baker* (two vols., New York, 1931), II, 366.
17. Laughlin to Lansing, October 15, 1918, *Foreign Relations, 1918,* Supplement I, I, 365–367.
18. *Idem.*

criticized also because "he won't treat with the Hohenzollerns—thus making sure of Bolshevism." The Field Marshal wanted France and England to send a note to President Wilson that would put him "in his proper place." He was unable, however, to persuade Lloyd George and the others to "put the truth baldly before Wilson [who] . . . is now taking charge in a way that terrifies me, as he is only a super-Gladstone—and a dangerous visionary at that." [19]

In the United States, Senator Lodge liked Wilson's note, "genuinely pleased that the President takes the ground he does." [20] "The outburst on Monday," he wrote to Roosevelt, referring to the resolution he had introduced into the Senate asking for unconditional surrender, "was what sent him back, made him drop the armistice and say he would not treat with the German Government as now constituted. We got back from the edge of the precipice but we are still in constant danger of a negotiated peace. The times are very anxious and the Germans are doing everything they possibly can to create a situation to justify their entering into further negotiations." [21] Senator Harding, who was to be Wilson's successor, thought that the second note was "more like the real spirit of America." To Senator Borah, it was "fine"; and an approving letter he wrote to Wilson evoked a note of gratitude from the President. To Senator Poindexter, the President's note was "the most refreshing utterance from him I have seen for some time"; the demands for adequate guarantees removed his doubts as to Wilson's standing firm.[22]

American and Allied approval of the second note is the measure of Germany's deep disappointment. The Germans had more to decide now than how a reply to Wilson should be worded. The issue had become whether to continue negotiations or to fight on to the end. No Government could have a graver decision to make.

That question was to be debated in Berlin on October 17, perhaps the most trying day that patriotic and conscientious Germans had to struggle through in the war. Ludendorff was to come to Berlin for these fateful conferences. The Government prepared another list of questions for him to answer; and he, in turn, put to the Government two questions that had been

19. Callwell, *Field-Marshal Sir Henry Wilson,* II, 136–137.

20. *New York Times,* October 15, 1918.

21. Lodge to Roosevelt, October 19, 1918, *Selections from Correspondence of Roosevelt and Lodge,* II, 542.

22. *New York Times,* October 15, 1918. See also Baker, *Wilson,* VIII, 486.

drafted even before Wilson's latest note had been received. They were:

1. Does the internal situation allow the removal of all troops from the east to the west, or is there danger that Bolshevism will come into the country?

2. Will the German people, not only the educated circles but the masses in general, take up the fight to the bitter end when it is realized that then our military situation would be sufficiently strong to bar the enemy from crossing our borders, or is their moral power of resistance so exhausted that this question cannot be answered unconditionally in the affirmative? It is not a matter of compulsion, but one of voluntary action.[23]

A preliminary Cabinet meeting was held on October 16 to discuss the situation. Ludendorff's two questions came up for debate. Solf believed that they were "extremely dangerous." Between the lines, he said, could be discovered an attempt to shift responsibility from the Army Command to the people. The questions looked to the renewal of fighting; if they were answered negatively the fault would lie not with the Army but with the people. He pointed out that they were in very poor accord with the view expressed earlier by both Ludendorff and the Minister of War, that a *levée en masse* was not possible.

Scheidemann wanted no answer made to Wilson until everything had first been discussed with Ludendorff. He admitted that the note from the American President was harsh; but the enemy had a right to be angry after the sinking of the *Leinster*. He believed that the submarine war should cease immediately. Secretary Gröber agreed with Solf, but argued "it is not enough to question His Excellency Ludendorff only; his judgment is no longer authoritative. We must get in touch with other Army leaders in the west. The Cabinet needs this kind of protection and should have it in the records. . . ."

Both Scheidemann and Gröber agreed that the morale of the nation was deplorable. But the former blamed it less on the demands being made by the enemy than on the failure of the Government to make long-needed reforms. It was questionable whether the people could be aroused to fight on to the very end in case the Entente demands appeared unacceptable. Gröber could see little reason for making such an appeal to the nation when

23. Document 54, *Amtliche Urkunden.*

some of the most serious internal problems remained unsolved. As a symbol of the reforms needed he asked that political prisoners be amnestied, particularly that Karl Liebknecht be released from prison. In this Scheidemann supported him.

Von Payer favored the motion that other Army leaders be heard and he made sure that the estimates already given by Ludendorff were a matter of record. It was objected that the current fighting was so serious that it would be impossible for generals to leave the front. And Ludendorff, everyone knew, would object strenuously to the suggestion that other generals be questioned.[24] But Prince Max conferred that day with the Kaiser about getting reports from other generals and the Emperor gave his approval.[25]

While these differences of opinion were developing in Berlin over the future of negotiations with Wilson, it seems that similar doubts existed within the Army Command at Spa. Baron von Lersner, Foreign Office Representative, telephoned during the afternoon of October 16 his belief that "the immediate cessation of the submarine war is practicable in case we should consider it necessary for political reasons"—a statement which suggests that the whole question was being debated at Spa. Lersner also wanted Ludendorff to be informed during the conference the following day "that the enemy might even demand the evacuation of German territory (for example, Metz and Strassbourg). It would be advisable to consider with the General how far such a demand could be complied with." Lersner still favored a continuation of negotiations via Wilson.[26]

On the morning of October 17 there was a session of the "inner Cabinet" at which the Chancellor reported that Ludendorff had threatened to resign and take Hindenburg with him when he learned of the official plan to consult other generals on the military situation. He had said that he would regard such an inquiry as a vote of no confidence. There was general agreement that it would be a catastrophe if the Government should lose both Generals, and particularly if Hindenburg should leave, although it was known that Ludendorff was "the man who makes the decisions." [27] There was no time to agree on what could be done to avert this disaster; preparations had to be made for hearing

24. See protocol of the meeting, *ibid.*
25. Max, *Erinnerungen,* p. 416.
26. Document 52, *Amtliche Urkunden.*
27. Document 55, *ibid.*

Ludendorff himself on the military situation in a full meeting of the war Cabinet.

The conference of the war Cabinet on October 17 is one of the most dramatic and moving events in Germany's history. The fate of a nation was being decided and the men who participated knew it, although they could not foresee the consequences of the decisions they had to make. It is one of the great human tragedies of our time that the formal deliberations attending the close of the war could not have preceded the opening of the struggle in 1914.

The following is the list of questions the Government prepared for Ludendorff to answer:

1. In continuing the war by the utmost exertion of the national strength, how long can it be so conducted as to keep the enemy away from German borders?

2. How strong is the Army in the west at the present time, including the troops in garrisons in Belgium and Northern France?

3. How strong are the forces stationed in the east?

4. How much time would it take for the so-called *levée en masse* to have any effect on our situation on the western front?

5. How much time would be required to transport to the west the troops not now needed in the east?

6. Can a guarantee be given that the western front will suffer no catastrophe before reinforcements come from the east and from home?

7. How many men can be brought to the western army:

   a. from home?
   b. from the east?

8. What value is to be given the fighting strength of reinforcements:

   a. from home?
   b. from the east?

9. Would the complete removal of German troops from districts in the east so imperil the transport of oil for military and domestic consumption that it would force us into a premature conclusion of peace or to the suspension of the submarine war?

10. How strong are the reserves now at the disposal of our enemies:

    a. The Americans?
    b. The English?
    c. The French?
    d. The Italians?

11. How much longer this year must we continue to expect major attacks on the western front?

12. If Austria-Hungary should drop out as our ally, is it likely that the Italian Army will be transferred to the western front?

13. What is the strength of the Italian Army?

14. Is there any possibility that a new southern front could be formed?

15. How high should the fighting power of the Russian Red Army be estimated?

16. Is there any possibility that a new eastern front could be formed?

17. Is there any possibility in the course of the next year that the European states which are still neutral will be compelled by our enemies to participate in the war against us?

18. How many Americans are being brought on the average each month to France?

19. How strong will the American Army presumably be by next spring on the western front?

20. How great will be the estimated strength next spring of the Allied Army on the western front (Americans, English, French, Italians)?

21. Will our military position be better or worse than now by next spring? [28]

The Chancellor opened the fateful meeting with the barbed remark that "the situation in which we find ourselves is the consequences of the step that we took on October 5. . . . There now lies before us a new note, one that contains increased demands on Wilson's part and about which we must reach a decision. Apparently, Wilson has got into a serious situation because of American chauvinists and because of pressure from France and England; and he hopes, as I hope, that we will give him a chance to continue negotiations with us and to overcome the opposition of those who want to keep on fighting. . . . Before we send a note to Wilson we must understand what Germany's military situation demands."

The discussion began with the first of the two questions that Ludendorff had asked the Government to consider: whether it would be possible to move troops from the east to the west. It was acknowledged that the troops in the east were better for defense

28. Document 56, *ibid.*

than for offense, but the basic question was whether Germany could afford to surrender the economic advantages of retaining control in the east and letting the people of those regions be at the mercy of Bolshevist propaganda. Scheidemann pointed out that the real question was neither food nor Bolshevism in the east but whether the western front could hold out three months longer and prevent a break-through. All that Ludendorff could reply was that a break-through was possible but not probable; at any rate, he was not afraid of it.

The Chancellor then took up Ludendorff's second question, whether the home front could supply the Army Command with the troops needed. The Minister of War said that the Army could get regular replacements of about 190,000 men a month without causing any great harm to the country's economic life; or, by disregarding the civilian economy, a single allotment of 600,000 men; after which, for the first half of the year perhaps, about 100,000 men a month would be available, a figure that could be raised to 150,000 a month with the class of 1901. But by the end of September the reservoir of manpower for the year 1919 would be exhausted.

"I am absolutely for the second method," said Ludendorff. "If we could have had estimates earlier we should not have had the crisis on the western front. And if I get these men, I shall look to the future with confidence. But I must have the men, and have them soon; then we can be optimistic again."

Colonel Heye asked how long it would take to supply the 600,000 men. Scheüch showed that it would be impossible to get them immediately: they must be taken from industry and agriculture; they must be trained; they must be transported to the front. All that would take time.

At this point Ludendorff spoke of the morale of the troops, which had been very bad on August 8 and was now much better. He was doing all he could to improve it, he said, and had urged Army Staffs to make sure "that the soldier in Belgium knows that he is defending German soil." Now he was hearing from many sides "that these armistice negotiations are having very bad consequences," for soldiers were wondering why they should keep on fighting if they must evacuate Belgium and even Alsace-Lorraine.

Gröber said that he had found the morale very bad during a special trip in the south to investigate it. He found particular fault with the differential treatment of officers and enlisted men, a source of complaint that was being quickly improved according to Ludendorff.

SCHEIDEMANN: I am willing to believe that we can mobilize hundreds of thousands of men for the Army; but we deceive ourselves if we think that these hundreds of thousands would improve the morale of the Army. The opposite is my firm conviction. The length of the war has already broken the spirit of the people, and to that [add] their disillusionment. They have been disillusioned by the submarine war, by the technical superiority of our opponent, by the defection of our allies or, at any rate, by their complete bankruptcy, and, in addition, by the increasing distress at home. Now the reaction is coming. Men on leave come from the Army with unpleasant stories; and they return to the Army bringing unpleasant news from home. This traffic in ideas depresses the morale. We should be deceiving ourselves if we tried to gloss it over. Workers are coming nearer and nearer to the point of view, "An end with horror is better than horror without end."

GENERAL LUDENDORFF: Could your Excellency not succeed in raising the morale of the masses?

SCHEIDEMANN: That is a question of potatoes.[29] We have no more meat. Potatoes cannot be delivered because we are short four thousand cars every day. We have absolutely no fats left. The distress is so great that one stands before a perfect puzzle when one asks: How does North Berlin live and how does East Berlin live? As long as this puzzle cannot be solved, it is impossible to improve morale. It would be the height of dishonesty if we left anybody in doubt on the matter.

Haussmann discussed the morale of the people, but he felt that the military situation was more decisive. "The tone of our negotiations," he said, "depends on how many days after satisfying the needs of the Army we shall have free for the negotiations."

LUDENDORFF: If the Army can get over the next four weeks and winter begins to come on, we are on safe ground. If we succeed in raising morale during these four weeks, it would be of extraordinary military value. I will do all I can to improve the provisioning

29. It is of interest to note that Scheidemann was using exactly the same argument that Ludendorff used earlier to explain poor morale in the Army. See document 57, *ibid.*

of the nation. I will discuss the matter immediately with the Director of Railways. How far it may be possible, I cannot foretell.

Von Payer, who had been quiet during the discussion of the military and economic situation, now spoke.

VON PAYER: I do not view things as darkly as Scheidemann. But one has to take note of changes. I recall the morale last summer, when nobody doubted that we would come out of the war as victors; but the war even then was troubling the people and morale was poor for that reason. Despite that nobody thought that we faced defeat.

When we despatched the first note, people asked one another, "What's happening? Things do not seem to be going so well." Soon their morale became uncertain. Then, when the second Wilson note came, their spirit collapsed; then it was clear that it was a matter of life or death. But even this feeling changed completely. Realizing that we were going to be destroyed as a nation, above all economically, everybody asked himself, "Do we have to endure that or is there a possibility of avoiding it?" If we tell people, "There is still a possibility of avoiding it if you only hold out; but if you cannot hold out a couple of weeks longer, then you can count on the fact that Germany will be virtually wiped out of the society of nations; you will have to reckon on a burden of reparations that will crush us," then we can have a good morale again.

If we succeed in so wording the note that the people get an assurance that we are indeed in a serious plight but that we do not give up the game, then everything is not yet lost.

GENERAL LUDENDORFF: The Vice-Chancellor has spoken my very thoughts. The only question is: How shall we do it? To that I can only repeat my plea: Get hold of the people, arouse them to the heights! Can't Herr Ebert do this? It must be done.

. . .

THE IMPERIAL CHANCELLOR: It is the opinion of Your Excellency that four weeks of high public morale are necessary?

GENERAL LUDENDORFF: It would be preferable to have it longer. In any case after that period the crisis at the western front will be at an end, even if we have to retire still farther. That is my feeling. The force of the attacks during the last few days has been slight.

THE IMPERIAL CHANCELLOR: But within a period of eight to ten days there will come a new wave of attacks, as Your Excellency told me yourself during our conversation.

GENERAL LUDENDORFF: It is coming. A new attack is now in progress on the Tenth Army front; how matters stand there, I do not know. Tomorrow there will be one against the Fifth Army; they do not cease.

THE IMPERIAL CHANCELLOR: It is a question, then, of whether the measures that you recommend will be sufficient so to block the attacks that we can be free to work politically. Your Excellency knows that at the time I was not in favor of the peace note, but I was told that every hour was costing so and so many hundreds of thousands of men, and that every moment might bring on a catastrophe. His Excellency von Hintze is my witness.

HIS EXCELLENCY VON HINTZE: That is so, Your Grand Ducal Highness.

GENERAL LUDENDORFF: The situation is such even now that we can be pushed back and beaten any day. Things went well the day before yesterday; they can also go badly for us.

THE IMPERIAL CHANCELLOR: While you say that we shall be in better shape after four weeks, the English may say that, if it goes on for six more weeks, it is no longer necessary for them to negotiate with the Germans. In any case, the Entente is doing all it can to prolong our negotiations with Wilson.

GENERAL LUDENDORFF: The conferences in Berlin have come to the ears of the Entente and have mightily increased their eagerness for attack. But it is still my opinion that every military reinforcement of the front also strengthens the position of Your Grand Ducal Highness in concluding peace.

THE IMPERIAL CHANCELLOR: That is correct.

GENERAL LUDENDORFF: Whether the reinforcement comes at the right time or not, I cannot say. I repeat that whatever comes is opportune.

THE IMPERIAL CHANCELLOR: How strong is the Army in the west?

COLONEL HEYE: The western front now consists of one hundred ninety-one divisions, of which four are Austrian and seven are from the east. They vary in strength. Twenty-eight divisions have a battalion strength of only 200 or 300 men. The others run approximately from 400 to 500.

GENERAL LUDENDORFF: If we had battalions of full strength, the situation would be saved.

THE IMPERIAL CHANCELLOR: Questions one to eight, that we had to put, have been disposed of by the discussion up to this point. I come now to the ninth question: Would the removal of troops from the eastern districts so imperil the transport of oil for military and domestic consumption that it would force us into a premature conclusion of peace or to the suspension of the submarine war?

Scheüch answered the question as well as he could. He admitted that it was impossible to discover exactly what the Army and the Navy would need in the way of oil in the coming months. Restrictions on civilian consumption would be serious, for it would now be necessary to curtail the lighting of homes and factories. Admiral Scheer reported that the Navy had enough oil to keep the submarines going even without additional supplies from Rumania; he admitted, however, that there was no sense in keeping that supply for the Navy if it meant that the Army could have none. Displeased by the vague estimates, the Chancellor insisted on getting precise figures on how long the Army, the Navy, and the home front could hold out if no more oil came from Rumania. The Minister of War promised to have them ready that afternoon.

The Chancellor now took up the question of the Ukraine. "Given the situation on the western front," he asked, "is the continued occupation of the Ukraine by twelve German divisions justified by Germany's need of supplies?"

SECRETARY OF STATE VON WALDOW: When the question is put in that form, I can answer it with a flat negative. We have included the food and fodder resources of the Ukraine in our economic scheme only as an emergency measure, to improve the situation for us. If, on the other hand, it is a question of entering upon a last desperate struggle, we could also give up the Ukraine and will then try to increase our resources by smuggling.

GENERAL LUDENDORFF: Again I call your attention to the fact that, at present, about one million people are supported by supplies from eastern territories, people whom we should otherwise have to support ourselves.

SECRETARY OF STATE VON WALDOW: In that case, I must first receive information as to the rations and quantities concerned.

GENERAL LUDENDORFF: I will have the Quartermaster General work out the question perfectly clearly with you. We have been told repeatedly by the War Food Administration that we must hold on to the Ukraine. We must have an absolutely clear understanding on that question. If we do not need the Ukraine in order to exist, the question becomes simply one of how many soldiers are needed to keep the danger of Bolshevism from the frontiers.

SECRETARY OF STATE VON WALDOW: When I affirmed the necessity of the Ukraine, the situation was quite different.

GENERAL LUDENDORFF: If we give up the Ukraine, our resources of livestock will be crippled. The question is one, however, not requiring a hasty solution. Austrian troops are also being transported from the Ukraine into Rumania. Only absolutely clear decisions have to be made.

Undersecretary of State Göppert minimized the economic value of the Ukraine for that year. He pointed out, however, that the prevailing conviction was that the withdrawal of German troops would open the way for Bolshevism.

The question of retaining control of Rumania was discussed. Ludendorff said there was no chance whatever of holding the country if the English fleet got into the Black Sea.

THE IMPERIAL CHANCELLOR: Now I come to another [the tenth] question: What is the situation of the Entente in regard to reserves?

COLONEL HEYE: Last week the French had forty divisions of reserves, the English twenty-five, the Americans eighteen, the Italians one; and in addition the Portuguese, the Poles, and other auxiliary troops, a total of eighty-seven divisions of reserves out of a full strength of two hundred twenty divisions.

GENERAL LUDENDORFF: We have one hundred ninety-one divisions on the western front. Thus the number of divisions is not so very different, their strength, however, is. The French division is also weak, not materially stronger than one of ours; the English division is stronger, and the forty American divisions are very strong.

To the eleventh question on how long major attacks could be expected in the west Ludendorff replied that he did not know. The Chancellor now asked his questions regarding the Italian armies.[30] Ludendorff had no fear of an Italian attack by way of Austria against Germany because the Italians were war weary. If they fought anywhere, he believed it would be on the western

30. These questions are numbered 12, 13, and 14. *Supra*, p. 142.

front. Neither did he have any fear of a Bolshevist Army in the east.[31]

The German Government had a very special interest in the American troops in France.[32] It was stated that 350,000 had come over each month during April, May, and June; and about 250,000 a month since that time. This was a notable increase over the 85,000 a month at the beginning of the year. Colonel Heye said that the American statistics had always proved dependable. By the spring of 1919 there would be 2,300,000 Americans fighting in France, with all their needed supplies.

THE IMPERIAL CHANCELLOR: So by next spring we can supply reinforcements of 600,000 or 700,000 men; the enemy 1,100,000 men, if we count the Americans only; perhaps the Italians may be added to these. Will our situation thus become better or worse by spring?

GENERAL LUDENDORFF: According to the figures it will be no worse. But we must further consider the effect of evacuation on our economic situation. If we retire, the state of our war industries will be impaired in the highest degree. It could always be foreseen that, if we come out of the war with our present boundaries, we shall be in a far worse military-political and industrial position than we were before. That result will be apparent now as a consequence of evacuation.

THE IMPERIAL CHANCELLOR: Up to the present Your Excellency has spoken only about manpower; but there is also the equipment to consider, airplanes, tanks, and other things.

GENERAL LUDENDORFF: The pilots of the two armies are at present in the ratio of about 1:3; none the less, the superiority lies with us. The figures that we give on enemy losses are far too low as we are later often able to determine from enemy reports. I am not frightened by all this.

THE IMPERIAL CHANCELLOR: And the tanks next spring?

GENERAL LUDENDORFF: It is my hope that, when our infantry recovers its strength, the tank panic, which was once overcome but has now returned, can once again be vanquished. It reappeared in full strength on August 8, by reason of the fog and who knows what else. But if the morale of the troops is restored, some branches of the Army, like the *Jäger* battalions and the *Garde-*

31. Questions 15 and 16. *Supra,* p. 142. Question 17 about neutral European states entering the war against Germany was not discussed.

32. Questions 18 and 19.

schützen, will make a regular game of shooting tanks. It is also an attractive sport for practical reasons, since there is always good food in the tanks. We could not keep up in tank construction because we had first to build auto trucks; but by next spring we shall be further along with such construction.

On one subject Ludendorff was not optimistic. "Should armistice negotiations take place," he said in answer to a question from Count Roedern, "the very promise to evacuate territory implies a serious deterioration in our military position." The General had come a long way since the first days of October, when he was exerting every pressure to have negotiations begin at once.

The demand for abandoning the submarine was as unwelcome to the Navy as the evacuation of territory was to the Army. "In the past two years," Admiral Scheer said, "the Navy has devoted itself solely to the service of the submarine war and has kept itself in perfect fighting trim at the same time. If labor conditions could be improved, we could double, yes, even treble, the construction of submarines. Now comes Wilson's demand that we give up the submarine war. If we yield, we sacrifice a very important instrument for exerting pressure and gain nothing by way of compensation for accepting an armistice in existing circumstances. For, in fact, the situation is such that the Army can hold its own. For that reason we do not need to agree to Wilson's second condition." Scheer hoped that 40,000 men could be employed in submarine construction in order to make better use of this one weapon.

THE IMPERIAL CHANCELLOR: Finally, I should like permission to ask the following question: If all measures are executed that Your Excellency [Ludendorff] has proposed, and if the front holds out for the next few months, does Your Excellency then believe that we shall have created in the course of the coming year a situation better than that in which we find ourselves at the present moment? We must understand fully that every effort now made that fails to pay in the end is a waste of our strength and would create a situation for which we bear the responsibility and which we must boldly face. Can we next year end the war under better conditions than now?

GENERAL LUDENDORFF: Every effort made now will improve our situation.

ADMIRAL SCHEER: It is certainly the general impression that

the enemy feels the submarine war very acutely, particularly Italy. That is a condition that will develop further in the immediate future, particularly with regard to America. But if we accept the terms that are offered us, we throw all this away.

THE IMPERIAL CHANCELLOR: That is no answer to the question I asked: Will we end the war under better conditions if we yield to the wishes of the Supreme Army Command? It is not now a question of a reply to Wilson's note.

ADMIRAL SCHEER: Our position will be better, while that of our enemy will be worse. That is the reason why our opponents are determined to end the war this fall.

Asked to explain the basis for his optimism Admiral Scheer said that the withdrawal of the submarine from the waters of the Mediterranean and from the coast of Flanders would allow a great concentration around the British Isles. Count Roedern referred to some unpleasant history when he reminded Scheer that promises had once been made that the submarine could keep American soldiers from landing in France.

The argument whether to end the negotiations or not went on.

VICE-CHANCELLOR VON PAYER: The impression made by the military situation today is decidedly more favorable than it was at the beginning of the month. Are there reasons for this from the military point of view?

GENERAL LUDENDORFF: At the front there is the unsuccessful attack of the enemy yesterday and the day before yesterday. The enemy did not take a big enough bite. If he had done all that he could have done, we should have been beaten. The fighting front of the Entente at this place was not at its former high level.

An additional reason is that the Americans are hard hit by the grippe. It is true that the grippe is beginning to spread in our lines, and that in a very serious form. Our soldiers are tired, and a tired man succumbs to contagious disease much more easily than a strong man.

THE IMPERIAL CHANCELLOR: So the situation is no longer the same as it was on October 5, when we were persuaded to make a peace offer to Wilson?

GENERAL LUDENDORFF: It is my impression that, before accepting the conditions of this note, which are too severe, we must tell the enemy: Win these terms by fighting for them.

THE IMPERIAL CHANCELLOR: And when he has won them, will he not then impose worse conditions?

GENERAL LUDENDORFF: There are no worse conditions.

THE IMPERIAL CHANCELLOR: Oh, yes; they can invade Germany and ravage the country.

GENERAL LUDENDORFF: Things have not gone that far yet.

COUNT ROEDERN: Up to the present we have talked only of victory or defeat. There is still a third possibility; we might retire slowly. That is the most likely thing, if we do not have to fear a break-through by the enemy. I regard it as improbable that we can drive the enemy back. So, assuming that we retire, that we fill our ranks, that our defensive power is strengthened, will America then be inclined to offer us better terms? America knows that we are using up our last reserves; she will bide her time.

GENERAL LUDENDORFF: But look how the situation appears in other countries. I have a report from an agent that in England and in France people are seriously afraid that, if the war lasts more than a month, Germany will bring the Entente to a halt while yet on enemy territory. There is in those countries a great fear that the present position may be reversed.

SECRETARY OF STATE SOLF: I have the responsibility of advising the Imperial Chancellor about the text and tone of the note we have to send to Wilson. For this task I am scarcely better prepared by the explanations of His Excellency Ludendorff than I was before.

At the beginning of this month the political head of the Empire was urged by the Supreme Army Command to ask our opponents for an armistice and to propose peace. Against his will and against his convictions, the Imperial Chancellor had to decide to accept the responsibility for this move. Then came the counterquestions [from Wilson], and even then we adhered to our conviction that, in our answer, we should simply keep to the conditions we had proposed. Now Wilson's answer has come, one that confronts us with serious decisions, and immediately the picture changes, so that we can now hold our own, yes, we shall even be in a much better position than before if we survive the next four weeks.

All this is a puzzle to me. What is the real reason that a thing can now be done which was formerly declared impossible?

GENERAL LUDENDORFF: I have always represented the lack of men to be the chief obstacle. Today I hear that the scarcity is not so great as I had assumed. Today I hear that I can get 600,000 men within a reasonable time. Why I was unable to get them earlier, I will not discuss. If I can get them now, the isolation of the Army will come to an end. In spite of the unfortunate things that have happened, the situation is changed because the enemy's fighting strength is diminishing at the same time.

I still believe as before that we must bring about armistice negotiations if it is at all possible. But we should enter upon such armistice negotiations as will permit an orderly evacuation of the country, consequently a respite of at least two or three months. And, further, we should not accept any conditions that make a resumption of hostilities seem impossible. But from the note we have to realize that such is the intention. The conditions are intended to put us out of the fight. Before we proceed further, the enemy must definitely state what his terms really are.

We should not break with Wilson abruptly. On the contrary, say, "Simply tell us what we are actually to do. If you demand anything contrary to our national honor, if you seek to make us incapable of fighting, then the answer is absolutely, No."

When I say this, I am not changing my previous position. I ask only that the measures proposed by the Minister of War be rapidly carried out.

SECRETARY OF STATE SOLF: But surely this measure was also taken into consideration even at that time.

GENERAL LUDENDORFF: Since April and even much earlier I have been fighting for men. They have not been given to me. It is still a fact that we are getting 70,000 too few men a month. If this deficiency is made good, we do not need to accept all the terms.[33]

THE IMPERIAL CHANCELLOR: Could the German Supreme Command put itself in direct touch with the American Command?

GENERAL LUDENDORFF: The Americans do not exercise the real command, but Foch. Would it not be better to put one more inquiry to the [American] Government?

MINISTER OF WAR SCHEÜCH: The time for asking Foch has not yet come. That would be an admission of defeat.[34]

Prince Max was not reassured by this conference, even if some of his colleagues were encouraged by Ludendorff's words. Still, the Chancellor felt relieved over the fact that the panic of the first days of October, when Ludendorff was pressing the Government to despatch its appeal to Wilson, had disappeared.[35]

33. Document 57, *Amtliche Urkunden,* ends here. The protocol of the meeting is continued in Max, *Erinnerungen,* pp. 442–444.

34. *Ibid.,* p. 443.

35. Niemann says that Ludendorff had recovered his old vigor when he reported to the Kaiser on October 17. Niemann, *Kaiser und Revolution,* pp. 101–102.

"Do you believe," he asked Ludendorff in a private conversation, "that we should be able next year to conclude the war on better terms than today?"

Ludendorff answered with a clear "Yes."

"You would then look with equanimity," the Chancellor continued, "on a rupture of relations with Wilson?"

Again Ludendorff answered with a clear "Yes."

The Chancellor was puzzled. He could see no real change in the military situation since October 5 or even since September 29. "We should not have raised the white flag on October 5. Even today it would have been unnecessary to raise it. But it is certain that the situation would be desperate after a couple of months." One thing seemed certain: "Negotiations with Wilson must go on. We turned to him; now it is a question of giving his good will a chance whether we have faith in him or not; our situation compels us to make the greatest sacrifices for peace. But if armistice conditions are made depriving us of honor, then *the people must be called out to make a last stand.*" Should it come to that, Prince Max was convinced that "Ludendorff was not the man to lead such a war of desperation." [36]

What troubled the Chancellor was that Ludendorff had shifted his ground since the time he had insisted upon an immediate plea for an armistice. Instead of admitting that he had lost his nerve between September 29 and October 3, Ludendorff now blamed everything on the lack of reserves. That was what he said on October 17, when for the first time, he asserted he learned that 600,000 men were available; had they been available earlier, there would have been no need for an armistice. So spoke Ludendorff, although he had been informed the evening of October 10 that Scheüch could get that number of men for him.[37]

The afternoon meeting of the Cabinet with Ludendorff brought no further satisfaction. Although willing to admit that "the defection of Austria would produce an unfavorable effect" from the military and economic points of view, Ludendorff said that no catastrophe could ensue for Germany. He still desired to have negotiations with Wilson continued. When Solf asked whether Germany should send a strong note "even at the risk of Wilson's breaking relations," Ludendorff said that Germany could take that responsibility. "If we give our note a sharper tone and Wilson breaks with us," Ludendorff explained, "we shall

36. Max, *Erinnerungen*, pp. 445–446.
37. *Ibid.*, pp. 448–449.

then see that he has not dealt with us honestly." The German note should insist that Wilson speak out clearly about the conditions of an armistice.

Colonel Heye tried to explain the Army's changed viewpoint. "When the Supreme Army Command decided on its peace proposal, it was done," he said, "in the belief that an honorable peace could be made. Now for the first time it appears to be a case of 'to be or not to be.' . . . We must accept a fight to the end if the terms offered should be dishonorable." [38]

Prince Max could not accept that interpretation. He was inclined to the view of Haussmann that the Army's earlier attitude had been a demand for diplomatic assistance to stave off military catastrophe; now the Army preferred military capitulation to dishonorable conditions. According to the Chancellor the Cabinet agreed on two things:

> First: Wilson should not be given any pretext for breaking off negotiations; that is, concessions in the submarine question are necessary. There were differences of opinion as to how far these concessions should go.
>
> Second: We cannot accept dishonorable conditions without being ruined forever. "Rather utter defeat than a surrender" must be the fundamental idea of the note.[39]

Members of the Government were also agreed that it was unnecessary at this time to consult generals other than Ludendorff before despatching the note to Wilson.[40]

In his memoirs, published about half a year later, Ludendorff, "astonished" by Solf's charge that he had reversed his attitude, replied that the Government too had been willing to fight on if the worst happened. Instead of attacking him for having reached more optimistic views of the military situation, Solf should have been grateful for a favorable judgment making it easier for him to carry on negotiations. "Besides," wrote Ludendorff, "at that time I was not thinking of breaking off [negotiations], but was insisting on clarity in our thinking and in our ultimate desires." [41]

Ludendorff had support for his opposition to Wilson's terms

38. From the protocol of the Cabinet meeting, document 58, *Amtliche Urkunden.*
39. Max, *Erinnerungen,* p. 449.
40. *Ibid.,* p. 451.
41. Ludendorff, *Kriegserinnerungen,* p. 609.

in a letter that von Tirpitz addressed to the Chancellor on October 17. According to the retired Admiral, Wilson's rising demands had taken on a character of "deliberate extortion." "Our latest offer of peace and armistice, which is so accommodating as to amount to a renunciation of any claim on our part to rank as a great power," he wrote, "has been answered bluntly by Wilson with a demand for our complete disarmament. He knows quite certainly that the cessation of the submarine war makes any further resistance on our part impossible. . . . Wilson's answer shows further that it was quite a mistake to assume, if anyone did assume, that the Entente would be so obliging as to concede us an immediate armistice on any terms that would admit of our putting our Army and our frontiers in a position of defence in case of the peace negotiations breaking down." The only way to secure the existence of German civilization was to issue an appeal to the whole nation to fight with determination in its last defense. He believed a dictatorship would be necessary for that final struggle.[42]

Apart from the difficulties raised by the Army and Navy, Prince Max found it hard to know what kind of answer Wilson really expected. The notes from the American President were not explicit with regard to the Kaiser or the German submarine; and for their significance the Chancellor had to look to neutral countries for light. Naturally these reports conflicted and added to the bewilderment. On October 17 a report from Brussels recommended the immediate abdication of the Kaiser and of the Crown Prince; that was a necessary condition for an armistice, and to delay was to play into the hands of the French and the English, who wanted to invade Germany and had made careful preparations for a big attack on November 1.[43] A report from Stockholm, dated October 16, stated that the demands of the Allies would increase as Germany retreated; that the French and the Americans desired to bring the war into German territory.[44] On October 18 the Chancellor received a report from a colleague who had been at The Hague and had spoken directly with one of the enemy diplomats. The report was thought to have a special value because it was the result of direct communication, involving no "confidential agent." According to this report Wilson and Foch were opposed to each other, the former seeking

42. Von Tirpitz, *My Memoirs* (London, 1928), II, 335–338.
43. Document 59, *Amtliche Urkunden.*
44. Document 53, *ibid.;* Max, *Erinnerungen,* p. 453.

"a just peace of reconciliation and understanding" and the latter demanding the "complete humiliation of Germany and the satisfaction of French vanity." In this conflict it was deemed advisable to satisfy Wilson, who was reported as desirous of concessions on two points only: the sinking of no more passenger ships by German submarines and the democratization of Germany, with the Kaiser retained as a constitutional monarch, the Crown to have in Germany the same role it has in England. France was represented as being the chief obstacle to peace. Since a strong military and diplomatic attitude on Germany's part would strengthen Wilson and weaken Foch, "friends of a just peace now advise us to proceed slowly, particularly in our desire for peace and armistice, and to do everything to enable the front to hold and the continued democratization of Germany to proceed in a calm and convincing fashion." [45]

Prince Max thought this report so significant that he immediately gave it to Field Marshal von Hindenburg, who distributed it in the form of a circular letter from Army Headquarters to all German Armies. In a covering letter Hindenburg stressed the great importance of maintaining present military positions for the success of the negotiations now being carried on with the enemy.[46]

On October 18 came a report from the Austrian Government that the early conclusion of peace was essential because the Entente could attack through Serbia toward Hungary and thus threaten the Central Powers from the south. The Austrians were convinced that "a maintenance of the western front alone was not enough." [47]

Under this barrage of conflicting reports and recommendations Prince Max found it difficult to answer Wilson's note. "All informants," he writes in his memoirs, "were in agreement on one point, that at the moment the Allies were debating fiercely with one another and with their people whether an armistice should be granted or not. Whether the will to peace would achieve its goal or not depended on the capacity of Germany's military and home fronts to resist." [48] He also believed it essential to support Wilson

45. *Ibid.*, pp. 453–454.

46. Document 59c, *Amtliche Urkunden.* The German Crown Prince seems to think the document was a page from his own diary and publishes it as such! Cf. *Memoirs of the Crown Prince,* pp. 268–270.

47. Document 59b, *Amtliche Urkunden.* In a marginal note to the document Ludendorff wrote that Austria had military power enough to maintain the Serbian frontier but questioned her will power. See also document 60.

48. Max, *Erinnerungen,* p. 453.

by making Germany more democratic and by imposing restrictions on the use of the submarine. "Our answer," he writes, "must be so framed that, if Wilson rejects it, his rejection will become a reason for an appeal to the German people to rise up as a nation" to defend their rights. Rejection because of inadequate concessions on the submarine issue would never serve as a basis for an appeal to the nation. "A *levée en masse* for the purpose of maintaining the submarine war is altogether impossible." If adequate concessions were made in this respect and with regard to Germany's democratization and if the Allies still rejected Germany's note, it would be clear that the enemy nations were continuing the fight not for Wilson's peace of justice but for Foch's military glory.[49]

With his legal adviser Simons, Prince Max drafted a reply to Wilson on October 18. This draft stated that when the German Government agreed to the evacuation of occupied territory, it had thought only of working out the details of that procedure and of an armistice with the Allied military experts. The President had not made it clear whether he rejected or approved a speedy solution by military experts of the technical questions involved. If this matter were to be the subject of open correspondence instead of direct negotiation between the belligerents, Prince Max said that he hoped Wilson and his Allies would state their demands; but he cautioned against demands injurious to German honor or irreconcilable with Wilson's peace of justice. Orders had gone out to all submarine commanders not to sink passenger ships but to confine themselves to the principles of cruiser warfare with the safety of noncombatants assured. The note reminded Wilson that German noncombatants were suffering from a war conducted contrary to the freedom of the seas and the principles of international law. As to the destruction of property committed by retreating German Armies in France and Belgium and the sufferings of the inhabitants, the German Government was not violating international law although it admitted excesses on the part of individuals, who were punished for them. The note recommended the appointment of neutral commissions to investigate and report on such charges. The Chancellor wanted to assure the President that the German Government had undergone a fundamental change, that "the final power of decision over all vital questions of the nation, particularly over war and peace, is today in the hands of parliament."

49. *Ibid.*, p. 455.

The answer being made to the President is made "in the name of a Government that is responsible to the people." No law can guarantee the continuation of the new system of government. "The assurance that the new system will not be revoked . . . rests on the fact that the declared will and the inner conviction of the great majority of the German people stand behind it. A relapse is to be feared only if Germany, to please other countries, permits the hasty and insincere imposition upon her of a constitutional form irreconcilable with her peculiar character and history." [50]

The Chancellor was pleased with this draft, sure of the approval of his colleagues and of the High Command. But within twenty-four hours he found himself opposed by his whole Cabinet and in such a violent dispute with the Army and Navy Commands that he had to place the matter before the Kaiser. Count Roedern argued that the note was not dignified; Scheidemann, that it was too challenging and would make Wilson sever negotiations, that its conclusion would arouse the suspicions of the enemy by its talk about changing the new system of government. The real fight, however, came over the decision "to conduct submarine war as cruiser war." Admiral Scheer and Admiral von Mann, the Minister of Marine, supported by Erzberger, opposed "any concession in the submarine question." The debate settled down to a choice between continuing negotiations with Wilson and modifying the German submarine war, whose value was challenged by Count Metternich, former German Ambassador at London, summoned with other ambassadors to give his opinion on the matter. The naval men said it was impossible for submarines to conduct cruiser warfare; it amounted to renouncing all use of the submarine. Solf then proposed "a public order that no passenger ships be torpedoed, a secret order that the submarine war be abandoned altogether." At last the Cabinet agreed that submarine commanders be ordered to sink no more passenger ships.

Admiral Scheer still refused to yield. He turned to the Army Command and to the Kaiser for help. General Ludendorff supported the Navy. In a telephone message delivered to Prince Max the morning of October 20, Hindenburg pointed out that Germany might soon be fighting alone, without allies. Still he favored fighting; for, even if beaten, "we should not really be worse off than if we were to accept everything as at present." The Germans should fight for their honor, to the very last man, rather

50. The draft of this long note is found *ibid.*, pp. 456–458.

than "surrender and so be delivered to destruction *before* doing the utmost in their power." By giving up the submarine without getting any compensation, he reasoned, "we adopt the latter course." Such a concession would have a harmful effect on the Army's morale; therefore he must oppose it. "If the Government, in adopting this view, must reckon with Wilson's breaking off negotiations, it must likewise be determined to fight through to the bitter end for the sake of honor." [51]

Prince Max says that he was profoundly surprised by the argument of the High Command that the German people should not "let themselves be forced to surrender and so be delivered to destruction *before* doing the utmost in their power." Those, he says, should have been the words of Ludendorff and Hindenburg on September 29, when they forced a Government determined to defend the nation to raise the white flag. It was in vain that the Chancellor spent the morning of October 20 trying to convince Ludendorff that the cessation of the submarine war did not mean surrendering to the enemy; that reports from abroad made it necessary to spare passenger ships in order to keep Wilson from breaking off negotiations and to strengthen him against French demands for a dishonorable surrender of the German Army; that the rejection of the note by Wilson after this concession would arouse the German people to fight whereas the submarine war was unpopular in the country and people would not fight to maintain it.[52]

The Cabinet was thoroughly aroused when it met that morning. The general opinion was that Ludendorff had outmaneuvered the Government. In the words of von Payer it meant that the civilian Government was being made responsible for "losing a war already lost." Erzberger asked that the public be told that the Army Command had forced the demand for an armistice; otherwise, German soldiers would say that the civil Government had sacrificed them to American shells. "The Cabinet must de-

51. *Ibid.*, pp. 458–461; also document 63, *Amtliche Urkunden;* Niemann, *Revolution von Oben*, pp. 162–163. Von Tirpitz has this comment to make on the fight over the answer to Wilson: "On October 17th and 18th the majority in the Imperial Government were in favor of negotiating sword in hand. On the 19th, however, the Scheidemann group, with the addition of Count Wolff-Metternich (a particularly unfortunate selection) succeeded in bringing the majority round. Wilson's desire, trading on our utter lack of political instinct, to render us defenceless before the negotiations opened, was fulfilled and with that our utter defeat was assured." Von Tirpitz, *My Memoirs*, II, 338n.

52. Max, *Erinnerungen*, pp. 461–462.

mand," said Erzberger, "that the Supreme Army Command accept the note without reservation."

Additional trouble developed for the Chancellor at noon, just after he had opened a session of the Bundesrat to explain and defend his note to Wilson. A special message from the Kaiser informed him that "His Majesty had adopted the attitude of the Navy and desired to hold a meeting of the Crown Council that afternoon at Potsdam should the Chancellor persist in his views." Prince Max replied that it was impossible to hold a Crown Council that afternoon because plans had already been made for meetings that could not be postponed. He desired that the Kaiser should come to Berlin. He made it clear that before he would change his mind on the submarine question he would resign even though he believed that revolution would follow the break-up of the Government.[53]

The Chancellor felt strengthened in his position by the knowledge that Solf had won parliamentary support for the note. He was also informed that there was a strong demand for constitutional regulation of the powers of the military Cabinet. A lengthy report on the military situation from Crown Prince Rupprecht of Bavaria showed that Ludendorff did not have the full support of the Army for his views. This report painted a dark picture of the military situation, saying it would not be possible to hold out through December. "I should stress the fact that even now our situation is a thoroughly dangerous one," wrote Rupprecht, "and that under certain circumstances it might become a catastrophe over night. Ludendorff does not understand the full seriousness of the situation. No matter what the circumstances are, we must obtain peace before the enemy forces his way into Germany; woe to us if he does!"[54]

In the early afternoon of October 20 the Kaiser saw Prince Max in Berlin. The latter had as his guest Count Lerchenfeld, the Bavarian Minister in Berlin, who had reported earlier on the longing of the people of Bavaria for peace.[55] Prince Max

53. *Ibid.*, pp. 463–464.

54. *Ibid.*, pp. 465–466. Solf had written to the Minister of War on October 18 that generals other than Hindenburg and Ludendorff should be heard. "The decision is of too much importance, it can be too fateful to be left to two men." Even at the risk of having them resign, the Government must inquire of others about the military situation. But, he added, that inquiry should not be held until after Wilson had made his reply to the German note then being discussed. Document 62, *Amtliche Urkunden.*

55. Max, *Erinnerungen,* p. 465.

asked the Count to be present during his talk with the Kaiser; he believed it proper since the Bavarian delegate to the Bundesrat was always chairman of the committee on foreign policy. Furthermore, the Kaiser and the Count were old friends. "His Majesty was taken aback by the presence of Count Lerchenfeld," writes Prince Max, "and greeted him with the words: 'I had no idea that you were an expert in naval affairs.' Then he expressed his views against the abandonment of the intensified submarine war. We explained our views to each other, and I added that I had to make my remaining in office contingent upon the Kaiser's agreeing to the concession I thought necessary. The Kaiser gave his assent, but only very unwillingly. At this point Count Lerchenfeld called attention to the dangerous tendencies in the Empire, tendencies which were directed expressly against the Emperor. His Majesty interrupted him; he knew this, he knew also that many people were demanding his abdication. But, he added with great earnestness, a successor of Frederick the Great does not abdicate. Then he left us and immediately received the head of the Admiralty Staff, whom he informed of his decision."[56]

Meeting in an afternoon session, members of the Cabinet were disturbed over Max's threat to resign. The Chancellor said he had acted alone because he had no desire to involve his colleagues in his resignation if it became necessary. So far as he was concerned, the matter was settled by the Kaiser's decision and he was sure that Ludendorff would yield.[57] Some members of the Cabinet wanted to compel Ludendorff to accept the note. But Haeften, who had tried repeatedly to make Ludendorff change his mind, reported that there was nothing that reason could do; Ludendorff was convinced that the time had come to break with Wilson. The Minister of War made a last effort to persuade the Quartermaster General to agree to the surrender of the submarine, but found he was wasting his time.[58]

While this debate was going on in Germany, the Entente Powers were making preparations for a mighty offensive through Lorraine. On October 18 Foch moved his Headquarters north-

56. *Ibid.*, p. 467. See also Niemann, *Revolution von Oben*, p. 163.

57. According to Niemann, Ludendorff said that "on the military aspect the matter is decided for me by the order of His Majesty; but His Majesty has no control over my conscience." Niemann, *Revolution von Oben*, p. 165. The words are also given in Max, *Erinnerungen*, p. 470.

58. Returning from his futile telephone conversation, Scheüch told Haeften that he did not envy him his battles with Ludendorff over the telephone. *Ibid.*, pp. 467–468.

ward from Bombon to Senlis, which was to be his last post of command during the war; he was to be here on November 7 when the German wireless message arrived asking him to fix the place of meeting for the armistice delegations. The Entente nations were counting on this offensive to end the war in 1919. Of these plans the Germans knew nothing. But they did know that Turkey had just asked Wilson for peace and that Austria was breaking up.

While they were speculating over possible terms from Wilson the Germans had learned a little of what lay in store for Austria-Hungary. On October 19 Wilson somewhat belatedly answered the Austrian request for an armistice. The President said that developments had caused him to modify Point 10 of the Fourteen Points, which had demanded for the peoples of the Dual Monarchy "the freest opportunity for autonomous development." Autonomy, said the President, was no longer enough; "nationalistic aspirations" had now to be recognized for the Czecho-Slovaks and the Yugo-Slavs.[59] This recognition set the seal on the long-pending dissolution of the Dual Monarchy; but, what was worse from the German point of view, it indicated that Wilson did not feel himself strictly bound by the Fourteen Points.[60]

The pessimism that grew out of these untoward developments had affected his colleagues so much, Prince Max has written, that they again attempted to modify the reply to Wilson. Late in the evening of October 20 the Chancellor learned that Solf had weakened in the presence of doubting Secretaries of State and was going to omit from the note two passages that the Chancellor wished to retain: one against dishonorable conditions and the other reminding Wilson that many Germans had suffered from the hunger blockade imposed in violation of international law and of the freedom of the seas. Angered by this second attempt of his colleagues that day to change the tenor of his note, Prince Max sent Solf a protest that arrived just before midnight and resulted in the retention of the passage about Germany's opposition to the imposition of dishonorable conditions. The reference to the blockade was eliminated. Twenty minutes after midnight on the night of October 20–21 Germany's third note was at last despatched to Wilson.[61] It read as follows:

59. Lansing to Ekengren, October 19, 1918, *Foreign Relations, 1918,* Supplement I, I, 368.
60. *Frankfurter Zeitung,* October 22, 1918, No. 293.
61. Max, *Erinnerungen,* p. 468.

In accepting the proposal for an evacuation of the occupied territories the German Government has started from the assumption that the procedure of this evacuation and of the conditions of an armistice should be left to the judgment of the military advisers and that the actual standard of power on both sides in the field has to form the basis for arrangements safeguarding and guaranteeing this standard. The German Government suggests to the President to bring about an opportunity for fixing the details. It trusts that the President of the United States will approve of no demand which would be irreconcilable with the honor of the German people and with opening a way to a peace of justice.

The German Government protests against the reproach of illegal and inhumane actions made against the German land and sea forces and thereby against the German people. For the covering of a retreat, destructions will always be necessary and are in so far permitted by international law. The German troops are under the strictest instructions to spare private property and to exercise care for the population to the best of their ability. Where transgressions occur in spite of these instructions the guilty are being punished.

The German Government further denies that the German Navy in sinking ships has ever purposely destroyed lifeboats with their passengers. The German Government proposes with regard to all these charges that the facts be cleared up by neutral commissions. In order to avoid anything that might hamper the work of peace, the German Government has caused orders to be despatched to all submarine commanders precluding the torpedoing of passenger ships, without, however, for technical reasons, being able to guarantee that these orders will reach every single submarine at sea before its return.

As the fundamental conditions for peace, the President characterizes the destruction of every arbitrary power that can separately, secretly, and of its own single choice disturb the peace of the world. To this the German Government replies: Hitherto the representation of the people in the German Empire has not been endowed with an influence on the formation of the Government. The Constitution did not provide for a concurrence of the representation of the people in decision on peace and war. These conditions have just now undergone a fundamental change. The new Government has been formed in complete accord with the wishes of the representation of the people, based on the equal, universal, secret, direct franchise. The leaders of the great parties of the Reichstag are members of this

Government. In future no government can take or continue in office without possessing the confidence of the majority of the Reichstag. The responsibility of the Chancellor of the Empire to the representation of the people is being legally developed and safeguarded. The first act of the new Government has been to lay before the Reichstag a bill to alter the Constitution of the Empire so that the consent of the representation of the people is required for decisions on war and peace. The permanence of the new system is, however, guaranteed not only by constitutional safeguards, but also by the unshakable determination of the German people, whose vast majority stands behind these reforms and demands their energetic continuance.

The question of the President, with whom he and the Governments associated against Germany are dealing, is therefore answered in a clear and unequivocal manner by the statement that the offer of peace and an armistice has come from a Government which, free from arbitrary and irresponsible influence, is supported by the approval of the overwhelming majority of the German people.

SOLF[62]

62. Oederlin to Lansing, October 22, 1918, *Foreign Relations, 1918,* Supplement 1, I, 380–381. For German original see document 64, *Amtliche Urkunden.*

VII

Pershing and the Allies Disagree with Wilson

THE third German note, sent on Sunday, October 20, was "undoubtedly known in Washington on the same day."[1] Because it made Germany appear to be far more democratically controlled than she actually was, one cannot say that it helped Germany's cause, either in the United States or in the Entente nations. Many members of the American Congress expressed open dissatisfaction with it. Commenting on October 21, Republican Senator Poindexter said, "If the President answers this note and undertakes to agree with Germany on the basis of it before her army is conquered and disarmed I should think he should be impeached."[2] That he meant what he said can be inferred from the resolution he offered in the Senate the same day:

Resolved, That no officer of the United States shall enter into any discussion with the Government of Germany as to terms of peace; and it is hereby made unlawful for any official of this Government to answer in any way any note, message, or representation from the German Government, or the German people, or from any official representing or purporting to represent them or either of them, on the subject of peace or an armistice between the German Government or the German nation or people and the Governments with which they are now at war, until and before such time as the German armed forces shall have surrendered to the allied nations in the war in which they are now engaged;

That the war against Germany shall be prosecuted by the United States with the utmost vigor and dispatch possible continuously until the armed forces of Germany shall have laid down their arms and surrendered to the commanding general in the field of the allied forces without condition or stipulation;

That German territory shall then be occupied and taken under control by the armed forces of the United States in coöperation

1. Baker, *Wilson,* VIII, 494.
2. *New York Times,* October 22, 1918.

with its allies, and that such occupation and control shall be continued until such time as the chosen representatives of the United States and the nations allied with the United States, in a conference appointed for that purpose, shall have formally agreed among themselves upon the specific terms of peace to be imposed by said allies upon Germany, and the practical and concrete application of the same in detail;

That no official of the United States shall agree that any representative of the German Government shall participate in said conference or have a vote therein or be present thereat, except for the purpose of conveying data or information to said conference when called on by the conference therefor.[3]

Wilson most certainly knew that his allies were looking with suspicion on his correspondence with Germany because of his failure to consult them about it. American representatives abroad were keeping Washington informed as to public and official opinion in the Entente nations. But Wilson did not know all that was going on. On October 16 Foch had written to Clemenceau to insist that the Commanders-in-Chief should make armistice terms. He had recommended occupation of the left bank of the Rhine pending the negotiation of the final treaty; now he wished to know what the Government's future policy was concerning the Rhineland. Would the territory be annexed to France? Or were buffer states to be erected there? If the French Government intended to separate the Rhineland from Prussia he believed the armistice should be framed accordingly. Clemenceau resented the questions about the Rhineland and curtly reminded Foch that his business was war and he should not interfere in other Government policy.[4]

The German note of the 20th alarmed Foch. He believed that Max von Baden had set a trap for the Allies and he thought it "high time . . . that the negotiations carried on for two weeks between Berlin and Washington should come to an end"; they could lead to nothing but confusion. "Furthermore," he went on, "it was undesirable that the Germans should come to look on President Wilson as a kind of arbiter between the Entente Governments and the Central Powers. In such a game the Entente

3. *Congressional Record,* October 21, 1918, p. 11402.

4. Foch, *Mémoires,* II, 276–279; R. Recouly, *Marshal Foch* (New York, 1929), pp. 52–55. Also Mordacq, *Le Ministère Clemenceau,* II, 284.

had everything to lose and nothing to gain; it was advisable, therefore, that without delay the military advisers should now have the say."[5]

Trouble for the President was also brewing in England. The British were having difficulty in formulating their own armistice terms; and the fear haunted them that Wilson would go ahead without consulting them. There was a long discussion of terms on October 19 in London, for which the British Commander-in-Chief, Haig, came over from France. He called on Field Marshal Wilson at the War Office and in the afternoon went with him to 10 Downing Street, where they conferred with Lloyd George, Bonar Law, Milner, Balfour, and Admiral Wemyss. It was Haig's conviction that the Germans were still strong, able to oppose considerable strength to the Entente armies, and therefore "not ready for unconditional surrender." He said that the French Army was "worn out . . . and not fighting latterly" because of a belief that the war was virtually over and peace in sight; that the American Army was not yet organized, was badly equipped and half trained, and lacked experienced officers and supply services. With the French and Americans incapable of making a serious offensive "now," it was up to the British to "bring the enemy to his knees," despite their lack of reinforcements. "But why expend more British lives? and for what?" he asked. In view of this situation Haig suggested the following armistice terms:

1. Immediate evacuation of Belgium and occupied French territory;
2. Metz and Strassburg to be at once occupied by the allied armies and Alsace Lorraine to be vacated by the enemy;
3. Belgian and French rolling stock to be returned and inhabitants restored.

He warned against the imposition of stiffer terms; the British should ask only "for what we intend to hold" and "set our face against the French entering Germany to pay off old scores," for "the British Army [will] not fight keenly for what is really not its own affair."[6]

Field Marshal Wilson was not satisfied with these mild terms. "Unless we held real guarantees, i.e. occupation of Boche territory," he argued, "we would never be able to enforce terms which would give us a durable peace." Lloyd George and Milner agreed

5. Foch, *Mémoires,* II, 275.
6. Duff Cooper, *Haig* (two vols., London, 1936), II, 394–397.

with Haig; Balfour and Bonar Law supported General Wilson. Admiral Wemyss presented the Admiralty proposal: surrender of virtually the whole German fleet and continued blockade. No final decision was reached at this session and another conference was set for October 21.

The meeting on Monday, October 21, was one of the longest Cabinet sessions on record, lasting from about 11 A.M. until after 6 P.M. The naval terms were apparently the main subject of discussion. Beatty, Commander of the Grand Fleet, and Wemyss wanted the German fleet and submarines handed over. It was an extreme demand, based on the reasoning that the Germans would have lost their entire fleet if they had dared engage in battle with the British.[7]

When the conference was resumed after lunch, the German note of October 20 was available. It was termed an "adroit" reply to President Wilson. "No mention of Alsace-Lorraine, nor any mention of the salt water." Field Marshal Wilson believed that the President was now "trapped" and that Lloyd George and Clemenceau must come to the rescue. Balfour got the Cabinet to approve a "VERY URGENT" telegram that was sent to Washington and presented to Secretary Lansing that same day. It pointed out that the Germans were seeking a conditional armistice, that they said nothing about naval terms, that they were assuming that only "occupied territories" should be evacuated, and were relying on a mere retreat to their own frontiers where they could easily organize a strong defense. It also demanded guarantees in the armistice in case the negotiations should break down and expressed the hope that President Wilson would make no commitments in these vital questions without first consulting his allies.[8]

Balfour had been so cautious about the Fourteen Points that there was reason to wonder what he thought of them. He threw light on his attitude toward one of them when, in a luncheon address before the Australian and New Zealand Club, he advised that the colonies taken from Germany should not be restored to her because it was absolutely essential to have the communications of the British Empire safe. If the colonies were restored, he asked, what security was there that their original oppressors

7. *Ibid.*, pp. 398–399; Lady Wester Wemyss, *Life and Letters of Admiral Wemyss*, pp. 385–387; Callwell, *Field-Marshal Sir Henry Wilson*, II, 138.

8. Baker, *Wilson*, VIII, 501; Callwell, *Field-Marshal Sir Henry Wilson*, II, 139–140.

would not use them as bases for piratical warfare? [9] On October 21 he was asked in the House of Commons whether Great Britain had approved or disapproved of the Fourteen Points; his only reply was that "it is not desirable at the present moment to discuss the matter . . ." When it was pointed out to him that demonstrations in London against the Fourteen Points required the Government to state its policy, he refused to be drawn out. He was equally reticent as to whether Wilson had approached the Government about the matter. [10]

It was in connection with his third note to Germany that President Wilson consulted his Cabinet for the first time during his armistice correspondence with Germany. This was in a two-hour session on October 22. "I do not know what to do," he said, opening the meeting. "I must ask your advice. . . . What do you think should be done?" There was a long silence, broken when Secretary of the Interior, Lane, said that the Allies should not treat with Germany until her troops were "across the Rhine." Secretary of Labor Wilson said that the Allies should be consulted. Houston, Secretary of Agriculture, spoke of his doubts about Germany's political reformation and went into great detail on the specific reforms that should be effected. McAdoo wanted the terms fixed by the military authorities. The most belligerent member of the Cabinet was Burleson, who insisted on absolute surrender and feared that terms worked out by Foch, Haig, and Pershing might be too lenient. Secretary Lane warned the President against proposing the kind of armistice that the Allies would not grant. The President told how he feared the spread of Bolshevism; he even said it was necessary to retain the Kaiser to keep it down. He was also deeply disturbed by the brutal demands appearing in the American press for the punishment of the Germans.[11]

The next afternoon the President discussed his reply with the "war cabinet." Mr. E. N. Hurley, chairman of the U. S. Shipping Board, who had written in the morning to the President that he should keep "the throttle of war and peace" in his own hands, has given an account of this session:

9. According to report in the *New York Times,* October 24, 1918.

10. *Parliamentary Debates,* House of Commons, October 21, 1918, col. 417.

11. *The Letters of Franklin K. Lane* (Boston, 1922), pp. 293–296; David F. Houston, *Eight Years in Wilson's Cabinet* (two vols., Garden City, 1926), I, 308–317.

The meeting was a most solemn occasion. The President seemed to be more nervous than usual. Discussion of the subject of his reply to Germany was broached as soon as we had assembled. The President stated that he desired an expression of opinion from each one present . . . Each man, with one exception, indicated his belief that the proposal for an armistice, in the form in which it had come from the German people, should be accepted by the United States. The dissenting voice came from a member . . . least expected . . . to suggest that we demand an unconditional surrender.

The President sat calm, and listened attentively to each member as he gave his opinion. The discussion that followed was general. Finally the President quietly drew from an inside pocket of his coat a typewritten memorandum. "Gentlemen," he said, "I have here the tentative draft of the note that I think I should send to Germany. I should like to read it, and since it is the consensus of your opinion that we should accept the proposal for an armistice, I shall be happy to receive your suggestions regarding any changes that you think should be made in the document." His utterances were slow and deliberate. He paused momentarily at the conclusion of each sentence, to enable his auditors to absorb its full significance. Not a man present failed to realize that in that note Woodrow Wilson had written a declaration that would end the great World War.

When he had concluded, the President laid the typewritten sheet upon the table before him and asked for suggestions for its improvement. I was enthusiastic over the character of the note, and so expressed myself. Others were equally warm in their endorsement. One member, however, suggested that while as a whole he would approve the contents of the note, at the same time he believed that it would be more helpful from a political standpoint if a certain change were made in one expression. The President shook his head in a most impressive manner. "No," he said decisively, "I am dealing in human lives—not in politics."

No one was able to offer a suggestion that we believed would improve the message. Not a word of it was changed from the form in which the President had drafted it. . . .[12]

Wilson's third note to Germany read as follows:

Having received the solemn and explicit assurance of the German Government that it unreservedly accepts the terms of peace laid

12. E. N. Hurley, *The Bridge to France* (Philadelphia, 1927), pp. 322–324. Hurley's letter to Wilson is found *ibid.,* 333–334.

down in his address to the Congress of the United States on the 8th of January, 1918, and the principles of settlement enunciated in his subsequent addresses, particularly the address of the 27th of September, and that it desires to discuss the details of their application, and that this wish and purpose emanate, not from those who have hitherto dictated German policy and conducted the present war on Germany's behalf, but from Ministers who speak for the majority of the Reichstag and for an overwhelming majority of the German people; and having received also the explicit promise of the present German Government that the humane rules of civilized warfare will be observed both on land and sea by the German armed forces, the President of the United States feels that he cannot decline to take up with the Governments with which the Government of the United States is associated the question of an armistice.

He deems it his duty to say again, however, that the only armistice he would feel justified in submitting for consideration would be one which should leave the United States and the powers associated with her in a position to enforce any arrangements that may be entered into and to make a renewal of hostilities on the part of Germany impossible. The President has, therefore, transmitted his correspondence with the present German authorities to the Governments with which the Government of the United States is associated as a belligerent, with the suggestion that, if those Governments are disposed to effect peace upon the terms and principles indicated, their military advisers and the military advisers of the United States be asked to submit to the Governments associated against Germany the necessary terms of such an armistice as will fully protect the interests of the peoples involved and ensure to the Associated Governments the unrestricted power to safeguard and enforce the details of the peace to which the German Government has agreed, provided they deem such an armistice possible from the military point of view. Should such terms of armistice be suggested, their acceptance by Germany will afford the best concrete evidence of her unequivocal acceptance of the terms and principles of peace from which the whole action proceeds.

The President would deem himself lacking in candour did he not point out in the frankest possible terms the reason why extraordinary safeguards must be demanded. Significant and important as the constitutional changes seem to be which are spoken of by the German Foreign Secretary in his note of the 20th of October, it does not appear that the principle of a Government responsible to the German people has yet been fully worked out or that any guarantees either exist or are in contemplation that the alterations of principle and of practice now partially agreed upon will be permanent. Moreover, it does not appear that the heart of the present difficulty has been reached. It may be that future wars have been brought under the control of the German people, but the present war has not been; and it is with the present war that we are dealing. It is evident that the German people have no means of commanding the acquiescence of the military authorities of the Empire in the popular will; that the power of the King of Prussia to control the policy of the Empire is unimpaired; that the determinating initiative still remains with those who have hitherto been the masters of Germany. Feeling that the whole peace of the world depends now on plain speaking and straightforward action, the President deems it his duty to say, without any attempt to soften what may seem harsh words, that the nations of the world do not and cannot trust the word of those who have hitherto been the masters of German policy, and to point out once more that in concluding peace and attempting to undo the infinite injuries and injustices of this war the Government of the United States cannot deal with any but veritable representatives of the German people who have been assured of a genuine constitutional standing as the real rulers of Germany. If it must deal with the military masters and the monarchical autocrats of Germany now, or if it is likely to have to deal with them later in regard to the international obligations of the German Empire, it must demand, not peace negotiations, but surrender. Nothing can be gained by leaving this essential thing unsaid.

ROBERT LANSING [13]

This message was sent on October 23. American critics of Wilson's foreign policy did not find it to their liking. "There is no German Government in existence," said Senator Lodge, "with which I would discuss anything. I deplore at this stage, when we are advancing steadily to a complete victory, any discussion or exchange of notes with the German Government. The only thing now is to demand unconditional surrender." [14] Former President Roosevelt was enraged by the note. In identical telegrams to Senators Lodge, Poindexter, and Johnson he "most earnestly" expressed the hope "that the Senate of the United States, which

13. Lansing to Oederlin, October 23, 1918, *Foreign Relations, 1918,* Supplement I, I, 381–383. The German translation is found in *Amtliche Urkunden,* document 76.

14. According to *New York Times,* October 24, 1918.

is part of the treaty-making power of the United States, will take affirmative action against a negotiated peace with Germany and in favor of a peace based on unconditional surrender of Germany . . . [and] that on behalf of the American people it will declare against the adoption in their entirety of the fourteen points of the President's address of last January as offering a basis for a peace satisfactory to the United States. Let us dictate peace by the hammering guns and not chat about peace to the accompaniment of the clicking of typewriters." As to the Fourteen Points, their language was neither straightforward nor plain, and most of them were thoroughly mischievous. To make them the basis of peace would signify the conditional surrender of the United States, not the unconditional surrender of Germany. They satisfied nobody but the Germans, and "every pro-German and pacifist and Socialist and anti-American so-called internationalist." He wanted war declared on Turkey immediately, saying that "the failure to do so hitherto has caused the talk about making the world safe for democracy to look unpleasantly like mere insincere rhetoric. While the Turk is left in Europe and permitted to tyrannize over the subject people the world is thoroughly unsafe for democracy." Roosevelt objected strenuously to the term "associate" instead of "ally." "We ought to make it clear to the world that we are neither an untrustworthy friend nor an irresolute foe. Let us clearly show that we do not desire to pose as the umpire between our faithful and loyal friends and our treacherous and brutal enemies, but that we are the stanch ally of our allies and the stanch foe of our enemies. . . . I hope," the telegram concluded, "the Senate and the House will pass some resolution demanding the unconditional surrender of Germany as our war aim, and stating that our peace terms have never yet been formulated or accepted by our people, and that they will be fully discussed with our allies and made fully satisfactory to our own people before they are discussed with Germany." [15]

It had been clear to Wilson for some time that the Republican opposition under Roosevelt's inspiration was planning to hamper his negotiations with Germany and his work for the kind of peace he had sketched in his speeches. With Congressional elections coming on November 5 action of some sort became necessary. On October 18 and 19 the President consulted with party leaders

15. The telegram is given in the *New York Times*, October 25, 1918.

about issuing an appeal to the American electorate for a Democratic Congress.[16] The appeal, addressed to his "fellow countrymen," was made public through the press on October 24. "If you have approved of my leadership and wish me to continue to be your unembarrassed spokesman in affairs at home and abroad," it read, "I earnestly beg that you will express yourselves unmistakably to that effect by returning a Democratic majority to both the Senate and the House of Representatives. . . . The return of a Republican majority to either house of Congress would . . . be interpreted on the other side of the water as a repudiation of my leadership." [17]

The challenge was accepted. "I am glad," wrote Roosevelt to Senator Lodge, "[that] Wilson has come out in the open; I fear Judas most when he can cloak his activities behind a treacherous make-believe of non-partisanship. I shall deal with him in my speech next Monday evening." [18] Republicans in Congress conferred and then issued a statement stressing the fact that "this is not the President's personal war" and assuring the nation that if Republicans were elected in November it would become clear that America intends to fight on to victory. The Republicans wanted Foch to arrange the question of surrender.[19]

The same day that the note was sent to Germany Secretary of State Lansing communicated to the Washington representatives of nineteen powers, including Great Britain, France, and Italy, the correspondence President Wilson had had with the German Government. The states associated with the United States, he told them, were not being forced into any premature armistice by the President; he hoped they would "acquiesce and take part in the course of action with regard to an armistice" as suggested in the note to Germany and "with regard to the manner in which the terms of an armistice are to be determined provided an armistice at this time is deemed possible from the military point of view." It was pointed out "that the President has endeavored to safeguard with the utmost care the interests of the peoples at war with Germany in every statement made in the enclosed correspondence; and that it is his sincere hope that your Government

16. Baker, *Wilson,* VIII, 487, 491.

17. *New York Times,* October 26, 1918.

18. Roosevelt to Lodge, October 25, 1918, *Selections from the Correspondence of Roosevelt and Lodge,* II, 542.

19. *New York Times,* October 26. The editorial for the same day stated that Wilson's appeal was justified by Roosevelt's telegram.

will think that he has succeeded, and will be willing to cooperate in the steps which he has suggested."[20]

This note opened the door for the entrance of the Allies into the armistice negotiations. To have delayed longer without consulting them would have been exceedingly risky. Their impatience was growing; and also their demands, according to General Bliss, the American Military Representative. "The views expressed by the military men as to conditions of so called armistice," he telegraphed to Secretary of War Baker on October 23, "are quite as much political as they are military and probably foreshadow peace demands that will be insisted on by the military parties of the Allies. These demands show a tendency to increase with every day's success in the present military operations." Bliss wanted to eliminate these political demands; he believed that the military men should have nothing to say beyond getting guarantees against any possible resumption of hostilities by Germany. If Germany surrendered by laying down her arms, they would have their guarantees, and their task would be done. Then the work of making peace could proceed.[21]

Later the same day General Bliss sent a letter by courier to Secretary Baker. "I wish to God," he wrote, "that the President himself could be here for a week. I hear in all quarters a longing for this. The people who want to get a rational solution out of this awful mess look to him alone. . . . In this dark storm of angry passion that has been let loose in all quarters I doubt if any one but he can let in the light of reason." He found the English "by far the most reasonable" and thought that the United States could reach an agreement with them "as to what is right and just for the present and which will tend to the future peace of the world." He said that the military group was now in control and would do things, if given the opportunity, that would shock the world's sense of justice. Bliss did not believe that "the question of conditions of so-called armistice should be left to the military men *alone*. The trouble is that it is not an armistice. It is an absolute surrender that we must have. But in order to get that surrender the conditions which are to follow it should be determined in advance and made known." He wanted "rational disarmament" to make it unnecessary to take away "this or that . . . of the defeated nation merely for the purpose of making it militarily

20. Lansing to Macchi di Cellere, October 23, 1918, *Foreign Relations, 1918,* Supplement I, I, 383.

21. Baker, *Wilson,* VIII, 508.

weak." He wanted the United States "to immediately take the lead . . . to act swiftly and determinedly." To illustrate how far the military men would go he enclosed a document from the French Military Representative who wanted an Inter-Allied aerial bombing force "to carry the war into Germany by attacking its industry, its commerce and its *population*." [22]

As soon as he had received Wilson's correspondence with Germany and his request to consider an armistice, Clemenceau called Foch and Pétain to the Ministry of War on October 24 and informed them that they must draw up detailed terms for an armistice at once so that the Allies would be in agreement whenever the German request for terms might be received. Foch reports that the three of them agreed orally on the conditions they wanted and the guarantees needed. "The blockade was to be maintained and the duration of the armistice was to be limited."

To get the opinions of the Commanders-in-Chief of the American, British, and French Armies Foch held a conference at Senlis the next afternoon.[23] Pétain, Field Marshal Haig, General Pershing, and Vice-Admiral de Bon, Chief of Staff of the French Navy, were present. General Gillain, Belgian Chief of Staff, could not arrive in time, but on the 26th he approved the text of Foch's recommendations.

According to Marshal Foch's account of the proceedings[24] Sir Douglas Haig spoke first. Believing that the Germans could "still offer serious resistance" and that the British Army was short of troops, the French Army exhausted, and the American Army "incompletely organized," he thought the conditions offered to Germany should be such that they could be accepted. And he proposed those he had already offered in London.[25] In case hostilities were renewed, the Allies could carry on the war in German territory and the American Army in the meantime would have been built up.[26]

22. Palmer, *Bliss, Peacemaker,* pp. 343–345.

23. Foch, *Mémoires,* II, 280; Mordacq, *Le Ministère Clemenceau,* II, 292–293.

24. Foch, *Mémoires,* II, 281.

25. *Supra,* p. 168.

26. Pershing, *My Experiences in the World War* (two vols., New York, 1931), II, 360–361. See also T. Bentley Mott, *Twenty Years as Military Attaché* (New York, 1937), pp. 277–278; Duff Cooper, *Haig,* II, 400. Field Marshal Haig learned a few days later that his remarks, given in French, had been "misinterpreted" so as to give the impression that the American Army had failed in France. He wrote a note to Pershing to explain that "such an idea never entered my head." *Ibid.,* pp. 401–402.

Pétain's suggestions were guided by the principle "that it must be made impossible for the Germans to renew hostilities." To weaken them by depriving them of their material, particularly of heavy guns and ammunition, he urged speedy withdrawal from occupied territory and from Alsace-Lorraine and provided a time schedule for that evacuation. Then the Allies should occupy the left bank of the Rhine and bridgeheads on the right bank. He also proposed that the Germans surrender 5,000 locomotives and 100,000 cars in perfect condition. Although he knew that the Germans might not accept these conditions, he said they were necessary.[27]

Pershing would have preferred a demand for the surrender of the German Armies; but he "accepted this as a conference to decide upon the terms in case an armistice should be granted." He believed that the military situation was favorable for the Allies and that the armistice conditions, in case an armistice were to be granted, should make it hard for Germany if hostilities were resumed. He therefore proposed the following:

1st. The evacuation of France and Belgium within thirty days and of all other foreign territory occupied by Germany without delay.

2d. The withdrawal of the German armies from Alsace-Lorraine and occupation of those territories by the Allied armies.

3d. Withdrawal of German armies to the east of the Rhine and the possession of such bridgeheads on the eastern side of the Rhine by the Allies as may be necessary to insure their control of that river.

4th. The unrestricted transportation of the American Army and its material across the seas.

5th. The immediate repatriation of all nationals of foreign territory now or heretofore occupied during the war by Germany.

6th. Surrender of all U-boats and U-boat bases to the control of a neutral power until their disposition is otherwise determined.

7th. Return to France and Belgium of all railroad rolling stock that has been seized by Germany from those countries.[28]

Pershing's reference to the surrender of German submarines caused Haig to interrupt, "That is none of our affair. It is a matter for the Admiralty to decide." Pershing replied that the question of submarines was a vital matter for American troops operat-

27. Foch, *Mémoires,* II, 281–282; Seymour, *House Papers,* IV, 112.
28. Pershing, *My Experiences,* II, 360, 362.

ing 3,000 miles across a sea where submarines "constituted a formidable menace to our sea communications." He was willing, however, to have naval authorities determine the number of German submarines to be surrendered. His views had the support of Foch.[29]

Marshal Foch did not give his own opinions of the armistice terms in this conference. Taking the suggestions of the Commanders-in-Chief into consideration, he drafted the following report:

After having consulted the Commanders-in-Chief of the American, British, and French Armies, I have the honor to inform you of the military conditions on which an armistice could be granted capable "of protecting, in a complete manner, the interests of the people concerned, and of assuring to the associated governments the unlimited power of safeguarding and of imposing the details of peace to which the German Government has consented."

I. Immediate evacuation of the countries invaded contrary to right: Belgium, France, Alsace-Lorraine, Luxemburg.

Immediate repatriation of their inhabitants.

The abandonment of a part of the enemy material in the evacuated region.

This evacuation must be made under conditions of time to make it impossible to the enemy to remove a large part of the material of war and supplies of every nature that are stored there, that is to say, in accordance with the following time-table:

At the end of 4 days the German troops must be withdrawn behind the line marked I. on the map attached:

At the end of 4 more days behind the line marked II.

At the end of 6 more days behind the line marked III.

Belgium, Luxemburg, Alsace-Lorraine will, in this way be liberated in a total period of 14 days.

This period will count from the day of the signing of the Armistice.

In all cases the total material abandoned by the enemy must amount to:

5,000 guns—½ heavy, ½ field:
30,000 machine guns:
3,000 minenwerfer[30]

29. *Ibid.*, pp. 362–363.

30. According to notes by Foch this meant one-third of Germany's artillery and one-half of the machine guns.

To be handed over *in situ*, under detailed conditions to be laid down.

The Allied troops will follow up through these countries the evacuation which will be effected in accordance with detailed regulations to be issued subsequently.

II. Evacuation, by the hostile army, of the country on the left bank of the Rhine.

The country on the left bank of the Rhine will be administered by the local authorities under the control of the Allied troops of occupation.

The Allied troops will assure the occupation of those countries by the garrisons holding the principal crossings of the Rhine (Mainz, Coblenz, Cologne, Strassburg), with bridgeheads at these points of 30 kilometre radius on the right bank—holding also the strategic points of the region.

A neutral zone will be reserved on the right bank of the Rhine between the river and a line traced parallel to the river and 40 kilometres to the east of the Swiss frontier and the Dutch frontier.

The evacuation by the enemy of the Rhine country will be carried out under the following time-limits:

To the Rhine, 8 days after the time-limit indicated above (22 days in all to date from the signing of the Armistice):

To behind the neutral zone: 3 more days (25 days in all to date from the signing of the Armistice).

III. In all the territories evacuated by the enemy no destruction of any kind will be committed, nor will any damage or injury be done to the persons or property of the inhabitants.

IV. The enemy will have to surrender under conditions to be laid down, 5,000 [31] locomotives and 150,000 wagons in good condition.

V. The German Command will be required to indicate the position of land mines and slow fuses left in the evacuated territory, and to facilitate their location and their destruction under penalty of reprisals.

VI. The carrying out by the enemy of these conditions will take altogether a period of 25 days. In order to guarantee the carrying out of these conditions the blockade will be completely maintained during the whole of this period. It will only be after this period is completed, and when the conditions are fulfilled, that the supply of

31. Of these quantities, 2,500 locomotives and 135,000 railroad cars represent the material removed from Belgium and France, the surplus is necessary for the train service in the country on the left bank of the Rhine. (Note of Marshal Foch.)

the enemy can be authorised in accordance with the special agreements which will regulate it.

VII. Allied prisoners will be given up in the shortest possible period under conditions, the details of which will be laid down later.

From the naval point of view the following conditions appear necessary and sufficient as bases:

> The enemy will surrender, under conditions to be laid down, 150 submarines, representing about the number which are at present in a condition to go to sea.
>
> All the German surface fleet will withdraw to the ports of the Baltic—the port of Cuxhaven and the Island of Heligoland will be occupied by the Allied Fleets.
>
> The enemy will indicate the positions of all his mine-fields and obstructions of every kind, with the exception of those moored in his territorial waters. The Allies will have the right of mine-sweeping wherever they consider necessary.

FOCH [32]

"I took these [conditions] myself to Paris on the afternoon of October 26th," writes Marshal Foch, "and I handed the text thus worked out to both the President of the Republic and the Prime Minister. During my conversation with Monsieur Poincaré, when he remarked that these conditions might be judged inacceptable and be rejected by the Germans, I replied: 'Then we will continue the war; for at the point the Allied Armies have now reached, their victorious march cannot be halted until they have made all resistance by Germany impossible and have got tangible guarantees of a peace obtained at the cost of great sacrifices.' " [33]

This same day Colonel House arrived in Paris, having been met the day before at Brest by General Bliss, who informed him as to what was going on. He came as President Wilson's "personal representative . . . to take part as such in the conferences of the Supreme War Council and in any other conferences in which it may be serviceable for him to represent" the President. Wilson had appointed him "a Special Representative of the Government of the United States of America in Europe in matters relating to the war," authorized and empowered "to execute and fulfill the duties of this commission with all the powers and privileges there-

32. Seymour, *House Papers,* IV, 143–145.
33. Foch, *Mémoires,* II, 283–284.

unto of right appertaining during the pleasure of the President of the United States. . . ."[34]

In Paris House took up his residence at 78 rue de l'Université, conveniently near the Foreign Office and the Ministry of War. On the day of his arrival he had lunch with important British officials, including Milner and Haig, "a delightful and important meeting." He found both Englishmen moderate in their views and "exceedingly reasonable"; he "did a great deal of talking" to bring them around to Wilson's views in order to have their support on Tuesday. At 6 P.M. he saw Clemenceau, who gave him a copy of the proposed armistice terms which Foch had just delivered. No one, the Premier told House, had seen the document except himself, not even the President of the French Republic. On Sunday, October 27, House sent a copy of the memorandum to Wilson.[35]

House noted the differences in views of the French and English officials he had seen. Whereas Haig "does not consider the German military situation warrants their complete surrender," Clemenceau expressed his own belief and that of Foch "that Germany was so thoroughly beaten she would accept any terms offered." Despite differences of opinion as to how severely Germany should be treated, House found the Allied leaders in general agreement that the request for an armistice should not be declined. He was soon to discover that the one exception was General Pershing, who on October 30 protested against an armistice.

On the 27th House continued his discussion of armistice terms with Allied leaders. He also had a long talk with General Bliss, who thought it would be better to ask for general disarmament without specifying terms.

On October 28, in compliance with a request from the Council of Ministers, General Bliss, the American Military Representative on the Council, submitted a memorandum of his views on armistice terms. He did not approve the Foch memorandum, which Colonel House had shown him; his objections were that the Marshal's terms actually forced Germany to take up a stronger position within her own borders, to concentrate her forces on a shorter and more strategic front with the organization of her Army, particularly her infantry, left intact. She would thus be in a position to re-arm and start fighting again; the essential

34. Seymour, *House Papers,* IV, 87.

35. *Ibid.,* pp. 92–93; Baker, *Wilson,* VIII, 520. According to Foch, the President of France knew of the memorandum.

thing was to make her incapable of resuming the war while peace was under discussion. It was a surprising argument in view of Foch's specific demand for extensive evacuation and partial disarmament.

Bliss's proposals were:

> First, that the associated powers demand complete military disarmament and demobilization of the active land and naval forces of the enemy, leaving only such interior guards as the associated powers agree upon as necessary for the preservation of order in the home territory of the enemy. This, of course, means the evacuation of all invaded territory, and its evacuation by disarmed and not by armed or partly armed men. The army thus disarmed cannot fight, and demobilized cannot be reassembled for the purposes of this war.
>
> Second, that the associated powers notify the enemy that there will be no relaxation of their war-aims but that these will be subject to full and reasonable discussion between the nations associated in the war; and that even though the enemy himself may be heard on some of these matters he must submit to whatever the associated powers finally agree upon as being proper to demand for the present and for the future peace of the world.[36]

Political leaders did not take Bliss's protest seriously, believing that Foch had made the Allies secure against any resumption of war on Germany's part.

On October 30 there was a second and stronger protest against the proposed armistice, from General Pershing. His proposals in the Senlis conference of October 25th with Foch and with other Allied Commanders-in-Chief had been made "in case an armistice should be granted." His conviction was that there should be no armistice and he wished to have that issue decided first. "Inasmuch as no intimation had been sent to me regarding the President's attitude toward granting an armistice to the German armies," he writes, "and feeling that I could not sit by without expressing my opinion, I prepared a letter to send to the Supreme War Council, giving my views for consideration in case a decision had not been finally reached." [37] General Pershing may have been

36. *Ibid.,* pp. 114–115, 146–147.

37. Pershing, *My Experiences,* II, 364; Mott, *Twenty Years,* p. 266. He telegraphed similar views to Secretary Baker on October 30. Baker, *Wilson,* VIII, 532.

encouraged to a step of this sort by President Wilson's invitation to "feel entirely free to bring to his attention any consideration he may have overlooked which in your judgment ought to be weighed before settling finally. . . ." Wilson asked for such advice at the same time that he said he did not approve all of Pershing's Senlis proposals; the President thought, however, that "the terms of the armistice should be rigid enough to secure us against renewal of hostilities by Germany but not humiliating beyond that necessity, as such terms would throw the advantage to the military party in Germany." The General was urged to discuss "all phases of this subject" with House.[38]

In a private code telegram of October 28 to House the President gave another argument for the kind of armistice he desired. While seeking to make any resumption of the war impossible for Germany, he favored an armistice "which will be as moderate and reasonable as possible within those limits, because it is certain that too much success or security on the part of the Allies will make a genuine peace settlement exceedingly difficult, if not impossible."[39]

After getting Mr. Wilson's request of the 29th for advice, Pershing gave Colonel House, for presentation to the Supreme War Council, the letter he had prepared:

Paris, October 30, 1918.

To the Allied Supreme War Council,
Paris.

GENTLEMEN:

In considering the question of whether or not Germany's request for an armistice should be granted, the following expresses my opinion from the military point of view:

1. Judging by their excellent conduct during the past three months, the British, French, Belgian and American Armies appear capable of continuing the offensive indefinitely. Their morale is high and the prospects of certain victory should keep it so.

2. The American Army is constantly increasing in strength and experience, and should be able to take an increasingly important part in the Allied offensive. Its growth both in personnel and matériel, with such reserves as the Allies may furnish, not counting the

38. Pershing, *My Experiences,* II, 364–365.
39. Baker, *Wilson,* VIII, 523.

Italian Army, should be more than equal to the combined losses of the Allied Armies.

3. German manpower is constantly diminishing and her armies have lost over 300,000 prisoners and over one-third of their artillery during the past three months in their effort to extricate themselves from a difficult situation and avoid disaster.

4. The estimated strength of the Allies on the Western Front, not counting Italy, and of Germany, in rifles is:

Allies 1,563,000
Germany 1,134,000

An advantage in favor of the Allies of 37 per cent. In guns:

Allies 22,413
Germany 16,495

An advantage of 35 per cent in favor of the Allies.

If Italy's forces should be added to the Western Front we should have a still greater advantage.

5. Germany's morale is undoubtedly low, her Allies have deserted her one by one and she can no longer hope to win. Therefore we should take full advantage of the situation and continue the offensive until we compel her unconditional surrender.

6. An armistice would revivify the low spirits of the German Army and enable it to reorganize and resist later on, and would deprive the Allies of the full measure of victory by failing to press their present advantage to its complete military end.

7. As the apparent humility of German leaders in talking peace may be feigned, the Allies should distrust their sincerity and their motives. The appeal for an armistice is undoubtedly to enable the withdrawal from a critical situation to one more advantageous.

8. On the other hand, the internal political conditions of Germany, if correctly reported, are such that she is practically forced to ask for an armistice to save the overthrow of her present Government, a consummation which should be sought by the Allies as precedent to permanent peace.

9. A cessation of hostilities short of capitulation postpones, if it does not render impossible, the imposition of satisfactory peace terms, because it would allow Germany to withdraw her army with its present strength, ready to resume hostilities if terms were not satisfactory to her.

10. An armistice would lead the Allied armies to believe this the

end of fighting and it would be difficult, if not impossible, to resume hostilities with our present advantage in morale in the event of failure to secure at a peace conference what we have fought for.

11. By agreeing to an armistice under the present favorable military situation of the Allies and accepting the principle of a negotiated peace rather than a dictated peace the Allies would jeopardize the moral position they now hold and possibly lose the chance actually to secure world peace on terms that would insure its permanence.

12. It is the experience of history that victorious armies are prone to overestimate the enemy's strength and too eagerly seek an opportunity for peace. This mistake is likely to be made now on account of the reputation Germany has gained through her victories of the last four years.

13. Finally, I believe the complete victory can only be obtained by continuing the war until we force unconditional surrender from Germany, but if the Allied Governments decide to grant an armistice, the terms should be so rigid that under no circumstances could Germany again take up arms.

Respectfully submitted:
JOHN J. PERSHING
Commander-in-Chief, A.E.F.[40]

On October 30 Pershing summoned Colonel Mott to Paris from his dinner at Foch's Headquarters, where he served as American liaison officer, and gave him a copy of the letter for Foch, with instructions to give it to the Marshal "as quickly as you can; tonight, if possible." It was not until eight the next morning that Foch could receive Mott. He read the letter and instructed Mott to "tell General Pershing that I am in agreement with his views, and he need not be anxious regarding this matter; what I am demanding of the Germans is the equivalent of what he wants and when I have finished with them they will be quite powerless to do any further damage." Mott "urged the importance which General Pershing attached to demanding unconditional surrender." But there was no time for discussion as Foch's car was waiting to take him to a meeting of the Supreme War Council.[41]

Colonel House received his copy of Pershing's memorandum just before he went to the afternoon meeting of the Council. He telegraphed the text immediately to the President and gave the

40. Pershing, *My Experiences,* II, 366–367. Also in *Lansing Papers,* II, 170–171.
41. Mott, *Twenty Years,* pp. 261, 266–267.

reactions of various people to it. ". . . when [Lloyd] George read this his comment was 'Political not military. Someone put him up to it.' When Clemenceau read it his comment was 'Theatrical and not in accordance with what he has said to Marshal Foch.' "[42] In the evening House informed Pershing "that the question as to whether an armistice should be granted was purely political and that all the Prime Ministers were in favor of it."[43]

The objections of General Bliss and of General Pershing resulted in no modification of the terms proposed by Foch. The conditions considered by the Prime Ministers and finally approved were the French terms.

"Technically," according to Colonel House, "the Allied Council which assumed responsibility for the armistice was still the Supreme War Council, enlarged on the political side by the representatives of Japan and the smaller Powers that were called in to its sessions. It met in the large room on the main floor of the Trianon Palace Hotel in Versailles, with its windows overlooking the garden. Down the length of the room extended a wide mahogany table, across which the delegates conversed; in the center sat Clemenceau and directly opposite him, Colonel House, next to the Italian Prime Minister, Orlando. Color was added by the uniforms of the generals and admirals, but the prevailing tone was somber and business-like, just as the predominant note of the discussions was that of a board of directors in a joint-stock company." [44]

The Allied Council, whose first formal session was held on October 31, "did not, as a matter of fact, draft the terms of the armistices. When it met, drafts were already prepared. 'Its sole function,' writes General Bliss, 'was to trim the edges and round off the corners, in doing which there was an opportunity to consider points raised by the smaller Powers that had not been represented in the preparation of the drafts.' The actual decisions were taken not in the formal meetings at Versailles but in the more informal conversations between the Prime Ministers and House, beginning on October 29. The formation of this steering committee resulted almost inevitably from the circumstances of the moment, which demanded speed and an absence of red-tape. . . . The meetings of the Prime Ministers and House, which

42. Baker, *Wilson,* VIII, 532–533.

43. Pershing, *My Experiences,* II, 368. Colonel House discusses the episode in Seymour, *House Papers,* IV, 95–96.

44. Seymour, *House Papers,* IV, 97–98.

generally included also Balfour, Pichon and Sonnino, the Foreign Secretaries, and almost invariably Sir Maurice Hankey, Secretary of the British War Cabinet, were sometimes held in Pichon's study in the Quai d'Orsay. . . . Sometimes . . . in Clemenceau's room at the War Office; more frequently in the salon of Colonel House's headquarters. . . . By gathering in a private house the political leaders were able to emphasize the informal character of the conversations, and to invite or exclude whom they chose, without hurting the feelings of any. . . . The meetings of this steering committee were generally held in the morning, and in these were discussed the topics to be formally approved by the Supreme War Council in the afternoon. Almost invariably the decisions reached by the small committee proved to be final."[45]

Although Orlando had not yet arrived, the Prime Ministers, their Foreign Secretaries, and House set to work on October 29. The first question which they took up was the relations between the great and small Powers and what part the latter should have in the deliberations. After an exchange of views Lloyd George's proposal was adopted; namely, that preliminary conferences should take place between the four Great Powers, France, Great Britain, Italy, and the United States, and that there should be no meeting of the Supreme War Council at Versailles until general agreement had been reached. Belgium and Japan were to be permitted to send representatives to Versailles and the minor nations could also be represented when questions affecting them were being discussed and if they demanded it.[46]

The next question that arose was the manner in which the various requests for armistices from Germany, Austria-Hungary, and Turkey should be dealt with. Clemenceau pointed out that the only communication before the Allies was that from President Wilson. Many people, he stated, were of the opinion that the entire matter should be left to Foch; but, he added, the Marshal was concerned only with purely military matters and, if he made the decisions, the Governments would be superseded. He proposed that the committee should consult anyone whose advice they desired and that they should send their conclusions to Wilson.

The British, however, were not impressed with the method of negotiating through the American President; they favored direct negotiation with Germany. Lloyd George asserted that the Ger-

45. *Ibid.*, pp. 97–99.
46. *Ibid.*, pp. 100–101.

mans would have to accept or refuse outright, and that, if the terms were published and the Allies did not insist on their integral acceptance, public opinion would be aroused to such an extent that the negotiations might fail.

House suggested the course which prevailed in the end; namely, that the terms should be communicated to Wilson for his approval, and that he should notify Germany that her request would be granted and that the terms of an armistice would be communicated directly to her by the Allies. Lloyd George liked this proposal. Clemenceau, however, disapproved of the suggestion that the Germans be invited to an armistice, saying: "There is one objection to his proposition: it is impossible. If we follow it out, it will be necessary for Marshal Foch to send a parliamentary to go to the German lines with a white flag to ask for an armistice. Marshal Foch would never do this and I would never permit him to do it."[47]

Lloyd George then suggested that the Allies should merely request President Wilson to ask the Germans to send a parliamentary to the French Marshal. This proposal was approved and accepted.

In the meantime Sonnino, in the absence of his Prime Minister, had become anxious lest Germany accept while Austria refused an armistice, in which event he saw Italy left to fight out the war alone with Austria. There was apparently some justification for this fear of the Italian Foreign Minister. On October 23, as a result of outside pressure, the Italians had started an offensive against the Austrians contrary to the military judgment of the Commander-in-Chief, General Diaz. The American Ambassador in Italy reported that the consequences might be serious in Rome if the campaign did not succeed and hoped that troops would be sent to quell the disturbances that were sure to develop if it failed.[48] House endeavored to assure Sonnino by reminding him that two days earlier Austria had agreed to accept any conditions that Wilson might impose.[49] This submissive attitude did not in-

47. *Ibid.*, pp. 102–103.

48. Page to Lansing, October 23, 1918, *Foreign Relations, 1918,* Supplement I, I, 386.

49. Seymour, *House Papers,* IV, 103. In fact it was on this very day, October 29, when President Wilson learned officially through the Swedish Minister in Washington that the Austro-Hungarian Government had "accepted all the conditions which the President had put upon entering into negotiations on the subject of armistice and peace" (including Wilson's virtual recognition of the Czecho-Slovaks and Jugo-Slavs in his note of October 19) and "declares itself ready to enter, without waiting for the outcome of other negotiations, into nego-

dicate that Austria-Hungary was an enemy greatly to be feared.

But Sonnino was still afraid that if Germany accepted first, Italy would find German soldiers in Austrian uniforms upon her front and that Austrian troops in Germany would be released to return to the Italian line. The Prime Ministers finally reassured him by promising that President Wilson would instruct Austria-Hungary to send a parliamentary to General Diaz at the same time that Germany sent one to Foch. The conference then adopted the following resolution:

"That the associated Governments should consider the terms of an armistice with Germany and the terms of an armistice with Austria. They should then forward these to President Wilson. If President Wilson agreed in the terms he should not notify them to the German or Austrian Governments, but should advise these Governments that their next step was to send parlementaires to Marshal Foch and General Diaz respectively." [50]

As it turned out, this procedure was not followed. On October 30, the day after this resolution was passed, Orlando arrived from Italy with the news that, while he was passing through Turin, General Diaz had telephoned him that an enemy officer had crossed the line with a letter from a general, not the Austrian Commander-in-Chief, asking for an immediate armistice. Fearing a trick on the part of the Austrians, the Italians had insisted upon having proper credentials before treating.[51] Lloyd George and Clemenceau told Orlando that Italy should have treated—it would be an advantage to prepare terms and to settle matters with Austria before entering upon negotiations with Germany. "I propose," said Lloyd George, "that these terms be submitted straightaway to Austria. As soon as Austria is out, Germany will capitulate at once. Therefore we ought to act before President Wilson has time to answer." [52]

Colonel House approved the suggestion. He was primarily interested in getting the Allies to accept the Fourteen Points before

tiations for a peace between Austria-Hungary and the Entente States and for an immediate armistice on all Austro-Hungarian fronts and begs President Wilson to take the necessary measures to that effect." Ekengren to Lansing, October 29, 1918, *Foreign Relations, 1918,* Supplement I, I, 404–405.

50. Seymour, *House Papers,* IV, 104.

51. For some of the details on this matter see telegram of Ambassador Page to Lansing, October 30, 1918, *Foreign Relations, 1918,* Supplement I, I, 441.

52. Seymour, *House Papers,* IV, 105.

signing an armistice but thought that they could be more appropriately considered in connection with the German armistice than with the Austrian. While military advisers drafted the military terms for Austria, the conference considered the naval terms, which called for the surrender of all submarines constructed since 1910, 6 battleships, 4 cruisers, and 9 destroyers.[53]

"We have left the breeches of the Emperor and nothing else," was Clemenceau's comment.

The terms were completed and presented at the first meeting of the Supreme War Council the following afternoon, when they were adopted and telegraphed to General Diaz. House communicated the decisions of the Supreme War Council to Wilson as he was instructed by resolution to do. "Fortunately," he wrote in his report to the President, "I was able [to prevent] discussion of political questions. I regard this feature as most favorable." [54] Because Colonel House "thought it best not to bring on a discussion of this matter at this time," the Austrian armistice was agreed to without any reference to the Fourteen Points, although Austria had sought to end the war on that basis. The question whether Wilson's program was to apply to the Austrian peace settlement was not answered now and was to remain unanswered and troublesome during the peace conference.

If Wilson had desired to make his Fourteen Points an essential part of the understanding with Austria, he acted far too slowly. When Secretary Lansing informed the Swedish Minister, Ekengren, in the early evening of October 31 that the Austrian request for peace and for an immediate armistice would be submitted to the Allied Governments,[55] these Governments had already acted. The terms for Austria had been drafted and arrived early next morning in Washington.[56] Austria was given until midnight of Sunday, November 3, to accept them; and it was agreed that terms for Germany would not be finally determined until Austria had accepted them.[57]

President Wilson had nothing to do with the armistice terms for Turkey, although the latter's request had been submitted to him by the Spanish Ambassador on October 14. On the 23d Wash-

53. *Ibid.*, pp. 105–106.

54. House to Lansing, October 31, 1918, *Foreign Relations, 1918,* Supplement I, I, 430-431.

55. Memorandum of Secretary Lansing, October 31, 1918, *ibid.*, pp. 429–430.

56. House to Lansing, November 1, 1918, *ibid.*, pp. 433–435. The Austrian terms are given in Appendix C.

57. House to Lansing, November 3, 1918, *ibid.*, p. 448.

ington learned that the Turkish Government had approached the British Government with the same request and that the British Admiral, Calthorpe, had been authorized by his government to discuss terms with accredited representatives of Turkey.[58] The English had already arrived at an understanding with France and Italy with respect to their demands. On October 25 the British Government instructed Admiral Calthorpe to conclude the armistice on the basis of the twenty-four clauses agreed to in Paris. He was advised, however, to get accepted "the first four conditions . . . [which] if immediately carried out will so inevitably make us master of the situation, that we do not wish you to jeopardize obtaining them, and obtaining them quickly, by insisting unduly on all or any of the rest" although it would be useful to get them all accepted "if only to enable us to satisfy the French and the Italians that we have done our best to proceed on the lines mutually agreed."[59] Although the French sent an admiral to Fort Mudros, on the island of Lemnos, the Turkish armistice delegates were accredited only to Great Britain and expressed a wish to treat solely with the British Government. There was a serious dispute between Lloyd George and Clemenceau in Paris on October 30 "as to who should accept the surrender of the Turks—the British or the French Admiral."[60] The final terms were agreed to by Admiral Calthorpe and the Turkish delegates on a British warship at Mudros on October 30. Turkey was to end all hostilities Thursday noon, October 31.[61] And so the armistice was already signed when on October 31 Lansing notified the Spanish Ambassador in Washington that Wilson would place before the warring Governments Turkey's request of October 12 for peace and armistice.[62]

58. The British Embassy to the Department of State, October 23, 1918, *ibid.*, p. 384.

59. Cited in Maurice, *The Armistices of 1918* (London, 1943), pp. 20–21.

60. For the differences between France and Great Britain, see *ibid.*, pp. 16–24. See also House to Lansing, October 30, 1918, *Foreign Relations, 1918,* Supplement I, I, 427.

61. House to Lansing, undated, but received at Washington November 1, 1918. *Ibid.*, p. 441. The Turkish armistice terms are given in Appendix D.

62. Lansing to Riaño, October 31, 1918, *ibid.*, p. 428.

VIII

Ludendorff Is Dismissed

THE division produced in Germany by Wilson's second note became clearer as time went on. In fact, it was the beginning of a cleavage that has endured in German history ever since. On the one side was the group, led by the Army and Navy Commands, that favored an end of negotiations with Wilson, because his demands had challenged those who wished to maintain the existing form of government and they thought accepting them was to place themselves and the nation at the mercy of the Entente. It was to be expected that conservative royalist groups would find Wilson's demands dishonorable and unacceptable. But even moderates were shaken by the excessive terms. The liberal *Vossische Zeitung* was convinced that a "war of the people" in defense of their homeland was near at hand; it asked that ministers of all parties visit the fighting front to explain the situation and to prepare for such a struggle by establishing closer relations between the Government at home and the soldiers in the field.[1] The *Frankfurter Zeitung* questioned whether Germany should accept the demands and so deliver herself to the arbitrary will of the Entente generals; Germany should give in only when it became physically impossible for the Armies to avert such a fate.[2]

In the face of this hostile attitude Prince Max and his Government decided to continue negotiations. At the same time they made it clear that they did not intend to accept dishonorable terms. They were determined, if a break should come, to place the responsibility for it on Wilson so that the German people would know beyond all doubt that their resistance was completely justified. The Chancellor differed, however, from the Army, who argued that the time for a break had already come.

The general public knew nothing about the struggle going on within the Government or about the reason for the delay in answering Wilson's note of October 14. The struggle came into the open with the publication on October 21 of Germany's third note. People acquainted with it knew that Germany's reply was that of

1. *Vossische Zeitung,* October 19, 1918, No. 535.
2. *Frankfurter Zeitung,* October 20, 1918, No. 291.

a civilian Government defying the military. In fact, that note in its abandonment of the submarine war can be regarded as the Government's declaration of independence of the Army. Ludendorff made a last-minute appeal to modify that part of the reply by suggesting a paragraph warning the Allies that Germany would employ the submarine again unless it got an armistice very soon. His proposal came too late; but in any event it would certainly not have gained approval.[3] Determined that the submarine should not induce Wilson to break off negotiations, the Government had the following instructions despatched to U-boat commanders:

> Return at once. Because of negotiations now in progress every kind of mercantile war prohibited. Submarines returning home may attack only ships of war in the daytime.[4]

Prince Max found himself under attack by the Pan-Germans for yielding to the enemy's shameful demands; they asked for a Government that would fight instead. His policy of continuing to negotiate with Wilson won him support, primarily from those who were beginning to realize how necessary peace had become to

3. Ludendorff would have inserted in the note after second paragraph concerning the U-boats:

"The President of the United States of America will see from these instructions issued to the U-boats that this obstacle to an understanding, mentioned by him, has also been removed. But the President should nevertheless realize that by letting pass passenger vessels which, as has been proved, also serve the purposes of war, the German Government, in the interest of humanity and for the prevention of further bloodshed, has relinquished a weapon which it was forced by England to employ on account of a blockade contrary to the law of nations and claiming thousands of innocent victims—women and children. The German people will find it impossible to dispense with a weapon forced upon it by its foe in a struggle for life or death against its numerous enemies, if some equivalent is not supplied at once by the inauguration of a general armistice. Thus, for reasons of equity and self-preservation, the German Government will be forced to have recourse to this weapon again, unless an armistice goes into effect within a brief period." Document 65, *Amtliche Urkunden.*

4. Document 74, *ibid.* It is not possible to ascertain the exact date for these instructions, which were sent out before October 24. Lersner, who represented the Foreign Office at Army Headquarters, reported to Berlin on October 24 having heard that all submarines had been recalled. Document 73, *ibid.* The American Vice-Consul at Zürich reported to Lansing on October 23 that all German submarines had been ordered home and that the Government had won Admiralty support for the action by refraining from any public announcement of the order. McNally to Lansing, October 23, 1918, *Foreign Relations, 1918,* Supplement I, I, 394–395. The message was not received in Washington until October 28. Austria is reported to have ceased its submarine war on October 21. Document 72, *Amtliche Urkunden.*

Germany. Professors in the University of Berlin issued an appeal to the nation to support the new Government.[5] The liberal *Frankfurter Zeitung*, which had wavered, applauded the German reply for warning Wilson not to approve any demand irreconcilable with the honor of the German people or with the realization of a peace of justice.[6] The Socialist *Vorwärts* was quoted as having nothing but praise for the decision to end the submarine war, which, in its opinion, "was to be condemned from the moral point of view and, wholly apart from the invasion of Belgium, was the greatest mistake committed by our military leadership." [7]

The Cabinet had full understanding of the nature of its differences with the military leaders and wanted to clinch its victory. In the morning session of October 21 there was strong insistence that the Army Command be compelled to accept the wording of the note it had opposed and thus to accept the consequences of negotiations initiated by Hindenburg and Ludendorff. To the majority of the Government it was a question of forcing the Army to acknowledge that the civilian authorities were supreme in Germany and to declare itself as having no direct influence in political affairs. As early as October 17 the *Berliner Tageblatt* had urged editorially that military authorities be subjected to parliamentary control. The note of October 20 was a symbol that this had now occurred. It appeared like sudden revelation to Erzberger that now "we are actually masters in our own house." He persuaded his colleagues to support a resolution that "the Supreme Army Command should declare itself to be no power in politics" in Germany. Over the telephone Colonel Haeften immediately acquainted Ludendorff with this decision and was authorized to make the following statement for the Army:

1. The Supreme Army Command regards itself as having no political power, consequently it does not have any political responsibility. Its political assent to the note [of October 20] is therefore unnecessary.

If a question is raised publicly—either in the Reichstag or in the press—as to the position of the Supreme Army Command, the Government may issue a declaration to that effect.

2. The Supreme Army Command will keep itself completely loyal toward the Government in the matter; it will avoid everything cal-

5. *Frankfurter Zeitung,* October 21, 1918, No. 292.

6. *Ibid.,* October 22, 1918, No. 293.

7. *Idem.*

culated to cause the Government difficulty in the eyes of the public with regard to responsibility for the note.

3. The declaration sought by the Imperial Government that the Supreme Army Command should confine itself to military matters and still acknowledge that the concession with regard to the submarines is necessary for the attainment of the *political* success of the note cannot be made by the Supreme Army Command because it lacks evidence on the basis of which it can pass judgment on the *political* aspect of the matter and consequently is not in a position to express an opinion.[8]

No one can say that this ungenerous and highly qualified declaration marked a victory for the civilian Government over the military; that was yet to be won. Perhaps the outcome might have been different if the Chancellor had threatened to reveal the fact that the High Command had insisted on an armistice at the very beginning. The unwillingness of the Army to yield to Prince Max becomes plain in the instructions prepared on October 23 by Ludendorff and Hindenburg for the German Armistice Commission. "The *military situation*," they began, "is of such a nature that the strength of the field army is no longer adequate to *assure* our holding our present position. For a long time replacements have not been equal to our losses. We could, of course, in order to close the most serious gaps, draft a still larger number of people from home by weakening war industries. But that would not suffice to bring the Army quickly back to needed fighting strength." For the enemy, it was pointed out, the question of manpower was different. With the relative strength of both armies changing to Germany's disadvantage, "the possibility of achieving our definite conditions of peace against the American-English-French Army no longer exists. In recognition of this situation the offer of peace was made. Nonetheless, we must obviously be always prepared to resume fighting if such conditions are offered us as destroy our future. Such conditions are presumably not in President Wilson's intentions. It is rather to be expected of France or of England that they will continue the war for the achievement of impossible conditions. In that case it is not unlikely that the United States will refrain from continuing to wage war. The fight against the French-English Army alone is not at all hopeless, especially if Belgium also withdraws and the war is confined to the regions near the Franco-German frontiers."

8. Document 66b, *Amtliche Urkunden;* Max, *Erinnerungen,* pp. 471–472.

The Army Command stated that the Government had accepted Wilson's Fourteen Points without reservations, without explanation, without knowing whether other demands would also be made, and had declared its readiness to evacuate without condition all occupied enemy territory. Germany might be confronted with new demands after evacuating such lands and thus be forced to fight on her own frontiers under unfavorable conditions. Hence it was essential to get a clear idea of the peace terms before the enemy got to German territory. The best way to do that was to speed up negotiations for a preliminary peace instead of purposely prolonging negotiations concerning the territory to be evacuated. The Generals advised the Armistice Commission to deal honorably and loyally with the Americans in order to exploit any differences between the United States and the Allies. It was acknowledged that much tact would be required for this sort of diplomacy. The commission was instructed to make no effort to recover what had already been granted, but should, within the framework of the correspondence with Wilson, try to gain for Germany as much as possible. If additional concessions were to be made, special instructions for each instance would come from the Army or Naval Command. Wilson was represented as wanting to begin armistice negotiations only after occupied territory had been evacuated, and as meaning by an armistice the definitive end of hostilities. What the German High Command desired, on the other hand, was an immediate cessation of the fighting on existing battle lines; after getting that kind of truce, the German Armistice Commission was to arrange for the evacuation of territory and the kind of final armistice on Germany's borders that Wilson wanted.[9]

With the Army Command and its many supporters headed for what might become open revolt against the Government, Prince Max confronted great difficulties when he appeared before the Reichstag on October 22, the first session since October 5, when the nation had been informed that peace and an armistice had been requested. The Chancellor had to discuss many matters; he had to justify his dealings with Wilson and at the same time make it clear that there were some terms Germany would refuse to accept, even if it meant prolonging the war. He had to introduce constitutional amendments by which Germany would be transformed into the democratic state described to Wilson on October 20. The Cabinet was anxious about this session and about the

9. Document 76a, *Amtliche Urkunden.*

speech; the Secretaries of State knew that debate could not be avoided as on October 5. Apart from the critics of negotiations with Wilson there were discontented groups such as the Independent Socialists who craved for Germany the kind of revolutionary state the Russians had created; there were the minority groups of Danes, Poles, and Alsatians—all discovering in the Empire's impending collapse their opportunity to compel consideration of their particular claims.

Wiser by reason of his experience in drafting a reply to Wilson's second note, Prince Max was not disposed to consult his ministerial colleagues about his speech. He knew it would be impossible for many minds to agree.[10]

The Chancellor began his speech by referring to his correspondence with Wilson and to the question whether the peace to come would be "a peace of right or a peace of force." It was not clear from what Wilson had written, he said, which point of view would triumph; he hoped the President's next note would bring certainty with it. Meanwhile, the Germans must be prepared for the possibility "that enemy Governments want to continue the war and that no other choice remains but to defend ourselves with the whole power of a people being driven to extremes. If this necessity arises, I have no doubt that the German Government will issue its call for national defense in the name of the German people just as it had to speak in the name of the German people when it undertook negotiations for peace. . . . The German people must not be led blindfolded to the conference table. The nation has today the right to ask the question: if a peace on the basis of Wilson's conditions should now come about, what does it signify for our lives and for our future?" The Chancellor did not agree with critics who said that the acceptance of Wilson's conditions "would mean subjection to a tribunal hostile to Germany which would decide the question of right solely from the viewpoint of selfish interests." He made it clear that for Germans the standard would no longer be "what we ourselves regard as right but only what would be recognized as right in open discussion with our enemies." The kernel of Wilson's program was the league of nations, which required the surrender by nations of a part of their sovereignty if justice for all were to be realized. "If we really understand that the significance of this frightful war is, above all, a victory for

10. Scheidemann believes he worked it out in consultation with such intimate advisers as Hahn and Simons. Scheidemann, *Memoiren eines Sozialdemokraten* (two vols., Dresden, 1929), II, 234.

the idea of justice, and if we submit to this idea without resistance, without mental reservations but with all our will, we shall then find in it a remedy for our sufferings in the present and a task for our powers in the future. . . . If today in this hour of difficulty for our people I represent the idea of a league of nations as a source of comfort and of new strength, I do not wish for a moment to brush aside the tremendous obstacles yet to be overcome."

Prince Max then came to the matter of internal reform, on which he had worked with the Majority parties since taking office. He informed the Reichstag that "universal, equal, direct, and secret suffrage" in Prussia was as good as assured. He referred to steps he had already taken to liberalize the Government: granting autonomy to Alsace-Lorraine, taking personal responsibility for the maintenance of civil liberties and removing restrictions on their exercise so far as the war permitted, pardoning political prisoners. He urged the enactment of two bills that "ought to free our new form of government from the constitutional obstacles still in its way." Under the first measure members of the Reichstag could become members of the Government without losing their seats; under the second, the Reichstag would have concurrent power with the Bundesrat in questions of peace and war and in making treaties of alliance. "If you . . . give your assent to these measures," he said, "government by the people will be firmly anchored in the laws of the Empire. . . . The German people have been sitting in the saddle for a long time; now they should ride." The changes were recommended not just to appease public opinion abroad or to meet the cruel demands of the moment, but because they were supported by the "inmost convictions" of the nation and were the expression of Germany's "peculiar character and history." [11]

The labor and anxiety of these days proved too much for Prince Max. In the evening after his speech he fell ill of influenza. For almost a fortnight he was confined to his room, keeping in touch with events only through assistants who reported to him constantly. It was a critical time for the head of the Government to be out of direct touch with developments that seemed for the first two or three days to be the prelude to *Finis Germaniae.*

The debate that followed the speech showed the existence of

11. *Reichstagsverhandlungen,* October 22, 1918, pp. 6159–6161; Max, *Erinnerungen,* pp. 478–486; *Foreign Relations, 1918,* Supplement I, I, 386–391. For the constitutional changes finally adopted see *infra,* p. 225 *n* 13.

great opposition to the Government; even the Social Democrats differed from the Chancellor in spite of their participation in the regime. Their leader Ebert protested that the two constitutional amendments offered by Prince Max did not go far enough. He suggested changes that he and his party wanted: that it be made perfectly clear that the Chancellor could be named or dismissed by vote of the Reichstag; that the legislative body acquire the right to hold the Chancellor or his representatives responsible in a court of law; that the military authority cease to be "a state within a state" and come under the direct control of the Chancellor and the Reichstag; that women be given the right to vote. He criticized the police, the censorship, and all other interference with civil liberties, even in Finland, where Social Democrats had been condemned to death by the German officers in the army of occupation. He was not satisfied with the Chancellor's statement that the franchise was virtually assured in Prussia—he wanted it granted immediately. While praising the Government for releasing Karl Liebknecht after two years' imprisonment, he demanded the release of many other political offenders, including some men jailed for participating in the naval mutiny of July, 1917. He warned Pan-Germans that they might be brought to trial for opposition to the new Government. He viewed with less calm than Prince Max the possibility of a war of desperation because "the first German Government in which Social Democrats participate should be a government of peace." He warned the Entente against brutal treatment of defeated Germans. Like Wilson, Ebert and his party wanted an end to arbitrary rule in Germany and said they had been making this demand ever since the Kaiser's irresponsible *Daily Telegraph* interview of 1908;[12] there was no place in Germany for personal rule and for the policy of the mailed fist.[13]

Stresemann, leader of the National Liberal party, supported the new Government, expressing both willingness and eagerness to coöperate although he and his party remained monarchists. In fact, he even said that such coöperation was the best way to preserve the monarchy.[14]

12. In this interview of October 28, 1908, the Emperor, indiscreetly and at length, found fault with the British press for misrepresenting his peaceful intentions toward England. What he said led to a crisis in Anglo-German relations, and his manner of saying it caused a major political crisis at home.

13. *Reichstagsverhandlungen,* October 22, 1918, pp. 6161–6166.

14. *Ibid.,* p. 6172. Stresemann distrusted Wilson and the Fourteen Points. He believed that Wilson would increase his demands and seek greater concessions from Germany. See his *Vermächtnis* (3 vols., Berlin, 1932–33), I, 12–13.

The Conservative leader, Count Westarp, attacked Ebert, the principle of parliamentary government, and the political reforms already instituted. As official opposition to the new Government he and his party would fight the constitutional amendments that had been offered. He held the Government responsible for an unnecessary request for armistice although, according to Prince Max, he was well acquainted with the facts. He criticized the correspondence with Wilson and said that the next note would force the German people to fight because they did not have to capitulate or accept conditions incompatible with their honor or with the principles of a just peace. Only in such a struggle would his party support the Government.[15]

The first speaker on the second day of debate, Haase of the Independent Socialist party, seemed to find a genuine pleasure in the predicament of the Government. He said that the German people had no idea why they had been defeated after all the reports of great victories. His criticisms of the Government were many: for the treaties of Brest-Litovsk and Bucharest, for unrestricted submarine warfare, for interference with civil liberties, for the limited amnesty. He attacked Westarp for saying that the Government had asked for an armistice when it was known that Ludendorff and Hindenburg were responsible for it. He did not want Social Democrats to have credit with the working classes for the effort to end the war. "It is not correct," said this political extremist, "that this present new Government made this offer on its own initiative. That issue lay before the former Government, which had already prepared the first draft. In fact, gentlemen, when the representatives of the Majority parties met together to participate in the new Government, they were not thinking about making a peace offer; rather, they wanted to get together to organize for national defense, that is, to intensify and prolong the war." From the military point of view, he said, all future bloodshed was absolutely useless and senseless. He pleaded that the wrongs done to Danes, Poles, and Alsatians be righted, but found fault with the Poles for asking too much. As for the government of Germany in the future, he thought it ridiculous that Germany alone should have a crowned ruler when republics were springing up everywhere and crowns were rolling in the dust.[16]

Vice-Chancellor von Payer agreed with Prince Max in criticizing Haase for his antimonarchist views, but gave more qualified

15. *Reichstagsverhandlungen,* October 22, 1918, pp. 6178–6180.
16. *Ibid.,* October 23, 1918, pp. 6182–6190.

support in suggesting that the constitutional amendments proposed be studied carefully and acted on with caution.

Representatives of the Polish, Danish, and Alsatian minorities spoke also, stressing a long history of wrongs and joyfully greeting the new day that was coming. The speaker for the Poles said that the Germans had long acted on the principle that "where the German once puts his foot, that is and remains German territory." He foresaw difficulties between the two peoples in the immediate future, for he knew that the Germans were organizing themselves into protective leagues against the Poles. In the plebiscites to be held to determine Polish territory, he said that "even the dead shall vote." [17]

The Alsatian Ricklin rejected autonomy for Alsace-Lorraine and placed his trust in the solution offered by President Wilson in the Fourteen Points. The Dane Hanssen talked at great length on the history of northern Schleswig, whose people had never been granted the plebiscite promised to them when annexed to Prussia in 1866.[18]

Westarp and Solf tried to answer these nationalists. Solf's criticism of Polish demands aroused great excitement; one Pole became so abusive that a member of the Right shouted, "Kick the dog out!"

Scheüch, making his first Reichstag appearance, spoke for the Government and pleaded that full support be given the Army at the front. Remarks directed against critics were resented by the Independent Socialists, their leader Haase interrupting the speaker so much that he had to be called to order. Ledebour spoke for the Independents in reply to the Minister of War, in terms unflattering to the military. Noske, although a Social Democrat and supposedly a supporter of the Government, felt the sting of Scheüch's attack on critics and made a long speech in which he attacked the Cabinet, the Minister of War, Government policy toward Poland, the excessive demands of the Poles, and so on. His words about supporters of the old system of government continuing in the new were disturbing. Prince Max says the house was shocked when this "administration Socialist" attacked the conservatives and their demand for a strong monarchy. "It would be dishonest," said Noske, "not to say that only one single grand

17. *Ibid.*, pp. 6193–6197.
18. *Ibid.*, pp. 6203–6205.
19. *Ibid.*, pp. 6206, 6210–6211.

gesture by the wearer of the imperial crown would evoke the approval of millions." [20]

Such were the divisions of opinion in Germany on October 24, when Wilson's third note was being circulated in the corridors of the Reichstag. The unity that the moment demanded was nowhere evident. It was hopeless even to think that it could be created.

The Chancellor found Wilson's answer shrewd, its language of the kind used by one "who regards his enemy's resistance as broken. And the worst of it was . . . [that] our people have been so far broken that in this 'humiliating' note with its 'excessive demands' they will discover no incentive for a fight to the very end." [21] "It was a telling answer to our unmanly attitude," wrote Ludendorff.[22] Members of the Reichstag sought to discuss the note, but the President of that body would not allow it.[23]

Members of the German-Conservative party in the Reichstag lost no time in informing Prince Max of their views. "Wilson's note, made public today," read a resolution addressed to the Chancellor, "demands an unconditional surrender, the abdication of the Kaiser, the dismissal of our Army commanders, and our complete submission to a peace of force. Germany is first to be dishonored and disarmed, and then humiliated. The acceptance of these conditions would surrender every German for generations to a deprivation of political rights and to economic slavery. . . . German honor commands the Government to reject such demands; the security of the Empire requires the Government to summon the people to their final battle." [24]

The divided opinion of the Reichstag on negotiations with Wilson and on the position of the Kaiser was reflected in the daily press. The nationalist *Tägliche Rundschau* of October 25 found Wilson's demand for shameless capitulation and for the removal of military and monarchical authorities intolerable; "we must," it affirmed, "whether we wish it or not, prepare for the final fight for life and honor." [25] The conservative *Lokal-Anzeiger*

20. *Ibid.,* October 24, 1918, pp. 6211–6218. Prince Max's account of the Reichstag debate is given in his *Erinnerungen,* pp. 486–491. He differs from the official account in a number of particulars.
21. Max, *Erinnerungen,* p. 494.
22. Ludendorff, *Kriegserinnerungen,* p. 611.
23. *Reichstagsverhandlungen,* October 25, 1918, pp. 6250–6251.
24. Quoted in the *Frankfurter Zeitung,* October 25, 1918, No. 297.
25. *Tägliche Rundschau,* October 25, 1918, No. 546.

urged the Government to learn the precise armistice conditions as soon as possible. "Then the Government has to decide whether it can accept these conditions or whether they so deprive Germany of both honor and arms that they must be rejected." In the latter case the war would be continued.[26] The *Frankfurter Zeitung*, after pointing out that the Entente Powers had never declared their acceptance of Wilson's Fourteen Points, said that it was clear that armistice conditions like those already imposed on Bulgaria would be imposed on Germany. "They are conditions," the newspaper said, "which a free and brave people can accept only when it must and there is no sense in concealing the fact that these notes and answers from Wilson are certainly the most humiliating thing that Germany has experienced since the days of Napoleon." [27]

Wilson's second note had been taken by some Germans to mean that the removal of the Kaiser was an essential preliminary to negotiations for peace. The third note was thought to be even clearer in the political implications of its demands. The *Frankfurter Zeitung* said that Wilson was directing his words to the Kaiser, who should realize that he was blocking the road to peace. "If it is really a question now of whether Germany should surrender or whether peace is to be negotiated, the choice between the alternatives rests primarily with the Kaiser. Upon his decision much will depend for Germany's future and, above all, for the development of peace. This decision could make people forget much that the Kaiser has said and done in the last decades and we would like to hope that it will be made soon and wisely." [28] On the same day *Vorwärts* said that Wilson was wrong if he believed that Germany's former masters would have a decisive role in days to come; in the future the only power in Germany would be the German people and the Government dependent upon them for support.[29]

Prince Max was unwilling to face the issue of abdication just now; instead, he ordered his supporters to speed the reforms for a democratic Germany. He also instructed Simons to draft a reply to Wilson. The President's latest note would not serve as the basis for an appeal for a *levée en masse*. A break must be avoided if possible; but, if it should come, Prince Max wanted the German people to see that Wilson was responsible for it. He was sure that

26. *Lokal-Anzeiger*, October 25, 1918, No. 547.
27. *Frankfurter Zeitung*, October 25, 1918, No. 296.
28. *Idem.*
29. *Vorwärts*, October 25, 1918, No. 294.

the soldiers and workers believed that Germany could have peace by making the state democratic; and he thought that Wilson desired to see Germany democratic in order to have a platform from which he could oppose the harsh terms that Foch favored. The reply should make it clear that the German people did not put themselves entirely at the mercy of the enemy, that the democratization of the country was proceeding, and that the American President should refrain from asking the Germans to adopt constitutional changes merely to influence people outside Germany.[30]

With regard to the Kaiser the Chancellor was sure to have difficulties with the Social Democrats. He knew that definitely on the afternoon of October 24, when Colonel Haeften rushed to his bedside from the Reichstag to warn him that next day the Social Democrats were going to demand the Kaiser's abdication. Haeften explained that he had been talking with Foreign Secretary Solf when Noske appeared with the first copy of the note from Wilson. Solf became more and more serious as he read it. But Noske said it was not so bad; if the Kaiser got out, Germany could get a good peace. Haeften urged Prince Max to withhold the note from publication so as to give the Emperor an opportunity to abdicate of his own free will, before any pressure was applied by the Social Democrats. "But if the Kaiser does not make up his mind right away, the only thing to do is to break with Wilson. And all we can do then is to remove our hats in prayer." [31]

Disappointed in his failure to persuade Prince Max to adopt his suggestions, Colonel Haeften informed Ludendorff at Spa that hurried and decisive resolutions would have to be made in Berlin, a report that led Ludendorff to declare that he and Hindenburg wanted to come to Berlin immediately. Haeften informed Prince Max of this decision, which the Chancellor disapproved so strongly that he ordered the two Generals to postpone their journey to the capital; he did not wish it to appear that the decisions being made during these days were made under pressure from the military.[32] Above all he wanted to draft his reply to Wilson without interference from the Supreme Army Command. This was the way to show Wilson that Germany was free from the arbitrary control of those responsible for the war.

30. Max, *Erinnerungen,* p. 497.

31. *Ibid.,* pp. 497–498.

32. *Ibid.,* p. 498. The presence of Ludendorff and Scheer in Berlin when Wilson's second note was under consideration had been interpreted by the American Chargé at The Hague as "activity of the military party." Bliss to Lansing, October 19, 1918, *Foreign Relations, 1918,* Supplement I, I, 372–373.

On the evening of October 24 there was a meeting of the Cabinet at which von Payer presided. Those who attended were disturbed over the disappearance on the home front of the will to fight on. The people, argued Haussmann, minister without portfolio and member of the Democratic party, do not comprehend the intolerable character of Wilson's conditions because of the vague language that expressed them. He believed that these demands, when worked out in detail, would make a break with Wilson both possible and necessary. Scheidemann was worried about the popularity of Karl Liebknecht. He had himself helped to have Liebknecht released from prison. But the gesture failed of its intended effect and the radical Liebknecht became increasingly popular with workers and soldiers. Erzberger dismayed the meeting by saying that the Centrist party had declared itself unanimously opposed to a war of national defense. The Minister of War reported that the soldiers were weary; if they could get some rest, much would be gained. "The majority of the Secretaries of State," wrote the Chancellor, "were of the opinion that we should not answer Wilson in such a way as to commit ourselves to a continuation of the war. For an evaluation of the military situation it was not enough to have the opinion of General Ludendorff; he had given indications of not being sure of himself. All agreed on the need of getting the views of other Army commanders immediately."

The question was asked as to whether Ludendorff could then remain in office. The decision was that he should get out; but no one wanted the Cabinet to take the initiative. Instead, the Ministers preferred to let events take their natural course and hoped for a solution with the summoning of other generals.[33]

The indecision of the Cabinet as to what should be done was not reflected in the High Command. Hindenburg wanted the nation to fight; by their unity and energy the people at home should inspire the Army and impress the enemy with their determination to resist. He too was worried about the disappearance of the will to fight. Writing later, he argued that the home front collapsed sooner than the Army.

In a last effort to secure the coöperation of the Government Field Marshal Hindenburg wrote the following letter on October 24 to the Imperial Chancellor:

I cannot conceal from Your Grand-Ducal Highness that I failed to

33. Max, *Erinnerungen,* pp. 498–500.

hear in recent Reichstag speeches any appeal for support of the Army and that it hurt me.

I had hoped that the new Government would call on the whole nation for all its strength to defend our Fatherland. That has not happened. On the contrary, with few exceptions, the talk is only of reconciliation, not of fighting the enemy threatening our country. It had a depressing effect on the Army at first; then it shattered their morale. It is proved by serious symptoms.

For leadership in the defense of the country the Army needs not only men but a conviction that it is necessary to fight and the moral energy for the great task.

Your Grand-Ducal Highness will agree with me that the Government and the representatives of the people must recognize the overwhelming significance of morale for a nation in arms and they must inspire and maintain such a spirit in the Army and in the people at home.

I earnestly beg Your Grand-Ducal Highness, as head of the new Government, to rise to the height of this holy task.[34]

At the same time there was published in the *Kreuzzeitung* another letter that Hindenburg had written to the Chancellor. It was also an appeal for unity on the ground that the enemy were taking advantage of the divisions within Germany to attack more fiercely and to increase their demands. It warned the nation that it had to choose between an honorable peace and a fight to the end. Since the letter was given some publicity, the *Frankfurter Zeitung* asked whether it did not constitute evidence that the military was interfering with the Government.[35]

Just before leaving Spa for Berlin the evening of October 24 in defiance of explicit orders of the Chancellor, Ludendorff and Hindenburg issued a proclamation to the troops. It read as follows:

FOR THE INFORMATION OF ALL TROOPS

Wilson says in his answer that he is ready to propose to his allies that they should enter into armistice negotiations, but that the armistice must render Germany so defenseless that she cannot take up arms again. He will negotiate with Germany for peace only if she concedes all the demands of America's allies as to the internal

34. Hindenburg, *Aus meinem Leben* (Leipzig, 1920), p. 396.
35. *Frankfurter Zeitung,* October 25, 1918, No. 296.

constitutional arrangements of Germany; otherwise, there is no choice but unconditional surrender.

Wilson's answer is a demand for unconditional surrender. It is thus unacceptable to us soldiers. It proves that our enemy's desire for our destruction, which let loose the war in 1914, still exists undiminished. It proves, further, that our enemies used the phrase "Peace with Justice" merely to deceive us and break our resistance. Wilson's answer can thus be nothing for us soldiers but a challenge to continue our resistance with all our strength. When our enemies know that no sacrifices will achieve the rupture of the German front, then they will be ready for a peace which will make the future of our country safe for the great masses of our people.

At the front, October 24, 10 P.M.[36]

This proclamation, which called for a virtual rupture of correspondence with Wilson, was issued to the troops the evening of the 24th and given to the press at noon the next day. Newspapermen were informed at the same time of a telegram in which Hindenburg complained to Prince Max of "reports to the effect that the General Field Marshal had made a personal demand for an *immediate* peace proposal and had indicated at the same time that it was a matter of hours." [37] The Government did not learn of the proclamation until it was issued to the press. When the Army Command discovered that the Cabinet was far from advocating a break with Wilson, it ordered that the proclamation be withheld; the instructions came too late, however, to keep the statement from some of the armies. Members of the Cabinet were angered by what appeared to be the High Command's interference in a political matter outside military jurisdiction for the purpose of anticipating, if not of forcing, the decision of the Government in Berlin.

Prince Max was far more offended, however, by the decision of the two Generals to disregard his specific orders by coming to

36. Document 76b and note, *Amtliche Urkunden;* Max, *Erinnerungen,* pp. 500–501. Ludendorff thought that the proclamation expressed the views of the Government in Berlin and Max seems somewhat inclined to accept the explanation that an error by Colonel Haeften had given Ludendorff an incorrect understanding of the Government's attitude. See *ibid.,* p. 501 and an appendix (inserted *ibid.* between pp. 683 and 684), in which Haeften explains how the Army leaders got the impression that the Cabinet was going to break off negotiations with Wilson. Ludendorff has explained his position in his *Kriegserinnerungen,* pp. 614–615. Hindenburg explained the circumstances in a letter to the Chancellor on November 1, 1918; it is found in Ludendorff, *Urkunden,* pp. 578–579.

37. Document 80, *Amtliche Urkunden.*

Berlin. When he learned early on the 25th that they had left Spa the night before, he was convinced that "this journey would end only in the dismissal of General Ludendorff." Without informing the Cabinet of his intentions, he sent the Kaiser a letter demanding that the Emperor either dismiss Ludendorff or accept the Chancellor's resignation. He begged the Kaiser to do all he could to retain Hindenburg, despite some pressure to have him replaced by General Gallwitz.[38]

Upon their arrival in Berlin Ludendorff and Hindenburg went immediately to Schloss Bellevue, where they demanded that the Kaiser discontinue negotiations with Wilson. Refusing to make such a decision, the Emperor referred the two importunate Generals to Prince Max. The latter had been so anxious to continue negotiations that he had prepared special instructions, which were actually never sent, for the German Minister in Berne to arrange that Wilson be informed in absolute confidence "that all U-boats have received orders to return and to refrain from every kind of mercantile war because of the negotiations with the President." [39]

Prince Max was ill and arranged to have Vice-Chancellor von Payer speak with the two Generals at 9 P.M. Before the meeting there was a telephone call from von Lersner, who said that the Supreme Army Command was absolutely "wild" and would insist upon the rejection of Wilson's armistice. He recalled his own long experience at General Headquarters when he uttered "the *most urgent* warning against granting credence to any possible promises of the Supreme Army Command, or permitting ourselves to be diverted in the least from the peace policy we have adopted." The military situation was as bad as it had been three weeks earlier, no improvement could be expected, and it was only a question of weeks or a few months before the enemy would be on German soil. When asked about the possible effect on the Army of a change in the Army Command, von Lersner replied that the larger part would like it, "as men had lost confidence in the present Supreme Army Command." [40]

The evening session lasted, in the words of von Payer, "a couple of serious hours." The Generals came accompanied by Minister of War Scheüch and Admiral Scheer. Ludendorff was greatly agitated. He said that Wilson's note signified nothing but capitula-

38. Max, *Erinnerungen,* p. 500. Stresemann was afraid that Hindenburg would resign with Ludendorff. Stresemann, *Vermächtnis,* I, 12–13.

39. Max, *Erinnerungen,* p. 501; document 75, *Amtliche Urkunden.*

40. Document 79, *ibid.*

tion for Germany, its terms were insulting and dishonorable. He and Hindenburg wanted an end to the negotiations and urged that an appeal be made to the German people by the Kaiser, the leaders of the German states, the German Government, the heads of the Army and Navy, and the Reichstag to summon all their strength and determination to continue the war. Scheer supported the Generals, while Scheüch sided with von Payer in opposition to the plan. The two Generals said that the western front could be held through the winter. The Vice-Chancellor got no satisfactory answer when he asked what chances Germany would have for a better peace if she continued to fight. Hindenburg and Ludendorff called attention to a number of factors that made the enemies' situation unfavorable: shortage of coal, declining offensive power, differences between Clemenceau and Foch, a report from France that the country would have to yield in four weeks, the possibility of internal disorders in France. Von Payer suggested that when Wilson's specific terms became known in detail and people saw clearly that they were intolerable, there might be a greater determination on the part of the nation to fight on. Ludendorff tried to bind the Vice-Chancellor to a *levée en masse* in that case. That promise von Payer refused to give, saying that he wanted the War Cabinet first to question other generals about the military situation. Ludendorff saw it was hopeless.

"Then, Your Excellency," he said, "in the name of the Fatherland I throw the shame of it on you and your colleagues. And I warn you, if you let things go like this, in a few weeks you will have Bolshevism in the country. Then think of me!"

"Come now, Your Excellency," replied von Payer, "I'm not afraid of that. Furthermore, you'll have to leave the interpretation of such matters to me. I understand them better."

"There is no sense in talking further with you, Herr von Payer," concluded the irate General. "Neither of us understands the other and will never do so. We could never get together; we live in different worlds. I'm through talking with you." [41]

Ludendorff was deeply disappointed as well as angry. "There is no hope," he said as he came away. "Germany is lost." [42]

Solf and Roedern were at the bedside of Prince Max the next

41. This account comes from Rear Admiral von Levetzow and is found in Niemann, *Revolution von Oben,* pp. 181, 411–412. See also Payer, *Von Bethmann Hollweg,* pp. 141–144. Von Payer's report on the conference to Prince Max is given in the latter's *Erinnerungen,* pp. 503–504; his report to the Cabinet is found in document 82, *Amtliche Urkunden.*

42. Ludendorff, *Kriegserinnerungen,* p. 616.

morning when von Payer gave his report of the session with the Generals. Suddenly Colonel Haeften rushed into the room in great excitement, exclaiming, "General Ludendorff is dismissed!"

"And Hindenburg?"

"He remains."

Everybody present jumped up with the cry, "Thank God!"[43]

Ludendorff gives the following account of his dismissal:

> On the morning of October 26, at eight o'clock, while still in the mood of the previous evening, I wrote out my resignation. In it I proceeded from the feeling that, in the talk of the day before with von Payer, I had become convinced that the Government would not bestir itself to any action, that His Majesty, the country, and the Army were thus put in an untenable position, that I was regarded as one who would prolong the war, and that, given the policy of the Government toward Wilson, my departure might perhaps make things easier for Germany in the future. For these reasons I asked His Majesty to accept my resignation.
>
> At nine o'clock the morning of the 26th, the General Field Marshal came to see me as usual. I had put my letter of resignation aside, having made up my mind to speak to him only when the letter was in the hands of His Majesty. The General Field Marshal was master of his own destiny; I had no desire to influence him. But he saw the letter. Its form caught his attention. He requested me not to send it off; that I should remain; that I must not leave the Kaiser and the Army. After a rather long inward struggle I gave in. I became convinced that I must retain my office and proposed to the General Field Marshal that we should try again to see Prince Max. But he would not receive us; he was still sick. While I was waiting for information on the matter, Colonel Haeften reported to me that the Government had got His Majesty to remove me, the ostensible reason being the already-mentioned order issued to the Army.[44]

Haeften had learned early in the morning that the Chancellor was insisting upon Ludendorff's dismissal; he got the news, not directly from Prince Max, who wished "to spare him scruples of conscience," but indirectly, in the office of the Chancellor's Adjutant. Thereupon he hurried off to warn Ludendorff "so that the final scene might be played in as dignified form as possible."[45]

43. Max, *Erinnerungen,* p. 504.
44. Ludendorff, *Kriegserinnerungen,* pp. 616–617.
45. Max, *Erinnerungen,* p. 504. Prince Max says that he tried to have Ludendorff call so that he could explain matters, but that the General did not come.

The General was summoned to Schloss Bellevue for an interview with the Kaiser, whose attitude he found completely changed from the day before. The Emperor criticized the Army order of October 24. "There followed," writes Ludendorff, "some of the bitterest moments of my life. I told the Emperor in a respectful manner that I had got the painful impression I no longer had his confidence and accordingly begged most humbly to be relieved of office. His Majesty accepted my resignation." [46]

At the request of Hindenburg, the Kaiser appointed General Groener to be Ludendorff's successor as First Quartermaster General. Groener said he was named without being asked and without having an opportunity to confer about the matter.[47]

With Ludendorff deprived of all authority, Prince Max felt himself in a position to give Wilson the sort of reply he thought proper. Under instructions from the Chancellor, Simons drafted a reply informing Wilson that governmental powers were now in the hands of a people's Government and that this popular Government would conduct peace negotiations. The note concluded: "The German Government consequently awaits proposals for an armistice, not a demand to lay down arms. If the armistice is to open the way for a peace of justice corresponding with the principles of the President, it should not deprive the German people of the possibility of giving their free assent to the details of the peace treaty." The Chancellor said that he made a distinction between armistice and capitulation because of the need of warning the Americans that the Germans should not be driven to desperation.

When the note was placed before the Cabinet in the morning session of October 26, great opposition was expressed to it. Scheidemann objected, according to the Chancellor, because it was too strong; he and his party desired a note that would bring peace and win support for the Government among the working classes, who were flocking to the Independent Socialists. After long and warm discussion, mainly to overcome the arguments of Erzberger and Scheidemann, the following draft was agreed to:

The German Government has taken note of the reply of the President of the United States. The President is acquainted with the pro-

46. Ludendorff, *Kriegserinnerungen,* pp. 616–617. The Kaiser's role in this incident is recounted in Niemann, *Revolution von Oben,* pp. 182–185.

47. Hans Herzfeld, *Die deutsche Sozialdemokratie und die Auflösing der nationalen Einheitsfront im Weltkriege* (Leipzig, 1928), p. 373.

found changes that have taken place and are taking place in Germany's constitutional life. The negotiations for peace will be conducted by a democratic Government, whose powers are decisive and are anchored permanently in the constitution of the German Empire. The German Government therefore awaits proposals for an armistice, not for a capitulation. Only in that way can an armistice lead to a peace of justice, such as the President has described in his addresses.

While the note was being put into cipher that evening, Solf had dinner with a number of prominent officials whom he acquainted with its contents. Disapproval was unanimous. It was agreed that the news which had just come of Austria's impending collapse made it impossible for Germany to adopt such a firm tone. "We must not run the risk," Solf's friends told him, "of Wilson's breaking off [the negotiations]; the German people could not stand it." On his own responsibility Solf held up the despatch of the note and got Cabinet support the next day for his action; the Secretaries of State agreed that an explicit warning against a demand for Germany's capitulation was no longer possible. The Chancellor threatened to send no note unless it stressed the distinction he wished to make between an acceptable armistice and an unacceptable capitulation, but he was won over with the argument that the people were expecting the note and should not be disappointed. At last Solf prepared a new draft that the Chancellor could accept.[48] It was sent off the afternoon of October 27. It read:

The German Government has taken cognizance of the reply of the President of the United States. The President knows the far-reaching changes which have taken place and are being carried out in the German constitutional structure. The peace negotiations are being conducted by a government of the people in whose hands rests, both actually and constitutionally, the authority to make decisions. The military powers are also subject to this authority. The German Government now awaits the proposals for an armistice, which is the first step toward a peace of justice, as described by the President in his pronouncements.[49]

48. Max, *Erinnerungen,* pp. 505–509.

49. Oederlin to Lansing, October 28, 1918, *Foreign Relations, 1918,* Supplement I, I, 395–396. The German original is document 85, *Amtliche Urkunden.*

The dissolution of Austria-Hungary, which led so directly to the postponement and modification of Germany's reply to Wilson, had been progressing irresistibly; the various nationalities were proclaiming their independence and winning recognition for their new status. The imperial armies broke up as bodies of troops decided to return home. The Italian attack on the Piave front October 23 met with decreasing resistance. Moved to desperation, the Emperor appointed Count Julius Andrassy to succeed Count Burian in the Foreign Office. Regardless of what happened to Germany, Austria was determined now to have a separate peace and Andrassy was to abrogate the Austro-German alliance of 1879 that his father had worked with Bismarck to create.

On October 26 the German Ambassador in Vienna telegraphed to Berlin that Andrassy had said it was his task to liquidate the war. "The monarchy is done for; if it fails to conclude peace immediately, there is no escape from revolution in Hungary, Croatia, Bohemia, and even in Vienna." Andrassy had heard in Switzerland that "perhaps the monarchy could get tolerable conditions if it separated itself from Germany." He relied on reports that the Entente Powers were agreed as to what should be done with Germany but lacked a definite program toward Austria-Hungary.[50]

In the evening of October 26 the Austrian Ambassador in Berlin, Prince Hohenlohe, talked with Prince Max, who found him "a broken man." He said he would not dare to appear again on the streets of Berlin, for people would spit at him because of the Emperor's irrevocable decision to seek a separate peace. He gave the Chancellor a copy of the message that Emperor Karl had addressed to the Kaiser explaining why it was imperative for the sake of order in Austria and for the monarchical principle to end the war immediately. Prince Hohenlohe added that every possible effort had been made to change the Emperor's mind, but in vain. The news about Austria was not made public that evening; but it went the rounds of political circles and everywhere people were shocked by the thought that Austria might make peace even before Turkey.[51]

On October 27 Solf prepared a reply for the Kaiser to send to Karl, to prevent the severance of the alliance with Germany and the making of a separate peace. Less than an hour after the de-

50. Document 79a, *Amtliche Urkunden.*

51. Max, *Erinnerungen,* pp. 507–508; document 83, *Amtliche Urkunden.*

spatch of the fourth note to Wilson on October 27, the Kaiser sent his message to Vienna. "By carrying out this intention," the Kaiser told his "dear friend," "You would open the way for the plan of our enemy aiming at the separation of our countries in order the more easily to subject our lands to their will and to put into effect their antimonarchical purposes." After reminding his ally that the people of Germany also longed for an immediate peace, the Kaiser continued: "The action recently initiated in coöperation with Your Government is seeking to bring about an armistice and a peace immediately afterward; the negotiations are in progress and may come to a conclusion in a few days. The coöperation of our Governments up to the present, for which the prospects do not appear unfavorable, would be most dangerously threatened by independent action on the part of Your Government at the present moment. As soon as our enemies hear that our alliance is broken, the conditions for the armistice will become *ipso facto* much more severe. That affects our countries in the same degree. I therefore urgently beg You to refrain from any step that must give the impression that we are no longer united. The more closely we coöperate from now on, the greater are the prospects that our opponents, who are likewise suffering terribly from the costs and horrors of the war, will come to an agreement on peace conditions that will be in harmony with the honor and interests of our peoples. I am expecting from You that You will immediately have Your Government, only in complete agreement with Mine, continue the negotiations that have been initiated with the United States." [52]

The people in Vienna were in desperate need of bread. On October 25 a delegation of twelve Austrians had arrived in Berlin and asked for a trainload of grain. They had been assured the day before by the German Ambassador that Germany would assist them with food. On October 27 the Cabinet discussed this request at great length before reaching a decision to ship food to the wavering ally. Germany's Food Administrator, Waldow, said Germany simply "could not give any supplies away." One of his reasons was that such shipments of food would make a bad impression on working classes at home. Scheidemann urged that the food be sent: the German working classes could be taken care of. Von Payer also approved. Knowing that the food could not be easily spared, the Cabinet at last voted to send enough grain to

52. Document 84, *Amtliche Urkunden.*

meet demands in Vienna and German-Austria for about four weeks.[53]

To make certain that German military interests would not suffer from Austrian defection, Hindenburg on October 29 asked the German Government to arrange with Austria for the return of German troops fighting in Italy; transportation back to Germany of soldiers stationed in Hungary, Rumania, and the Ukraine, or provision for their care; and assurance that goods could be shipped from Rumania and the Ukraine through Austro-Hungarian territory.[54]

It was impossible to keep Austria from making her separate peace. The retreat that had begun when the Italians opened their attack was turning more and more into a rout. The officer who crossed to the Italian lines with a white flag in the evening of October 29 was sent back because his credentials were not deemed satisfactory. The next day, equipped with the proper papers, General von Weber and other plenipotentiaries came with the white flag and negotiations for an armistice were begun. On October 30 Emperor Karl reported by telegram to the Kaiser that he had suggested an armistice to the Italians that morning because the military situation had become untenable. "But," he assured the Kaiser, "should the Italians require that the railways through the Tyrol and Carinthia (the Tauer Railway, the Brenner Railway, and the Southern Railway) be opened for the passage of hostile troops against Your territories, I will place Myself at the head of My German-Austrians and prevent such passage by arms. You can have complete confidence in that. In such a case the troops of other nationalities could not be relied on." [55]

No faith whatever was placed in these assurances. When the Emperor informed the German Ambassador in Vienna on October 29 that the enemy could not use his lands for an attack on Germany, the Ambassador commented, "it is uncertain how one can judge this declaration on the basis of earlier experience." [56]

The Kaiser continued to observe the proper forms in his telegram of October 30 to Emperor Karl:

It is with emotion that I have read Your telegram with its news about the request to the Italians for an armistice. I am convinced

53. Max, *Erinnerungen*, pp. 517–518; Payer, *Von Bethmann Hollweg*, pp. 265–266.

54. Document 86a, *Amtliche Urkunden.*

55. Document 88, *ibid.*

56. Document 89a, *ibid.* See also the assurance given by Carl in document 87.

that Your German-Austrians under the command of their Imperial Master would rise as one man against shameful [armistice] conditions, and I thank You for the special assurance You have given Me." [57]

As October came to an end it was being borne home to the Germans that they were fighting alone against a world of enemies. A month earlier Bulgaria had signed an armistice. On October 30 Turkey came to terms with the enemy. And Austria was making her way out of the war by separate negotiations. On Sunday, November 3, Austria agreed to the Allied armistice, General Pietro Badoglio of the Italian Army signing in behalf of the Entente. The terms became effective November 4 at 3 P.M. "Germany now stands alone!" wrote the editor of the London *Times*. At the same time Colonel House informed President Wilson by telegram that the Allied leaders in Paris had approved a plan for military operations against Germany by way of Austria and would agree on armistice terms for Germany that afternoon.[58] If Germany had ever faced encirclement, it was now.

At last on October 28, after much talk about it, the Cabinet had come to the point of questioning other generals than Ludendorff on the military situation. The men consulted were General von Mudra, Commander of the Seventeenth Army, and General von Gallwitz, Commander of the Fifth Army, both with excellent military records. Gallwitz had behind him many years of service in the War Ministry, where his achievements had made him highly respected among political leaders. Before conferring with the Cabinet, the two Generals called on Prince Max, with whom they talked about the armistice appeal and the "frightful" effect it was having on Army morale; they spoke as if the Government bore the responsibility for initiating it. "I told them," writes the Chancellor, "the true story with all its ramifications. The men looked at each other in amazement: neither one had been asked about it." [59]

The long Cabinet conference with the two Generals did not lead to any change of policy. Gallwitz and Mudra took the point of view that Ludendorff had expressed in the conference of October 17, after he had changed his mind as to the need and desirability

57. Document 89, *ibid.*

58. House to Lansing, November 4, 1918, *Foreign Relations, 1918,* Supplement I, I, 460–461.

59. Max, *Erinnerungen,* p. 519.

of an armistice and had asked for a national uprising against the enemy. They spoke of the depressing effect of the armistice request on the men at the front, of the bad morale produced by visits of fighting men to their homes, of the need of getting fresh recruits. They admitted the impossibility of achieving a military victory over the enemy; the most they could promise was stiff resistance, to convince the enemy that intolerable terms would not be accepted. They recommended a break with Wilson, but only after receiving his reply to the latest note. Then a stirring appeal should be issued to the people by the Government to rise up in a last struggle. The Generals admitted that if Austria withdrew from the war, the situation would be much darker; but they doubted that their ally could commit so unworthy an act.[60]

Prince Max supplies some interesting details of the conference that are missing from the official protocol. At one point in the conference, General von Gallwitz "turned to Scheidemann and demanded the coöperation of the Social Democrats for national defense, since everything depended on stirring up new strength by getting the masses to exert themselves." Scheidemann realized, however, that this meant greatly prolonging the war; he saw no advantage to be gained by an appeal to the nation. It was fundamentally a matter of arousing factory workers who could not be aroused because they had already fought at the front and knew what continuing the war involved. The prospect looked hopeless to Scheidemann, particularly with the impending collapse of Austria. If it should be possible, he argued, to conclude peace on the basis of the negotiations with Wilson, even Army leaders should be satisfied. Gallwitz later blamed the Social Democrats for not being willing to rouse the nation to continued resistance against the enemy. The Chancellor agreed with him, convinced that "the Social Democrats held the key to the situation." Scheidemann, says the Chancellor, was so dominated by the fear that Bolshevism would spread among the workers of Germany that he could think of nothing else during the crisis. To end the war would be the best means of retaining his hold on the working classes. The Socialists abandoned national defense, writes the Chancellor; as evidence he quotes the words of *Vorwärts* on October 28: "Even without weapons the German people would be a significant factor in the peace conference. . . . Even without weapons we would not be without means of defense at the peace conference table." Whereas the Army had recovered from

60. Document 86, *Amtliche Urkunden.*

the defeatism that produced the armistice offer, concludes the Chancellor, the home front never recovered; it collapsed.[61]

There was nothing to cheer the Germans at the end of October. Confidential reports from abroad showed no rift in the clouds. On October 30 the Army Command transmitted to Berlin a report that had been received on the 25th from one of their agents in Berne. It referred to the conference of Allied Commanders-in-Chief at Senlis on that day and purported to give a few of the conditions that generals had agreed to impose on Germany. All conditions could not be given, said the report, because the conference had not yet concluded its discussions! In view of the special pains taken by Foch to keep the terms a secret, it is amazing that the German Military Intelligence Service should have come so close to the actual terms in those that it reported:

> 1. Absolute refusal to negotiate with Ludendorff or other members from [German Army] Headquarters. Willingness, on the other hand, to negotiate with a committee appointed by the Reichstag for this purpose.
> 2. Withdrawal of German troops to the frontiers.
> 3. Immediate occupation of this evacuated territory by the Allies.
> 4. All German war material to remain in the territory to be evacuated.
> 5. Evacuation of Alsace-Lorraine and occupation of the cities of Metz and Strassburg by the Allies.[62]

Reports from The Hague, based on information obtained from English Embassy circles, told of disagreement between Pershing and Wilson. Pershing was said to be in close touch with members of the Republican campaign committee and to be giving them propaganda in favor of continuing the war. He was also reported to have demanded "the occupation of fortresses on the Rhine as far as Wesel."[63]

Another report on October 30, from Amsterdam, brought further disquieting information. Serious complications were said to have arisen in the interallied armistice discussion. "Chauvinist tendencies in the United States, let loose largely by Republican election propaganda, have confronted the Associated Govern-

61. Max, *Erinnerungen,* pp. 522–524.

62. Document 93, *Amtliche Urkunden.* For comparison with the conference at Senlis, see *supra,* pp. 179–181.

63. Document 86c, *Amtliche Urkunden.*

ments with new decisions, particularly because a group of people in the British Government, men like Balfour, Churchill, Cave—not to mention Northcliffe and his satellites—are urging a consideration of the American knock-out policy on the Prime Minister, who has recently been following a middle course." According to the report, "the French Government believes that the occupation of Alsace-Lorraine, after occupied territories have been evacuated, would suffice to maintain the military supremacy of the Entente Armies." The British Admiralty was represented as demanding the surrender of the submarines and the occupation of Helgoland. "In regard to the question of the German throne," the report ended, "the position of the Entente Governments is not clear. The English and French Governments do not regard the question as very important. Wilson's attitude is not yet defined. It is indeed possible that the present chauvinist tendencies might force him to regard abdication by the Emperor and the Crown Prince as a *conditio sine qua non.*" [64]

64. Document 86e, *ibid.*

IX

Enlightening the Kaiser

OPPOSITION to the Kaiser had existed in Germany for a long time, mainly from parties of the Left. These critical views were not taken seriously by others until the impending collapse of Germany in 1918 made people ask questions about the responsibility of the Emperor for the ominous situation. Wilson's notes and speeches had focussed attention on William II, but his language was not explicit. While one group cited passages to show that Wilson was demanding abdication, supporters of the monarchy and of the Hohenzollern dynasty could cite others to indicate that the President wanted a limited monarchy and would be satisfied to have the Kaiser retained if only he were made a constitutional ruler.

As early as October 11 the sociologist Max Weber wrote that, although he was a convinced monarchist who favored constitutional monarchy, it was his firm conviction that the Kaiser should abdicate for the sake of the Empire and his own dynasty—and immediately, before any pressure was put upon him. The consideration that better peace conditions would result from his doing so was a matter of secondary importance to Weber. Should the Kaiser fail to withdraw, he believed, any appeal to the nation to make a last stand would result in the secession of Bavaria, where Catholic and dynastic particularism had traditionally opposed the Prussian and protestant king who became German Kaiser in 1871.[1]

The Kaiser knew that the demand for his abdication was growing, particularly in the press of the Left.[2] He felt that Wilson was also insisting on it. The question was being more or less publicly discussed by October 21, when the Emperor first received the members of Prince Max's parliamentary Government. His brief formal address seems to have been dictated in part by his desire to keep the throne by claiming credit for creating Germany's first parliamentary regime with his decree of September

1. Marianne Weber, *Max Weber, ein Lebensbild* (Tübingen, 1926), pp. 635–636; Max Weber, *Gesammelte Politische Schriften* (München, 1921), pp. 477–479.

2. For newspaper opinion on the question the best study is Adolf Stutzenberger, *Die Abdankung Kaiser Wilhelms II* (Berlin, 1937).

30. The ministers had been called by the people, he said, to establish a new order in Germany, for the German people were to be second to none "in political freedom." "With you, gentlemen," the Emperor concluded, "I know that I am of one mind in the sacred determination to guide the German Empire out of the need of this time into a quiet and peaceful development. I hope we shall succeed, in passionate love of country and in a feeling of great responsibility, to discover for the new Germany a way to a bright and happy future. We are determined to put all our strength into that task, prepared to follow the way of peace, but equally prepared, if our enemies would not have it otherwise, to fight to the very last breath and blow." [3]

The Cabinet got into warm debate over the publication of the speech. Nobody was really favorably impressed by it. "If only this speech had been made three months earlier!" exclaimed Haussmann. The Chancellor opposed publication on the ground that the Kaiser should have as little publicity as possible at a time when Wilson was apparently suggesting that he abdicate. The Kaiser insisted that it be made public: if the people knew that he stood at the head of the new Government, their talk and intrigue against him would cease. The Cabinet was not impressed by the argument and voted against immediate publication.[4]

Prince Max carefully avoided reference to the Kaiser in his discussion of constitutional reforms on October 22, psychologically unable by reason of kinship and background to criticize the person and position of the Emperor. The issue was brought forward in the debate when the Independent Socialists, through their spokesman Haase, made it clear that they opposed Germany's having a crowned ruler at a time when "crowns were rolling in the dust." The Majority Socialists were far more tactful. They criticized the Kaiser's arbitrary rule but refrained as a Government party from asking that he abdicate. The climax was reached on the 24th, after the arrival of Wilson's third note, when Noske hinted that the Kaiser's abdication would please millions of Germans; Haeften even got the impression that the Social Democrats would demand abdication the following day and spoke to the Chancellor about it. The latter still did nothing

3. Max, *Erinnerungen,* pp. 473–474; Niemann, *Revolution von Oben,* pp. 194–195; Scheidemann, *Memoiren,* II, 230–233.

4. Max, *Erinnerungen,* pp. 473–474; Scheidemann, *Der Zusammenbruch,* p. 189. The speech was published November 4. Stutzenberger, *Die Abdankung Kaiser Wilhelms II,* p. 67.

except to urge the speedy enactment of constitutional reforms, believing and hoping that Wilson would be satisfied with them.[5]

In an evening session October 24 the Cabinet discussed the fourth note to Wilson. A few minutes before the Secretaries of State assembled, Haussmann told Prince Max of his confident opinion that "the German people will not cast their Emperor aside at the behest of the enemy." In the Cabinet discussion Scheidemann expressed the view, according to Max, that it was possible to get around the problem of the Kaiser, that leaders of his party had instructed the Socialist press not to complicate peace negotiations by discussing the abdication.[6] Scheidemann gives a slightly different report. Not a single voice, he said, was raised to ask that the Kaiser remain; opinion favored abdication in the interests of a decent peace, but did not wish to go to the length of forcing it. Scheidemann says he argued in favor of getting the Kaiser to abdicate, but without success; in the very difficult situation in which Germany found herself, he could not make an issue of the matter at this time.[7] It had become his conviction ever since Wilson's note of October 23, he writes, that "the Kaiser *must* go." [8]

On October 25, according to the Chancellor, the press abandoned all its self-imposed restraint and began to discuss the question of the Kaiser with utter frankness and directness. The *Frankfurter Zeitung* demanded that the Kaiser abdicate and that the Crown Prince renounce the throne so that Wilson could have the democratic guarantees he wanted. Prince Max still clung to the hope that the German people would never make such demands. He says he could have mentioned the matter in the letter he wrote to the Kaiser demanding the dismissal of Ludendorff, but decided to say nothing.

It was on this day that the Chancellor received important documents claiming to interpret Wilson's mind on this difficult question. One of them arrived in the middle of the afternoon, sent from Switzerland by the Chancellor's cousin, Prince Hohenlohe-

5. The Chancellor's distaste for public discussion of the Kaiser may well have been the reason why the Reichstag was not allowed to discuss Wilson's note. *Supra*, p. 203.

6. Max, *Erinnerungen*, p. 498, and note.

7. Scheidemann, *Memoiren*, II, 240–241; Scheidemann, *Der Zusammenbruch*, p. 200.

8. Scheidemann, *Memoiren*, II, 262. Ballin of Hamburg wrote to a friend on October 27 that the Kaiser should abdicate in favor of his grandson because "he now stands . . . in the way of the destiny of seventy million people." Stubmann, *Ballin*, p. 277.

Langenburg, who, as head of the German mission, had been negotiating in Berne with delegates from the United States concerning prisoners of war. He wrote that "the conclusion of Wilson's note means only that the one way to anything like a tolerable peace is through the resignation of the Kaiser." Wilson was represented as knowing that Germany's form of government corresponded with the history and needs of the German people; but propaganda had assigned to the Kaiser an influence that the American President could not disregard. His abdication "would make it easier for Wilson to influence the Senate in favor of his peace plans, that body having recently influenced opinion in favor of a complete overthrow of Germany. At the same time such a move would strengthen peace sentiment in the other Entente countries. Thus the maintenance of the dynasty would be assured, which . . . would be endangered . . . if the belief could be created [by the enemy] that peace was wrecked because of the person of the Kaiser." Hohenlohe added that Germany's military position was known to be so weak that the Entente had confidence in their ultimate victory; Germany's collapse was only a matter of time. "An effort to prolong the final struggle would be looked upon only as new evidence that military influence was dominant and would strengthen the suspicion that no faith could be placed in the constitutional changes Germany was then making." [9]

The second message for Prince Max came at 6.10 P.M. from Treutler, the Prussian Minister at Munich, who said "that here in Bavaria Wilson's reply . . . is interpreted by those able to judge as being in its last section directed against the person of our Emperor. The Prime Minister and the Minister of War hold the opinion that the wording of the note allows no other interpretation; by its veiled language the opportunity is simply being offered to us of taking this painful step of our own free will. In any case the gentlemen mentioned hold the view that His Majesty should be candidly informed that the enemy will approve of no acceptable peace if the great sacrifice is not made. If His Majesty renounces his Imperial title he would be acting only in the spirit of his twenty-six years of labor for peace and thus crown his endeavors." [10]

Both messages were forwarded to the Kaiser without comment by the Chancellor.[11]

9. Max, *Erinnerungen,* pp. 501–502; document 78, *Amtliche Urkunden.*
10. Max, *Erinnerungen,* p. 502; document 77, *Amtliche Urkunden.*
11. Max, *Erinnerungen,* p. 503.

On the same day the Supreme Army Command received news indirectly from The Hague that "all Entente Governments have adhered to the principle of the United States to make no peace with the Kaiser and the Crown Prince." [12]

In his speech of the 22d Prince Max, as has already been said, avoided this grave issue; instead, he speeded the constitutional reforms through the Reichstag, where the three readings were completed in three days.[13] The speed, wrote Max, was "hard to reconcile with the constitution and impossible to reconcile with our dignity." A letter from Hindenburg calling attention to the risks involved in the proposed curtailment of the Kaiser's military powers could not hold the Chancellor back. Speed was all-important to stay the demand for the Kaiser's abdication. Later the Chancellor expressed regret that he did not recognize soon enough the necessity for the abdication, that he had not acted on the evening of October 24 after getting Haeften's warning.[14]

By October 27 the public was determined, according to the Chancellor, that the Kaiser must go, convinced that "if the Emperor abdicated, we shall get a good armistice." Official efforts to control the press were made in vain because the demand for abdication was coming from people who were beyond the influence of German newspaper opinion. On the 27th two emissaries from Prince Hohenlohe-Langenburg called on Prince Max with another message interpreting Wilson's note of the 23rd. Wilson was represented as opposing his own allies and people in his own country who wanted unconditional surrender. His opponents would never consent to negotiating an armistice or peace with the Kaiser, the Crown Prince, or Ludendorff; all three must go in order to strengthen Wilson's hand in favor of a negotiated agreement rather than capitulation. If Germany failed to meet these conditions Wilson would break off negotiations and Germany would find it impossible to renew them. The Entente knew that an appeal to the German people to resist to the end could accomplish nothing, that Germany was too weak to do much. If the war

12. Document 76c, *Amtliche Urkunden.*

13. As finally passed on October 26, the reforms amended six articles of the constitution. The changes gave the Reichstag concurrent power with the Bundesrat in declaring war and in making treaties; they made the Chancellor dependent on the support of the Reichstag; they held the Chancellor responsible for the political acts of the Kaiser; they gave the Chancellor greater control over the appointment, promotion, and retirement of officers and officials in the Army and Navy. See *Anlage* 1984, *Reichstagsverhandlungen, Anlagen zu den stenographischen Berichten,* Vol. 325, p. 3142.

14. Max, *Erinnerungen,* pp. 510–511.

continued, Entente propaganda would manage to convince the discontented German people that the struggle was concerned only with the person of the Kaiser, who would be represented as the "greatest obstacle to the conclusion of peace." Wilson was said to be appealing to the Germans to make his fight for a just peace easier. The two emissaries pleaded with Prince Max to make his decisions soon lest within a few days, or a few hours, Germany be confronted with Foch's armistice terms.[15]

The Chancellor was greatly disturbed by this message from Hohenlohe. He had informed the Kaiser of the significance of Wilson's note, although he had not advised him regarding abdication. Was it now too late to do so in order to influence the armistice terms? On the other hand reports from Holland said that Wilson was not demanding abdication—he would be satisfied with the abolition of "Kaiserism" or the arbitrary rule symbolized by the Emperor. In his perplexity Prince Max decided to get in touch with a young American diplomat who had been in Germany before the war and was said to have been much distressed when Germany and the United States went to war. This was Lithgow Osborne, Second Secretary of the American Legation in Copenhagen. On the morning of October 28 the Chancellor sent one of his most intimate advisers, Kurt Hahn, to discuss matters with Osborne. He decided not to see the Kaiser until Hahn's expected return on the evening of the 29th.[16]

15. *Ibid.,* pp. 512–516. These views were repeated in a despatch from von Romberg, the German Minister in Berne, sent late on October 28 and received at the Foreign Office early on the 29th. This telegram said that "several members of the Federal Council . . . had stated that they no longer saw any possibility of avoiding the abdication of the Kaiser. . . . The dynasty might yet be saved and the hopeless final struggle avoided if we now made the sacrifice ourselves of our own free will. It is their opinion that, if His Majesty the Emperor sacrifices himself and in a proclamation commits his young grandson to the loyalty of his people and of the Army, particularly of Field Marshal Hindenburg, he would thus arouse not only strong sympathy abroad but would also stifle the spirit of revolution in Germany." Document 94, *Amtliche Urkunden.*

16. Max, *Erinnerungen,* p. 517. According to the report sent to Lansing about this meeting, Hahn described what had happened in Germany and what Prince Max's fears were. He said that the reforms made in the Government were sincere but that "the declaration of a republic merely to impress the Entente . . . would be insincere . . . [and] would not represent the demands of the people now." He told Osborne that the proposed constitutional changes would take the Army command away from the Emperor, would subordinate the military to the civilian authorities, would make the Chancellor responsible to the Reichstag, and require that the Chancellor counter-sign papers emanating from the Emperor. To prove to the Americans that Max was sincere in his opposition to the militarists Hahn pointed out that he had effected the dismissal of Ludendorff by threatening to resign if Ludendorff remained. Max's hold on the German people,

During the afternoon of October 28 the Chancellor had a talk with General von Chelius, who had just arrived from Brussels and insisted on making a special report. The General said he was perturbed over information coming to him from a trusted American who had foretold exactly the contents of each of Wilson's notes. This American stated positively that "without the abdication of the Kaiser the war will continue or Germany will get a terrible armistice and likewise a frightful peace." It was difficult for von Chelius, who had for many years been a special aide-de-camp to the Kaiser, to report such things. "I begged the General," writes Prince Max, "to go immediately to Hausminister Count August Eulenburg and through his mediation and, if possible, with his assistance, to report his views to His Majesty. It seemed important to me that men whom the Kaiser regarded as his personal friends and in whom he saw the pillars of his throne should first show him the honorable solution." [17]

The Chancellor also had an interview with the Court Chaplain, von Dryander, who for decades had been closely associated with the Emperor. Prince Max desired to have the Chaplain suggest abdication, provided it was his belief that the interests of the monarchy demanded this sacrifice. The Chaplain said he was not the proper person for the task, but asked for time to think the matter over more thoroughly. Later in the day he wrote that he could not undertake the mission "not only because such action was contrary to the obligations of my position but also because I was firmly convinced that the abdication of the Kaiser (and that was the issue) would destroy the Army's fighting resistance and at the same time loosen the bond uniting our people at home," a bond that the German people needed more than ever now that they faced the violence of their enemies.[18]

With the others who were to advise the Kaiser to abdicate the Chancellor had no better success. Late in the evening of October 28 he received a candid letter from Count August Eulenburg, Minister of the Royal Household, returning the letter from

he said, depended on their belief in the sincerity of President Wilson. If degrading armistice terms should be imposed, Wilson's peace program would be discredited, Prince Max would be discredited, and the German people would be permanently embittered. The Americans were virtually asked to help the Germans to maintain and to extend the freedom they had newly won so that German militarism would remain discredited. Grant-Smith to Lansing, October 29, 1918, *Foreign Relations, 1918,* Supplement I, I, 416–418.

17. Max, *Erinnerungen,* p. 518.

18. *Ibid.,* pp. 519, 526; D. Ernst von Dryander, *Erinnerungen aus Meinem Leben* (Bielefeld and Leipzig, 1922), pp. 316–317.

Hohenlohe-Langenburg that General von Chelius had asked him to transmit to the Kaiser. He suggested that the Chancellor send it "privately" to the Kaiser along with the news that Chelius had brought from Brussels. "If Your Grand-Ducal Highness should think it necessary to influence His Majesty in the sense of these papers, documentary support of that nature is absolutely essential; without it one would always get the same answer, that a soldier should not leave his post at the moment of danger—even if the sacrifice demanded is made 'voluntarily'—no guarantee is offered that the easy peace sought would be attained." Eulenburg "did not believe that efforts to get an abdication would be successful unless the price the Entente is prepared to pay for it appears more certain and definite."

The Chancellor eagerly awaited news from von Chelius himself. The General made his report on the 29th. "He began," writes Prince Max, "with the statement that under no circumstances should the Kaiser abdicate, for that meant the dissolution of the Army and of the Empire. I asked him to give me an explanation of this change in his views, whereupon he replied that yesterday he had been under my influence and, thus influenced, has spoken differently. To that bewildering explanation there was nothing for me to do except to ask whether he or I had come from Brussels to Berlin to demand the abdication of the Kaiser as Germany's only means of salvation and to support this demand with documents brought along for the purpose." [19]

Thus the first efforts of the Chancellor to have others "enlighten" the Kaiser ended in failure; they only made the Emperor more determined to resist. As a matter of fact he acted on October 28 as though he had never heard of intimations that he should step down from the throne. Late that day the Chancellor received the text of a decree under which the Kaiser wished the newly accepted constitutional amendments published. Max said it could be regarded as his "answer to the request that he abdicate . . . an answer that said: 'I intend to remain at my post and to cooperate loyally with the Government.' " The Emperor professed to see in the constitutional reforms "a *new* order in which fundamental rights are transferred from the person of the Kaiser to the *people*." "Thus," the proclamation went on, "a period comes to an end which will be held in honor in the eyes of all future generations . . . [a period which] rendered possible for our people that mighty development which has made an indelible impression

19. Max, *Erinnerungen*, pp. 526–527.

in the wonderful achievements of this war. . . . At the end of this time the German people has the right to claim that no right shall be denied it that ensures a free and happy future. To this conviction the proposals of the Federal Governments, accepted and enlarged by the Reichstag, owe their origin. With my august confederates I give my assent to these resolutions of the people's representatives, in the firm determination to coöperate as best I can in their *full execution*, convinced that I am thereby serving the welfare of the German people. The Kaiser is now the servant of the people. May the new order thus set free all the forces for good which our nation needs in order to face the difficult tests required of the Empire and to win for itself a bright future as it firmly steps out of the darkness of the present." [20]

The Chancellor believed this document to be a last effort on the part of the Kaiser to win popular support for his cause. Debate arose within the Government over whether the proclamation should be made public. The majority in the Cabinet felt that publication at this particular time was undesirable; it was better for the Kaiser to remain in the background and not to draw attention to himself.[21]

Prince Max decided on October 29 that he himself must see the Kaiser. While he was waiting, however, for Hahn to return with information from Copenhagen, at about 5 P.M. Grünau, who attended the Kaiser as Representative of the Foreign Office, suddenly appeared with the report that "His Majesty is going to Spa today." Surprised, the Chancellor asked if it was a bad joke. Grünau replied that he had learned of the trip half an hour earlier. Major Niemann had telephoned and said that Grünau was to accompany him. Grünau had asked whether the Chancellor knew of the trip and had approved it; he warned that the Kaiser's sudden departure would alarm the public and would be taken to mean he was placing himself under the Army's protection. Major Niemann had replied that Hindenburg wanted the Kaiser to come, and that he would be back in Potsdam in four or five days.[22]

The Chancellor now tried to block this "flight to Varennes." He sent his Foreign Secretary, Dr. Solf, to Count Eulenburg and to von Delbrück, Chief of the Kaiser's Civil Cabinet, for this purpose. He telephoned to the Ministry of War; Scheüch knew nothing of the Kaiser's proposed trip, but he got the news con-

20. *Ibid.*, p. 525.
21. *Ibid.*, p. 526. Niemann, *Revolution von Oben*, pp. 196–197.
22. Max, *Erinnerungen*, p. 527.

firmed by von Marschall, who happened at the moment to be in the Ministry. Scheüch tried to calm the Chancellor by saying that no difficulties could arise if the Kaiser were absent only three days. The Chancellor said he believed the Kaiser would never come back; Scheüch remained confident he would return right away.[23]

After that, Prince Max writes, "I got into telephone connection with His Majesty and told him how taken aback I was at this new decision and particularly at its being formed so suddenly and without my knowledge. The Kaiser answered that speedy decisions were made in time of war, that the Supreme Army Command desired his presence at the front, that the Kaiserin had likewise been surprised. I begged him urgently to postpone the journey—at this moment it would make the worst possible impression. In the next few days questions of the greatest importance had to be settled, questions that we could not possibly settle over the telephone. The Kaiser said: 'You removed Ludendorff, now I have to install Groener.' My answer was that the Field Marshal could surely do that by himself; I begged to have a personal audience. The Kaiser then mentioned his doctors who feared the danger of infection from influenza—'besides, you must take care of yourself.' In spite of all that, I begged for permission to see him. His Majesty declined. His voice contained no tone of personal criticism. I pressed him once again: 'We are now approaching our most difficult times, when Your Majesty cannot be absent.' The Kaiser parried: 'If you do what I have advised you to do, everything can still turn out well.' This remark was a reference to a note that His Majesty had addressed to Solf, in which he advised a change of front in our foreign policy, namely, to base our peace action on England."

"During our talk over the telephone I was several times about to hand in my resignation. I decided against it because it was not yet the proper time. I did not wish to throw away the last means I had to bring pressure."[24]

In the evening the Chancellor received a telegram from the Kaiser, who had not yet left Potsdam. It read:

> Since important conversations are taking place tomorrow at Spa, in which the question of Ludendorff's successor is also going to be discussed, I am going there. [I am also going] to thank my brave

23. *Ibid.,* pp. 527–528.
24. *Ibid.,* p. 528.

troops in the name of the Fatherland for their superhuman achievements, since my duty directs me to them in a difficult time. Ludendorff has had to go to make the situation easier for you; his departure is, from the military point of view, a great loss for the Army. It is my duty to replace him and it is essential to initiate the man who replaces him; that is why I am leaving this evening. It was quiet on the whole front today. You have, no doubt, received my proposals regarding England.[25]

The Chancellor, pondering over the Kaiser's resolution to go to Spa, at first believed that the Supreme Army Command was behind the move because it wished to keep the Kaiser out of reach of the Chancellor's advice. But the Army Command turned out to be just as surprised to receive the Kaiser as others were to see him leave Berlin. It had been rumored that the Minister of War had desired the Kaiser's removal from the capital because he no longer could assure him of protection, but the report proved false. Max's only explanation—which he arrived at much later—was that the plan was carefully prepared and quickly executed by a group that was determined to keep the Kaiser out of Berlin. "My efforts to persuade Dryander, Count Eulenburg, and von Chelius to penetrate the mists that surrounded the Kaiser had failed; but they certainly had the effect of making known to the immediate entourage of the Emperor where I stood in the question of abdication. These gentlemen must have known that it was a matter of hours only or days at the most before the decisive step would be taken by the Kaiser." [26]

The Kaiser departed for Spa in the evening. At about the same time Prince Max received a letter from Scheidemann asking that he recommend voluntary abdication to the Kaiser without communicating anything to the press.[27] "Thus on the same day," writes Prince Max, "my policy was thwarted by the Kaiser and by my Social Democratic colleagues." On the morning of October 30 the Chancellor persuaded Scheidemann after some argument to withdraw the letter. Its withdrawal, he knew, was only a formality; sooner or later the Social Democrats would officially demand the Kaiser's abdication.[28]

25. *Ibid.*, p. 529.
26. *Ibid.*, pp. 529–530.
27. In *Der Zusammenbruch,* pp. 201–203, Scheidemann incorrectly dated the letter October 20; he corrected the date in *Memoiren,* II, 253–255.
28. Max, *Erinnerungen,* pp. 531–532.

In the morning Hahn made his impatiently awaited report. He had talked with two American diplomats and with the German Minister to Denmark, Brockdorff-Rantzau. The latter's opinion affected Prince Max deeply; Brockdorff-Rantzau reasoned that the German people would not be in a position to defend themselves against dishonorable armistice conditions if the Kaiser postponed his abdication. From the two American diplomats "X" and "Y," it was learned that "Wilson is still sticking to his peace of justice and is fighting an up-hill battle against the Entente chauvinists, who are at present in control in France and in England." Chauvinism was said to be strong also in the United States; "Foch is today just as great a man in America as is Wilson." It was possible that Wilson had become personally convinced of Germany's democratization but it was apparent that his conviction could not affect armistice terms; it would be different with the peace terms. It would be possible for Wilson to make headway against the extremists in the United States if he could win the support of the middle groups, who wished to have better evidence than had yet been given of Germany's democratization. "This unequivocal evidence would be the abdication of the Kaiser and the renunciation by the Crown Prince." It was pointed out that "for hundreds of thousands of people everything that is hateful and dangerous in Germany is incarnate in the personalities of the Kaiser and of the Crown Prince." If Wilson failed to persuade his allies to accept his point of view after Germany had become a democratic state, the war would be continued by Lloyd George and Clemenceau at great risk. " 'X' called the offer of an armistice a mistake because it gave encouragement to hostile chauvinists." Twice he had advised "that the armistice terms should be answered by the counterquestion whether the Allies have taken their position on the basis of Wilson's conditions for peace." The interview had closed with the appeal, "For God's sake, do something to make Wilson strong against the Entente militarists, who are in power in France and in England." American chauvinism would be an easy problem to handle after the abdication of the Kaiser and the Crown Prince.[29]

The Chancellor now felt that he had made a grave mistake in not compelling the Kaiser, at no matter what cost, to remain in Berlin. Like the members of the Cabinet he hoped that it was still possible to bring about a "voluntary" abdication. In an effort

29. *Ibid.*, pp. 532–534.

to persuade the Kaiser to return to Berlin he sent the following telegram on Wednesday the 30th:

The public is disturbed by rumors of a military blow aimed at the popular government.

Your Majesty's journey to Headquarters will strengthen these reports, I fear, as soon as it becomes known, and will create the impression of a refusal to support the policy of the new government. This impression cannot be erased by public statements.

Furthermore, the enemy's armistice terms, which we expect at any hour, as well as the difficult questions connected with the political changes at home require the presence of the monarch for direct and immediate discussion.

Under these circumstances with Your Majesty absent, I see no possibility of being able to finish the task of making peace at home and abroad, a task assigned to me when I was appointed Chancellor.

I therefore most humbly beg Your Majesty to return as soon as possible. An absence extending beyond Thursday could not, in my opinion, be justified; at any hour we may be confronted with decisions on which the fate of Germany depends, decisions that can be made only through the coöperation of Crown, Imperial Chancellor, and the Government. In this situation I cannot possibly leave Berlin myself.[30]

The reply came immediately, through von Delbrück. The Emperor informed the Chancellor that he had to go to Army Headquarters because of questions connected with the peace and armistice, that he had no intention of remaining any longer than necessary. Reports of an intended military *coup* against the new Government were thoroughly ridiculous. His Majesty had repeatedly declared his intention of accepting the changes that had been made in the constitution and "statements in this sense have not been published despite his own expressed wishes and despite the opinion of parliamentary members of the so-called War Cabinet." The Kaiser repeated his request for publication and sent a new statement to the Chancellor for the purpose.[31]

The Chancellor sensed from this letter that the Kaiser felt deeply hurt. But he too felt hurt; there was no longer any doubt that the Kaiser saw in Prince Max one who opposed him, despite many years of friendship and service.

30. *Ibid.*, pp. 534–535.
31. *Ibid.*, p. 535. *Supra*, pp. 221–222, 228–229.

Certain circles in Switzerland felt no doubt as to what Wilson desired. Early in the morning of October 31 there came another telegram from the German Minister at Berne, saying that representatives of the Swiss Government "do not understand how it is still possible for any doubt to exist as to the meaning of Wilson's note." The dismissal of Ludendorff was said to have made a bad impression on Americans in Berne; they took it to mean that the Kaiser would let his best men go to save himself. Even Hindenburg's dismissal was a possibility. The Kaiser was believed to be opposed to the democratization of Germany and to be doing all he could "to rescue the old system" of government. For the present, the report went on, it is futile to try to make America understand that the changes in the German constitution have at last overthrown the old regime, which, in the eyes of Americans, is embodied in the person of the Kaiser; only his elimination would carry conviction. It urged the greatest possible speed in getting rid of the Kaiser, and warned "that Wilson could not have been clearer [in expressing his demand for the Kaiser's abdication] without being tactless." It also pointed out that the German press was right in believing that Wilson sought the Kaiser's removal.[32]

What seemed so clear to people in Switzerland and to parts of the German press was not so plain to members of the Government; they were honestly perplexed. The fact was that "in none of the communications received up to now from President Wilson is the renunciation of the throne by the Kaiser expressly demanded." Because of that fact Solf drafted a memorandum containing those passages in Wilson's notes and speeches that bore on the question. "Up to the present," the memorandum stated, "it has been impossible to determine clearly whether in these phrases the President was striking at the system and its constitutional provisions or whether he had particular personalities in view." Efforts to establish definite conclusions failed. It was reported in neutral countries that Wilson was demanding the Kaiser's abdication chiefly because he wanted to win the Congressional elections on November 5 in favor of his kind of peace by defeating the Republicans, who were demanding the unconditional surrender of Germany. Since the German Emperor is in American eyes the personification of autocracy and militarism, his "abdication, as an undeniable achievement of Wilson's policy, would strengthen his position and presumably enable him to

32. Document 95, *Amtliche Urkunden.*

carry out his program despite all opposition. Without such a reinforcement of his position it is to be feared that Wilson must yield to pressure and that severe peace terms of the sort desired by the Entente will be imposed on Germany."[33]

Although less was said in public about the Kaiser's journey to Spa than the Chancellor had feared, there was nonetheless a feeling that it was motivated by the desire not to surrender his throne. Agitation for his abdication grew. The press of the Left demanded it with increasing violence. As this pressure increased hour by hour, it became a matter of principle with the Kaiser to resist. How long it would be before he was forced to yield depended upon the Social Democrats. The Chancellor wondered anxiously when they would bring the issue into the open. He made up his mind to commit Scheidemann to an agreement not to exert pressure upon him. He opened the session of the Cabinet on October 31, the first meeting he had been able to attend since his illness, with a discussion of the abdication. It was his conviction "that an abdication by His Majesty the Kaiser must be a voluntary one" and he demanded that his own freedom of action be unimpaired, that no pressure be put upon him.

Scheidemann spoke at some length. While he had no desire to apply pressure on the Emperor, he felt the latter should be advised. The demand for the abdication, he asserted, did not originate with the working classes but among the bourgeoisie and the peasants of southern Germany, particularly in Bavaria, where separatism from the Empire and from Prussia was very strong. Although he said he did not favor putting pressure on the Kaiser, Scheidemann gave the Chancellor the impression that he would resign from the Cabinet if the Kaiser did not abdicate.[34]

In the general debate that followed, the Cabinet found itself hopelessly divided over the issue. Nor was it capable of reaching any agreement over the kind of Government that should follow the Kaiser's abdication. The Imperial Constitution contained no provision for a regency whereas the Prussian did. These legal complications led to long and inconclusive debate which ended only when a message came asking for a postponement of the decision until the arrival of important news by courier from Army Headquarters.[35]

In this impasse Prince Max decided to hold a secret conference

33. Document 96, *ibid.*
34. Max, *Erinnerungen,* pp. 536–540.
35. *Ibid.,* pp. 543–544.

in the afternoon with a selected group of men—Vice-Chancellor von Payer, Foreign Office Counselor Simons, Minister of War Scheüch, Prussian Minister of the Interior Drews, Undersecretary of State and Head of the Chancellery Wahnschaffe, Secretary of State Friedberg, who was also Vice-President of the Prussian State Ministry—men "who had not been raised to eminence by the panic of the last days in September, but had been summoned after unhampered study by the Kaiser." The Chancellor put special faith in the opinion of Drews, a man "who embodied the best tradition of Prussian officialdom." Prince Max explained what he wanted them to discuss: Would the people fight against hard armistice terms under a Kaiser whom they regarded as responsible for those harsh terms? Would not conditions be made easier if the Kaiser should abdicate?[36]

Drews spoke, writes Prince Max, "like a man acting under the compulsion of conscience; often his voice almost failed him." He said it was clear that the movement for the Kaiser's abdication was spreading daily among the people, not only among the working classes but also among the bourgeoisie. He was sure that the Government would soon be confronted with a demand from the Social Democrats that the Kaiser and the Crown Prince abdicate. Neither the Social Democrats nor the Independent Socialists would support a war against unacceptable armistice conditions. Everywhere, Drews said, even in heavy industry and high finance, the conviction was spreading that "the person of the Kaiser is the obstacle to peace." Explaining that the subject was the hardest one possible for him to talk on, Drews gave the opinion "that with the person of the Kaiser at the head a summons to a final struggle would not get the necessary general support among the people."

Von Payer pointed out how opposed people in south Germany were to the Kaiser. Solf thought that the abdication should come in time to enable Wilson to win a victory in the Congressional elections of November 5. Others supported Scheüch, who opposed abdication, stressing particularly the harmful effect on the Army.[37]

Summing up the sense of the meeting, Prince Max noted that opinions differed here as well as in the Cabinet as a whole. It was his own conviction "that an abdication of His Majesty is possible only if it takes place voluntarily. . . . My chief concern," he

36. *Ibid.*, pp. 544–545.
37. *Ibid.*, pp. 545–547.

explained, "is not to produce at home the situation where the people demand abdication. Such a situation would lead to civil war, because there are millions in the country who hold closely to His Majesty." The Chancellor could promise only to consider the views his colleagues had expressed.[38]

After the meeting Drews was on the verge of collapse. Nevertheless, Prince Max asked him "to go to Army Headquarters in the evening as Minister of the Interior to inform his King on the state of mind in the country." He also asked Count Lerchenfeld, the Bavarian representative in the Bundesrat, to accompany Drews, but the Bavarian could not get permission from his Government and Drews had to go alone.

Having come to feel that he could not himself approach the Kaiser about abdication, since the Emperor had lost faith in him, Prince Max sought feverishly to find somebody who could carry out the mission for him. He had even asked August William, the fourth son of the Emperor, to make it clear to his father that he should abdicate before pressure came from Parliament. The Prince naturally refused to do so. On October 30 Prince Max had appealed to the Grand Duke of Hesse, who also was unwilling. At last the Chancellor turned to Prince Friedrich Karl of Hesse, who was the Kaiser's brother-in-law and had close connections with the Army. The Prince asked to be given time to consider the matter. On the morning of November 1 he consented to undertake the delicate mission to Spa and it was arranged that he should leave in the evening, accompanied by Simons. The Chancellor refused to be dissuaded from his purpose by a warning from Army Headquarters that the Army would not tolerate the Kaiser's abdication. He said he found himself in the dilemma of having to choose between the Army that would not fight if the Kaiser went and the people who would not fight if the Kaiser remained. He believed that the only way out of this dilemma was for the Kaiser as he abdicated to issue an appeal to the soldiers and workers to make a last effort in behalf of the country. At the same time he could tell the nation that he was renouncing the throne for the sake of peace and could urge them to continue the struggle if his sacrifice proved futile and a dishonorable armistice were proposed. Much time that day was spent in preparing documents for Prince Friedrich Karl to submit for the Kaiser's signature.[39]

38. *Ibid.,* pp. 549–550.
39. *Ibid.,* pp. 544, 551–552.

At 11 A.M. on November 1 the Chancellor met with the leading members of the Bundesrat at the Bavarian Embassy. He told them about the position of the Kaiser, and the possibility that Scheidemann might at any time demand his abdication. He asked the delegates to consult the princes they represented about their attitude in case Prince Max himself should have to see the Kaiser and present a demand for abdication. They were to report to him by telegram. At the end of the session the Bavarian Minister told Prince Max in confidence that the King of Bavaria had already made known his agreement with the proposed policy. Prince Max came away from the meeting feeling that the German princes in general would support him, a feeling that was to have its confirmation in the next few days.[40]

But all the Chancellor's hopes were set on the success of the mission of Prince Friedrich Karl of Hesse. In the afternoon the documents which the Prince was to lay before the Kaiser for signature were at last prepared. One was an appeal to the people of Prussia, another an appeal to the German Army. In the former the Kaiser was to state that he was giving up the Prussian Crown as well as the Imperial Crown because the enemies' hatred of him might result in harsh conditions of armistice and peace. The appeal to the German Army stated that if Germany received acceptable and honorable terms from the enemy, credit should go to the heroism of the soldiers. If, however, the terms should prove unacceptable, the Kaiser urged the soldiers to defend the homeland with all their strength, assuring them that the home front would give them full support. The third document was a memorandum from the Government to the Kaiser explaining that the armistice terms would be so harsh that people would blame him for them and demand his abdication, and that the demand would become stronger when people came to believe there was a choice between the Kaiser and a tolerable peace. Immediate abdication might so strengthen the morale of the nation that Germany would be able to reject unacceptable conditions and continue the fight with a united front. Prince Friedrich Karl was to decide for himself whether to make use of this memorandum.[41]

Toward evening the Prince arrived, not to set out on his difficult mission as Prince Max desired, but to inform the Chancellor that he had changed his mind during the day because he feared the harmful effect of abdication on the Army. The Chancellor

40. *Ibid.*, pp. 552–556.
41. *Ibid.*, pp. 556–559.

summoned Simons, who was to accompany the Prince and had assisted in the preparation of the documents, and told him the news. Simons exploded in anger. The Prince said he could not convince the Kaiser since he was not convinced himself of the need for abdication. Simons thereupon canceled the arrangements for the special train that was to have taken them to Spa.

The Chancellor was in despair. Under the strain of anxiety and overwork his health broke down again. A doctor gave him a drug to assure him of a good rest; but it had an unexpectedly violent effect on his weakened constitution and he fell into a deep sleep that lasted thirty-six hours.[42]

On November 1 Drews arrived at Spa, where he delivered his message to the Emperor. In his memoirs the Kaiser makes this reference to the meeting: "Drews . . . suggested to me that I myself should decide to abdicate in order that it might not appear that the Government had exerted pressure upon me." [43]

After referring to the fateful consequences sure to follow his abdication, the Kaiser asked Drews how it was possible for him to reconcile his advocacy of abdication with his oath as a Prussian official. The Minister was embarrassed by the question, but replied that he came under orders—somebody had to tell the Kaiser. The Emperor then said that as a descendant of Frederick the Great he could not abdicate. He added that the Army would then dissolve, and he summoned Hindenburg to support the argument. The Field Marshal asserted that nothing could hold the Army together after abdication, that the men would return home as a mob of plunderers. General Groener also stated his opposition, and allowed himself some bitter criticism of the Government for its failure to restrain agitation in the public press. Drews became angry; he turned on Hindenburg and the Kaiser and burst out, "Who asked for this Government?—You! Who telegraphed and telephoned incessantly [to get an immediate armistice]?—You!" Even Hindenburg became heated for a moment, but he soon calmed down. Drews then asked to be permitted to resign. "No,"

42. *Ibid.,* pp. 559–560. While Prince Max was unconscious, Colonel Haeften and von Payer prepared a minor coup d'état in the form of a bulletin for the press. The fact of the Chancellor's illness was to be made public and it was stated that von Payer, Vice-Chancellor, would be acting Chancellor during this illness. An aide of the Chancellor prevented the publication of this document. When Haeften suggested to Prince Max on Sunday, November 3, that he could resign by reason of the Kaiser's failure to abdicate, Max refused to do anything of the sort; it was impossible for him to place the responsibility of government on others in such a crisis. *Ibid.,* p. 561.

43. William II, *My Memoirs,* pp. 274–275.

said the Kaiser sharply, "nothing of the sort. We have been only explaining things to one another. Give my opinion to the gentlemen in Berlin."

When the painful interview was over, the Kaiser went outside, where he told Major Niemann what had taken place, how General Groener had told Drews that the greatest danger for Germany was not the superior might of the enemy but internal collapse and the spirit of rebellion on the home front. "That it was actually a south German general," the Kaiser went on, "who stood up for the German Emperor and the King of Prussia, that did my heart good." [44]

On Saturday, November 2, Drews made his report to Payer and Wahnschaffe on the failure of his mission; the Chancellor of course was not there because of his illness. Drews told them that the Kaiser would not abdicate and that the Emperor's sons had promised their father not to assume a regency. Before letting Drews go the two Secretaries summoned Scheidemann and got him to promise that the Social Democrats would refrain from demanding abdication until after the armistice was in effect. They discussed how to keep the newspapers from making the crisis more acute. On November 1 the press had commented freely on the abdication, revealing important information: that the Government had considered the question several times; that the Emperor's departure for Spa had made it difficult to confer with him on the matter; that Scheidemann had written to the Chancellor demanding abdication. And the Socialist *Vorwärts* wondered when Scheidemann's letter would be answered. Prince Max had convinced himself that everything depended upon Scheidemann, who, he said, was as much influenced by the masses as they were by him. The workers were causing more and more trouble—aroused by the Government's failure to reply to Scheidemann's letter and by the failure to bring about peace—and were reported ready for revolutionary uprisings for which they had already stolen weapons. When Scheidemann was asked why trade-union leaders did nothing to quiet them, he replied that efforts to calm them would be futile so long as the Kaiser refused to abdicate.[45]

44. Max, *Erinnerungen,* pp. 561–562; Nowak, *Les Dessous de la Révolution,* pp. 82–85; Niemann, *Kaiser und Revolution,* p. 123. The Kaiser might have had a different opinion of Groener if he had known that immediately after the interview Groener told others that he thought the Kaiser should go to the front and seek death in battle. Stutzenberger, *Die Abdankung Kaiser Wilhelms II,* p. 152.

45. Max, *Erinnerungen,* pp. 562–563.

When Prince Max woke from his long sleep on the evening of November 3, it was to learn of events that would have staggered a Rip Van Winkle. Germany's position was weakening under blow after blow. Turkey had surrendered on terms that enabled the Entente Powers to make free use of the Bosporus and the Dardanelles, to supervise transportation and communications, to occupy all strategic points in the country. On the afternoon of November 3[46] Austria had also accepted an armistice, and the enemy could now advance on Germany by way of Austrian territory. Reports stated that Bolshevism was spreading rapidly into Europe from Russia; moderate Socialists appealed to German workers not to succumb to the propaganda and urged measures to control the propagandist activity of the Russian Embassy in Berlin. There were reports of unrest in the German Navy, but of a character so vague as to make it impossible to determine their significance. There were reports that Bavaria might conclude a separate peace with the enemy.[47] On the 2d the Prussian representative in Munich had telegraphed that Independent Socialists in Bavaria were going to demand the abdication of the Kaiser.[48] Because it was known that armistice conditions would soon be presented by the enemy, the War Cabinet had discussed the matter on November 2 and agreed on the principle that a representative of the civil Government should be present when terms were offered so that the military could not use the harsh conditions as a reason for breaking off negotiations. The civilian was to ask questions about points that could not be clarified immediately so that the negotiations would have to go on.[49]

These crowding developments convinced Prince Max that he would have to see the Kaiser himself. "But I saw no way," he writes, "to compel the Kaiser to return home. On October 29 my resignation could perhaps have changed the Emperor's mind; today I had the definite feeling that it would be accepted. And what then? Not until later did I learn that Scheidemann had been sounded at this time on behalf of the Chief of the Civil Cabinet as to whether the Kaiser could be retained if, he, Scheidemann, were to take over the chancellorship.[50]

Nevertheless the Chancellor made one more attempt to per-

46. Prince Max erroneously gives the date as November 2.
47. *Ibid.*, pp. 563–570.
48. Document 97, *Amtliche Urkunden.*
49. Document 96b, *ibid.*
50. Max, *Erinnerungen,* p. 570.

suade the Kaiser to return to Berlin. He had Delbrück and Solf send him a communication on the 3d saying "that the arrival of armistice conditions was expected any day and that in the opinion of the Cabinet negotiations regarding an armistice could not be conducted without the presence of Your Majesty." It was even suggested that a governmental crisis might arise out of the armistice conditions, which could not be resolved without the Emperor's aid.[51]

The Chancellor writes that he was "obliged to conclude that the situation was more hopeless than on the evening when the Prince of Hesse refused to take his journey." He was disposed to put the blame for his failure to convince the Kaiser on Army Headquarters. The latter had not only defeated him at Spa—they had even won supporters among people close to him.[52]

A report from Berne, which arrived in the early morning hours of November 4, could have been of no comfort to the harassed Chancellor. Several confidential agents, independently of one another, said that "Wilson's decisive influence was considerably endangered and that because of his lack of success in the matter of abdication he would be forced to the second alternative mentioned, namely, unconditional surrender." The Entente Powers were reported to be "harmfully affected" by the failure of the Bavarian Federal Council to achieve anything by demanding the Kaiser's abdication and by the belief held in prominent circles in Bavaria that the Kaiser was planning to overthrow the new German Government. Separatist tendencies in Bavaria were said to be taken seriously by the Entente.[53]

On November 4 Prince Max telegraphed General Groener—who had done so much to wreck Drews's mission—to come to Berlin as quickly as possible. He wanted a report on the military situation; but above all he wanted to inform the Quartermaster General about the internal situation, which was now becoming serious. The General, who in times past had enjoyed the confidence of the trade-unions, now seemed to be out of touch with the domestic situation. The Chancellor reasoned that the General would realize that the military front could not solve its problems if the home front broke down; he believed it possible to convince Groener that the home front would crash if the Kaiser failed to

51. *Ibid.*, p. 570 and note.
52. *Ibid.*, p. 563.
53. Document 98, *Amtliche Urkunden.*

abdicate and the Social Democrats consequently left the Government; and he hoped that Groener, thus divested of the "illusions of Army Headquarters," would acquaint the Kaiser with the situation as it actually was.[54]

Still shying away from the unpleasant task, Max was trying to get others to "enlighten" the Emperor.

54. Max, *Erinnerungen,* pp. 570–571.

X

Germany in Revolution

ON Sunday evening, November 3, Prince Max received vague reports telling of the refusal of a few sailors on some ships at Wilhelmshafen to obey orders. The information was so fragmentary that the Chancellor could not tell whether it was a case of Bolshevist agitation or of minor local discontent. He was soon to learn, however, that it was the first sign of the revolution that was to shake Germany to her foundations; also, that he had been kept in ignorance of the truth for several days. The sailors were in mutiny, not against the Government of Prince Max in Berlin that was trying to conclude the war by negotiations with Wilson, but rather against their own naval officers who would have endangered those negotiations by sending the German fleet against the British fleet in a final effort to stave off defeat or to prevent the surrender of the Navy without a fight.[1]

The Naval High Command parted ways with the Government in Berlin when the latter wished to surrender the use of the submarine after the sinking of the *Leinster*. Admiral Scheer, who had hauled down his flag as Commander-in-Chief of the German fleet on August 7 in order to assume the post of Director of Naval Operations, had been assured at the time the armistice was requested that the submarine program was to continue. The Admiral was on his way to Berlin when he learned of Wilson's note of October 14 with its criticism of Germany's use of the U-boat. He believed it impossible for the submarine to confine itself to the sinking of ships of war and to let passenger ships go unmolested; it was suicidal for a submarine to rise to the surface to

1. Max, *Erinnerungen*, p. 568. The question whether the mutiny was caused by revolutionary propaganda coming from some central source outside the Navy or by dissatisfaction within the Navy—on account of rigid discipline, poor food, unequal treatment of officers and men, etc.—was studied by the Reichstag Committee of Investigation and reported in *Die Ursachen des deutschen Zusammenbruches*, Vol. IX, Parts I and II, and Vol. X, Parts I and II. The mutinies of both 1917 and 1918 were investigated. Part II of Volume X is a reprint of a diary kept during the entire war by a sailor on the *Helgoland*, Richard Stumpf. Except for a few paragraphs omitted because of objections from some members of the Investigating Committee, the diary is printed as written—misspellings and bad grammar—and constitutes a fascinating document of great psychological significance.

establish the facts that would spare the one and sink the other. To ask for a cessation of attacks on passenger ships was equivalent to asking the Navy to abandon all use of the submarine. And the Navy had no intention of doing that unless it got an armistice as compensation. According to Scheer, Prince Max agreed with this point of view when it was explained to him and invited the Admiral to attend the important meeting on October 17, when Ludendorff was to answer questions regarding the military situation in preparation for the answer to be made to President Wilson's second note.[2]

Scheer came away from that critical conference of October 17 with the definite conviction that the submarine was not to be abandoned and that the Government was determined to oppose the imposition of dishonorable conditions in the armistice negotiations. He sent his Chief of Staff, von Levetzow, to Wilhelmshafen with the reassuring news about the submarine war. The next day he told the Kaiser at Potsdam that the submarine was still to be employed, although he expressed a fear that the Cabinet might end the submarine war without getting the compensating armistice. The Navy would be free, he said, to continue fighting and to give aid to the Army even if it were decided to give up all use of the U-boats, whose protection had been its chief responsibility hitherto. The Kaiser, says Scheer, agreed with these views. However, when he heard that the Government was seriously considering a plan to restrict the submarine to cruiser warfare, Scheer decided to remain in Berlin to make certain that the reply given to Wilson's note of the 14th corresponded with the decision of the conference of October 17 not to abandon the submarine.[3] Hot debate resulted on the 19th, when the Cabinet discussed a draft of a reply promising to sink no more passenger ships and to restrict the U-boat to cruiser war. The Chancellor feared any move that might result in rupturing negotiations with Wilson; the submarine was the one issue over which no break must be permitted, for the people would not fight for the retention of the "sinister" weapon that drove the United States into war with Germany. In the final showdown Admiral Scheer lost, in spite of having the support of both von Payer and Erzberger.

2. Kutscher, *Admiralsrebellion,* pp. 16–18; Admiral Scheer, *Deutschlands Hochseeflotte im Weltkrieg* (Berlin, 1919), pp. 488–489.

3. Scheer, *Deutschlands Hochseeflotte,* pp. 489–491; Scheer, *Vom Segelschiff zum U-Boot* (Leipzig, 1925), pp. 274, 355.

He did not give up the fight. He sent a telegram to the Army High Command stating that he would not approve the sacrifice of the submarine unless the Army Command demanded it.[4] Hindenburg and Ludendorff both responded, and made final efforts by telephone and telegraph to have the Cabinet's note to Wilson modified. Pressure was put on the Kaiser, who came to Berlin in an effort to persuade Prince Max to change his mind; the latter said he would resign rather than yield. The civilian Government was not to be moved; orders recalled the submarines to their home bases, allowing them to attack only ships of war on their homeward journey.[5] Germany had definitely given up the U-boat.

Admiral Scheer issued the recall order, hoping, however, that it would not be for long. He now informed the Chancellor that the German High Seas Fleet had lost its primary function of protecting the submarines and had recovered its full freedom of action.[6] That was all he said—and Prince Max could not be expected to deduce from it that he was planning to send the fleet against the enemy. Scheer believed that the time had come to make use of the Navy; it could not remain inactive while the hard-pressed Army was still fighting. He believed that the striking power of the German fleet had by now been so greatly increased that it might even win a victory over the British. And there was also the consideration that success at sea would have a most favorable influence on the negotiations for peace and armistice, that the demands of the enemy would depend on the resistance offered by Germany. And so, on the very day that the German Government despatched their reply to Wilson, the Naval Command sent the following terse order to Wilhelmshafen: "The power of the High Seas Fleet should be made ready for an attack on the English fleet." [7]

Admiral Hipper, who had succeeded Scheer as Commander-in-Chief of the High Seas Fleet, approved this decision. The order was brought to him on the morning of October 22 by Cap-

4. Kutscher, *Admiralsrebellion,* p. 65.

5. Document 74, *Amtliche Urkunden.*

6. The Navy people made much of this statement, even to giving the impression that they would have engaged the British fleet much earlier but for the fact that the German fleet was wholly occupied with protecting the submarines. But they never have been able to reconcile that view with their unqualified hostility to the Government's surrender of the submarine during these October days.

7. Kutscher, *Admiralsrebellion,* pp. 26–29; Scheer, *Deutsche Hochseeflotte,* pp. 493–494; Scheer, *Vom Segelschiff,* pp. 275–276. There is an informing study of the reasons for this order to the Navy in Joh. Victor Bredt, "Der geplante Flottenvorstoss Ende 1918" in *Preussische Jahrbücher,* May, 1927, pp. 189–206.

tain von Levetzow, who described the difficult conferences in Berlin and the debate over the submarine question. The decision having been made to employ the fleet in a final desperate gamble, choice had to be made between two plans of operation: one aiming at the east coast of England, the other aimed at British ships at the lower end of the North Sea, between the Thames estuary and the coast of Flanders. The second plan was favored; and Scheer was to notify the Army High Command when he returned to Spa.[8]

Von Tirpitz, who had seen the Navy of his solicitous creation "wrapped in cotton" during the war, who had criticized Wilson's demands as "deliberate extortion," and who had objected to the surrender of the submarine on the ground that "it makes any further resistance on our part impossible," must have been stirred by this tardy move; he had favored "negotiating sword in hand."

The details for the operation were prepared by Admiral Hipper on October 24 on the basis of plans worked out in March, 1918, as a means of bringing assistance to the German Army in Flanders.[9] The fleet was to gather at Schillig Road, not far from Wilhelmshafen, on October 28. That would allow time for submarines to return to their home ports and for other vessels to lay in necessary supplies. The purpose of the plan was to draw the British fleet into battle under conditions favorable to the German fleet. Light surface vessels were to open the operation by attacks on the Flemish coast and in the Thames estuary. It was hoped and believed that the English fleet would pursue these ships,[10] which would retreat and draw the British ships after them, late in the afternoon of the second day, to a place off Terschelling, one of the Dutch Frisian Islands, where the waters would be mined and occupied by submarines. When mines and submarines had greatly weakened the admittedly far superior British fleet, the German battle fleet was to engage it in a final struggle and presumably win a great victory.

Wilson's third note to Germany, which arrived on October 24, contained nothing to make the sponsors of the plan abandon it. That note, according to Scheer, aimed at Germany's capitulation,

8. Rear Admiral von Levetzow, "Der letzte Akt," *Süddeutsche Monatshefte,* April, 1924, p. 67.

9. The detailed plan is found in Kutscher, *Admiralsrebellion,* pp. 29, 48–52, and in Charles Vidil, *Les Mutineries de la Marine Allemande* (Paris, 1931), pp. 152–154. See also Scheer, *Deutsche Hochseeflotte,* p. 494.

10. Scheer admits there was a possibility that the enemy might not come out and fight. See his *Vom Segelschiff,* p. 276.

which the nation was honor-bound to resist. As we have already seen, Ludendorff and Hindenburg concurred in this opinion;[11] and convinced that the Government would stand firm and that important military decisions would be made for continuing the war, the two Generals insisted on coming to the capital for conferences. They asked Admiral Scheer to accompany them. The three men had lunch together on the train and discussed Wilson's latest note. "We could not imagine," writes Scheer, "that our Government would do anything but reject this new demand in a way in keeping with the honor of the nation and its military power."

Ludendorff and Hindenburg came away from their audience with the Kaiser the afternoon of the 25th under the impression that he would follow the decisions of the Government; he was not to be persuaded to break off negotiations. This disappointing news they discussed with Admiral Scheer and Colonel von Haeften at 6 P.M. in the building of the General Staff; they decided to interview Prince Max to keep the Government from making the wrong decision. Since the Chancellor was ill they saw von Payer instead, and used every available argument to convince the Vice-Chancellor "that our national honor demanded of us that we reject the conditions proposed by Wilson." All in vain; von Payer could not be persuaded.[12]

For his defiance of the civil authorities Ludendorff was dismissed the next morning. Had the Navy committed an overt act of rebellion like the proclamation issued to the Army by the High Command, it is possible that similar strong action might have been taken with regard to the Navy Command. But the "revolt" of the latter was a close secret, known only to a very few. Not even the Kaiser was aware of what was being planned, although Scheer could have informed him on two occasions.[13]

On October 26 the fleet began to assemble at Schillig Road. The first signs of trouble appeared the next day, when some forty stokers failed to report for duty at the time the small cruiser *Strassburg* was to sail for the fateful rendezvous. The missing men were located on shore, not far from the ship, and were brought aboard without offering any opposition. The reason

11. Scheer, *Deutsche Hochseeflotte,* p. 494. Also *supra,* pp. 207–208.

12. Scheer, *Deutsche Hochseeflotte,* pp. 494–495; Payer, *Von Bethmann Hollweg,* pp. 141–144; Levetzow, "Der Letzte Akt," pp. 68–69. Cf. *supra,* pp. 209–210.

13. Kutscher, *Admiralsrebellion,* pp. 78, 80.

for their behavior, they explained, was a report that their commander was planning to risk his ship in battle to avoid handing it over to the English under the armistice.[14]

To keep the men in ignorance of the real purpose for which the ships were gathering, officers and men were told that certain maneuvers, worked out in September, were to be executed to test the ability of the fleet to meet a mighty British attack. Not even squadron leaders and commanders knew the real intent until the afternoon of the 29th, when Admiral von Hipper described the operation in a conference on the flagship. Ranking officers were then instructed to reveal it to the officers and men in their command only after all connection with land had been broken. The actual operation was to begin the morning of the 30th.[15]

During the evening of October 29 von Hipper, on his flagship *Baden* at Schillig Road, received reports of trouble on the small cruiser *Regensburg*, one of the ships at Cuxhaven taking on a cargo of mines. Reports of worse disturbances were to follow. He was soon to learn that men on several battleships of the Third Squadron had objected to being ordered out to sea. Even before he had met his officers in conference over the proposed naval operation, there had been an incident on the battleship *König*. Some of the sailors had made it clear that they would disobey orders if commanded to go beyond Helgoland or the mine fields. Order was restored, but not until several men had been placed in chains. An outbreak had also occurred on the *Kronprinz Wilhelm*. The mutineers on this ship had somehow become convinced that the fleet was to be uselessly sacrificed in battle with the more powerful British Navy in an operation that would be very much on the order of a coup d'état against the Government in Berlin. On the *Grosser Kurfürst* members of the crew insulted their officers and some revolutionary placards were discovered. The most serious disturbance took place on the *Markgraf* where sailors gathered on deck in the evening and one of their number shouted to an officer that they had no desire to participate in the "death cruise" next day. When questioned later, this sailor said that the officers had sworn to seek an honorable death in battle with the enemy rather than surrender the fleet. He thought such a sacrifice futile although he and other sailors were ready to fight if the English should attack. Reporting on the attitude of

14. *Ibid.*, p. 53.
15. *Ibid.*, pp. 53–54.

their crews, some officers said they had heard the word "revolution" a number of times.[16]

By midnight the 29th even the flagship was affected although no open break had occurred. When Admiral Hipper learned how extensive the disaffection was, he ordered that the operation be postponed and that preparations be made for special naval maneuvers next day instead; to do nothing at all would indicate to the mutineers that their opposition had been successful.

But on the morning of October 30 even these proposed maneuvers had to be put off for a while because of heavy fog. The bad morale, worst among the sailors of the Third Squadron, did not improve, but spread to ships in other squadrons. When the weather cleared somewhat, around eight o'clock, and the order was given to prepare for maneuvers, part of the crew of the *Thüringen* of the First Squadron refused to obey. Some gathered in the forward battery, where they sang songs in defiance of officers and orders. Only gradually could they be persuaded to return to their duties. A similar refusal to obey orders occurred on the *Helgoland*, whose commander later reported that his men believed they must prevent any naval operation sure to accomplish nothing beyond rendering armistice negotiations more difficult. This rebellious spirit among the men and the uncertain weather at noon led to the abandonment of the maneuvers set for the day and their postponement to the next morning.[17]

In the meantime the submarines and the torpedo boats had taken the stations assigned to them in the plan to attract and destroy British ships. On these vessels there had been no disaffection; their crews had always had plenty of action to occupy their minds. They too were now ordered to postpone action.

At the time that naval maneuvers were called off Admiral Hipper sent a statement to the commanders of rebellious crews to counteract the discontent. This document, which was either read to the men or posted where they could read it themselves, did not specifically deny the existence of a naval move against the English. It stated that the British Navy wanted no peace until the German fleet had been defeated. The German Navy had to be prepared for an attack, to keep the British at a distance from the German coasts, to keep them out of the North Sea, either by stubborn defense or by a mighty counterattack. All the men were urged to do their best at this critical time when the German

16. *Ibid.*, pp. 54–57.
17. *Ibid.*, pp. 58–61.

Navy was merely making a defensive move against attack by the British fleet.[18]

This appeal failed to quiet the men. When orders were given to the First Squadron to set out at 10 P.M., October 30, for what was to be the beginning of planned operations against the British Navy, open mutiny manifested itself aboard the *Thüringen* and the *Helgoland*. Part of the crew of the former gathered in the forward battery again; the electric lights were extinguished; sabotage made it impossible to weigh anchor; stokers refused to get up steam. The same thing happened on the *Helgoland*. Some of the men even got weapons. Officers of the *Thüringen* got the rebels under control in the morning with the aid of marines and it was hoped that those responsible could be identified and arrested. On the theory that those who had disobeyed the night before would disobey again, the officers decided to weigh anchor in the early afternoon of the 31st. The sailors barricaded themselves again in the forward battery. Marines were now called aboard; three torpedo boats and a submarine stood by with guns ready to open fire on the mutineers. Suddenly the guns on the *Helgoland* were aimed at the submarine. The squadron chief then signaled that the submarine would send a torpedo into the *Helgoland* if the latter should open fire. The big guns on the battleship returned to their position of rest, not only because of the threat but because of lack of munitions for the guns. Seeing how risky their situation had become, the mutineers on the *Thüringen* and on the *Helgoland* surrendered and were taken away.[19]

The utter hopelessness of bringing off the projected naval attack on the British Navy now became perfectly apparent. It was thought hazardous even to keep the fleet together, and it was decided to split it up. The Third Squadron, commanded by Admiral Kraft, was sent to its home base at Kiel in the belief that morale had fallen because the men had seen too little of their homes and that a brief period in the home port would enable the officers to get control of the situation.[20]

Sending the ships to Kiel was fatal; that was the worst possible port for the rebellious sailors. The city was full of revolutionaries. There had been a serious strike in January. The twenty thousand sailors who lived there got along well with the workers,

18. *Ibid.*, pp. 63–65.
19. *Ibid.*, pp. 66–70.
20. *Ibid.*, pp. 70–71.

each group sympathizing with the other. The Governor of the port, Admiral Souchon, who had made history in the early weeks of the war as commander of the *Goeben* and *Breslau* in the Mediterranean, warned Admiral Kraft about the situation; but the warning was not heeded. On November 1 the ships of the Third Squadron steamed through the Kiel canal, with people on shore wondering why they had come. As the vessels made their slow way through the canal, word was passed to the sailors that there was to be a meeting that evening at the Trade-Union House. Souchon informed Kraft of the situation and recommended that the sailors be denied leave to go ashore. Kraft did not agree, convinced that refusal to grant shore leave would make a bad situation worse; he let his men go on land, but only in small groups.[21]

Ashore, many of the sailors attended meetings at the headquarters of the trade unions, which the Commandant had neglected to place out of bounds despite the warning he had received. Here and there on the streets a good deal of political haranguing went on, the theme being that there was no sense in performing regular duties any more since the war would soon be over. Because many of the sailors returned late if they returned at all, the Admiral issued orders forbidding them henceforth to attend meetings at the Trade-Union House. Patrols were sent out to gather in the delinquents; about one hundred men were rounded up and brought on board under arrest. Sympathetic comrades sent a delegation to the Admiral to seek their release, but met with refusal. They also expressed concern about the fate of the one hundred and fifty mutineers who had been removed from the *Markgraf* and imprisoned in the Naval Guard House. Anxious about the prisoners on shipboard, Admiral Kraft summoned a company of marines to escort them to fortresses ashore. The first company refused to obey orders after coming on board ship and a second detachment had to be called.[22]

On Saturday, November 2, the situation got further out of hand. The streets of Kiel were filled with crowds—with women and children, and particularly with sailors on leave. There was a sort of holiday spirit in the air. Only an occasional patrol was seen. Here and there meetings were held. Sailors who sought to

21. For an account of the activities at Kiel see Charles Vidil, *Les Mutineries de la Marine Allemande,* pp. 157–172. A much more dramatic and picturesque narrative of the essential events is given in Paul Schubert and Langhorne Gibson, *Death of a Fleet* (London, 1932?), pp. 94–154.

22. Haussmann says that the revolution in Kiel had its origin in this desire to effect the release of prisoners. Haussmann, *Journal,* p. 312.

enter the headquarters of the trade-unions found the door closed and a picket on guard, all according to orders from Souchon. But the Governor could not prevent meetings by simply closing one hall. Word went around that a meeting would be held about three o'clock in the park called the Waldwiese. Some thousand people gathered to hear speeches from workers and sailors. The most important speaker was a stoker named Artelt, who talked in revolutionary phrases and demanded the release of the naval prisoners, even including the men imprisoned for participation in the mutiny in the summer of 1917. Another meeting was set for the same time and place the next afternoon. Souchon sent troops to disperse the crowd, but when they arrived the meeting was already over.

In the evening Souchon and Kraft met to discuss the situation. The Governor wanted military aid brought in from the Ninth Army Corps barracks at Altona; Kraft opposed the summoning of outsiders, saying that the marines were loyal and quite adequate to suppress any disturbances. Souchon suggested that shore leaves be denied sailors of the Third Squadron, but Kraft was opposed to this too. He said he had instructions to quiet the unrest by leniency. Both men agreed to sound a general defense alarm Sunday afternoon at four to effect a return of the sailors to their ships and enable the authorities to arrest the ringleaders of the agitation.

In the course of Saturday afternoon Artelt had got assurances of support from the Independent Socialist party. Notices were distributed that evening inviting sailors and workers to a meeting Sunday afternoon at 4.30 "to protest against the arrest of our comrades of the Third Squadron." Sunday morning more sailors than ever asked for shore leave and the commanders dared not deny it to anyone. The streets of the city were crowded. Anticipating a move on the part of the authorities to suppress the demonstration in the afternoon, the organizers distributed handbills requesting soldiers not to fire upon the others. The "general defense alarm" that was sounded as Kraft and Souchon had agreed was ignored. Souchon then tried to get control of the situation by sending out patrols to order the sailors to return to their quarters at once. The patrols were swallowed up in the crowds. Armed men were sent out to defend the prisons and a call was sent to Altona for troops. In the meantime crowds moved toward the Waldwiese, where about twenty thousand people had gathered by five o'clock.

The meeting was a disorderly one. One speaker, Garbe, President of the trade-unions, asked that action be postponed. His speech led to argument. Artelt called for volunteers to free the *Markgraf* prisoners in the Naval Guard House in Feldstrasse. His extreme views won much support and soon the crowd followed Artelt toward the prison singing the "Internationale." There were cries of "Long live the Republic!" and "Down with the Kaiser!" Near the prison the mob met an armed patrol whose commander ordered the crowd to disperse. The warning was not heeded. A volley was fired, but with blank cartidges. Since the crowd still refused to leave, live ammunition was used in the next volley and a number of people were killed or wounded. This was the first blood shed in the German revolution. Armed men in the crowd fired back, killing or wounding some of the patrol. At last the crowd dispersed. Believing that the trouble was over, Souchon telephoned to Altona to cancel the order for troops.

The ringleaders were not arrested. That evening Artelt and the Workers' and Sailors' Soviet, as they now called themselves, were free to hold a meeting to formulate their demands: recognition of the Russian Soviets, the abolition of the salute, equality of rations for enlisted men and officers, the closing of the officers' messrooms, freedom of speech, the release of the men under arrest, and the abdication of the Emperor. The demands were no longer limited to naval grievances; they were becoming political in character. A mutiny was becoming a revolution.[23]

Only after all this had happened did Prince Max receive vague reports of disturbances in the fleet. They did not appear to have any real significance, and nothing was done about them.

The disturbances were not confined to Kiel alone or to the Navy. Less violent discontent was manifesting itself at Brünsbüttel and at Wilhelmshafen, where other squadrons had put in. The Army was also confronted with mutinous conditions. On October 31 Groener had reported the breakdown of discipline and the weakening of morale, which he ascribed to the demand for the Kaiser's abdication.[24]

On November 1 an officer reported that soldiers were deserting; that, without Army leaves and without tickets, they took control

23. Cf. the demands listed in Haussmann, *Journal,* pp. 312–313.

24. See Groener's telegram in Martin Hobohm, *Soziale Heeresmissstände als Teilursache des deutschen Zusammenbruches von 1918,* in the Reichstag investigation, *Die Ursachen des deutschen Zusammenbruches im Jahre 1918,* XI, Pt. I, 411–412.

of railway trains, which were many hours late in consequence; the railway officials were helpless. In one place soldiers, having removed their insignia, crowded into the bars, and refused to salute their officers any more.[25]

The publication of the Austrian armistice terms on November 4 further stirred the growing discontent. The *Vossische Zeitung* announced them under a headline informing the people that the enemy would march through Austrian territory into Germany. It pictured the enemy as being at the very door.

There was intense speculation about the terms Germany might expect. Nothing certain or specific was yet known about the results of the prolonged conferences at Versailles. On November 4 the *Berliner Tageblatt* printed Lord Northcliffe's thirteen-point program as given in the London *Times* and pointed out how widely it differed from Wilson's Fourteen Points, particularly in omitting to specify the kind of internationally organized world that was to come into being. The perplexing American system of government was carefully explained in the press so that people could follow the Congressional elections on which Germany's fate might hang.

It had become clear by November 4 that great changes like those in Austria-Hungary were impending in Germany: Bavaria was discussing a parliamentary regime and might seek a separate peace; Baden was facing a constitutional crisis. Debate on the question of the Kaiser's abdication was becoming intense.

Such was the explosive state of affairs in Germany when "Red Monday" dawned on November 4. Unrest had become so widespread that the Government had to turn its attention from the military situation to conditions within the country. Signs of revolution were multiplying. Demonstrations had been planned in Berlin for the 4th and the Government had to take steps to render them harmless. A lengthy appeal to the people, signed by members of the Cabinet, listed the great achievements of the new parliamentary government and stated that there was much yet to be done to complete the transformation into a people's government; self-restraint and self-discipline were essential to maintaining order and fulfilling the Government's task. The people were asked not to let themselves be carried away to destruction in the direction of communism by senseless and profit-

25. This document is given in full, *ibid.*, p. 412.

less visionaries. "With the conclusion of peace," they were assured, "an improvement in the supply of food and in other vital matters will result." [26]

The Social Democrats were likewise afraid of communist activity and appealed to the workers not to participate in demonstrations the Communists were arranging.[27]

The Chancellor was particularly alarmed by a report in a Berlin newspaper that a Munich mob had marched out to release prisoners in one of the city's jails. To publish such a report at this time seemed to Prince Max to show a complete lack of scruple. When General von Winterfeldt told Scheidemann that harsh armistice terms were expected and should be rejected by the people, the Socialist leader replied: "The Supreme Army Command needs to be informed about the situation at home. We are no longer able to resist. The situation has become very acute." [28]

It was on this morning of November 4 that the Minister of Marine, von Mann, informed the Chancellor about the situation at Kiel. He told of the revolutionary demands being made, of the fighting that had resulted in killed and wounded, and asked that the Social Democrats send a representative to calm the people since the Naval Command had lost control of the situation. The Cabinet accepted Scheidemann's motion that Noske be sent, accompanied by Secretary of State Haussmann as representative of the Government. Noske had been long interested in naval matters and had the good will of the sailors. He took with him a proclamation signed by the Chancellor, von Mann, and Scheidemann, which, it was believed, would scotch the rumor "that the officers intended to destroy the fleet to avoid surrendering it" in the armistice. The statement said that the officers were in agreement with the Government's peace policy; claimed that the Government was doing all it could to prevent the further shedding of blood; and explained that the armistice had not yet been signed because the enemy had not specified its terms. There was a warning against civil war: "We do not desire to conclude an international war in order to commence a civil war." The sailors' complaints would be investigated; they were asked in

26. This appeal is found in many places: *Frankfurter Zeitung,* November 4, 1918, No. 307; *Berliner Tageblatt,* November 5, No. 566; Lutz, *Fall of the German Empire,* II, 406–408.

27. *Frankfurter Zeitung,* November 4, 1918, No. 306.

28. Max, *Erinnerungen,* p. 571.

return to help the Government settle internal affairs without bloody strife.[29]

It was generally believed in Berlin that Noske would be absent for only a day. Noske himself had no real understanding of what had taken place, for no one could tell him about it. He and Haussmann arrived at Kiel Monday evening. They were expected and warmly greeted, especially Noske. Troops of the Ninth Army Corps who arrived on the same train were also greeted by the throng and then disarmed.[30] Artelt was on hand to welcome Noske and drove away with him. During the ride he explained what had happened in the course of the day. He mentioned a meeting to be held at eight that evening, at which Noske himself was expected to speak. Everywhere there were red flags and many unarmed sailors, but it did not look at all to Noske as if a great revolution had broken out. He had got no clear picture of what had occurred and could therefore speak only in general terms and briefly to the evening gathering of the rebels. Afterward he was taken to a conference with about a dozen workers and the same number of soldiers, who were engaged in the formation of a soldiers' council. At this meeting he learned in greater detail what had occurred earlier in the day.[31]

Much had happened. In the morning some sailors had obtained arms and had moved toward the naval prison. They were stopped. Then other sailors got arms and refused to be stopped. The efforts of one commander to persuade the men to return to their duties were shouted down. A delegation appeared and made the following demands: abdication of the Hohenzollerns, votes for women, the release of prisoners of the Third Squadron and of the mutineers of 1917. During the day Governor Souchon, who was greatly surprised by the revolt and was undecided as to what was to be done, received representatives of the sailors and apparently promised them that no troops would be called from outside Kiel

29. Max, *Erinnerungen,* pp. 572–573, and note on p. 572. The Chancellor's judgment on the Kiel outbreak is interesting. He has no criticism of the officers who planned the naval operation against the British fleet, except to say that they were more optimistic than he was, and particularly that they should have informed him. Instead, he blames the mutineers in the Navy for "breaking the backbone of national defense." He sums up the responsibility of the sailors in this fashion: "Without Kiel, no revolution; and without the revolution, no surrender on November 11." *Ibid.,* pp. 572–576.

30. *Ibid.,* p. 585.

31. Noske, *Von Kiel bis Kapp* (Berlin, 1920), pp. 9–12; Vidil, *Les Mutineries,* pp. 162–163.

and that the prisoners would be freed. There was not much else he could do since some twenty thousand sailors were parading about the city with arms they had taken and were threatening to bombard the town from the warships in the harbor if force were used against them. This threat would not have meant much, for the officers had rendered the guns useless. There had been violence in other parts of the city during the day, and occasional shots fired; but no harm appears to have resulted.[32]

At nine o'clock Noske and Haussmann met with the Governor, the naval officers, representatives of the sailors and of both the Social Democratic and Independent Socialist parties. The representatives of the mutinous sailors were alarmed over the possibility of troops being brought in from outside. It was impossible to get them to talk quietly and reasonably until Noske assured them that no soldiers would attack the city. Haussmann promised to explain to the Government in Berlin what had happened and to seek an amnesty for all political prisoners. After the meeting Noske and Haussmann went to their hotel to draft their report to Berlin, a task punctuated by random shooting that went on all night. It was agreed that Haussmann should return to Berlin the next day to make the report while Noske remained at Kiel.[33]

During the night the mutineers strengthened their positions by setting up machine guns in various parts of the city. There was intermittent shooting and officers were roughly handled. In the morning all the ships but the *König* were flying the red flag.[34] About eight o'clock, when the imperial standard was raised on the *König*, a sailor appeared with a red flag to be raised instead. The commandant shot the man, whereupon the captain and another officer were shot and killed.[35]

Noske went in the morning to the Trade-Union House, where the Soldiers' Council was said to be in session. The building was filled with arguing soldiers, everybody asking for information that nobody was in a position to give. There was no trace of any responsible authority—only confusion. No arrangements had been made for feeding the sailors. Something would have to be done, or they would pillage the city. The rebel leaders, Artelt and

32. Noske, *Von Kiel bis Kapp,* pp. 12–13; Vidil, *Les Mutineries,* pp. 161–163. Cf. Max, *Erinnerungen,* pp. 577–578.

33. Noske, *Von Kiel bis Kapp,* pp. 13–14; Max, *Erinnerungen,* pp. 578–579.

34. Vidil, *Les Mutineries,* p. 171.

35. Noske, *Von Kiel bis Kapp,* p. 15; Vidil, *Les Mutineries de la Marine Allemande,* p. 171; E. O. Volkmann, *Revolution über Deutschland* (Oldenburg, 1930), p. 35.

Garbe, asked Noske to take control of affairs. Noske was willing but he wanted some kind of popular approval for such assumption of power. Speaking to a large crowd in the afternoon he referred to the need of some authority and said he would be willing to assume the responsibility if the people showed that they had confidence in him and would send representatives to coöperate with him. The mob shouted its approval and soon offices were set up in the first floor of a naval building, with a desk and telephone for Noske's use. There was little violence during the day; there was some indiscriminate firing, but only one person was killed so far as Noske could discover.[36]

In the afternoon some fifty to sixty soldiers, selected by their ship comrades or their military formations, came to help Noske administer the government of Kiel. He thought the group too large to function effectively, and suggested a council of seven or nine members to sit under his presidency. When this suggestion was approved, Noske proceeded to select the men from those present, guided only by their appearance. Some of the men of course proved to be no help whatsoever. Other problems arose to make Noske's task difficult. He could do little work because people crowded into his office and his telephone rang constantly. His greatest problem was to overcome the sailors' fear that soldiers were being summoned to attack the city and suppress the mutiny; they even believed that troops were already concealed in a forest near by awaiting the proper moment for attack.[37]

It was not until Tuesday the 5th that Berlin papers began to publish anything like detailed reports of the revolutionary events taking place in Kiel and elsewhere. But rumors had been multiplying. The Chancellor was especially disturbed over reports of the spreading propaganda in Pomerania, where agitators were said to be asking for a division of land according to the principles adopted in Soviet Russia. He knew for a certainty, he said, that the center for much of the agitation was the Russian Embassy in Berlin; evidence to support that belief had been accumulating for several weeks. Scheidemann, fearing as always that extremists would have more influence with the working classes than he, suggested a method to put an end to this Russian propaganda. He urged that a railway station porter be so trained that it

36. Noske, *Von Kiel bis Kapp*, pp. 15–18.

37. *Ibid.*, pp. 18–20. See Vidil, *Les Mutineries de la Marine Allemande*, pp. 164–165.

would have all the appearance of a regrettable accident if he caused one of the hundreds of inviolable diplomatic boxes coming to the Russian Embassy to fall, break open, and reveal its incriminating contents. The Cabinet members laughed at the proposal; but a few days later, on November 5, Dr. Solf reported just such an incident and the discovery of revolutionary documents calling for an uprising in Germany and for the assassination of certain leaders. A political *cordon* was placed around the Russian Embassy and on November 6 the Ambassador was informed that he must leave Berlin. It was during the discussion of these matters that Scheidemann made the statement, "Bolshevism is a greater danger today than the Entente." [38]

The Chancellor shared much of Scheidemann's fears. "Indeed," he wrote, "there was no one of us who was not convinced of the need of strengthening the Social Democrats against the Independents." But the difficulty of coöperating with the Majority Socialists was their insistence on the abolition of the monarchy. Prince Max found himself in an awkward situation, needing the support of those with whom he differed over a fundamental matter. On November 5 he received the Kaiser's reply to his appeal of the 3d that the Emperor should return to Berlin. "The inclination of the Kaiser to return is now slight," the despatch read; "its explanation is to be found in the feeling produced by the sending of Minister Drews and by the opinion that some time will elapse before armistice conditions come." Should no progress be made with regard to an armistice, which was for the armies to arrange, the Kaiser desired that negotiations for peace should continue. The Emperor's visit to the soldiers at the front, it was said, had been very successful because officers had got the impression that the Kaiser had deserted them and needed the encouragement of a visit from him.[39]

The Kaiser explained his views on peace and armistice somewhat more fully during November 5 to von Grünau. He believed that the armistice terms would be harsh, to judge from those that Turkey and Austria had just received. It was possible they would prove to be so objectionable that the Army would reject them and put itself in opposition to the civil Government and the people desiring peace. A dispute of that sort within Germany might be the intent of the Entente Powers. If negotiations for an armistice should be broken off, the Kaiser urged that negotiations

38. Max, *Erinnerungen,* pp. 579–580; Scheidemann, *Memoiren,* II, 251–253.
39. Max, *Erinnerungen,* pp. 580–581, 589–590 and note.

for peace be carried on; they might even produce a good armistice eventually. He wished to know how the Government regarded this suggestion. No answer was ever made, for events made it unnecessary: Wilson's note had already arrived and an armistice commission had been appointed.[40]

The Kaiser was relying upon General Groener to explain his position when he went to Berlin the morning of the 5th on Prince Max's summons. The General painted a dark picture to the Chancellor: Germany being rapidly encircled by the Entente, assisted by Bolshevism on the east, by Rumanians and Czecho-Slovaks—and even by Germany's former allies, through their acceptance of the armistice conditions imposed upon them. Although he thought it might be necessary to recall German troops from the east, he hesitated because some soldiers stationed there were infected with Bolshevism and because the Bolsheviks would take over any evacuated territories. Whether they should be recalled or not, he thought, was for the Cabinet to decide. Touching briefly on the need of defense against enemy attack through Austria-Hungary, Groener said that troops for such an operation would have to be taken from the western front, where unfortunately the Entente's superiority in numbers was very great. Despite the sacrifice of supplies and other materials, the Supreme Army Command had decided to retire to a shorter line in the west. If heavy battles could be avoided for two weeks or so, it would be possible to give the soldiers in the west some much-needed rest. Groener thought that the morale of the Army was getting poorer, because of the armistice proposals, "the cowardly and dissatisfied utterances of the press," the effect of conditions at home on men returning to the front, and the Bolshevistic spirit of the men coming from the east. He and Hindenburg were convinced, he said, that "the worst enemy against which the Army has to guard itself is the danger of being unnerved by influences from home and the threat of Bolshevism." The most he could promise was gaining time for negotiations with the enemy. He did not see how the military situation could improve. Von Payer tried to force the General to say how much time Germany had before she must surrender, but he got no satisfactory reply. Erzberger had no better luck when he sought to learn how soon she might have to give up if the most unfavorable circumstances operated against her.[41]

40. Document 99 and note by Solf, *Amtliche Urkunden.* See *infra,* p. 320, on the appointment of the armistice commission.

41. Max, *Erinnerungen,* pp. 581–584; document 100, *Amtliche Urkunden.*

According to Prince Max, General Groener had left Spa for Berlin authorized to promise the return of the Kaiser to the capital on twenty-four hours' notice. But he had no sooner arrived at the railway station in Berlin than this authorization was withdrawn. The Quartermaster General raised the question in talking of the military situation. "The Field Marshal has asked me," he declared with deep feeling to the assembled Secretaries of State, "to state in so many words with regard to the matter of the Kaiser's abdication that he would look upon himself as a scoundrel if he deserted the Kaiser; and, gentlemen, I think the same and so do all other honorable soldiers. . . . If the agitation against the Kaiser does not cease, the fate of the Army is sealed. It will fall apart. The very beast in man will break out in the soldiers coming back to their homes." When the Chancellor tried privately to convince the General that the Kaiser must abdicate, Groener replied that even to discuss the question revealed a complete lack of consideration for the soldiers at the front. It seemed, wrote Prince Max, almost as though the General had bound himself at Spa by a promise not to give in under any circumstances.[42]

In the afternoon and evening the Government learned what the actual situation at Kiel was. Haussmann made his report to the Cabinet in the afternoon, in the presence of Groener. About midnight Noske telephoned from Kiel and told von Payer about latest developments. On his arrival, he said, there was no authority in the city: the Navy had lost its influence and the rebels were without responsible leaders. In this situation he took over control and had already managed to quiet things down during the day.

Noske and Haussmann were certain that the Social Democrats could calm the people, whom the Independent Socialists were trying to stir up. Both men pleaded that no troops be sent to quell disturbances—that would merely multiply difficulties. Noske knew that his leadership depended upon his protecting the sailors and being the spokesman of their demands, particularly in insisting upon the abdication of the Kaiser and the amnesty of the mutinous sailors under arrest. Although abdication was listed first among the demands, Noske said that amnesty should be granted first, by Wednesday the 6th—or he could no longer remain at Kiel. Haussmann had also insisted on that in his afternoon session with the Cabinet. Members of the Government were divided over the issue. The Secretaries for the Army and Navy wanted force used against the Kiel mutiny and were more or less supported by

42. Max, *Erinnerungen,* p. 581.

Erzberger. Doubt was expressed, however, whether there were enough troops fit for such an undertaking against the city where it was believed that forty thousand "well-armed, well-fed, and well-rested" sailors were capable of offering effective resistance. Despite strongly expressed opinions for and against it amnesty was granted the next day.[43]

By Wednesday Groener's view of the situation had become even more gloomy. Max and he talked matters over in the garden of the Chancellery. The General reported that just after his arrival in Berlin he had received from the Kaiser a message expressing the belief that the German Army must approach the enemy and inquire about armistice conditions. A similar telegram had been sent to the Foreign Office. Unwilling the day before to identify himself with such a move, Groener now thought that "we must cross the lines with the white flag."

"But certainly not for a week," suggested Max.

"That is too long," replied Groener.

"But still, not before Monday [November 11]," pleaded the Chancellor.

"Even that is also too long," Groener replied. "Saturday is the very last day."[44]

Groener was present when Prince Max informed the Cabinet of this "terrifying" disclosure. The Quartermaster General explained his change of opinion. "I too had hoped," he said, "that we could wait eight or ten days, until we had established ourselves in a new line. After all I have found out in the meantime about Kiel, the Tyrol, and morale at home, particularly in Bavaria, with its far-reaching political consequences, I am convinced that we must take the step, however painful it is, and ask Foch."

The Chancellor explained that Groener was convinced Germany must withdraw behind the Rhine. He was still determined to carry on the struggle, for asking Foch for armistice terms was not the same as accepting them. Whether they should be accepted or not would depend on their character.[45]

Prince Max was convinced; it was impossible to wait longer. "Under any circumstances," he said, "negotiations with Foch must be initiated by the morning of Friday, November 8." He wanted the armistice delegation to leave that very day. If no reply

43. *Ibid.*, pp. 584–588; Noske, *Von Kiel bis Kapp*, p. 19; Payer, *Von Bethmann Hollweg*, p. 156.

44. Max, *Erinnerungen*, pp. 589–590.

45. *Ibid.*, p. 590.

came from Wilson before Friday, he thought the Germans must raise the white flag and get negotiations started for an armistice, possibly even for surrender. The decision was approved unanimously by the War Cabinet and later by the High Command.[46]

At noon in the Chancellery leaders of the Social Democratic party and of the trade unions met with Groener. The meeting had been arranged before Groener had decided an armistice was necessary, with the idea of convincing him that the home front had broken and that the only way to keep it united was by persuading the Kaiser to abdicate. The friendly feeling that had existed in the past between the General and the workers reappeared as soon as Groener entered the room.

The question of abdication was immediately brought up. Rightly or wrongly, the people held the Kaiser responsible, said Ebert, and wanted him removed. He proposed that the Kaiser announce his abdication the next morning at the latest. The Emperor could name one of his sons as deputy, either Oskar or Eitel Friedrich. "The Crown Prince is now impossible, because he is too much hated by the masses of people." Groener said that abdication was a matter not to be discussed; it was impossible to deprive the Army of its Supreme War Lord. Everyone continued to press the General. They were not opposed to monarchy: getting rid of the Kaiser was not abolishing the monarchy. They said that many Social Democrats could get along perfectly well with a king committed to a progressive social program and a parliamentary system.

The discussion was becoming more and more academic, when Scheidemann returned, pale and excited, from a telephone conversation to which he had been called as the session opened. "The abdication," he said, "is now no longer a matter for discussion; the revolution is spreading. Sailors from Kiel have taken control in Hamburg and Hanover also. Gentlemen, this is not the time for further discussion; it is time to act. We do not know whether or not we shall still be sitting in these chairs tomorrow."

Although a republican, Ebert, supported by the tearful pleas of others, now pleaded with Groener to try to save the monarchy and arrange immediately to have one of the princes entrusted with the regency.

46. Prince Max does not tell the precise circumstances under which he decided to ask Foch for an armistice and appointed the Armistice Commission. Erzberger says that the decision was made in the meeting of the Cabinet on Wednesday the 6th just before noon. M. Erzberger, *Erlebnisse im Weltkrieg* (Stuttgart, 1920), p. 325.

The General was not to be moved. He had been authorized to say that all the princes had taken a pledge not to assume the regency in case their father were forced to abdicate.

"Under these circumstances," said Ebert, "there is no point to further discussion. Events must now take their own course." "We thank you for these frank words," he said, turning to Groener, "and will always with pleasure remember our work with you during the war. From now on we go separate ways and who knows whether we shall ever see each other again."

The meeting broke up, most of the men leaving the room lost in thought and incapable of saying a word.[47]

47. The story of this conference is found in Max, *Erinnerungen,* pp. 591–593. Groener said later he wished he had accepted Ebert's proposal. *Ibid.,* note on p. 592.

XI

The Fourteen Points

AFTER the Germans had stated their willingness to accept Wilson's Fourteen Points and other principles "as a basis for the peace negotiations," it was the President's great concern to get a similar acceptance by the Powers associated with the United States in the war. The German High Command had wanted to know whether the Entente Powers had accepted that program, but Wilson needed no such prompting. He believed in his program and was determined to make it the foundation of world peace. The unselfish, ideological character of his principles was to stand out in sharp contrast to the British concern about the German Navy and the French concern about the German Army; it reminds one of the role ascribed to the Germans over a century ago by those who said they sought dominion over the clouds while the English sought control of the sea and the French control of the land.

The President knew that he was in for a difficult time—with political opponents in America, with critics in England, France, and Italy, with those who wanted a clear interpretation of the Fourteen Points in order to see their application to the problems of the world after the war. That his program needed interpretation and elucidation was virtually admitted by the President himself, who set the example by informing Austria-Hungary, as we have already seen, that Point 10 with its promise to the peoples of the Dual Monarchy of the "freest opportunity for autonomous development" was no longer adequate; the right of the Czecho-Slovaks and the Jugo-Slavs to determine their own destiny must be recognized. In a letter to Senator F. M. Simmons the President explained that Point 3, which called for "the removal as far as possible of all economic barriers and the re-establishment of an equality of trade conditions" did not mean the abolition of tariffs; nations could still have tariffs, but they should not be permitted to discriminate against other countries.[1]

Wilson thought he could best deal with American opposition to his program by asking for and getting a Democratic Congress

1. Simmons' letter and Wilson's reply are found in the *New York Times*, October 29, 1918.

in the elections of November 5. Even with such a victory, the President would still have powerful opponents at home, even in his own household. His own Secretary of State, for example, objected to the Fourteen Points as "too indefinite in specific application." [2]

The primary problem was to get the Fourteen Points accepted abroad, and the President knew it was not to be easily solved. Near the end of October he wrote to a friend that the disposition to make "an absolutely and rigorously impartial peace . . . is growing less and less on the other side of the water." [3]

Persuading the Entente Powers was practically the main purpose of House's mission to Europe. "It seems to me of the utmost importance," he wrote in his diary on October 28, "to have the Allies accept the Fourteen Points and the subsequent terms of the President. If this is done the basis of a peace will already have been made. Germany began negotiations on the basis of these terms, and the Allies have already tentatively accepted them, but as Germany shows signs of defeat it is becoming every day more apparent that they desire to get from under the obligations these terms will impose upon them in the making of peace. If we do not use care, we shall place ourselves in some such dishonorable position as Germany when she violated her treaty obligations as to Belgium." [4]

To meet the criticism that the Fourteen Points represented a vague program, House arranged in Paris to have them explicitly interpreted in a lengthy memorandum by Walter Lippmann, Secretary of "The Inquiry," [5] and Frank I. Cobb, editor of the *New York World*. This commentary was ready by October 29, when House transmitted it to President Wilson for his approval "at the earliest possible moment." [6] Wilson found it a "satisfactory interpretation of the principles involved" but thought that the "details of application mentioned should be regarded as merely illustrative suggestions and reserved for [the] peace conference." [7]

2. Robert Lansing, *The Peace Negotiations* (Boston, 1921), pp. 43–45, 190–198.

3. Wilson to Dr. E. P. Davis, October 26, 1918, Baker, *Wilson,* VIII, 518.

4. Seymour, *House Papers,* IV, 150–151.

5. This name was given to the body of American experts organized in the United States by Colonel House to study the problems connected with the peace settlement.

6. House to Lansing, October 29, 1918, *Foreign Relations, 1918,* Supplement I, I, 405–413; Seymour, *House Papers,* IV, 154–158, 192–200. The Cobb-Lippmann memorandum is found in Appendix E.

7. Wilson to House, October 30, 1918, *Foreign Relations, 1918,* Supplement I, I, 421.

During the armistice discussions House had the memorandum on the table so that he could refer to it whenever a question arose as to the implications of any particular point.

The British were the first to raise objections to the Fourteen Points when their endorsement was sought. Late on October 27, the day after House's arrival in Paris, Sir William Wiseman, British expert on American affairs, informed him that the British Cabinet had had "stormy sessions over the President's peace terms." He said they rebelled against the freedom of the seas and wanted to include reparations for losses suffered at sea. House replied "that if the British were not careful they would bring upon themselves the dislike of the world," that "the United States and other countries would not willingly submit to Great Britain's complete domination of the seas any more than to Germany's domination of the land, and the sooner the English recognized this fact, the better it would be for them." He even suggested that the United States "if challenged, would build a navy and maintain an army greater than theirs." On October 28 and 29 he made it plain to other British leaders and "to the French and Italians as well, that he meant to insist upon the Fourteen Points as a condition of the United States joining in the Armistice negotiations." [8]

At a luncheon with British leaders on October 29 House learned from Lloyd George "that it was his opinion that if the Allies submitted to Germany's terms of armistice without more [discussion?], Germany would assume that the Allies had accepted President Wilson's fourteen points and other speeches without qualification." The British Premier made it clear that Point 2, dealing with the freedom of the seas, could not be accepted without qualification, unless it were incorporated into the constitution of a league of nations satisfactory to the British. He did not wish to discuss freedom of the seas with Germany and would not agree to it as a condition of peace.[9]

After luncheon, in a conference at the Quai d'Orsay, Clemenceau with his Foreign Minister Pichon, Lloyd George with Foreign Secretary Balfour, Italy's Foreign Minister Sonnino, and Colonel House discussed Wilson's program. Clemenceau and Sonnino were "not at all in sympathy with the idea of a league of nations." House got the impression that the Italian Premier would "submit many objections to the Fourteen Points."

8. Seymour, *House Papers,* IV, 160.

9. House to Lansing, October 30, 1918, *Foreign Relations, 1918,* Supplement I, I, 421; Seymour, *House Papers,* IV, 161.

"Should we not make it clear to the German Government," Lloyd George asked, "that we are not going in on the Fourteen Points of peace?"

Clemenceau said that Wilson had never asked him whether he accepted the Fourteen Points. In answer to Clemenceau's direct question Lloyd George said he had never been asked either.

"Do you think," the British Prime Minister asked, turning to Colonel House, "that if we agree to an armistice we accept the President's peace terms?"

"That," replied House, "is my view."

Clemenceau insisted upon having the Fourteen Points read. "Yes," added Sonnino, "and the five more and the others." The reading began, and in answer to the objections that were made House read from the commentary that had been prepared. Lloyd George again objected strongly to Point 2.

"We cannot accept this under any circumstances," he said, repeating what he had told House at lunch; "it takes away from us the power of blockade. My view is this, I want to see the character of [the] League of Nations first before I accept this proposition. I do not wish to discuss it with Germany, I will not make it a condition of peace with Germany." House spoke frankly, to the effect that future British interference with American trade during another war might find the United States taking sides with Great Britain's enemies. The French and the Italians joined in the discussion, not because they were concerned about freedom of the seas but rather because they objected in principle to virtually everything involved in the Fourteen Points. Sonnino wished to have President Wilson informed that his program was unacceptable because it was impossible to agree upon a peace program while engaged in drafting an armistice. House was determined not to have agreement on Wilson's principles postponed. If the Powers associated with the United States persisted in their objections, he said, President Wilson would be forced to say to Germany: "The Allies do not agree to the conditions of peace proposed by me and accordingly the present negotiations are at an end." Then, House explained, the President would be "free to consider the question afresh and to determine whether the United States should continue to fight for the principles laid down by the Allies." His warning had "an exciting effect on those present."

Balfour came into the discussion at this point to say "that it was clear that the Germans were trying to drive a wedge between the President and the Allies and that their attempts in this direction must be foiled." House then proposed that the proper course would be "for France, England, and Italy to get together to limit their acceptance of the fourteen conditions; that would be the first preliminary to working out the Armistice." He offered to withdraw from the conference so that the others would be free to discuss the matter among themselves without the embarrassment of his presence; but they asked him to remain since "they had no secret from America." Seeing the risks of a division of the Allies over this issue, Lloyd George became conciliatory and intimated that British objections were confined to the one issue of freedom of the seas. He suggested, however, that France, Great Britain, and Italy should state their objections "and see to-morrow whether we cannot agree upon a common draft." [10]

In a private conversation with House the same day Lloyd George showed that he and Wilson were worlds apart in their principles and policies. This is what House reported to the President:

> In my private conversation with Lloyd George . . . he said that Great Britain desired the United States to become trustee for German East African colonies. That Great Britain was unwilling that they should be turned back to Germany for the reason that the Germans had used such inhuman methods in their treatment of the natives. He said by right [South West] Africa and the Asiatic islands belonging to Germany must go to the South African Federation and to Australia respectively; that unless this was done Great Britain would be confronted by a revolution in those dominions.
>
> He added that Great Britain would have to assume a protectorate over Mesopotamia and perhaps Palestine. Arabia he thought should become autonomous. France might be given a sphere of influence in Syria.
>
> My [opinion, based on] his suggestion regarding German East Africa, is that the British would like us to accept something so they might more freely take what they desire.
>
> George also thought the Allies should get together before the peace conference and thresh out their differences. He believed the peace conference itself need not last longer than one week. The preliminary conference he thought could be finished in three or four weeks.
>
> I strongly advise against this procedure and for reasons which will be obvious to you.[11]

10. Seymour, *House Papers,* IV, 161–167; House to Lansing, October 30, 1918, *Foreign Relations, 1918,* Supplement I, I, 421–423.

11. House to Lansing, October 30, 1918, *ibid.,* p. 424.

House was distressed by the opposition of the Allies to Wilson's program. American newspapermen realized also how unpopular the Fourteen Points were; through Cobb they told House on the 29th that the "general opinion of all American correspondents in Paris is that the one definite policy of the Allies at this time is to take control of the peace negotiations out of the [hands] of President Wilson." Americans returning from London had come to the same conclusion.[12]

House had no intention of yielding in the fight for the President's program. And he was strengthened in his determination by the following code telegram from Wilson on the 29th:

Can be no real difficulty about peace terms and interpretation of fourteen points if the Entente statesmen will be perfectly frank with us and have no selfish aims of their own which would in any case alienate us from them altogether. It is the fourteen points that Germany has accepted. England cannot dispense with our friendship in the future and the other Allies cannot without our assistance get their rights as against England. If it is the purpose of the Allied statesmen to nullify my influence force the purpose boldly to the surface and let me speak of it to all the world as I shall. League of nations underlies freedom of the seas and every other part of peace programme so far as I am concerned. I am ready to repudiate any selfish programme openly, but assume that the Allies cannot honorably turn the present discussions into a peace conference without me. Please do not use wireless.[13]

When Wilson began getting reports about the opposition of the Allies to his program, he showed he was going to fight for his principles with all the Presbyterian stubbornness of his nature. On the 30th he sent the following code message to House:

I feel it my solemn duty to authorize you to say that I cannot consent to take part in the negotiation of a peace which does not include freedom of the seas because we are pledged to fight not only to do away with Prussian militarism but with militarism everywhere. Neither could I participate in a settlement which did not include league of nations because peace would be without any guarantee except universal armament which would be intolerable. I hope I shall not be obliged to make this decision public.[14]

12. House to Lansing, October 29, 1918, *ibid.*, p. 413.

13. Wilson to House, October 29, 1918, Baker, *Wilson,* VIII, 529.

14. Wilson to House, October 30, 1918, *Foreign Relations, 1918,* Supplement I, I, 423.

Even before he received this defiant telegram, Colonel House had been pondering the situation. He had been deeply disappointed and depressed by his talks of the 29th. As he considered everything, he came to the conclusion that his best hope lay in reaching an understanding with the British, who had intimated that an agreement with Wilson might be possible on all points but freedom of the seas and reparations. By satisfying Lloyd George in these two matters, House believed he could count on British help to persuade the French and Italians to abandon their objections to the Fourteen Points. The problem was on his mind when he went to bed on the 29th; it prevented his sleeping again after he had been awakened by the noise of motorcycles around three o'clock in the morning. "It then occurred to me," he writes, "there was a way out of the difficulty. I would tell them that if they did not accept the President's Fourteen Points and other terms enunciated since January 8, I would advise the President to go before Congress and lay the facts before it, giving the terms which England, France, and Italy insisted upon, and ask the advice of Congress whether the United States should make peace with Germany now that she has accepted the American terms, or whether we should go on fighting until Germany had accepted the terms of France, England, and Italy, whatever they might be. . . . I turned over and went to sleep, knowing I had found a solution of a very troublesome problem." [15]

Later in the day House informed Wilson by telegram of his intentions. He knew that the Allies would fear to have it published to the world by the President of the United States that "their conditions of peace are essentially different from the points you have laid down and for which the American people are fighting. . . . I told the British privately," his telegram went on, "you anticipate that their policy would lead to the establishment of the greatest naval program by the United States that the world had ever seen. I did not believe that the United States would consent for any [power] to interpret for them the rules under which American commerce could traverse the sea. I would suggest that you quietly diminish the transport of troops[16] giving as excuse the prevalence of influenza or any other reason but the real one. I would also suggest a little later that you begin to gently shut

15. Seymour, *House Papers,* IV, 167, 169.

16. Pershing had asked for 350,000 American soldiers for January, 1919, and Wilson had already assured the country that there would be no diminution of effort while negotiating with Germany.

down upon money, food and raw material. I feel confident that we should play a strong hand and if it meets with your approval I will do it in the gentle and friendly [way] almost certain [to prevail?]." [17]

Just before the morning's conference at the Ministry of War, Lloyd George gave House the British draft of a reply to President Wilson's request of the 23d for views on his correspondence with Germany about an armistice:

The Allied Governments have given careful consideration to the correspondence which has passed between the President of the United States and the German Government. Subject to the qualifications which follow they declare their willingness to make peace with the Government of Germany on the terms of peace laid down in the President's address to Congress of January 8, 1918, and the principles of settlement enunciated in his subsequent addresses. They must point out, however, that clause two, relating to what is usually described as Freedom of the Seas, is open to various interpretations, some of which they could not accept. They must therefore reserve to themselves complete freedom on this subject when they enter the Peace Conference.

Further, in the conditions of peace laid down in his address to Congress of January 8, 1918, the President declared that invaded territories must be restored as well as evacuated and freed. The Allied Governments feel that no doubt ought to be allowed to exist as to what this provision implies. By it they understand that compensation will be made by Germany for all damage done to the civilian population of the Allies, and their property by the forces of Germany by land, by sea, and from the air.

House was pleased with the moderate tone of this draft, which was "in marked contrast" to the position Lloyd George had taken the day before.

In the conference of Clemenceau, Lloyd George, and House that followed, it developed "that Clemenceau was having prepared an elaborate brief setting forth France's objections to the President's Fourteen Points."

"I promptly pointed out to Clemenceau," House reported, "that undoubtedly Sonnino was preparing a similar memorandum and that if the Allied Governments felt constrained to submit an

17. House to Lansing, October 30, 1918, *Foreign Relations, 1918,* Supplement I, I, 423–424.

elaborate answer to the President containing many objections to his program, it would doubtless be necessary for the President to go to Congress and to place before that body exactly what Italy, France, and Great Britain were fighting for and to place the responsibility upon Congress for the further continuation of the war by the United States in behalf of the aims of the Allies. As soon as I had said this George and Clemenceau looked at each other significantly." [18]

House's 3 A.M. solution worked. "Clemenceau at once abandoned his idea of submitting an elaborate memorandum . . . and apparently accepted the proposed answer drafted by the British." House telegraphed the text of the draft, now approved by Clemenceau, to Wilson and suggested that if all the Allies should adopt it as their answer to his communication of October 23, he accept it "without alteration."

Wilson replied by telegraph the next day. He made it clear that he sympathized with "the exceptional position and necessities of Great Britain with regard to the use of the seas for defence both at home and throughout the Empire" and that he also realized "that freedom of the seas needs careful definition." He was not convinced, however, that Lloyd George's proposed reply "definitely accepts the principle of freedom of the seas and means to reserve only the free discussion of definitions and limitations." He urged House to "insist that that be made clear before I decide whether to accept the reply or go again to the Congress who confidentially will have no sympathy whatever with spending American lives for British naval control."

"Terms one, two, three, and fourteen," the President said, "are the essentially American terms in the programme and I cannot change what our troops are fighting for or consent to end with only European arrangements of peace. Freedom of the seas will not have to be discussed with Germany if we agree among ourselves beforehand but will be if we do not. Blockade is one of the many things which will require immediate redefinition in view of the many new circumstances of warfare developed by this war. There is no danger of its being abolished" as the British fear.

The President made it clear that he could not "agree to George's programme of a general settlement among ourselves before the general peace conference." He said he was "entitled to take personal part in the real settlement and such preliminaries

18. House to Lansing, October 30, 1918, Seymour, *House Papers,* IV, 170–171; *Foreign Relations, 1918,* Supplement I, I, 425–426.

would make the final conference a mere form." He closed the telegram with an assuring pat on the back for House, "I am proud of the way you are handling things." [19]

Now that the French had accepted the British draft House sought Italian support for it. The Italians objected to it in the afternoon meeting on the 30th and produced a memorandum on Point 9, concerning their frontiers. Disregarding protests, Sonnino insisted upon reading the draft he had prepared. History, geography, security, and nationality were all invoked to support Italy's claim to extensive territories on the eastern shore of the Adriatic. Warm discussion followed, and would have been prolonged had not Clemenceau suddenly interrupted:

"Are we agreed respecting the reply to Germany? I accept. Lloyd George accepts. [Turning to Orlando] Do you accept?"

"Yes," said Orlando.

And so by this somewhat abrupt procedure the Italians were prevented, for the time being at any rate, from attaching reservations to the pre-Armistice agreement.

House was elated over his victory. "Everything is changing for the better since yesterday," he cabled triumphantly to Wilson on October 31, "and I hope you will not insist upon my using your cable except as I may think best." He asked for a free hand in dealing with the immediate negotiations. "I can assure you," he informed the President, "that nothing will be done to embarrass you or to compromise any of your peace principles. You will have as free a hand after the Armistice is signed as you now have. It is exceedingly important that nothing be said or done at this time which may in any way halt the Armistice which will save so many thousands of lives. Negotiations are now proceeding satisfactorily." [20]

When the final terms of armistice for Austria were drafted that same day, House was proud of his success in keeping all discussion of the Fourteen Points out of that question.[21] It was his de-

19. Wilson to House, October 31, 1918, *ibid.*, pp. 427–428. The complete text is found in Baker, *Wilson,* VIII, 537–539. Cf. Seymour, *House Papers,* IV, 171–172 and note.

20. *Ibid.*, pp. 172–174.

21. Whether the Fourteen Points were legally a part of the Austrian armistice or not is a difficult question to answer. Like Germany, Austria had asked Wilson for an armistice and peace on that basis. Charles Seymour writes that "Colonel House evidently regarded the Allies as bound to the President's terms in the case of Austria." *House Papers,* IV, 177–178. This view is not entirely consistent with the satisfaction House derived from the fact that he kept the Fourteen Points out of the discussion of Austrian armistice terms. The text of

sire to have them accepted at the time the Allies agreed to armistice terms for Germany. The final phase of his fight for the Fourteen Points started on November 1, when the Supreme War Council met at Versailles to consider Germany's armistice. Clemenceau, who presided, took up the first item of business, namely, the approval by the Council of Lloyd George's draft reply to Wilson.[22] Hymans of Belgium touched off the debate.

HYMANS: I wish to state some reservations concerning article 3 [removal of economic barriers] and article 5 [concerning the interests of native populations in the adjustment of colonial matters] of the Fourteen Points of President Wilson.

Article 3 abolishes all economic barriers; I should like to call your attention to the fact that, as a result of the ravaging and pillaging of Belgium, we must adopt special measures to prevent the invasion of our country by German products; we must ask our allies for preferential treatment.

Article 5 refers to colonies, proposing a free adjustment. In this matter we must maintain our absolute rights to our colonial domain whose integrity we insist upon. Furthermore, these rights have been recognized by our allies.

LLOYD GEORGE: I would have, in that which concerns me, an observation to make on article 3. We are all in the same condition. By way of introduction I should like to ask Mr. House to clear up this point for us. We are going to be short of raw materials, among them, wool, tin, tungsten, manganese, cotton also, perhaps. We have a certain amount but not enough to give some to everybody. What does the article say on this point? After the peace is signed, must we make an equal distribution of available stocks among all peoples? Germany is already at an advantage because her machines are intact whereas in Allied countries and particularly in Belgium, a large part of the factories are either destroyed or deteriorated.

HOUSE: I do not have my notes with me, but I am quite ready

House's telegram to Lansing on October 31 quoted in the *House Papers* (p. 178) differs from that given in *Foreign Relations, 1918* (p. 431) so that House's opinion on the matter is not perfectly clear.

22. The protocol of the session of November 1 is found in Mermeix, *Les Négociations Secrètes* (Paris, 1919), pp. 226–239. According to Mermeix, p. 226, the version that Clemenceau read was a slightly revised one and differed from the first draft (*supra*, p. 273) only in the last sentence, which read as follows: "By it they understand that compensation will be made by Germany for all damage suffered by the civilian population of the Allies and by their property as the result of Germany's invasion of Allied lands, either on land, or on the sea, or in consequence of operations in the air."

to give detailed explanations of Wilson's Fourteen Points to whoever desires it.

LLOYD GEORGE: In the newspapers I have seen that certain persons have interpreted the articles of Mr. Wilson in question as proposing the abolition of all commercial tariffs. That is not the case; but does President Wilson mean that after the peace is signed no country must have preferential tariffs?

HOUSE: It is impossible for me to answer now, I do not have my notes.

LLOYD GEORGE: Are we to send, for example, as much wool to Germany and to France as we keep for ourselves? I think we must first talk these matters over before we send our message to the President.

VESNITCH: I am anxious to point out to you that, so far as article 3 is concerned, Serbia finds herself in the same position as Belgium.

ORLANDO: I wish to remind you that during the meeting of Government heads in which we prepared this note, the Italian Government made reservations about article 9 [re-adjustment of Italian frontiers] which lends itself to various interpretations. At that time I was told that the note concerned Germany only and that the article was thus not under consideration.

Since this note is now being examined in plenary session, I insist that notice must be taken of the reservations that I previously made on the subject of article 9.

CLEMENCEAU: Mr. House will give explanations on all the points.

LLOYD GEORGE: It is my belief that articles 9 and 10 [autonomy for the peoples of Austria-Hungary], 11 [Roumania, Serbia, and Montenegro] and 12 [Turkey and the Dardanelles] have nothing to do with the document we must send to Germany. Would it not be preferable to add a paragraph saying that we have no desire to discuss with Germany clauses that do not concern her?

Clemenceau now turned the discussion from the Fourteen Points to the military and naval terms to be imposed on Germany.

Complying with Wilson's request that Lloyd George's position with regard to Point 2 be made perfectly clear, Colonel House, upon his return that night from the conference at Versailles, summoned Sir William Wiseman "and told him that unless Lloyd George would make some reasonable concessions in his attitude upon the 'Freedom of the Seas,' all hope of Anglo-Saxon unity would be at an end; that the United States went to war with England in 1812 on the question of her rights at sea, and that she had gone to war with Germany in 1917 upon the same question." If Lloyd George expressed the British viewpoint as he indicated, House warned "there would be greater feeling against Great Britain at the end of the war than there had been since our Civil War . . . [and] our people would not consent to allow the British Government, or any other Government, to determine upon what terms our ships should sail the seas, either in time of peace or in time of war." Wiseman promised to discuss the matter with "his people" immediately and to report on his efforts in the morning.[23]

After lunch the next day House worked with Wiseman and with Lord Reading, who was Lord Chief Justice and had served as special envoy to the United States, for two hours on the issue, but "got nowhere." House told Reading that the English attitude was like Germany's toward her Army in the spring of 1914: that she needed an army because Europe was armed against her and that her Army did not exist for aggressive purposes. "But Germany came to grief," warned House, "and in my opinion it was inevitable that Great Britain would likewise have cause to regret such an arbitrary attitude."[24] Instead of having debate on details occupy the time of the formal sessions, as on the day before, House sought to arrive at agreement on difficult questions in private talks of this sort. He reported to Wilson that he spent "almost every minute" outside the time for conferences in discussing Point 2 with the British. An agreement with them was essential, for "Clemenceau and Orlando will accept anything that the English will agree to concerning article 2. . . . I am insisting," he told Wilson, "that they must recognize the principle, that it is a strong case for discussion[25] at the peace conference or before and I am having the greatest difficulty in getting them to admit even that much. . . . I believe if I could get the matter postponed until you come that some satisfactory solution might be arrived at."[26]

The meeting to be held the afternoon of November 3 was a critical one, as House realized. "I was fully prepared," he said

23. Seymour, *House Papers,* IV, 179–180.
24. *Ibid.,* p. 180.
25. "that it is a subject for discussion" is the reading in House, *ibid.,* p. 175.
26. House to Lansing, November 3, 1918, *Foreign Relations, 1918,* Supplement I, I, 448; Seymour, *House Papers,* IV, 175–176.

in his report to President Wilson, "to exert strong pressure in order to secure from the Allies an acceptance of the President's fourteen points. . . ." Lloyd George opened the discussion by saying that he would stand by the position taken in the draft note he had given House on October 30.[27] House said that the draft did not make it clear that the Allies accepted the principle of the freedom of the seas when it said that they must "reserve to themselves complete freedom on this subject when they enter the peace conference." House then read a paraphrase of Wilson's telegram of October 31, omitting the sentence in which the President threatened to place the whole matter before the American Congress "who confidentially will have no sympathy whatever with spending American lives for British naval control."

Lloyd George stood by his reservation. "This is not merely a question for Great Britain," he said, looking for the support of Orlando and Clemenceau, "but also for France and Italy. We have all benefited by the blockade which prevented steel, copper, rubber, and many other classes of goods from entering Germany. This has been a very important element in the defeat of the enemy."

"Yes," said House, "but the President does not object to the principle of blockade. He merely asks that the principle of the Freedom of the Seas be accepted."

Clemenceau interjected: "I do not see any reason for not accepting the principle. We accept"; and, turning to Lloyd George with his frank and pleasant manner: "You do also, do you not?"

But Lloyd George stood his ground, not to be charmed from his position. "No," he said, "I could not accept the principle of the Freedom of the Seas. It has got associated in the public mind with the blockade. It's no good saying I accept the principle. It would only mean that in a week's time a new Prime Minister would be here who would say that he could not accept this principle. The English people will not look at it. On this point the nation is absolutely solid. It's no use for me to say that I can accept when I know that I am not speaking for the British nation."

House then wanted to know whether the British would discuss the principle freely at the Peace Conference if they could not accept it now. Or was the British reservation a challenge to Wilson?

"This formula does not in the least challenge the position of

27. This conference of November 3 is described in Seymour, *House Papers*, IV, 176–177, 182–185 and in House's despatch to Lansing, November 3, 1918, *Foreign Relations, 1918,* Supplement I, I, 455–457.

the United States," said Lloyd George. "All we say is that we reserve the freedom to discuss the point when we go to the Peace Conference. I don't despair of coming to an agreement."

"I wish you would write something I could send the President," said House.

"Will he like something of this kind?" returned Lloyd George: " 'We are quite willing to discuss the Freedom of the Seas and its application.' " If so, he said he would be willing to say that to President Wilson and would instruct the British Ambassador in Washington so to inform the President. House said he preferred to have Lloyd George give him the information so that he could himself inform Mr. Wilson.

As a result of this understanding, House received the following letter from Lloyd George:

British Embassy
Paris, November 3d, 1918.

My Dear Colonel House: I write to confirm the statement I made in the course of our talk this afternoon at your house when I told you that "We were quite willing to discuss the Freedom of the Seas in the light of the new conditions which have arisen in the course of the present war." In our judgment this most important subject can only be dealt with satisfactorily through the freest debate and the most liberal exchange of views.

I send you this letter after having had an opportunity of talking the matter over with the Foreign Secretary, who quite agrees.

Ever sincerely,

D. Lloyd George

On November 3 Orlando made another unsuccessful attempt to enter a reservation on Point 9. Neither Lloyd George nor Clemenceau could see that any reservation on this article was pertinent to armistice terms for Germany. That should have been a part of the Austrian armistice terms; but those had already been despatched to the Austrians. In fact, they were accepted at three o'clock that very afternoon.

Lloyd George thought that President Wilson might be reminded that Point 9 had no bearing on Germany.

"I think," suggested House, "that it would be better to say nothing at all on this matter to President Wilson. It would be inadvisable to increase the number of exceptions."

"Yes," agreed Clemenceau, "it is desirable to suggest as few changes or reservations as possible to the Fourteen Points."

And so Italian objections to the Fourteen Points had to await the peace conference.

Lloyd George and Hymans brought up article 3 again. The latter wanted an arrangement that would enable Belgium to secure raw materials and would protect her against dumping during the period of reconstruction: specifically, a barrier against German goods that might swamp Belgian markets. House argued that Germany would have to export goods. "We have got to remember," he explained, "that Germany must necessarily pay out thousands of millions and that she must be in a condition to pay them. If we prevent her from making a living, she will not be able to pay." The French and Belgians found that a difficult argument to answer; they looked upon themselves as future beneficiaries of German reparations. When attention was called to the fact that Point 3 asked for "the removal so far as possible of all economic barriers" the qualification made further reservation unnecessary.

"I think," said the Belgian Foreign Minister, "that we should have a more ample phrase than merely 'damages to the civilian population.' "

"It is then for indirect compensation that you ask?" said Lloyd George.

"I do not ask for it now," replied Hymans, "but I should like to have a phrase referring to it."

"I think it will be a mistake to put into the Armistice terms," insisted Lloyd George, "anything that will lead Germany to suppose that we want a war indemnity."

Thus Italian and Belgian reservations to the Fourteen Points and to Lloyd George's proposed note to Wilson were eliminated. There remained the two reservations that the British insisted upon: the right to complete freedom in defining "freedom of the seas" in the peace conference, and the explanation that the evacuation of occupied territory by Germany carried with it the obligation on Germany's part to pay for the direct damage done to the civilian population.

House was still not satisfied with the British reservation on the freedom of the seas. Nevertheless, in his report of November 3 to Wilson he advised the President to accept the note. "If I do not hear from you to the contrary," he cabled, "I shall assume that you accept the situation as it now is. This I strongly advise.

Any other decision would cause serious friction and delay." Lloyd George's letter to House on the free seas issue "must not be published unless it becomes necessary." [28]

Wilson was disappointed in his failure to get an unqualified acceptance of Point 2. On November 4 he authorized House to inform the Allies that if they did not accept it they could "count on the certainty of our using our present equipment to build up the strongest navy that our resources permit and as our people have long desired." [29] But the President gave in to House's recommendation that the agreement be accepted in order to avoid friction and delay.[30]

How Colonel House felt about his failure to get agreement with the English on the question is clear from his diary entry for November 4:

> It is difficult to fully tell of the tense feeling that has prevailed due to the discussion of the Fourteen Points. George and I, and Reading and I have had many conferences, separately and together. . . .
>
> Lloyd George said that Great Britain would spend her last guinea to keep a navy superior to that of the United States or any other Power, and that no Cabinet official could continue in the Government in England who took a different position. I countered this by telling him it was not our purpose to go into a naval building rivalry with Great Britain, but it was our purpose to have our rights at sea adequately safeguarded, and that we did not intend to have our commerce regulated by Great Britain whenever she was at war.
>
> After we had this debate, George sent Reading around to argue the matter with me. . . . I told Reading he was wasting his breath, that in no circumstances would we yield the point about the Freedom of the Seas being a matter for discussion between our two Governments. I insisted that sooner or later we would come to a clash if an understanding was not reached as to laws governing the seas. I let him know that it was not my intention to budge and that I had the backing of the President.[31]

On the afternoon of November 4 House, reporting on the procedure to be followed in informing the Germans how they could get an armistice, told Wilson that Lloyd George's draft letter

28. House to Lansing, November 3, 1918, *Foreign Relations, 1918,* Supplement I, I, 455–457.

29. Quoted in Seymour, *House Papers,* IV, 179.

30. Wilson to House, November 4, 1918, Baker, *Wilson,* VIII, 550.

31. Seymour, *House Papers,* IV, 180–181.

had been accepted, the only change being the insertion of the italicized words to make the last sentence read: "By it they understand that compensation will be made by Germany for all the damage done to the civilian population of the Allies and their property *by the aggression of Germany* by land, by sea, and from the air." "This," said Colonel House, "with Lloyd George's letter [declaring England's willingness to discuss the freedom of the seas] . . . makes the situation quite satisfactory for the moment." [32]

House was overjoyed. His private-code message to Wilson carried a note of triumph:

I consider that we have won a great diplomatic victory in getting the Allies to accept the principles laid down in your January eighth speech and in your subsequent addresses. This has been done in the face of a hostile and influential junta in the United States and the thoroughly unsympathetic personnel constituting the Entente governments. I doubt whether any other heads of the governments with whom we have been dealing realize how far they are now committed to the American peace programme. . . . Both French Prime Minister and George wanted to make the League of Nations an after consideration, and not . . . a part of the Peace Conference. . . .[33]

In his diary for November 4 House wrote that he was "glad the exceptions were made, for it emphasizes the acceptance of the Fourteen Points." [34]

The Allies were now no longer free to do as they pleased with Germany; when Germany accepted the agreement and proceeded to conclude the armistice, the Entente nations were bound morally and legally to a pledge that peace with Germany would be made on the basis of the Fourteen Points.[35]

Wilson informed the Cabinet on Tuesday, November 5, of the victory House had won for his program in Paris, and said that the two reservations made to his Fourteen Points were satisfactory. Writing about that day's session of the Cabinet, Secretary of the Interior Lane said that the President was "in splendid humor and good trim—not worried a bit. And why should he be,

32. House to Lansing, November 4, 1918, *Foreign Relations, 1918,* Supplement I, I, 460–462.

33. House to Wilson, November 5, 1918, Baker, *Wilson,* VIII, 554.

34. Seymour, *House Papers,* IV, 188.

35. Cf. Charles Seymour, *American Diplomacy during the World War* (Baltimore, 1934), pp. 393–394.

for the world is at his feet eating out of his hand! No Caesar ever had such a triumph." [36] The Secretary of Agriculture, David F. Houston, said, "The President came in looking well and happy. He acted as if a load had been taken off his mind. He appeared to be less hurried and less under a strain than I had seen him for years." [37]

But this day of victory was also a day of defeat. On this day, when Wilson notified Germany that the Allies would "make peace . . . on the terms of peace laid down" in the Fourteen Points except for the two reservations, the American people gave their answer to his appeal for the return of a Democratic Congress to support him and his principles. They elected an overwhelmingly Republican Congress—and Wilson stood repudiated at home just when he was being accepted abroad.

36. *The Letters of Franklin K. Lane,* pp. 297–298.

37. D. F. Houston, *Eight Years with Wilson's Cabinet,* I, 320.

XII

Drafting Armistice Terms for Germany

DRAFTING the armistice terms for Germany was a difficult matter. On Tuesday, October 29, House met with the Prime Ministers (except Orlando, who had not yet arrived) and the Foreign Ministers to discuss the proposals. There was a general predisposition to accept the military terms of Marshal Foch; they seemed to offer adequate guarantees against any resumption of the war by Germany. There was more difficulty with the naval terms, which the British had been working on since October 6. Admiral Wemyss and Sir Eric Geddes brought them to Paris on the 27th and Wemyss had no doubt that the Allied Naval Council would approve them the next day and the Supreme War Council would ratify them soon thereafter. He recognized the "fact that so far as the naval terms are concerned it is impossible not to embody terms of peace." But the approval of the Naval Council was not so easily achieved; Wemyss found the Americans "tiresome" and "sententious," the Italians "grasping." Even Lloyd George, although firm with regard to the freedom of the seas, was inclined to think the proposed naval terms too hard.[1]

Taken together, the military terms of Foch and the naval terms of the British appeared to the members of the conference on October 29 too severe.

"Do you think," Balfour asked Clemenceau, "that there is the smallest prospect of the Germans accepting these terms?"

"They won't the first day," replied Clemenceau, "but they will somehow or other contrive not to let the conversations drop." He suggested, however, that the naval terms were "rather stiff."

Lloyd George then read the terms, as drafted by the British and approved by the Naval Council; they called for the surrender of 150 submarines, 10 battleships, and 6 battle cruisers, besides lighter craft.

"What are the Allies going to do," asked Colonel House, "with the ships they take from Germany?"

"They will divide them," replied the British Prime Minister.

1. Lady Wester Wemyss, *Life and Times of Admiral Wemyss*, pp. 386–387.

"You can sink them if you like; you must take them away from Germany."

"Well," said Balfour, "I do not think Germany will agree to these conditions. They are stiffer than those imposed on France in 1871; you will have to beat them in the field worse than they are beaten now." [2]

The same day Marshal Foch wrote the following letter to Clemenceau:

I had the honor of sending you on October 26 the military conditions of the armistice.

It is likely that naval conditions will be added. The latter cannot be accepted without examination; for if they are too severe, it would result in the continuance by the land forces of a costly struggle for advantages of questionable value.

I ask therefore to be heard before the final draft of the terms of the armistice is fixed.[3]

Others shared these views. "We are all agreed," wrote Colonel House in his diary that evening, "that the articles drawn up by the navy are entirely too severe and we propose to soften them. We plan to eliminate the German battle cruisers and submarine fleet which will be all that is necessary." [4]

He reported these difficulties to President Wilson in a long telegram on October 30:

. . . I ascertained that George and Clemenceau believed that the terms of the armistice, both naval and military, were too severe and that they should be modified. George stated that he thought it might be unwise to insist on the occupation of the east bank of the Rhine. Clemenceau stated that he could not maintain himself in the Chamber of Deputies unless this was made a part of the armistice to be submitted to the Germans, and that the French army would also insist on this as their due after the long occupation of French soil by the Germans; but he gave us his word of honor that France would withdraw after the peace conditions had been fulfilled. I am inclined to sympathize with the position taken by Clemenceau.

I pointed out the danger of bringing about a state of Bolshevism in Germany if the terms of the armistice were made too stiff, and

2. Seymour, *House Papers,* IV, 117–118.
3. Foch, *Mémoires,* II, 284.
4. Seymour, *House Papers,* IV, 118.

the consequent danger to England, France, and Italy. Clemenceau refused to recognize that there was any danger of Bolshevism in France. George admitted it was possible to create such a state of affairs in England, and both agreed that anything might happen in Italy.[5]

The first formal session of the Allied Supreme War Council was held the morning of October 31 at Versailles. Just before the meeting opened news came that Turkey had signed an armistice and that Austria had asked for one. Although the business of the conference was to consider the terms for Austria, Foch was asked to describe the general military situation. The favorable news that had come in made the task easier, says Foch. His description follows:

Today is October 31, and since July 18 we have forced the enemy to retreat. We have attacked him along 400 kilometers and we are continuing to do so on the same front. Since July 18 the enemy has lost more than 240,000 men, perhaps 280,000. I am sure of the first figure, but I think the second is correct. He has left in our hands more than 4,000 cannon, perhaps 4,500. An army which during three months is forced to retreat, which is undergoing losses, which can no longer straighten its line, is a beaten army; but, however, it is bent upon a methodical destruction, accepting battle everywhere. To the prisoners must be added losses in men, in material, in supplies, in munitions, of which the number is considerable and which we have not been able to total at this time.

Military disorganization is therefore an accomplished fact, but the struggle continues and is prolonged.

On our side, we are able, with the coming of winter, to continue this 400 kilometer battle; the effective force of our armies permits us to do so. The French and British Armies have suffered losses, to be sure, but they can continue; the American Army is still fresh and its reserves are coming daily. The morale of the troops is excellent, our soldiers are aware of their ascendancy over the enemy. Some time ago the situation was not the same: thus, in Flanders we were on wet ground; on the banks of the Yser, the British and Belgian Armies, after four years of war, found themselves in a swamp. If we had not gotten out of there a month ago, perhaps we might not get out today; today we are in a rich country. To march for-

5. *Ibid.*, pp. 118–119.

ward we have the material, the communications, and a good morale; that allows us to continue.

On the Italian front the situation is very favorable. We learned today that the enemy armies were cut in two by the capture of Monte Grappa which allows us to march on Belluno and Vittorio.

In the east the situation is secured: the defeat of Bulgaria permits the liberation of Serbia and the line of the Danube is occupied by us; communications between the Central Powers and southern Russia have been cut by our troops.

You know what the situation is in Turkey. The victories in Palestine have destroyed the Turkish Army; they have hardly any troops left in Europe and, having no other solution, they are ready to capitulate.

Therefore the war is over in the east and it is favorable to us in the west. We can continue it, if the foe desires it, right up to their complete defeat; our enemies are now possibly limited to but one, Germany.[6]

At this meeting Colonel House put a question which drew a reply of great significance.

"Will you tell us, M. le Maréchal," said House, "solely from the military point of view, apart from any other consideration, whether you would prefer the Germans to reject or to sign the armistice as outlined here?"

"Fighting," replied Foch, "means struggling for certain results (*On ne fait la guerre que pour les résultats*). If the Germans now sign an armistice under the general conditions we have just determined, those results are in our possession. This being achieved, no man has the right to cause another drop of blood to be shed." [7]

The next morning, to prepare for the formal meeting of the War Council in the afternoon, the heads of government met at House's headquarters with Foch, Weygand, and Sir Eric Geddes, who represented the Naval Council. Foch's recommendations were taken up first. Lloyd George found them "rather stiff," charging Foch with seeking to occupy far too much of western Germany. ". . . would it not be possible," he asked Foch, "to secure the

6. Cited in Mermeix, *Les Négociations Secrètes,* pp. 205–206; Foch, *Mémoires,* II, 284–285.

7. Seymour, *House Papers,* IV, 89, 91; Foch, *Mémoires,* II, 285. Charles Seymour gives the date of this interchange as November 1; Foch says it is October 31. Cf. R. S. Baker, *Wilson,* VIII, 534–535. For Foch's later defense against having made a premature armistice see Recouly, *Marshal Foch,* pp. 43–48.

bridgeheads required for military purposes without occupying the great cities?" Believing with Marshal Haig that the Germans were far from being beaten and that the British and French Armies were very tired, the British feared excessive demands that might lead to a rupture of the armistice negotiations. Foch argued at length against Haig's views and said it was essential to Allied military supremacy to occupy the bridgeheads and other German territory. "If Germany should break off the peace negotiations," he said, "the Allies ought to be in a position to destroy her." House "was not disposed to take from Germany more than was absolutely necessary, but he was disposed to leave the matter in Marshal Foch's hands." Clemenceau's view was that Allied morale, although good at the moment, might deteriorate if the armies had to fight again. At the end of the lengthy discussion Lloyd George said that he was prepared to accept Foch's terms, though he had thought it worth while to give Marshal Haig's views full consideration first.[8]

The meeting had much more difficulty with naval terms than with the military ones. Sir Eric Geddes presented the naval program. He said that the number of German ships to be surrendered was arrived at by calculating the losses the German High Seas Fleet would have suffered had it engaged the British Grand Fleet in battle. One reason for the drastic terms was the desire to keep the Germans from renewing the war under better conditions than now existed. Sir Eric also made the point that the German fleet was superior in battle cruisers and the Allies faced the choice of making the Germans surrender theirs or else building some of their own.

Foch now turned their own argument against the British; the terms were too severe, the Germans would never consent. Although he appreciated the submarine threat and was in favor of taking submarines from Germany, Foch wondered why there was any fear of a fleet that had not left its home ports during the war. "What will you do," he asked, "if the Germans, after having accepted the severe and ample conditions that I propose, refuse to subscribe to the additional humiliations you suggest? Will you on that account run the risk of a renewal of hostilities with the useless sacrifice of thousands of lives?" It was wrong, he asserted, "to ask the armies to fight again in order to secure these conditions."

8. The detailed account of this discussion is found in Seymour, *House Papers*, IV, 119–124.

When Geddes declared that the German fleet had been a far more serious factor than Foch had thought, the Marshal proposed that the German High Seas Fleet be shut up in certain designated ports in the Baltic while the Allies occupied Helgoland and Cuxhaven. Sir Eric answered that the strain of war would still continue; the British Navy would still have to be on its guard. Lloyd George suggested a compromise involving the surrender of German submarines and battle cruisers and the internment of battleships. He then proposed that the Allied Naval Council meet again and reëxamine the question. The results of the morning discussion were placed before the Supreme War Council in the afternoon for formal adoption.[9]

Clemenceau presided at the afternoon meeting. After some consideration of the Fourteen Points the Council turned its attention to the armistice terms.[10] Each article was read and discussed, then voted on.

ARTICLE 1. Cessation of operations on land and in the air six hours after the signature of the armistice.

(Adopted without remarks.)

ARTICLE 2. Immediate evacuation of invaded countries: Belgium, France, Alsace-Lorraine, Luxembourg, scheduled in such a way as to be completed in a period of fourteen days, to date from the signature of the armistice.

German troops who have not evacuated the above-mentioned territories in the period fixed will be made prisoners of war.

The occupation of these territories by troops of the Allies and of the United States will follow the process of evacuation.

CLEMENCEAU: It is not a question of Russia in this paragraph. We should add an article saying that the treaties of Brest-Litovsk and Bucharest are abolished.

SONNINO: I propose the addition of: "All invaded territories shall be evacuated."

HOUSE: I approve that proposal.

SONNINO: I think we should dot our i's, because of the two treaties in question, and say: "All the territories taken from Russia by virtue of the Treaty of Brest-Litovsk, must be evacuated."

9. *Ibid.*, pp. 127–130.

10. The protocol of the meeting comes from Mermeix, *Les Négociations Secrètes*, pp. 229–234. Colonel House says very little about this meeting. Seymour, *House Papers*, IV, 124–125.

FOCH: I think it is useless to mention that in this paragraph. It can be made the object of another article.

(Adopted without change.)

ARTICLE 3. Repatriation, beginning immediately and to be terminated in a period of fourteen days, of the inhabitants of the countries listed above (including hostages and accused or condemned prisoners).

(Adopted.)

ARTICLE 4. Surrender by the German Armies of the following war material in good condition:

5,000 cannons (2,500 heavy and 2,500 field)
30,000 machine guns
3,000 minenwerfers
2,000 pursuit and bombing airplanes, in the first place all the D 7's and all the night bombing airplanes.

To be delivered on the spot to the Allied and United States troops.

(Adopted.)

ARTICLE 5. Evacuation by the German Armies of the country on the left bank of the Rhine.

The countries on the left bank of the Rhine will be administered by the local authorities under the control of the armies of occupation of the Allies and of the United States.

The troops of the Allies and of the United States will assure the occupation of these countries by garrisons holding the principal crossings of the Rhine (Mainz, Coblenz, Cologne) with, at these points, bridgeheads of a radius of 30 kilometers on the right bank, and garrisons also holding the strategic positions of this region.

A neutral zone will be reserved on the right bank of the Rhine, between the river and a line traced parallel to the river and 40 kilometers to the east from the Dutch frontier up to the parallel of Gemersheim, and only 30 kilometers to the east of the river from that parallel to the Swiss frontier.

The evacuation by the enemy of the countries of the Rhine shall be determined in such a way that it will be completed in a period of 11 more days, that is to say, 25 days after the signature of the armistice.

(Adopted.)

ARTICLE 6. In all the territories evacuated by the enemy, all evacuation of the inhabitants shall be prohibited. No damage or injury shall be done to either the persons or the property of the inhabitants.

No destruction of any kind shall be done.

Military establishments of all sorts shall be surrendered intact; as well as military supplies, foods, munitions, equipment, which were not removed in the period fixed upon for evacuation.

Stocks of food of all kinds for the civil population and livestock, etc., must be left on the spot.

Industrial establishments must not suffer any damage nor the personnel thereof any change.

(Adopted.)

ARTICLE 7. Roadways and all means of communication, railroads, waterways, roads, bridges, telegraphs and telephones must not suffer the slightest damage.

All civil and military personnel employed now are to be maintained.

There must be surrendered to the Associated Powers 5,000 locomotives, 150,000 railroad cars and 10,000 motor trucks in good working condition and supplied with all spare parts and necessary accessories in the period fixed for the evacuation of Belgium and Luxembourg.

The railroads of Alsace-Lorraine shall be surrendered in the same period, supplied with all pre-war personnel and material.

In addition, all material necessary to the exploitation of the country on the left bank of the Rhine will be left on the spot.

All supplies of coal, of repair parts, of tracks, of signals and shops shall be left on the spot and maintained during the whole period of the armistice.

All barges taken from the Allies shall be returned.

HYMANS: We count on demanding the restitution of our rolling stock.

CLEMENCEAU: That is included in our lump demand, and the division will be made between France and Belgium.

(Adopted.)

ARTICLE 8. The German Command will be obliged to notify us of all mines or delayed action fuses in the territories evacuated by German troops and to hasten their search and destruction.

It will also note any injurious measures which may have been taken such as the poisoning or pollution of springs or wells, etc.

All this under penalty of reprisals.

(Adopted.)

ARTICLE 9. The right of requisition shall be exercised by the Allied and United States Armies in all occupied territories.

The maintenance of the armies of occupation in the Rhine country (not counting Alsace-Lorraine) will be at the expense of the German Government.

(Adopted.)

ARTICLE 10. Immediate repatriation, without reciprocity, under conditions to be determined, of all Allied prisoners of war. The Allied Powers may dispose of them as they see fit.

Enemy prisoners will not be returned until after the signature of the preliminary peace.

(Adopted.)

ARTICLE 11. Sick or wounded who cannot be evacuated shall be cared for by German personnel which shall be left on the spot with the necessary supplies.

(Adopted.)

CLEMENCEAU: No mention is made of the restitution of stolen objects or of reparation for damages.

LLOYD GEORGE: I agree with the restitution of stolen objects but reparation for damages is a condition of peace.

CLEMENCEAU: In our factories of the north all our machines have been dismounted and carried off into Germany where they are at present at work.

HYMANS: Mr. Lloyd George has just made a very apt distinction between restitution and reparation. Thus, they took from us the cash of the *Banque Nationale* which is at present deposited with the *Deutsche Bank.*

HOUSE: General Bliss calls my attention to the fact that if we accept this addition, the restitutions will make an extremely great delay necessary and that the armistice will never end.

SONNINO: Armistice means that we must bring the enemy to the peace; therefore let us not encumber it with conditions which will retard the conclusion of peace.

PICHON: We could add a phrase something like this: "From now on, and under reservation of future modifications, we demand the immediate delivery of all documents, securities, papers, objects, etc., belonging to the public or private administrations of the invaded territories which are at present in the hands of the German authorities, soldiers or private individuals."

HYMANS: These restitutions will make life easier during the period of the armistice.

ORLANDO: I consider, and M. Sonnino agrees with me, that that is a condition of peace. The armistice only views military questions and should tend to bring us nearer to peace. However, if M. Hymans holds to this paragraph, I am willing to accept it.

HYMANS: We should be able to find a formula capable of covering these desiderata while avoiding the difficulties which have just been considered.

CLEMENCEAU: M. Hymans will propose a text tomorrow when we are discussing the second reading.

(This proposition is accepted.)

CLEMENCEAU: I now propose to you the addition of the following paragraph: "Sick and wounded who cannot be evacuated shall be cared for by German personnel which shall be left on the spot with the necessary supplies."

(This paragraph is accepted.)

On the proposal of Mr. Lloyd George, asking that mention be made of the conditions for the eastern front, Russia, Rumania, etc., a discussion begins at the end of which Marshal Foch is instructed to propose a text on this subject for the second reading.

FOCH: I should like, before solving this question, to know the ideas of the Governments. Evacuation of the eastern countries, Russia, Poland, Rumania, is all very well but are we going to take these countries over on our own account? Rumania may be able to extricate herself from the affair alone, but what about the others? Are we to abandon them to themselves?

HOUSE: That is a very delicate question, for the retreat of the troops would be followed by a Bolshevist regime.

CLEMENCEAU: I see exchanges of telegrams every day on this subject. To believe in the Bolshevist danger in these territories is to let oneself be lured by German propaganda.

SONNINO: The principle must be inserted in the armistice conditions. The Bolshevist menace is old German strategy; we must not fall into the trap. The conclusion of an armistice which we have just made with Turkey reëstablishes our liaison with South Russia and Rumania and allows us to consider a reorganization. We must accept the principle of evacuation and the restitution of prisoners. All the former frontiers must be restored during the armistice. A condition of this kind must be inserted.

FOCH: The principle of evacuation, I can understand that, but the restitution of prisoners, to whom are we going to make it? It would run the risk of leading the whole world to Bolshevism.

SONNINO: I am of the same opinion as Marshal Foch concerning the prisoners.

HOUSE: I propose an addition to paragraph 2 [11] "or in all other regions occupied by the Germans and which may be designated by the Allies."

(After discussion the matter is referred to the Marshal who is to propose a text at the second reading.)

The discussion was resumed the next day, November 2, at Versailles after consideration of a matter connected with the Turkish armistice.[12]

CLEMENCEAU, presiding: I now wish to return to the question of restoration and reparations of the damage caused, brought up yesterday by M. Hymans. People here in France would not understand our not including a clause to that effect. What I ask of you is simply the addition of the three words "reparation for damages," without other comment.

HYMANS: Would that be a condition of the armistice?

SONNINO: That is more a condition of peace.

BONAR LAW: It is useless to insert a clause in the armistice conditions which could not be fulfilled in a brief period.

CLEMENCEAU: I only wish to mention the principle. You must not forget that the French population is one of those which suffered the most; it would not understand our not making an allusion to this clause.

LLOYD GEORGE: If you consider that principle of reparations on land you must also mention that of reparation for ships which have been sunk.

CLEMENCEAU: I include all that in my three words: "reparation for damages." I beg the Council to put itself in the mind of the French population. . . .

HYMANS: And Belgian. . . .

VESNITSCH: And Serbian. . . .

SONNINO: Italian, also. . . .

HOUSE: Since it is an important question for all, I propose accepting it.

BONAR LAW: That has already been said in our letter to Presi-

11. This is the second clause of those concerning the eastern front, or Article XIII in the final draft.

12. The following account is based on Mermeix, *Les Négociations Secrètes*, pp. 241–250. See Seymour, *House Papers,* IV, 125–126.

dent Wilson, who will communicate it to Germany. It is useless to say it twice.

ORLANDO: I accept in principle although it has not been mentioned in the conditions of the armistice with Austria.

(The addition "reparation for damages" is accepted.)

CLEMENCEAU: M. Klotz,[13] who has a proposal to make, now has the floor.

KLOTZ: I think it will be necessary to add to the armistice conditions a very brief clause demanding the return of documents, specie, etc. The enemy has, in fact, some presses and is making bank notes. We have some cities which have had to issue numerous notes during the occupation: for instance, the communities of Roubaix, Lille, Tourcoing have issued more than a thousand million francs. I propose the following wording: "Return of all documents, specie, securities (personal or fiduciary with the assets of issue) touching on public or private interests in the invaded regions."

(This text is adopted.)

KLOTZ: I consider it needless to remind you of a clause of the armistice of 1871: "During the period of the armistice nothing will be diverted from public securities which might serve as a pledge or a payment of war reparations."

(This text is adopted.)

BALFOUR: I should like to make some observations before we settle the final armistice conditions.

The first observation concerns territory to be evacuated by the enemy on the eastern front. All the information that we get in the Foreign Office, like that which M. Pichon must receive at the French Foreign Office, agrees in saying that when the Germans evacuate these regions, they will become the prey of Bolshevism, the populations having neither army nor police. We run a danger of imposing a more harsh regime than the German regime and, despite the hatred of the latter, the people will likely prefer the German rule to that imposed upon them by a Bolshevik authority.

We have made an effort to persuade the Scandinavians to intervene either by sending arms for which we would pay or by sending police. I do not believe that they will accept either one of these requests. The only solution we can consider in case of refusal is to allow the people certain arms so that they will not give in without resisting the first invader who comes.

13. French Minister of Finance.

CLEMENCEAU: That is a question about the eastern front. Marshal Foch has been instructed to prepare a text for us. We have not yet discussed that question. When we get there, we shall bear Mr. Balfour's proposition in mind.

BALFOUR: I have one other observation to make. I learned this morning that the Germans are doing what we have feared for a long time. They are selling their merchant marine to neutrals. We must say that we do not accept the change of flag.

CLEMENCEAU: That is a naval question. We shall examine it later.

I wish now that we should specify a time limit for the armistice, that is to say, a period for a reply to this armistice. Mr. Lloyd George and I propose three days, that is to say, seventy-two hours to date from the hour of notification.

(This proposition is accepted.)

HYMANS: You instructed me to give you a text concerning certain restitutions that my Government had asked me to submit to you and which are aimed as far as possible to restore the economic situation in the invaded regions during the period of the armistice. I know that the Council is opposed to that idea because of the difficulty of executing and controlling it.

I should wish, however, that this question be treated in the first preliminaries of the peace treaty so as not to lose precious time.

KLOTZ: I support M. Hymans' proposal. This question must be treated in the preliminaries to the peace treaty if we are not to lose precious time.

VESNITSCH: Will there be a second reading of the general text?

CLEMENCEAU: Certainly, we shall review all these points.

CLEMENCEAU: Mr. Lloyd George proposes the acceptance of the following clause: "Unconditional capitulation of all the German forces operating in East Africa."

(This proposition is accepted.)

CLEMENCEAU: I now propose the examination of the naval conditions. Admiral Hope has the floor.

HOPE: The continuous pressure of the fleets has contributed as much as the actions of the armies to the present crumbling of the Central Empires. At the beginning of the war, Germany had 13 cruisers of the "dreadnought" type; at the end of the war, including those which she is building, she will have 25, 12 of which are of the most modern and powerful type in the world. As for the battle cruisers, she had 4 at the beginning of the war, at the end she will have 9. If we took 6 from her she would then finish the war with 3, that is to say, 1 less than at the beginning. It follows then that unless the German Navy is reduced at the peace in the proportion proposed by the Interallied Naval Council, Germany will emerge from the war stronger than she entered it and will remain a permanent menace to the future peace of the world.

Concerning the armistice, the British Admiralty considers that it is absolutely necessary that the German fleet should be put out of harm's way during the entire period of the armistice, this to allow some rest to be given to the Grand Fleet. We can obtain this result only by reducing the German Navy by the number of ships proposed in the Naval Council either by handing them over to the Allies or by interning them in neutral ports under our surveillance, it being understood that in the end they will not go back to Germany. Doubtless, surrender would be the better method.

LLOYD GEORGE: The armistice conditions to be imposed upon Germany depend to a great extent on what will happen with Austria. If Austria accepts our conditions, or if the Italian successes continue we shall, perhaps, be in a position to enforce harder conditions.

On the other hand, if Austria does not give in and continues the struggle, then we shall find ourselves faced with grave decisions to make. Until we know that, we cannot decide about what we are going to demand of Germany. We must ask ourselves whether we want to make peace right away or whether we wish to continue the war for a year. I would not wish to make a decision before the Austrian reply. It may be very tempting to take a certain number of ships, but that is not the root of the question.

At the present time each one of our armies is losing each week more men than in any other weeks of the first four years of the war. We must not lose sight of that.

At the right time I shall be able to assume responsibility, in spite of the clamorings, but today I do not wish to decide. If Austria falls we shall know where we are; Monday we shall know where we stand.

HOUSE: But the Germans will know what's what before we do and will know what Austria is going to do. What advantage is there for us to wait for?[14]

LLOYD GEORGE: But I, I don't know what Austria is going to do. The modification that the Austrian reply may bring is in the

14. House explains his opposition to Lloyd George's request for postponement. Seymour, *House Papers,* IV, 130–131. Austria had until midnight, November 3, to accept the armistice. She actually accepted at 3 P.M.

form which we will give to our conditions. Thus, if we can march on Munich and Dresden, we shall be able to impose stiffer conditions.

CLEMENCEAU: I propose the adjournment of all naval questions to Monday and to pass now to the questions of the eastern front.

(This proposition is accepted.)

CLEMENCEAU: Marshal Foch has the floor.

MARSHAL FOCH: With the exception of certain reservations as to the time for the execution, on account of the distances, this is what I propose:

Clause I. Evacuation by German troops in a period of . . . (three weeks?) of Rumania in its pre-war boundaries, including Bessarabia.

(Adopted.)

Clause II. Evacuation by German troops in a period of . . . (15 days?) of all the territories of Poland, including Old Poland, as she existed before the first partition, with Danzig.

PICHON: I wish to insist that, in the evacuated territories, all territories are clearly included which formed the Kingdom of Poland before the first partition of 1772.

Moreover that springs from the declarations and original agreements of all the governments at the beginning of the war; the United States has accepted it. I desire the restoration of Old Poland with access to the sea. It is one of the war aims of the Allies, and President Wilson has entirely approved of it. The Poles who have remained on the spot, the Polish Council of Paris which we have recognized, consider that we owe them this pledge. There is need for mentioning this clause in the armistice conditions in order to avoid all discussion at the time of the examination of the peace terms.

BALFOUR: I have listened to this proposition with anxiety; the Poland of 1772, you say, must be the Poland of 1918. It is not to that that we pledged ourselves. We pledged ourselves to restore a Poland composed of Poles. That of 1772 did not correspond to this aim; it was not composed solely of Poles. Non-Polish territories were included while Polish ones were not included. This formula would therefore offend by its insufficiency as well as by its excess. The exact delimitation of these frontiers of this new Poland is such a complicated subject that I entreat you not to introduce it into the armistice clauses. I propose to sum up in one sentence, taking in the whole of the eastern front, what Marshal Foch said: "All the

German forces in the East must return within their frontiers such as they were before the month of August 1914."

We shall leave the task of studying this question to the Inter-allied Conference, which must necessarily meet before the Peace Conference.

HOUSE: I accept the proposition of Mr. Balfour.

PICHON: If we adopt such a general formula, the question is modified. I do not insist, as this résumé takes in everything. All I want is that it is clearly understood by the Polish people that we are not renouncing anything which we have promised to them.

(The proposition of Mr. Balfour is accepted.)

Clause III. Immediate setting on foot of the evacuation by the German troops and the recall of all instructors, prisoners and German civil and military agents who are on Russian territory (within the boundaries of before 1914).

(Accepted.)

Clause IV. Liberation on the spot and maintenance of all Russian prisoners with a prohibition on their being subjected to any work, until a decision for their repatriation is made by the Allies and the United States, with the concurrence of a regular Russian Government.

(Accepted.)

Clause V. Immediate cessation on the part of the German troops of all requisition, seizure of or search for food products and all other products, intended for German consumption, in Rumania, Poland, and Russia (limits of before 1914).

PICHON: M. Klotz offers me a very wise observation. Germany must be deprived not only of food products but of all products. I move we strike out the words "food products."

(This proposition is accepted.)

Clause VI. Renunciation in principle of the Treaties of Bucharest and Brest-Litovsk and of the complementary treaties.

(Accepted.)

SONNINO: Germany has taken all the Russian gold stock and has collected indemnities the total of which I do not know exactly. Couldn't we find a formula to obtain restitution of these funds to Russia and Rumania?

KLOTZ: I propose the following text: "Restitution of the gold handed over to the Germans by the Russians. This gold will be taken in charge by the Allies until the signature of peace."

(This proposition is accepted.)

BALFOUR: I now ask to take up the question again of which I spoke to you a little while ago; it is to supply a certain quantity of arms to the population of the evacuated countries to permit them to defend themselves against Bolshevist or other bands.

SONNINO: We shall have to determine the quantity of the arms and who is to receive them.

BALFOUR: Perhaps the military representatives can advise us about this subject.

CLEMENCEAU: No, we will charge Mr. Balfour with submitting a text for the second reading.

(At the end of the meeting Mr. Balfour submits the following text, which will be discussed at the second reading.)

"When the Germans, according to this agreement, shall evacuate the territories on their eastern frontier, they must leave a third of their arms in the hands of local authorities to be designated by the Allies, in order to permit the population to defend itself against all disorders and aggressions."

BALFOUR: I wish to submit another point which is intimately linked with the preceding question. If we do not consider a special clause, the Allies will be cut off from Poland and the neighboring countries. We ought to insist upon keeping contact with them, by Danzig, for instance, or by any other means of access, which would allow us to send to these countries arms and police, if a special need became apparent, or food supplies if tonnage permitted us.

(This principle is accepted and Mr. Balfour submits at the end of the session the following text which will be examined at the second reading.)

"The Allies will have free access to the territories evacuated by the Germans on their eastern frontiers, either by Danzig or by the Vistula, in order to be able to provision the populations of these countries, or for any other reason."

FOCH: I ask to make an observation on the subject of the paragraph about the restitution of the gold taken from the Russians which we previously accepted. If we demand from Germany the restitution of the gold taken from the Russians and she answers us 'We haven't any,' what will you do? In my opinion this clause should not appear in an armistice.

SONNINO: If the Germans reply that they haven't any gold, we shall take cognizance of it.

KLOTZ: It would be wise to place at the head of the financial questions a clause reserving the future claims of the Allies and I propose the following text: "Under the reservation of all subsequent claims and demands on the part of the Allies."

(This addition is accepted.)

On November 3 the Prime Ministers met with their naval and military experts to discuss naval terms. Although it had been agreed to postpone final decision on the matter to the next day, ostensibly to hear beforehand what reply Austria would make to the terms offered her, Lloyd George was looking for a compromise that would satisfy the experts who were demanding that Germany surrender battle cruisers and battleships.

"Our admirals have their tails up," said the British Prime Minister, "and will not move. We might suggest that instead of confiscating cruisers and battleships we intern the whole lot."

"That is what I think," said House, "and leave the ultimate disposition of these ships to the Peace Conference."

"There will be no place in the Society of Nations," added Clemenceau, "for a country with 32 dreadnoughts."

The compromise plan suggested by Lloyd George found support in Admiral Benson, the American naval expert, a man in whom Colonel House had great confidence. Discussing the events of these days later, Admiral Benson described his views thus: "I was in favor of sinking all German war craft. The majority of the Committee on naval terms wanted the vessels divided up. I did not feel that after peace any naval armaments should be increased." On November 2 Benson had spoken with Sir Eric Geddes about the German ships to be surrendered. "He assured me," Benson wrote Colonel House, "with the utmost frankness and candor that the disposition of these ships should not be used for augmenting European armament after the war and that in his opinion none of the European Powers have so anticipated. He stated frankly that in his opinion they should be destroyed when final decision is reached. . . . The word 'surrendered' was used in order that there might be no possible misinterpretation by Germany as to the terms imposed." [15]

Benson's attitude was the consequence of careful thought about naval terms on the part of the American Naval Planning Section, which sent the Admiral on October 30 the following memorandum:

15. Seymour, *House Papers,* IV, 131–132. On the 4th Colonel House told Geddes that he would have accepted England's naval terms just as he had accepted Foch's military terms. *Ibid.,* pp. 135–136.

1. We deem it highly important that the following principle be accepted now by all concerned:

"No vessel surrendered by Germany shall ever be used to increase the naval armaments of any power whatever."

COMMENT

The distribution of vessels surrendered by Germany will serve to increase the armaments of the Powers participating in the distribution. It is highly improbable that the United States will participate in such a distribution; in fact, we consider it undesirable that she should so participate. In consequence, we shall find ourselves at the end of this war, if distribution does take place, in a position of great naval inferiority not consistent with our interests at sea and overseas.

With Germany disarmed, there is no occasion for Great Britain to possess a fleet greater than her present fleet, unless the power of that fleet is designed to restrain us.[16]

On November 4 Colonel House and the Prime Ministers met again to continue their discussion of the disposition of the German Navy. The Allies had no intention of returning the vessels to Germany. If the Germans objected to the "surrender" of their ships, Admiral Benson thought a good verbal compromise would be the "internment" of the vessels, as Lloyd George had suggested.

BENSON: It is held that it is impossible to decrease the number of vessels to be surrendered. As a matter of fact all of the German fleet will, by the requirements, be rendered harmless under either condition imposed.

The point at issue is, shall the ten battleships be surrendered or shall they be interned in a neutral port?

In any case the final disposal of all vessels must be decided by the Peace Conference.

To intern the ten battleships will increase the probability of acceptance of the terms of the Armistice. In order to save life every possible effort should be made to submit such terms as will satisfy our requirements and at the same time bring an end to hostilities.

16. Publication No. 7, American Naval Planning Section, London (Washington, Government Printing Office, 1923), Memorandum No. 64, p. 456. The detailed reasons for this American policy are given in Memorandum No. 65. See Appendix F.

The British, French, and Italian proposals consider the surrender to the Allies and to the United States of sixteen dreadnoughts [six battle cruisers, ten battleships], eight light cruisers including two minelayers, and fifty destroyers. These proposals are in complete agreement with my own, except in respect to the sixteen dreadnoughts which I wish to have interned and not surrendered to the Allies. I think that the internment of all the dreadnoughts might be required rather than the surrender of sixteen.

FOCH: Shall the war be continued for the sole advantage of interning these ships in a neutral port? I myself cannot see the advantage of this, especially as the ships have never been used.

LLOYD GEORGE: Yes, but if these German battleships had not existed, Great Britain could have furnished 350,000 more men, possibly 500,000, and we should have had ample supplies of coal, oil, and other commodities.

FOCH: But the German battleships never left their ports and naval warfare now is conducted by submarines. German battleships have no doubt kept the British fleet in home waters, but their action was virtual not actual. Are we to continue the war simply to suppress this virtual influence? Should the Germans refuse to surrender their fleet, what should we do? If we obtain satisfaction for our military conditions the war is ended whether the enemy accepts the naval clauses or not. Otherwise we should continue the war to pursue the capture of ships which are blockaded in their ports, when the acceptance of the military conditions alone is enough to carry the day.[17]

LLOYD GEORGE: If the Germans say to us: "We accept your military conditions but we cannot accept your naval conditions," we shall then see what we must do. But we are assuming a grave responsibility in rejecting the unanimous recommendations of the admirals. I propose that we ask them to review their documents on the basis of the disarmament of the German cruisers and their internment in a neutral port. This solution will undoubtedly give rise to difficult questions, for neutral waters do not belong to us, and our surveillance could only be exercised from the outside. We shall consult the diplomats about that and those who are versed in international law.

CLEMENCEAU: And if Germany does not accept our naval conditions, we shall meet again to take a new decision. Does the Marshal accept that?

FOCH: Yes.[18]

17. Seymour, *House Papers,* IV, 132–133.
18. Mermeix, *Les Négociations Secrètes,* p. 263, note.

There were three proposals before the Premiers: that of the Naval Council, the original British plan, calling for the surrender of the German ships; that of Lloyd George and Admiral Benson, who thought the first plan too harsh and suggested the internment rather than the surrender of the ships; and that of Marshal Foch, who believed it was both useless and dangerous even to intern the German ships, which had performed no real function during the war. A compromise had to be found. "After listening to Marshal Foch," writes Charles Seymour, editor of the *House Papers*, "Mr. Lloyd George proposed that Germany should surrender the stipulated number of submarines, but that all the other war craft in question, battle cruisers as well as battleships, should merely be interned in a neutral port. Clemenceau, Orlando, and House agreed that this course should be followed, if the naval advisers could be persuaded to yield." [19]

This was the solution that was presented to the Supreme War Council on the afternoon of November 4, when it met to give final form to Germany's armistice. One wonders what might have been the turn of discussion and the decision had the Allied leaders known that at that moment German revolutionaries, and not the German Government, were in control of the German Navy.

It seemed so possible that Germany might not agree to the armistice terms that plans were also worked out in the morning for a drive from the south, by way of Austria, now that armistice terms with the latter made such an attack possible.[20] A plan for an offensive through Lorraine already existed. Every military precaution had now been taken against Germany.

On the afternoon of November 4, the plenary session of the Supreme War Council was held at Versailles. Here, one by one, the clauses of Germany's armistice were discussed and adopted.[21]

CLEMENCEAU: The session is opened. I move to give the floor to M. Orlando.

ORLANDO: In the armistice with Germany a condition has been inserted which is not included in the Austrian armistice, it is that of reparation for damages.

19. Seymour, *House Papers,* IV, 133–134.

20. Details of this plan for a drive on Germany by way of Austria are given in Mermeix, *Les Négociations Secrètes,* pp. 284–286, note.

21. Although the document adopted here differs in only minor points from that eventually signed by the Germans, the numbering and order of the clauses do not necessarily correspond. The account of the discussion is taken from Mermeix, *Les Négociations Secrètes,* pp. 252–266.

When we examined this question, at the time of the discussion of the clauses for Austria, it had been decided that that was, rather, a clause of peace; today, being given the invasion and devastation of Belgium and of France, it has been thought useful to register the principle in the clauses of the armistice. Our Italian people will note this difference and will think that it was done on purpose. We do not know the damage done to us, but now that we have reconquered the invaded regions in Italy as well as in Serbia, we are taking stock of what they have done and I can assure you that the Austrian devastations are just as bad as the German ones.

The Austrian armistice being signed, we cannot reopen the matter and I should like to have this conference admit that the principle of indemnification is fully acknowledged and that it will be officially understood in the preliminaries of the peace *pourparlers*. I should like to be able to make an official declaration on this subject.

VESNITSCH: I ask leave to speak in order to associate myself in the name of the Serbian Government to the demand of M. Orlando.

CLEMENCEAU: Since no one makes any objection, this proposition is accepted.

CLEMENCEAU: Let us now pass to the second reading of the military clauses.

The text is read.[22]

Part A. The Western Front

Clause 1. [Cessation of hostilities on land and in the air six hours after the signature of the armistice.]

(Accepted without modification.)

Clause 2. [Evacuation of invaded territory: Belgium, France, Alsace-Lorraine, Luxembourg. Occupation of these territories by Allied troops.]

(Accepted without modification.)

Clause 3. [Repatriation of all the inhabitants of the above-named countries.]

VESNITSCH: I ask you to add the words: "as well as the Allied and Associated countries" after the words "of the above-named countries."

MILNER:[23] We must avoid inserting in an armistice clauses

22. A synopsis, in brackets, of each clause is added to make the discussion clear.
23. Lloyd George had already returned to England.

whose fulfillment is quite impossible; the repatriation in question does not seem to me to be possible in fourteen days.

HYMANS: If we extend the clause to the other countries, the fourteen days will not be enough, but for us, Belgians and French, this period is sufficient.

CLEMENCEAU: We shall discuss this proposition among the clauses referring to the East.

Clause 4. [Surrender of armament: 5,000 guns, 30,000 machine guns, etc.]

(Accepted without modification.)

Clause 5. [Evacuation of left bank of Rhine; bridgeheads; neutral zone on right bank.]

(Accepted without modification.)

Clause 6. [Prohibition on the evacuation of people from the territories evacuated by the enemy; on doing any damage to their persons or properties, or damage of any kind. Surrender intact of all military depots and supplies which have not been removed in the period specified. Neither industrial establishments nor their personnel to suffer the slightest damage or change.]

(Accepted without modification.)

Clause 7. [Railroads and communication of every nature are not to suffer the slightest damage, personnel thereof to be maintained. Surrender of 5,000 locomotives, 150,000 railroad cars, etc. The railroads of Alsace-Lorraine to be surrendered with all pre-war personnel and equipment. All supplies of coal, spare parts for signals, and shops to be left on the spot and cared for by Germany during the armistice. All barges taken from the Allies to be returned.]

(Accepted without modification.)

BALFOUR: I wish to make an observation. We say that we are taking all the railroads, all the communications, all the rolling stock, and on the other hand we give the Germans fourteen days to bring back all civil and military prisoners and at the same time to evacuate hundreds of thousands of soldiers.

Therefore, two movements, one from east to west, the other from west to east without the means of executing them.

FOCH: The observation does not seem to me to be well founded, for we do not ask them for the transportation of our prisoners but only that of the hostages and inhabitants.

WEYGAND: There will certainly be two currents of transportation: the one from west to east of the German troops, who will return on foot; the period which we have fixed for the evacuation is based on stages of 15 kilometers a day. The material which has not been evacuated during this period will be captured.

The other current from east to west will bring back our refugees and civilians, who will use trains which we shall keep.

CLEMENCEAU: No one, I believe, will complain if the German troops go back on foot.

MILNER: You say that the railroads of Alsace-Lorraine are to be surrendered with their pre-war personnel. To do that you will have to resurrect the dead.

WEYGAND: A personnel of equal numbers is understood by that.

Clause 8. [German Command to reveal all mines and delayed-action fuses, poisoned wells, etc.]

(Accepted without modification.)

Clause 9. [The Allies to exercise the right of requisition in all occupied territories. Germany to pay for costs of occupying armies.]

(Accepted without modification.)

Clause 10. [Allied prisoners of war to be repatriated without reciprocity. Enemy prisoners will not be returned until after the signing of the preliminary peace.]

PICHON: I propose the suppression of the second paragraph of this clause which binds us to return the prisoners after the signature of the preliminary peace. I think it is useless to mention it now.

(This suppression is adopted and Clause 10, thus modified, is accepted.)

Clause 11. [Sick and wounded who cannot be evacuated to be cared for on the spot by German personnel with the necessary supplies.]

(Accepted without modification.)

Clause 12. [Under the reservation of all subsequent claims by the Allies, reparation for damages.

During the period of the armistice nothing is to be diverted from public or private securities which might serve as security for the recovery of reparations.

Return of all documents, specie, and securities bearing on public or private interests in the invaded territories.

Restitution of the gold handed over by the Russians to the Germans.

This gold shall be taken in charge by the Allies until the signing of the peace.]

HYMANS: I have reviewed the wording of this clause with M. Klotz; I think some modifications should be made in it.

Thus, in paragraph 3, we must specify that it is in occupied territories.

In paragraph 4, we must say: "return and restitution." I make a distinction between these two terms. In fact by "return" I have in mind the return of that which they have in hand, while by "restitution" I mean the return of that which has been taken.

And so I am led to speak to you again of the claim I informed you of the other day concerning the question of the cash in our bank. I am all the more concerned about it because Baron Sonnino has asked for the insertion of a clause concerning the Russian gold. The Germans took from us by force eight to nine hundred million marks; they had demanded that we give them this sum but the reply was made that we would yield only to force, and they took it from us.

I therefore permit myself a most emphatic insistence before the conference that my request be taken into account.

I propose the following text: "Restitution of the cash of the *Banque nationale de Belgique* and of the *département d'émission de la Société générale.*"

KLOTZ: I am not opposed to this text, but I draw your attention to the fact that we have some credit companies in the same situation. In my opinion the words "return of specie" covers this claim.

CLEMENCEAU: I don't think that in French we make a distinction between "return" and "restitution."

HYMANS: My claim is extremely important. The *Banque* had a deposit of a large amount of marks as a result of the recovery of Belgian securities. I do not ask the addition of this clause for a private institution but for our *Banque nationale,* something like the *Banque de France.* I beg the conference to take our serious situation into account and to accept the addition of this clause.

PICHON: I accept . . . even though it creates a special case.

CLEMENCEAU: M. Sonnino proposes the following text: "Immediate restitution of the cash of the *Banque nationale de Belgique* and, in general, immediate return of all documents, specie, etc. . . ."

(This wording is accepted.)

KLOTZ: For the greater clarity I propose to add to paragraph 2: "Nothing is to be diverted from public securities by the enemy which could serve as security for the Allies. . . ."

(This wording is accepted.)

SONNINO: I propose the following wording for the restitution of the gold: "Restitution of Russian or Rumanian gold taken by the Germans or handed over to them."

(This modification is accepted and the whole of Clause 12 is adopted.)

Clause 13. [Time allowed to Germany for reply: seventy-two hours from the time of notification.]

CLEMENCEAU: We must now discuss the duration of the armistice. What does Marshal Foch propose?

FOCH: The present armistice is valid for a period of thirty days.

SONNINO: I think it would be preferable, instead of adopting a fixed period, merely to provide a clause permitting breaking off the *pourparlers* after three days' notice, for instance.

FOCH: The two ideas could be linked and we could say that, in the event of non-fulfillment of the clauses, the *pourparlers* shall be broken off after two days' notice.

MILNER: From the moment that we fix on forty-eight hours' notice it is useless to specify a fixed period of thirty days which might, at some time or other, be annoying to us.

FOCH: We consent to stopping hostilities for thirty days on the condition that certain clauses are fulfilled; if not, we take back our freedom of action. This period of thirty days allows the enemy to make his calculations.

HOUSE: I propose that we make it thirty days with option of extending it.

FOCH: I propose the following text:

"The duration is fixed at thirty days, with the option of extending it. If, during this period, the clauses are not fulfilled, the armistice may be denounced by one of the contracting parties, which must give notice forty-eight hours in advance."

(This text is accepted, and Clause 13, at the request of the Marshal, is placed at the end of the general text.)

The discussion then turned to the clauses affecting the eastern front.

Part B. The Eastern Front

Clause 1. [German forces in the East to retire within their frontiers as they were in August, 1914.]

PICHON: I wish to point out that we have specified absolutely nothing about Rumania; I ask that this omission be rectified. Furthermore, I have received a most pressing letter on this subject from the National Council of the Rumanian Union, over which M. Take Jonescu presides. I think we should keep here paragraph 1 of the first draft.

SONNINO: This question is much more in its place in the execution of the Austrian clauses.

I wish to point out that the phrasing that we have is not very clear. What do the words "in the East" mean? Is it a question of the old eastern front? It must be defined. For instance, Rumania is at peace with Germany. The Germans will have the right to tell us that they are in friendly country and that, therefore, the armistice does not apply to this case.

BALFOUR: I propose to strike out the words "in the East." That makes the German troops go home and gives satisfaction to everybody. If, on the other hand, you are speaking of Russia, we will have to determine whether Estonia, for instance, or Courland is a part of it.

MILNER: I propose the following wording:

"All German troops which are at present in the territories which, before the war, were a part of Russia, Rumania, or Turkey, must return within the German frontiers such as they were on August 1, 1914."

(This text is adopted.)

Clause 2. [Evacuation by Germany of all instructors, prisoners, civil and military agents on Russian territory in the boundaries before 1914.]

(Adopted with the final modification "in the boundaries of August 1, 1914.")

Clause 3. [Cessation of requisitions by Germany in Rumania, Poland, and Russia in the boundaries before 1914.]

BALFOUR: To be logical, the word "Poland" should be omitted, since this country was included in the Russia of August 1, 1914.

(Accepted, the last line to read: "in Rumania and in Russia, within the boundaries of August 1, 1914.")

Clause 4. [Renunciation in principle of the Treaties of Bucharest and Brest-Litovsk.]

(Accepted after the deletion of the words "in principle.")

Clause 5. [On evacuation, Germans to leave one third of their arms with local authorities with which to protect themselves against disorder and aggression.]

BALFOUR: If you accept the principle of my proposal, I shall merely ask for slight modifications in the text.

PICHON: I consider this proposal very dangerous; the arms which you will leave in these countries, if the Allies are not there, will serve the Bolshevists only, and other governments in which we cannot have any confidence.

SONNINO: If we do nothing, the situation will be still more serious, for the Germans will organize Bolshevism themselves.

ORLANDO: Mr. Balfour's thought is generous and I do not see the possibility of applying it; there are, besides the Bolshevist and anti-Bolshevist parties, five or six other opposed parties; we shall greatly risk mixing ourselves in internal political questions which it is preferable to avoid.

CLEMENCEAU: The Allies not being on the spot, we shall not know to whom to turn over the arms.

VESNITSCH: I wish to support the proposition of Mr. Balfour. A great part of Russian Bolshevism has been made in Germany. We all wish to see the Russia of other days revive; such has been our line of conduct up to this day.

PICHON: We are not at all in agreement.

BALFOUR: I am not thinking of Russia at all in making this proposal, but of the small peoples who aspire to autonomy, such as the Estonians and the Letts. I am not thinking at all of mixing in the internal affairs of the Ukraine or of Russia.

HOUSE: I propose that we specify that the handing over of arms be optional, depending on the request of the Allies.

PICHON: You will see as soon as this clause is published the bad effect it will have, and how the Bolshevists will know how to make use of it to say that we have all decided in common to organize civil war among them.

FOCH: The introduction of all these clauses makes our document chimerical, since the greater part of the conditions cannot be carried out. We must be sober about these unrealizable prescriptions.

BALFOUR: I yield before the authority of Marshal Foch's words and withdraw my proposal.

Clause 6. [Allies to have free access to evacuated territories on Germany's eastern frontier.]

(Adopted without modification.)

(The whole of the military clauses is accepted.)

The Council now discussed at length the naval clauses of Germany's armistice.

Clause 1. [Immediate cessation of hostilities on sea; report of location and movements of German ships; notice to neutrals that Allied ships may navigate in territorial waters without raising questions of neutrality.]

(Accepted without modification.)

Clause 2. [Restitution, without reciprocity, of all naval and mercantile marine prisoners of war.]

(Accepted without modification.)

Clause 3. [Surrender to the Allies of 160 submarines, including all submarine cruisers and mine layers with their armament, crews, etc.]

(Accepted without modification.)

Clause 4. [Surrender to the Allies with armament and crews intact of 6 battle cruisers, 10 cruisers, 8 light cruisers (including 2 mine layers), 50 destroyers of the most recent type to be designated by the Allies and to be placed under the surveillance of the Allies. Military armament of all the auxiliary fleet to be removed.]

CLEMENCEAU: This morning at the conference of Prime Ministers the question came up whether the German ships were to be interned in neutral ports, or whether we should take some of them. This question was submitted for examination to the Naval Council.

GEDDES: Did the Prime Ministers and Mr. House *decide* this morning that the surrender of the battleships was not possible and that only their internment had been considered?

I wish to specify clearly that that was not a recommendation of the Naval Council.

HOUSE: That was decided.

SONNINO: I have the text of the resolution which reads:

"The Interallied Naval Council will examine the naval terms of an armistice with Germany on the following basis, that the total of the ships designated in Article 4 of their note of November 1 shall be disarmed, then interned under the surveillance of the Allies, in neutral ports to be designated by the Allies and having only caretakers on board."

GEDDES: The Naval Council understood that this text meant that surrender was impossible, and that that was decided. We are not at all of the same opinion.

HOUSE: Personally, I understood that that was decided, and I think that Mr. Lloyd George, who proposed it, has left convinced that that had been decided.

CLEMENCEAU: I have the same impression, but the conference is free. Our naval experts, this morning, were not minded to modify their first recommendations; they did so only at the request of the governments.

LEYGUES: Here is the document:

"The Interallied Naval Council has received and examined the request of the conference of Prime Ministers relative to a revision of their proposals concerning the naval clauses of an armistice with Germany.

"The Interallied Naval Council is disposed to accept the revision of paragraph 1, of Clause 4, of the document of November 1, entitled: 'Résumé of the naval clauses and report on the subject of the surrender of the warships or of their internment in neutral ports,' in such a way as to demand the internment of the ships indicated in a neutral port instead of their surrender pure and simple, *but on the condition* that it is here a question only of an armistice clause and that these ships shall under no circumstances return to the Germans at the end of the armistice or at any other time.

"Under these conditions the Council is disposed to accept the text of Clause 4, revised as follows:

> 'The German surface warships which shall be designated by the Allies and the United States, shall be disarmed and interned in neutral ports indicated by the Allies and the United States of America, and they shall remain under the surveillance of the Allies and of the United States—only caretaking detachments being left on board.'

"These ships to be interned are: 6 battle cruisers, 10 cruisers, 8 light cruisers, of which 2 are mine layers, 50 destroyers of the latest type.

"All the other surface warships, including river ones, shall be returned to German naval bases designated by the Allies and the United States of America, where they shall be completely disarmed in personnel as well as in material and placed under the surveillance of the Allies and of the United States of America.

"The military armament of all the auxiliary fleet (trawlers, motor ships, etc.) shall be removed."

CLEMENCEAU: I am sure that the fate of the fleet has not been decided by us in the sense recommended by our naval advisers. We have all agreed that the Peace Conference shall be the sole judge of the fate of these ships. There is, however, one point with which I am preoccupied: it is a point of law.

What are the laws which permit us to keep the enemy ships in a neutral port under our surveillance?

DE BON: I have not adhered to the opinion of the Naval Council, for, precisely, I don't see how we shall intern these ships. Furthermore, at the first conference, we were all agreed to demand the surrender of a certain number of ships, for it was our unanimous opinion that the German Navy could not be permitted to emerge from this war as strong as, or even stronger than when she entered it.

What is the object of this internment? To put the German fleet out of harm's way. There are two solutions to that: either we seize the ships, or we leave them in German ports, disarmed and under our control.

If we intern them, the Germans will think, seeing their ships in neutral ports, that we have our eyes on these vessels, and the same impression will be produced on them as if we took them outright.

That is why I could not adhere to the opinion of the Naval Council.

To sum up, I ask the surrender of the ships mentioned in Article 4, or general internment, after disarmament, of the whole German fleet in German ports under our control.

ORLANDO: It was this morning that this question was examined by the Prime Ministers. We all agreed against surrender and the Marshal expressed the same opinion in very firm words.

Concerning internment in neutral ports, what are our guarantees? Will the neutral be responsible for the internment or must we maintain our blockade on the sea?

HOPE: I accepted this modification only because I understood that the heads of the governments had flatly refused the surrender of these ships and wished only to intern them; I now propose disarming them first. They must, therefore, be assembled at a place indicated by the Allies, their armament must be removed, their personnel disembarked, and then convoyed to a neutral port.

CLEMENCEAU: I propose giving up the neutral ports and designating Antwerp, if that is possible from the naval point of view.

DE BON: We should have to verify that, but I don't think they can enter this port on account of their draught.

CLEMENCEAU: We discussed the matter thoroughly this morning in the presence of Lloyd George. Now, Mr. Lloyd George has left. This evening, after fresh study, we see that that solution is no longer possible and that we cannot embarrass a neutral country which will have nothing to gain from this operation. I confess that this legal point makes me change my mind.

MILNER: Why do you say that that is impossible? Admiral Hope thinks that it is possible and I don't think that a neutral would refuse since it would bring about the end of the war.

BENSON: If the two groups of belligerents agree, why should a neutral refuse?

GEDDES: I wish to point out once more that the Naval Council, without adhering to it, merely submits to the decision of the ministers.

CLEMENCEAU: Then we shall stick to what was decided this morning.

GEDDES: It has also been proposed to insert an article prohibiting the transfer of flag.

CLEMENCEAU: This clause has been accepted.

SONNINO: Aren't we going to stipulate anything about the Russian ships?

CLEMENCEAU: We cannot mix ourselves up in that. There is no war between Germany and Russia. We cannot ask Germany to return them to Russia, or to turn them over to us.

BALFOUR: What did the Naval Council think of this? These ships, are they Russian or German?

GEDDES: We assumed that the Russian warships were German. As for the merchant marine, we have a clause concerning it.

LEYGUES: I propose that Germany hand over to our consuls all the ships which are in neutral ports. We shall find there a compensation for all the losses suffered by Allied shipping.

CLEMENCEAU: That is a condition of peace; we shall examine it later.[24]

Clause 5. [Right of the Allies to sweep for mines outside German territorial waters. Mine fields to be indicated by Germans.]

Clause 6. [Free access to the Baltic for Allied naval and mermantile ships.]

Clause 7. [Maintenance of blockade; German merchant ships found at sea subject to capture.]

24. Cf. Seymour, *House Papers,* IV, 134–135, for brief comment on this discussion of naval terms. On November 13 the Germans were ordered to send these surface ships to a rendezvous off the Firth of Forth. Since the sailors had gone Bolshevist, it was difficult to get the vessels disarmed and made ready for their last cruise; but the efficient Noske managed to succeed even in this task of persuasion, chiefly by pointing out that the Allies would otherwise occupy Helgoland. The ships—reduced by accidents beyond German control to 69 from the stipulated 74—passed through long lines of Entente ships on November 19 in what was made to resemble a formal surrender of Germany's naval might. Then they were ordered to Scapa Flow in the Orkneys since no neutral power was said to be ready to intern them. Spain was apparently the only neutral sounded on the question. The ships arrived at the bleak Orkney naval base on November 27; and here they remained, manned by shadow crews of homesick and discontented Reds who had believed in the early days of Germany's revolution that they could persuade British sailors to seize control of their ships. On June 21, by order of Admiral von Reuter, who had been made responsible for the ships at Scapa Flow, they were scuttled to avoid the surrender called for in Article 184 of the Versailles Treaty.

Clause 8. [Concentration and immobilization at German bases designated by the Allies of all aerial forces.]

Clause 9. [Abandonment by Germany of all port and river material, of all commercial vessels, tugs, lighters and equipment, of naval aeronautical ships and material of every nature in evacuating the Belgian coast and ports.]

Clause 10. [Evacuation of all ports of the Black Sea, return of all Allied shipping, etc.]

Clause 11. [Restitution without reciprocity of all Allied commercial vessels actually in the hands of Germany.]

Clause 12. [Prohibition of destroying any ships or material before evacuation, surrender, or restitution.]

(All of the naval clauses, thus modified, are thus accepted.)

HOUSE: Before the session rises I desire to submit to the Council the text of a wish that President Wilson has instructed me to transmit to you to the end that the Allies will immediately co-operate in the sending of various supplies, of food and of other things, to Austria-Hungary for the relief of the population.

BALFOUR: I agree with Mr. House's proposal, for the enemy will gather that there is an advantage in making peace. It is necessary, however, to word the text carefully for there are questions of tonnage and supplies which must be carefully examined so that we shall not make a proposal and a promise which we shall be unable to carry out later.

CLEMENCEAU: We have a clause maintaining the blockade, on the other hand you promise them provisions.

PICHON: Here is a text which is proposed:

"If the peoples of Bulgaria, Austria-Hungary, and Turkey make an appeal to the Allies and Associated Powers to furnish them with provisions, the Allies and Associated Powers will do all in their power to help them in the interests of humanity."

CLEMENCEAU: We accept this text, but it must not be part of the conditions of the armistice.

(This proposition is accepted, and the discussion is closed.)

At the morning session in Colonel House's headquarters November 4 the procedure to be followed had been settled on.

"The Supreme War Council decide as follows:

(a) To approve the attached terms for an armistice with Germany.

(b) To communicate the terms of armistice to President Wilson, inviting him to notify the German Government that the next step for them to take is to send a *parlementaire* to Marshal Foch who will receive instructions to act on behalf of the Associated Governments.

(c) To communicate to President Wilson the attached memorandum [of] observations by the Allied Governments on the correspondence which has passed between the President and the German Government, in order that they may be forwarded to Germany together with the communication in regard to an armistice.

(d) To invite Colonel House to make the above communications on their behalf to President Wilson.

(e) To authorize Marshal Foch to communicate the terms as finally approved to envoys properly accredited by the German Government.

(f) To associate a British admiral with Marshal Foch on [the] naval aspects of the armistice.

(g) To leave [discretion to] Marshal Foch and the British admiral in regard to minor technical points in the armistice.[25]

The "memorandum of observations" sent to Wilson and to be sent by him to Germany was the pre-armistice agreement, in which the Allies stated their qualifications of the Fourteen Points as a suitable basis for the peace. As finally modified and transmitted to Germany on November 5, it read as follows:

The Allied Governments have given careful consideration to the correspondence which has passed between the President of the United States and the German Government. Subject to the qualifications which follow they declare their willingness to make peace with the Government of Germany on the terms of peace laid down in the President's address to Congress of January 1918, and the principles of settlement enunciated in his subsequent addresses. They must point out, however, that clause 2, relating to what is usually described as the freedom of the seas, is open to various interpretations, some of which they could not accept. They must, therefore, reserve to themselves complete freedom on this subject when they enter the peace conference.

Further, in the conditions of peace laid down in his address to Congress of January 8, 1918, the President declared that invaded territories must be restored as well as evacuated and freed; the

25. House to Lansing, November 4, 1918, *Foreign Relations, 1918,* Supplement I, I, 461. Also in Mermeix, *Les Négociations Secrètes,* pp. 275–276.

Allied Governments feel that no doubt ought to be allowed to exist as to what this provision implies. By it they understand that compensation will be made by Germany for all damage done to the civilian population of the Allies and their property by the aggression of Germany by land, by sea and from the air.

"I immediately gave orders," writes Marshal Foch, "for receiving any German *parlementaires* that might suddenly present themselves at our front lines; and as I intended, if warned beforehand of their coming, to direct them along the line Givet-La Capelle-Guise, I sent special instructions to General Debeney. At the same time we cautioned the armies against false rumors which the enemy might spread regarding the expected conclusion of an armistice." [26]

26. Foch, *Mémoires,* II, 289. There were rumors in Paris that the armistice was signed. By November 7 "most of the officials in Paris and practically every non-official person" believed them. It is highly doubtful that the rumor originated with the enemy. About 10 A.M. on November 7 Secretary Lansing learned of the report from a telegram that the War Department had received from its military attaché in Paris. The Secretary knew it to be false because "it was physically impossible for the German parliamentaries to have reached the French lines and much less to have conferred with Marshal Foch." A talk with the Chief of Staff, General March, confirmed his views. Telegrams of inquiry to Paris brought news from the military attaché at noon and from Colonel House at 2 P.M. that there was no truth in the report. By noon, however, American newspapers had published the report and given impetus to an emotional wave that swept the entire country. The papers received the news from Roy Howard of the United Press. Investigations in Paris revealed that the Naval Attaché in the American Embassy, Captain Jackson, had sent the news by telegram to Admiral Wilson at Brest. The Admiral had informed Roy Howard and even enabled him to cable the news to the United States by sending an aide with him to the censor's office. According to the *New York Times* of November 8, 1918, the cablegram arrived at 11.56 A.M., was passed by the censor at 11.59, and immediately broadcast over news wires to the nation. See memorandum of Secretary Lansing, November 7, 1918, *Lansing Papers,* II, 171–173; Lansing to House, November 7, 1918, *Foreign Relations, 1918,* Supplement I, I, 480; Lansing to Sharp, November 7, 1918, *ibid;* House to Lansing, November 8, 1918, *ibid.,* p. 483; Mordacq, *L'Armistice du 11 Novembre 1918,* 107–109.

XIII

Erzberger Seeks an Armistice

AN armistice that brings all hostilities to an end is usually concluded by the Commanders-in-Chief of the belligerent powers after their respective governments have given them specific authority to do so. Believing in early October that the end of the war was near, the German High Command appointed an Armistice Commission. Difficulty had arisen over who should be head of the Commission because the first two people suggested were not available. The Kaiser thereupon suggested the Infantry General von Gündell. He was appointed and Colonel von Winterfeldt was made his Chief of Staff. The other members were commissioned officers. As we have already seen, this Commission proceeded with its work by establishing in a meeting on October 7 the principles to guide the negotiations with the enemy.[1]

When the correspondence with Wilson showed what kind of armistice the Allies wanted, the High Command underwent a change of mind and indicated its desire to have negotiations broken off. In the meantime the Government had become convinced of the necessity for continuing its dealings with Wilson and was equally determined to avoid a break. To deprive the generals of the opportunity to make the strong terms of the Allies an occasion for a rupture, the Government stipulated on November 2 that a civilian should be named to the Armistice Commission. Erzberger suggested Haussmann for that position.[2]

When Prince Max suddenly decided on the 6th that the war must be ended immediately, Erzberger was surprised to hear himself named representative of the War Cabinet on the Armistice Commission. He protested and again suggested Haussmann's name. In the end he had to yield to the insistence of his colleagues.[3] He did not succeed in getting from the Cabinet any instructions beyond the general one that an armistice must be con-

1. Document 35a and footnote, *Amtliche Urkunden. Supra,* pp. 97–98.
2. Document 96b, *ibid.*
3. The Chancellor says that General Groener had suggested Erzberger's name. Max, *Erinnerungen,* p. 594. See M. Erzberger, *Erlebnisse im Weltkrieg,* p. 325.

cluded under any circumstances.[4] Since it was deemed advisable to have the Foreign Office represented on the Commission, the German Minister to Copenhagen, Count Brockdorff-Rantzau, was proposed. When it turned out to be impossible for him to get ready in time, Count von Oberndorff, the German Minister to Bulgaria and a close friend of Erzberger's, was selected instead. General von Gündell was still first plenipotentiary.

Having received no plenipotentiary powers as late as three in the afternoon, Erzberger informed the Chancellery that he would not leave until he had got them. He was then directed to the Foreign Office, where nothing was known of the matter. The most he could get was a promise that the necessary documents would be in his hands before five o'clock. They were brought to him just before his special train left the station. He was given full powers signed in blank by the Chancellor.

For a letter of introduction to Foch he was given a copy of the American note of November 5, which reached Berlin just before he left. The note was not entirely unexpected, for Berlin newspapers had reported on Tuesday that the Entente Powers had agreed upon armistice terms and would make them public within a few days.

This fourth and last note from the United States read as follows:

Washington, November 5, 1918

Sir: I have the honor to request you to transmit the following communication to the German Government:

In my note of October 23, 1918, I advised you that the President had transmitted his correspondence with the German authorities to the Governments with which the Government of the United States is associated as a belligerent, with the suggestion that, if those Governments were disposed to effect peace upon the terms and principles indicated, their military advisers and the military advisers of the United States be asked to submit to the Governments associated against Germany the necessary terms of such an armistice as would fully protect the interests of the peoples involved and ensure to the Associated Governments the unrestricted power to safeguard and enforce the details of the peace to which the German Government had agreed, provided they deemed such an armistice possible from the military point of view.

The President is now in receipt of a memorandum of observations

4. *Ibid.*, pp. 325–326.

by the Allied Governments on this correspondence, which is as follows:

"The Allied Governments have given careful consideration to the correspondence which has passed between the President of the United States and the German Government. Subject to the qualifications which follow they declare their willingness to make peace with the Government of Germany on the terms of peace laid down in the President's address to Congress of January 1918, and the principles of settlement enunciated in his subsequent addresses. They must point out, however, that clause 2, relating to what is usually described as the freedom of the seas, is open to various interpretations, some of which they could not accept. They must, therefore, reserve to themselves complete freedom on this subject when they enter the peace conference.

Further, in the conditions of peace laid down in his address to Congress of January 8, 1918, the President declared that invaded territories must be restored as well as evacuated and freed, the Allied Governments feel that no doubt ought to be allowed to exist as to what this provision implies. By it they understand that compensation will be made by Germany for all damage done to the civilian population of the Allies and their property by the aggression of Germany by land, by sea and from the air."

I am instructed by the President to say that he is in agreement with the interpretation set forth in the last paragraph of the memorandum above quoted. I am further instructed by the President to request you to notify the German Government that Marshal Foch has been authorized by the Government of the United States and the Allied Governments to receive properly accredited representatives of the German Government, and to communicate to them the terms of an armistice.

ROBERT LANSING[5]

A special train took Erzberger and members of the Army High Command to Spa, where they arrived at 8 A.M., Thursday morning, November 7. Shortly after midnight the Government sent a radio message to Marshal Foch, naming the members of the German Armistice Commission and informing him that the delegation was ready to leave at once for the place agreed upon. "The German Government would be happy," the message read, "if in the interest of humanity the arrival of the German delegation on the

5. Lansing to Sulzer, the Swiss Minister, November 5, 1918, *Foreign Relations, 1918,* Supplement I, I, 468–469.

Allied front would bring [about] a provisional suspension of arms."

In less than an hour Foch made his reply:

If the German plenipotentiaries desire to meet Marshal Foch to ask for an armistice they shall present themselves to the French advanced posts by the Chimay-Fourmies-La Capelle-Guise [road]. Orders have been given to receive them and to conduct them to the place fixed for the meeting.[6]

This route was chosen because it was said to be the shortest as well as fairly safe. It ran from northeast to southwest, practically at right angles across the front, a few miles south of the British Army and into the area held by General Debeney's First Army. In a straight line the distance from Chimay to Guise was over 50 kilometers, sufficiently great to allow for a rapidly shifting front. In fact, on November 1 the battle line passed through Guise; it was beyond Chimay when the armistice took effect.

During the morning Foch had been informed that the German delegation would leave Spa at noon and expected to arrive in front of the French line between four and five in the afternoon. Arrangements were made by both French and German commanders to stop the gunfire on each side during the passage of the delegation. At five Foch himself left his headquarters at Senlis for the rendezvous, accompanied by three members of his staff, General Weygand, and the British Admiral Wemyss, First Sea Lord of the Admiralty.[7]

When he arrived at Spa Erzberger found that no preparations whatever had been made for other members of the Armistice Commission. The Foreign Office Representative at Spa, von Hintze, advised him not to take General von Gündell with him. The change was effected by telephone call to Berlin and the consequence was that Erzberger, a civilian, found himself named head of the German Armistice Commission. General von Winterfeldt, former military attaché in Paris, was also named to the Commission. In his conferences at Army Headquarters Erzberger found over two dozen officers who wished to accompany him. Believing it inadvisable for a large number of German officers to appear in France at this time, he decided that only Count Oberndorff, Gen-

6. *Ibid.,* p. 481. See also Foch, *Mémoires,* II, 289. Also *Vossische Zeitung,* November 7, 1918, No. 571.

7. Foch, *Mémoires,* II, 289, 290.

eral von Winterfeldt, and Lieutenant Commander Vanselow should accompany him. A cavalry captain, von Helldorf, was to act as interpreter, and a Dr. Blauert as stenographer.

Hindenburg, who came in when the conferences were over, observed that it was probably the first time in history that political rather than military men were concluding an armistice. He had no objections to the arrangement, particularly now that the Supreme Army Command no longer determined the policy of the Government and because the Army needed a rest. "God go with you," he said, seeing Erzberger off, "and try to get the best you can for our country." [8]

After a short luncheon the delegation left Spa for the front in five automobiles. On the edge of the town an accident occurred which might have been serious. The car in which Erzberger and Oberndorff were riding failed to make a curve and was hurled against a house; the car behind crashed into it. Nobody was injured; but the two automobiles were so badly damaged that only the three remaining cars were available for the delegation. The journey through Belgium was continued, slowly, however, on account of the masses of retreating soldiers on the roads.[9]

After the Cabinet had sent off the Armistice Commission on the 6th, it devoted the afternoon to a discussion of the revolutionary uprisings occurring throughout Germany and the measures to be adopted to check them. Revolutionaries had seized the railway

8. Erzberger, *Erlebnisse,* p. 327. It was an unusual Armistice Commission that went to Foch under a civilian. Much has been made of that fact by Nazis who claim that civilians, not the Army, carried the white flag of surrender in 1918. Mordacq has argued at some length in his *L'Armistice du 11 Novembre 1918,* pp. 145–149, that the German High Command played a trick on Foch (who did not say so at the time) by informing him that General Gündell was to be head of the delegation and later appointing Erzberger instead so that the Army could maintain its prestige. He arrives at this conclusion partly by misinterpreting words of Erzberger, whom he quotes as his source, partly by neglecting the circumstances under which Erzberger was made a member and later head of the Armistice Commission. It is perfectly clear that the initiative for changing the personnel of the Armistice Commission appointed in early October came from the civilian authorities in Berlin. Many reasons account for that policy: the determination to keep the Army from dictating Government policies and from taking harsh armistice conditions as an excuse for breaking off negotiations with Wilson; the decision to appoint a civilian to the Commission to make sure those negotiations would continue; the knowledge that Wilson was unalterably opposed to the military masters of Germany; the eagerness of Prince Max on November 6 to get an armistice immediately in order to check the spread of revolution.

9. Erzberger, *Erlebnisse,* p. 327.

stations in Hamburg and Altona; they had taken control of the local government in Lübeck, Wilhelmshafen, Brünsbüttel, Cuxhaven, and other coast towns.[10] Prince Max compared the revolution in the north with the opening of a new military front. But, according to Noske, it was impossible to determine whether the disturbances were purely local in their nature or part of a general movement. Authorities in Berlin had no idea of their extent.[11] They did know, however, that the reports from Kiel and elsewhere greatly excited the populace of Berlin. The Independent Socialists had arranged five meetings in Berlin that evening, to celebrate the anniversary of the Russian revolution—incidentally, on the very day that the Russian Ambassador Joffe and his staff left Berlin by request of the Government. These meetings were prohibited by the authorities, who hoped in this way to avoid difficulties. Preparations were made to arrest sailors arriving in the city from the centers of revolution in the Hanseatic towns. To quiet the people with the information that the fighting would soon end, Chancellor Max and General Groener arranged to publish, late on November 6, the news about the Armistice Commission.[12] The statement read as follows:

President Wilson has answered the German note today and has informed us that his allies have agreed, with the exception of the freedom of the seas, to the Fourteen Points, in which in January of this year he summed up his peace conditions, and that the conditions of armistice can be given to us by Marshal Foch. Thus the preliminary requirement for peace negotiations and armistice negotiations is stated at the same time. To end the bloodshed the German delegation for the conclusion of the armistice and for the opening of peace negotiations has been named today and has already left for the west. The successful course of negotiations will be seriously jeopardized by disturbances and undisciplined behavior.

For over four years the German people have borne the most grievous sorrows and sacrifices of the war in unity and quiet. If these spiritual powers should fail in the decisive moment when only the absolute unity of the whole German nation can avert grave dangers for its future, then the consequences are not to be calculated.

To maintain order in the spirit of willing self-discipline as it has

10. Max, *Erinnerungen,* p. 595.

11. Noske, *Von Kiel bis Kapp,* p. 23.

12. Max, *Erinnerungen,* p. 594. A number of Berlin papers carried the news in their evening editions.

been maintained to the present is in this critical hour an indispensable demand that any popular government must make.

May every citizen be conscious of the high responsibility he bears to his nation in the fulfillment of this obligation.[13]

The moderate Socialists tried desperately to check the spread of the revolution to Berlin and to keep the Independents from getting control of the working classes. They issued an appeal to the people to maintain order, pointing out that disturbances would make it impossible to get peace, to solve economic problems, to get food, etc.[14] Wednesday evening they held a party meeting to determine policy. Scheidemann said he objected to the Cabinet's further postponing action on the question of abdication and he asked his party's permission to resign. He believed, he said, that only the immediate abdication of the Kaiser and a thorough democratization of all the states of the Empire could avert a catastrophe.[15] The party refused to allow him to withdraw; instead, they passed a resolution in favor of an immediate armistice, amnesty for people guilty of military misdemeanors, and the immediate democratization of the central Government, of Prussia, and of the other states. They voted to inform the Chancellor that they wanted an immediate settlement of the question of abdication. This "half-hearted" resolution, as Scheidemann called it, was presented to the Chancellor, who took what satisfaction he could from the fact that he had been given no ultimatum.[16]

Prince Max knew that the plight of Germany was desperate. The revolution was making great gains; those agitating for it justified themselves by placing all responsibility on the Kaiser. At any time he might be confronted with demands from the Social Democrats for the Kaiser's abdication; so he decided that the time had come for him to go to Spa. Before taking this step, however, he wanted to make sure that the Social Democrats would not confront him with an ultimatum before he could consummate the delicate mission. He conferred with Ebert and David, men who could, he thought, put aside party considerations when the nation was in danger. The Chancellor believed that he had a solution by which the Kaiser would be spared any political

13. *Ibid.*, pp. 598–599; also *Berliner Tageblatt*, November 7, 1918, No. 570.

14. *Frankfurter Zeitung*, November 6, 1918, No. 308.

15. Payer, *Von Bethmann Hollweg*, pp. 158–159.

16. Max, *Erinnerungen*, pp. 596–597; Scheidemann, *Memoiren*, II, 264–275; Scheidemann, *Der Zusammenbruch*, pp. 204–205.

pressure from below. The Emperor should first appoint a deputy and, as soon as possible, a new Reichstag should be elected to settle the issues raised by abdication. After these arrangements had been made, the Kaiser would abdicate. Prince Max believed that a call for a "constituent national assembly" would check the revolutionary movement and that the Social Democrats would agree to the scheme. He had his interview with Ebert on Thursday morning, the 7th, and told him of his intention to go immediately to Spa and lay his proposal before the Kaiser.

"If," he asked, "I should succeed in persuading the Kaiser, do I have you on my side in the struggle against the social revolution?"

Ebert's answer was clear and given without hesitation. "If the Kaiser does not abdicate, the social revolution is inevitable. I do not want it; in fact, I hate it like sin." Only *after* the Kaiser's abdication could he hope to bring his party and the masses of people to the support of the Government. Still, he wished Prince Max success on his mission to Spa. David, whom the Chancellor saw later, spoke much as Ebert had. The Chancellor felt, consequently, as though he had concluded something like an alliance with the Social Democrats to stand together in the task of saving the country from revolution.[17]

The attitude of *Vorwärts* on November 7 was not such as to fill the Chancellor with confidence about Socialist support. The paper took much satisfaction in Wilson's Fourteen Points and in the likelihood that "the last shot in the World War will probably be fired this week"; it had, however, profound misgivings about the Entente's reservations on the freedom of the seas and about their demand that Germany indemnify their civilians for damages suffered in the war. It also wanted the question of the Kaiser settled. "Germany cannot allow the conditions of peace to be made more stringent on account of one man," stated the editorial. "The war, which has inflicted such untold sacrifices and losses upon the nation, now demands a sacrifice from this one man, who with his six sons returned safe and sound." [18]

The situation became ever more threatening. Out of Munich came a report that workers, peasants, and soldiers had taken control of the Government and proclaimed a republic. The situation at Kiel was somewhat better, chiefly because of the work of Noske. Reports from elsewhere were alarming. In Hamburg the Inde-

17. Max, *Erinnerungen,* pp. 597–600.
18. Quoted in Lutz, *Fall of the German Empire,* II, 408–410.

pendents had got control and were making demands of a revolutionary character. Thousands of armed men were said to have left Hamburg for Berlin to start a revolution in the capital, and others were reported coming from Hanover. The Minister of Railroads had taken countermeasures by ordering tracks torn up at various places outside Hamburg and Hanover and by garrisoning the Lehrter Bahnhof in Berlin with strong troop formations. The President of the Berlin police reported the discovery of plans to seize control of the prisons and of police headquarters. That the plot failed of execution was ascribed to the expulsion of the Russian Ambassador, which deprived the Independents of competent advice. The Cabinet discussed ways and means of defense against the revolution and speculated on the possibility of getting military assistance from the front. Troops destined for the front were kept in Berlin.[19]

In the middle of Thursday afternoon the Secretary of the Admiralty, von Mann, conferred with some twenty sailors of the mutinous Third Squadron, who had come to Berlin from Kiel. There was very little of a political nature in the demands these men presented; they seemed to have come chiefly to explain what had happened and to apologize for it rather than to insist on demands. Haussmann, who participated in this conference, appealed to the men to preserve discipline because of the effect the agitation might have on the Government's peace policy. "We can still accomplish a good deal in our negotiations," he reasoned, "but only if we have you behind us. Clemenceau wishes to ruin Germany, Wilson wishes to restore her. Clemenceau will win if signs of dissolution appear in Germany. . . ." This appeal to the patriotism and intelligence of the sailors worked, and the favorable results were reported to the Chancellor, who took them as evidence of the good work of Noske.[20]

At five o'clock Undersecretary of State Wahnschaffe rushed into Prince Max's room at the Chancellery to report that Scheidemann and Ebert had telephoned from the Reichstag to ask that they be received immediately, to present an ultimatum of five demands from their party. It was apparent when they arrived that they were neither threatening nor defying the Government; instead, they came like men "overcome by sudden terror" at the thought that they and their party would lose influence with the masses of the people. Their demands were as follows:

19. Max, *Erinnerungen,* pp. 600–601.
20. *Ibid.,* pp. 602–603.

1. Immediate permission to hold the meetings that were prohibited for today.

2. Instructions to the police and to the military to exercise the greatest discretion.

3. Abdication of the Kaiser and of the Crown Prince by noon Friday.

4. Strengthening of Social Democratic influence in the Government.

5. The transformation of the Prussian ministry in accordance with the principles of the majority parties of the Reichstag.

If the ultimatum was not complied with by Friday noon, the Social Democratic ministers would retire from the Government.[21]

"The Kaiser must abdicate immediately," they argued; "otherwise, we shall have the revolution." This ultimatum had been drafted during a party session in the afternoon, at which Scheidemann had again asked for permission to resign from the Government. Instead of withdrawing from the Government immediately, it was decided to give the Chancellor an opportunity first to meet the demands of the Majority Socialists.[22]

"My answer was," writes Prince Max, "[that] the foundation of my chancellorship has been wrecked; I put a speedy end to the talk and was filled with indignation and bitterness. My journey [to Spa] had become purposeless."

But the Chancellor made one last effort to reach an understanding with the Social Democrats. Simons was instructed to ask Ebert to withdraw the ultimatum and to keep it secret. If that could be arranged, Prince Max promised to start for Spa that evening. Simons returned very soon. Ebert had declined the offer; he said that preparations had been made to publish the ultimatum at twenty-six mass meetings that night. "Otherwise everybody will leave us for the Independents." Ebert gave Simons the clear impression that he was seeking to have himself made Chancellor.

Prince Max now summoned Vice-Chancellor von Payer and told him his intention to resign immediately. Von Payer was deeply distressed, but appeared to Prince Max convinced that the Chancellor had no alternative. He was instructed to inform the members of the Cabinet of the decision. Then Prince Max telegraphed his resignation to the Kaiser:

21. *Ibid.*, pp. 603–604; Scheidemann, *Memoiren,* II, 279; *Vorwärts,* November 8, 1918, No. 308.

22. Stutzenberger, *Die Abdankung Kaiser Wilhelms II,* pp. 166–167.

Berlin, November 7, 1918

TO HIS MAJESTY THE KAISER AND KING,

Your Majesty knows that the so-called War Cabinet has, in spite of my most earnest and insistent warnings, for some time been making the August Person a subject of discussion. This occurred for the first time in my absence. But after the Secretary of State, Herr Scheidemann, had informed me in writing that his party expected me to advise Your Majesty's abdication, and my efforts to induce him to withdraw his letter had been in vain, I was obliged to define my position. I therefore read the Cabinet a declaration to the effect that I would neither permit pressure to be exercised upon Your Majesty in the question of abdication nor would myself yield to such pressure in advising Your Majesty.

Your Majesty's departure for General Headquarters, decided on as it was without my knowledge and carried out against my advice, rendered continuous communication with Your Majesty very difficult. On the other hand any absence from the capital on my part must inevitably involve considerable difficulties. In spite of this, having regard for the situation as a whole and after the most mature consideration, I had determined to set off this evening on a journey to Your Majesty in order to supplement the information with which the Ministers Delbrück and Drews, acting on my instruction, had supplied Your Majesty. However, this afternoon Scheidemann and Ebert brought me in the name of the Social Democratic party an ultimatum, containing among others the demand that the news of Your Majesty's abdication be announced to the people before tomorrow afternoon.

My efforts to convince the two party leaders of the fatal nature of this demand from the point of view of the Fatherland were fruitless. The party leaders are convinced that this very night in Berlin riots on a great scale will break out unless they can at least console the masses with the prospect of such news. They refuse to withdraw the ultimatum; on the contrary, moved by anxiety at the growing power of the radicals, they are firmly resolved to reap a tactical advantage from the fact of its having been presented by publishing it this very evening.

In these circumstances it is impossible for me to preserve the unity of the present Government any longer. The majority of the members of the Cabinet and of the Secretaries of State take an attitude of opposition to the Social Democratic step. Since I can administer the affairs of the Empire only so long as I enjoy the confidence and support of a solid majority in the Reichstag, and since as Imperial Chancellor I am obliged to hold fast to my decision not to allow any pressure to be put on me in the matter of the August Person, I therefore beg Your Majesty in the spirit of the deepest reverence most graciously to relieve me of my office as Imperial Chancellor.

I naturally regard it as my duty to retain in my hands the conduct of Imperial affairs in this time of stress until a decision is taken, especially as the armistice negotiations which are in progress might be endangered by a breach in the continuity of government.[23]

In the meeting of the Cabinet that evening Scheidemann acquainted his colleagues with his party's ultimatum and the reasons for it. He stressed the spreading revolt against the Government and asserted that the people in Berlin had been embittered by the military measures adopted by the Government and particularly by the prohibition placed on their meetings. He and his party saw no way of checking the revolution except by getting the Government to accept their demands. The Chancellor had done nothing but talk, and action had now become necessary. Since it was clear that Prince Max would not act to force the Kaiser's abdication, the Social Democrats had to act. Payer informed those present that the Chancellor had now decided to resign. Scheidemann expressed regret, adding that the Chancellor had his full sympathy. "But," he concluded, "we still feel that with regard to the Kaiser he has not shown the determination that is needed." Von Payer, Haussmann, and Count Roedern said that the Social Democrats assumed a grave responsibility in pressing their ultimatum at this critical time. Solf pointed out that the resignation of the Chancellor would have a bad effect abroad. He asked for a three-day extension of time, until the armistice had been formally concluded. Scheidemann desired to prevent the Chancellor's resignation. "The Government need not break up," he reasoned, "if the Imperial Chancellor remains. It is our conviction that a revolutionary collapse will occur if the Kaiser does not abdicate immediately." And then Scheidemann spoke words that Prince Max was never to forget: "Should he abdicate, we believe ourselves able to guarantee a favorable development of the situation." The arguments of his colleagues led Scheidemann to suggest a compromise: that an immediate report on the situation be made to the Kaiser and that neither the Chancellor nor the Social Democrats resign until the armistice had been concluded.

23. Max, *Erinnerungen,* pp. 605–606.

He promised to try to persuade his party colleagues to accept this proposal but said he could not give any assurances that he would succeed.[24]

Von Payer, Roedern, and Solf tried to convince Prince Max that he should withdraw his resignation, but the Chancellor replied that he could not act contrary to his convictions. He wished them to inform the Cabinet that the action of the Social Democrats had made it impossible for him to remain in office and that he had telegraphed his resignation to the Emperor. He said he would feel he had not served his country in vain if, as Chancellor, he had contributed something toward the ending of the war. Scheidemann regretted the Chancellor's move. He reported having heard from Ebert that the demands of the Socialists had already had a calming effect on the working classes; and he assured Prince Max that the Social Democrats were doing all in their power to restrain the masses.[25]

In the evening the Chancellor felt it necessary to telegraph a warning to the Kaiser, despite the provocation he had had, against taking action hostile to the Social Democrats or trying to govern without their support. Such a policy would create even greater dangers than the Socialist demand for abdication; it would lead to civil war and to Bolshevism. Difficult as it would be to coöperate with the party, Prince Max was convinced that no alternative existed.[26]

In the meantime the armistice delegation was with difficulty making its way toward the French lines. At 6 P.M. the party arrived at Chimay, where a German general informed Erzberger that he could not proceed that night. The roads were impassable, he said, because trees had been felled across them to cover the retreat of the troops. Erzberger insisted that he must continue his journey and, in the end, succeeded in doing so after telephoning to German commanding officers in the neighboring headquarters at Trélon.[27]

The delegation was in Trélon at 7.30 P.M. and Erzberger was told that all preparations had been made for crossing the front. Three German officers, carrying white flags, had gone ahead to report the coming of the Armistice delegation and to arrange for

24. *Ibid.*, pp. 607–611.
25. *Ibid.*, pp. 611–612.
26. *Ibid.*, pp. 612–614.
27. Erzberger, *Erlebnisse,* pp. 327–328.

firing to cease so that the delegates could get through safely. A detachment of pioneers had cleared the road of mines. The General at Trélon praised the valor of his troops very highly; they had been fighting for six weeks without respite, with the result that one division had been reduced to 349 men and another to 437. Their spirit was admirable, he said, and officers and men showed superhuman courage. The General knew hardly anything about events in Berlin and Kiel, and he asked Erzberger not to speak of them to his officers. After a brief halt the delegation pushed on at a faster pace, owing to the roads having been cleared.

It was 9.20 in the evening of November 7 [8.20 P.M. French time] when the delegation crossed the German front line. A man from Erzberger's home district, Swabia, gave him the last farewell. The fellow, very much surprised, asked him where he was going. Erzberger said he was going to conclude an armistice, whereupon the other replied in good Swabian dialect, addressing the two men in the first car: "What! You are going to do that, you two alone?"

After leaving the German lines the cars went forward very slowly, through a drizzling fog. Firing on both sides had ceased in this sector some hours before. A large white flag had been hoisted on the leading automobile, and a trumpeter stood on the running board and continually blew short blasts. Erzberger said that he found this journey much harder than that he had made three weeks earlier to the deathbed of his only son.[28]

About 150 meters from the German lines the first French soldiers appeared and halted the cars. An officer stepped forward and recognized the delegates. This was Captain Lhuillier, twenty-five-year-old commander of a battalion of the One Hundred Seventy-First Infantry Regiment. He got into the leading car and Bugler Corporal Sellier replaced the German trumpeter on the running board. Erzberger says that he was conducted very politely by two officers to the near-by town of La Capelle.[29]

There the Germans were met by Major de Bourbon-Busset, who had been sent out from First Army Headquarters for that purpose, and by Major Ducorne, Commander of the Nineteenth Battalion of *Chasseurs à pied* which had attacked in that sector

28. Erzberger, *Erlebnisse,* p. 328; Weygand, *Le 11 Novembre* (Paris, 1932), p. 26.

29. Erzberger, *Erlebnisse,* pp. 328–329; Weygand, *Le 11 Novembre,* p. 26, with pictures of La Capelle on pages 27–28.

during the morning. General Winterfeldt began talking with French officers. Before the war he had been military attaché in Paris and he spoke excellent French. He apologized for their coming late and explained why; then he introduced the members of the German delegation.[30]

Erzberger says that the first question put to him by several soldiers who came up to his car was: "Finie la guerre?" His automobile was greeted with applause, sign of the joy with which the end of the war was hailed. He heard several cries of "Vive la France!" but otherwise the soldiers were quiet and guarded. Many of them approached his car, some asking "What nation?" and others begging for cigarettes. Erzberger, however, had none to give them, for he did not smoke. The roads, he noted, still had German sign posts, and on a large building "Kaiserliche Kreiskommandantur" was written in big letters. Above this floated the tricolor which had been placed there that afternoon when the French had entered the town. The rain began to come down harder; so Major de Bourbon-Busset took the Germans to his temporary headquarters in the Villa Francport. Erzberger noticed that all the streets were decked with flags. Hostilities, in this sector, were suspended until midnight.

At the Villa Francport Erzberger found the three officers who had preceded him. Beneath a portrait of Napoleon III in general's uniform, which happened to be hanging on the wall, von Winterfeldt introduced himself and his colleagues. He was described by a French eyewitness as "tall, cold, and dignified." Erzberger, on the other hand, was "short, a bit fat, ruddy, and fidgety, seeming to be unacquainted with what was going on." Arrangements were made to leave the German cars, emblazoned with imperial eagles, behind and to continue the journey in French machines. While these preparations were being made, a German officer approached General Winterfeldt and said in a low voice something that was nonetheless audible about the armistice being indispensable on account of the state of affairs in the German Army.[31]

At 9 P.M. (French time), as the delegation was about to leave La Capelle, a crowd began to gather around the automobiles. Major de Bourbon-Busset asked them not to make any demonstration. After being photographed by the light of flares the

30. Weygand, *Le 11 Novembre,* p. 29.

31. Erzberger, *Erlebnisse,* pp. 328–329; Weygand, *Le 11 Novembre,* pp. 32–33.

Germans took their places in the French cars. Each German plenipotentiary had his own machine, and a French officer as escort. Major de Bourbon-Busset took his place beside Erzberger. As the cars rolled off, a voice from the crowd shouted: "Nach Paris!"

The cars went forward slowly, bumping over roads which were in very bad condition. Erzberger's hat was dented and he lost his glasses; when he grumbled about the roads, de Bourbon-Busset reminded him that it was the German Army which had plowed them up. De Bourbon-Busset was not able to say where they were going, but he did tell Erzberger that they had fifty kilometers ahead of them. He also taught him how to pronounce the name of General Foch.[32]

At no time during the trip were the German envoys blindfolded, and Erzberger took advantage of this to note as much as he could of the passing landscape. They went through Guise which, together with its bridges, was badly damaged. At midnight, they reached the Presbytery of Homblières on the eastern outskirts of Saint-Quentin. This was the headquarters of a French Army command; the building it occupied had also been badly damaged by the bombardment. While the Germans were eating their supper, two French generals, one of them Debeney, entered and told them that Marshal Foch was ready to receive them. Erzberger found the attitude of these officers very cold. Debeney pointed out that the supper was the same as that served in the French Army—to general and poilu alike. It consisted of soup, salt meat, and peas. Erzberger seems to have thought that Debeney's remark was in the nature of a thrust at the Germans.[33]

At 1 A.M. the delegation continued its journey, passing through Chauny, which was completely destroyed. It was a succession of ruins that looked ghostlike in the dim moonlight, and not a soul lived in the region. At three they arrived in the town of Tergnier, also completely destroyed, and stopped to ask the way to the station.

"Where are we?" said Erzberger.

"At Tergnier."

"But there are no houses."

"It's true. There was once a town here . . ."

32. Erzberger, *Erlebnisse,* p. 329; Weygand, *Le 11 Novembre,* pp. 33–34. Pictures can be found in Weygand, 27–28.

33. Erzberger, *Erlebnisse,* p. 329; Weygand, *Le 11 Novembre,* pp. 34–35.

At the station, which was lighted by torches, a company of *chasseurs* presented arms. Clambering over wreckage, the delegation reached their special train. This was made up of three coaches: a dining car, a sleeping car, and the coach of Napoleon III, upholstered in green satin and ornamented with the "N" capped by a crown. Just beside the track there was a huge shell hole.

"That was a delayed-action shell," de Bourbon-Busset explained to von Winterfeldt. "It exploded three weeks after the Germans left. I hope there are none under our train. I don't wish to blow you up, or to be blown up with you."

"The High Command," replied von Winterfeldt, "has never ordered destructions of this sort, which are very regrettable and must be ascribed to isolated persons."

French brandy was served to Erzberger and his colleagues, and orders were given to keep the windows shut. No one would tell them where they were going.[34]

At seven o'clock on the morning of November 8 the train arrived in a forest and ran onto the right-hand branch of a siding. About 100 meters away Erzberger saw another similar train. There was no station, no platform or shelter. The two tracks had been constructed for use by heavy railway artillery. Here the big guns could fire from the shield of the trees without being observed. Erzberger asked several times where he was; but the attendants told him they were from the north of France and did not know the region.

At eight o'clock Erzberger was informed that Marshal Foch would receive him at nine. When the hour approached, he and his companions walked in single file along the narrow duckboard that led to Foch's train. The civilians wore the clothes they had traveled in; the officers were dressed in field service uniform. They were ushered into a car where they found a large table, with four seats placed on each side. The car was really a dining car made over into a conference room. The Germans stood at one side of the table, behind the chairs tagged with their names. Weygand went to Foch's private car to tell him they were ready.

In a few minutes Marshal Foch entered accompanied by Admiral Wemyss, General Weygand, and two other British naval officers. He gave the Germans a military salute and bow. Erzberger describes him as "a little man with hard, energetic features

34. Erzberger, *Erlebnisse,* pp. 329–330; Weygand, *Le 11 Novembre,* pp. 35–36.

and who displayed, at first glance, the habit of commanding." Erzberger was surprised to note that no American, Italian, or Belgian was present; and he concluded that only the Allied High Command was going to take part in the negotiations.[35]

The meeting of the two delegations was reported to Clemenceau by General Mordacq, who, in Paris, kept in constant touch with the negotiations over a wire linking Foch's train with the Ministry of War.

After receiving the German credentials, Foch retired with his staff to an adjoining compartment to examine them. They read as follows:

(1) FULL POWER.

The undersigned, Chancellor of the German Empire, Max, Prince of Baden, hereby gives full power:

To Imperial Secretary of State Mathias Erzberger (as president),

To Imperial Envoy Extraordinary and Minister Plenipotentiary Count Alfred Oberndorff, and

To Major General Detlef von Winterfeldt of the Prussian Army, to conduct in the name of the German Government with the plenipotentiaries of the Powers allied against Germany, negotiations for an armistice and to conclude an agreement to that effect, subject to acceptance by the German Government.

Signed: MAX, Prince of Baden.

Berlin, November 6, 1918.

(2) FULL POWER.

The undersigned, Chancellor of the German Empire, Max, Prince of Baden, hereby appoints as additional plenipotentiary for the armistice negotiations with the Powers allied against Germany,

Captain Vanselow, Imperial Navy.

General Erich von Gündell, Royal Infantry, has been relieved of his post as plenipotentiary; consequently his name has been stricken from the power enclosed herewith.

Signed: MAX, Prince of Baden.

Berlin, November 6, 1918.

After Foch had examined these papers, he returned with his

35. Erzberger, *Erlebnisse*, pp. 330–331; Weygand, *Le 11 Novembre*, pp. 47–49, 53–58; Foch, *Mémoires*, II, 290–291. The most dramatic account of the signing of the armistice is found in Theodor Plivier, "Im Wald von Compiègne," *Neue Deutsche Blätter*, I (November, December, 1933), 145–156, 219–229.

staff to the table and asked Erzberger to announce the names of his delegates. They were:

Secretary of State Erzberger,
Major General von Winterfeldt,
Minister Plenipotentiary Count Oberndorff,
Naval Captain Vanselow,
Staff Captain Geyer,
Cavalry Captain von Helldorf.

Foch then announced the names of the members of the Allied delegation as follows:

Admiral Wemyss,
General Weygand,
Admiral Hope,
Naval Captain Mariott,

and as interpreters:

Commander Bagot,
Interpreter Officer Laperche.

The delegates then took their places opposite each other at the table in this order, with the interpreters at one end:

Weygand	Foch	Wemyss	Hope
Vanselow	Winterfeldt	Erzberger	Oberndorff

Marshal Foch, speaking French, opened the proceedings. "What brings these gentlemen here?" he asked. "What do you wish of me?"

Erzberger replied that he awaited proposals relative to the conclusion of an armistice on land, on sea and in the air, and on all fronts.

"I have no proposals to make," said Foch.

Erzberger then said that his delegation had come in answer to Wilson's last note, which he had Oberndorff read in the English text, and he added that he requested the communication of these proposals. Foch then ordered Weygand to read the armistice conditions in French, clause by clause, so that the interpreters could translate them.[36]

36. Erzberger, *Erlebnisse,* p. 331; Weygand, *Le 11 Novembre,* pp. 59–60. Foch's account (*Mémoires,* II, 291–294) is slightly different and emphasizes the fact that he forced the Germans to ask for an armistice in so many words:

"Marshal Foch asked the German delegates the purpose of their visit.

According to Weygand, there was complete silence, the silence of death, except for the voice that read the clauses. Heads were erect, faces impassive. Because he did not understand French, Erzberger had an opportunity to observe the demeanor of his adversaries. Wemyss, he writes, affected great indifference but could not conceal his inner emotion by toying with his monocle and tortoise-shell spectacles. Foch sat at the table as imperturbably calm as a statue. Occasionally he gave an energetic tug at his moustache. During the reading neither side spoke. Weygand says that tears poured down the cheeks of Captain Vanselow at the reading of the clauses providing for the occupation of the Rhineland.[37]

At the end of the reading Erzberger asked for an immediate suspension of hostilities and cited, in support of his plea, the disorganization of the German Army and the spread of revolution in Germany. The fighting ended, he said, the German Armies could prevent the invasion of Europe by Bolshevism. Foch replied that the fighting would not cease until after the armistice had been signed.[38]

Herr Erzberger replied that the German delegation had come to receive the proposals of the Allied Powers looking to an armistice on land, on sea, and in the air, on all fronts, and in the colonies.

Marshal Foch replied that he had no proposal to make.

Count Oberndorff asked the Marshal how he wished them to express themselves. He did not stand on form; he was ready to say that the German delegation asks for the conditions of an armistice.

Marshal Foch replied that he had no conditions to offer.

Herr Erzberger read the text of President Wilson's latest note stating that Marshal Foch is authorized to make known the armistice conditions.

Marshal Foch replied that he is authorized to make these conditions known if the German delegates ask for an armistice.

'Do you ask for an armistice? If you do, I can acquaint you with the conditions under which it can be obtained.'

Herr Erzberger and Count Oberndorff declared that they asked for an armistice."

General Mordacq gives the following account, written he says by a witness of the scene a few days after the signing of the armistice (*La Vérité sur l'Armistice,* pp. 50–51):

"Marshal Foch asks the Germans the object of their overture.

ERZBERGER: The delegation has come to receive the proposals of the Allied Powers with a view to reaching an armistice.

THE MARSHAL: I haven't any proposal to make, but if the German delegates ask for an armistice, I can make known the conditions under which it can be obtained.

ERZBERGER AND OBERNDORFF: The German Government asks for an armistice."

37. Erzberger, *Erlebnisse,* p. 331; Weygand, *Le 11 Novembre,* pp. 60–61.

38. Foch, *Mémoires,* II, 294–295; Erzberger, *Erlebnisse,* pp. 331–332.

Winterfeldt, who apparently thought that Erzberger had not made his plea strong enough, read a prepared statement calling attention to the large numbers of people who would be killed while armistice terms were being studied. Foch was firm. "The Governments have stated their conditions," he said. "Hostilities cannot cease before the armistice is signed." [39]

Erzberger then sought permission to send a radio message to the German Chancellor and to General Headquarters; he also requested that another meeting of the armistice delegations be held in the afternoon. Foch would not allow the armistice conditions to be transmitted to Germany except in code or by special courier. Erzberger pointed out that the length of the text made it impossible to use code. And since it would take a courier at least twelve hours to reach Army Headquarters, he asked that Germany be given four days in which to reply rather than the stipulated three days. This extension Foch refused, explaining that he had no authority to modify what the Allied Governments had fixed upon.[40] It was made clear that the German reply would have to come before eleven o'clock Monday morning, November 11.[41]

While this conference was taking place, the Allied armistice delegation was in continuous communication with Paris. At 9.30 A.M. General Mordacq telephoned Weygand that as a result of a demand of the Italian Government Foch was to insist on the withdrawal of Bavarian troops from the Tyrol. Shortly after that Weygand informed Mordacq that the Germans, instead of confining themselves to a discussion of the armistice terms, were trying to sound out Foch on the peace conditions to be imposed on them. Speaking for Clemenceau, Mordacq instructed Foch soon after ten o'clock that he was not to discuss peace conditions under any pretext. If the Germans returned to the subject, the Marshal was to avoid it by making them understand that he, as a soldier, could concern himself only with the armistice.[42] The German insistence on a suspension of hostilities before signing the armistice was relayed to Paris. After consultation General Mordacq replied within twenty minutes on behalf of Clemenceau that, once and for all, the Germans were to be informed that no suspension of hostilities would be granted until after the signing of

39. Foch, *Mémoires,* II, 295–296; Weygand, *Le 11 Novembre,* pp. 61–62.

40. Erzberger, *Erlebnisse,* p. 331–332; Foch, *Mémoires,* II, 296–297

41. According to Weygand, *Le 11 Novembre,* p. 62; Erzberger, *Erlebnisse,* p. 332.

42. Mordacq, *La Vérité sur l'Armistice,* pp. 19–20.

the armistice.[43] Foch made it perfectly plain that "negotiations concerning conditions were to be permitted under no circumstances; Germany could accept them or reject them—there was no third choice." [44]

Erzberger was given permission to send radio messages. Captain von Helldorf was instructed to take the armistice conditions back to Germany and to say that it was unlikely that Germany would be permitted to make counterproposals on essential matters; that, nonetheless, efforts would be made in personal talks to temper the conditions with a view toward maintaining internal order and averting famine; that the German delegates would try to get extensions of time [for evacuating territories?] and a reduction in the amounts of material to be surrendered; that they would endeavor to get what concessions were possible; and that, in accepting the armistice, they would declare it impossible to fulfill all the conditions that were being imposed.[45]

At one o'clock Captain von Helldorf, having been assured that his passage through the lines would be arranged by Foch's staff, set out with the armistice text. French officers calculated that he should reach the German lines in about five hours, an estimate that caused Erzberger incorrectly to deduce that the German delegation had been led by a roundabout route through northern France the night before. Helldorf reached the French front in good time. There he was held up, because no arrangements had been made for passing through the lines. The German soldiers "fired like the very devil" and for five hours kept their own courier from entering their lines despite his signals, his white flags, and his reckless exposure to danger.[46]

Meanwhile in Paris, where "great nervousness" prevailed as to whether Germany would accept or reject the proffered armistice terms, the authorities had been informed at noon that all was proceeding favorably and that a courier would soon arrive with an important message from Marshal Foch. The courier arrived at 3 P.M. Mordacq opened the envelope he carried and took the message upstairs to Clemenceau in his office on the second floor of the War Ministry. Here he found the Premier in conference with Pichon, the Minister of Foreign Affairs, and René Renoult, President of the Army Committee in the Chamber of Deputies.

43. *Ibid.*, p. 20.
44. Erzberger, *Erlebnisse*, p. 332.
45. *Idem.*
46. *Ibid.*, p. 332; Foch, *Mémoires*, II, 298.

"Good news, Mr. President!" cried Mordacq as he handed Clemenceau the message, which stated that the German delegates had accepted the terms of the armistice in principle.

"M. Clemenceau," writes Mordacq, "had hardly finished reading the report when I saw him staring at me long and fixedly. His eyes moistened, and, taking his head in his hands, he began to weep silently. Never, either before or during the war, had I seen him prey to such emotion. After a moment he pulled himself together and cried: 'It's absurd, I am no longer master of my nerves; it was stronger than I, but, all of a sudden, I saw 1870 again, the defeat, the shame, the loss of Alsace-Lorraine, and now all that is wiped out. Is it a dream?' " [47]

The wireless messages that came from Erzberger gave the Army Command its first report of the negotiations with Foch and repeated what Helldorf had been instructed to say. In case the Army Command decided not to reject the terms offered, Erzberger asked for "express authorization to sign at once with whatever ameliorations could be won in the practical execution of the terms." He also asked for permission to add to the protocol of the negotiations a declaration of the following nature: "The German Government will, of course, with all its powers arrange for the execution of the obligations it has undertaken. The undersigned, however, take it to be their conscientious duty in the interest of honorable relations between Germany and her opponents to point out even at this early time that the execution of these conditions will plunge the German people into famine and anarchy, and that, therefore, a situation may arise, without any fault of either the German Government or the German people, which may make impossible the further observation of all obligations." Erzberger made it clear that it was the task of the Army Command to decide what answer should be made to the armistice conditions and also whether the proposed declaration should be included even at the risk of rupturing the negotiations. Because of the little time available, he said that the final wording of the agreement would have to be left to the armistice delegation.[48]

A second telegram from Erzberger notified the Army Command that the armistice conditions being brought by courier to

47. Mordacq, *La Vérité sur l'Armistice,* pp. 23–25.

48. Document 103, *Amtliche Urkunden.* This document, which was telegraphed from Spa to the Foreign Office on November 8, did not arrive at its destination until midafternoon on November 10. One wonders whether the revolution was the cause of the delay.

Spa would have to be accepted or rejected by Monday noon and that the request for a cessation of fighting had been rejected.[49]

Immediately after Helldorf's departure the German delegates met together to formulate a program for the personal discussions scheduled to take place in the afternoon. Oberndorff and von Winterfeldt met with Weygand, and Vanselow talked with Admiral Hope. Oberndorff asked if the terms were made severe in order to force the Germans into refusing them. The reply he got was that the Allies were merely stating the terms and that they had no ulterior motives. He then asked if the Allies did not wish to have the armistice fail so that they could proceed at once with peace negotiations. He was informed that Foch had come to negotiate an armistice, and nothing else.

The Germans then presented their arguments for a mitigation of the severity of the terms. They were, briefly, as follows:

The presence of the German envoys was proof of their sincerity in desiring an armistice. The exhausted condition of the German Army with the consequent lack of discipline, coupled with traffic congestion of all sorts behind the front, rendered any rapid evacuation of territory impossible. Moreover, once the armistice was signed, the German Army would be incapable of resuming hostilities, and there was, therefore, no need for making the terms so severe.

The military terms were accepted with the exception of the number of machine guns (30,000) to be surrendered. This would almost deprive Germany of a weapon with which to preserve internal order, and which was essential under existing conditions at home. The number was later reduced to 25,000.

The Germans asked for enough time to make an orderly retreat, and enough of an organized army with which to suppress revolution and enforce order within their own boundaries. This would be an advantage to the Allies as well as to Germany.

The stipulations covering the blockade and the delivery of rolling stock were considered inhumane because they would paralyze the work of feeding the population and would inflict disease and suffering on women and children.

49. Document 104, *ibid.* There was some bewilderment at Spa over the time limits for accepting or rejecting the Allied conditions. It seems that the 72-hour limit appeared as a 12-hour limit—perhaps careless handwriting on the telegram explains the discrepancy—although the document specified Monday noon as the time by which a final answer was expected. This message was telegraphed to the Foreign Office from Spa on the evening of November 8 and reached Berlin twenty-six hours later.

These protests and demands were answered by the Allies with the statement that the disorganized condition of the German Army was the result of four months of Allied victories, and that it was the duty of the Allied High Command to safeguard, by the terms of the armistice, the advantages won on the field. Weygand also emphasized the point that the conversations just held were merely exchanges of opinions which were not binding on either side, and that all requests and observations must be put into writing.[50]

Commenting on these conversations, Erzberger says that the Allied representatives seemed unwilling to believe what the German delegates said; one of them went so far as to say frankly that the Germans were attempting to trap the Allies for the purpose of gaining time in which to reorganize their troops for a new attack. The Germans placed particular emphasis on the insufficient time allowed for the evacuation. They also spoke most earnestly to the British officers about the blockade, but Admiral Hope replied that he was not prepared to discuss the subject. The Germans pointed out that the Allies were making the same mistake that the former German Government had made in the spring of 1918 with regard to Russia; at that time Germany considered herself in a position to behave as a conqueror toward the Bolshevists, with the result that she herself was now the conquered one. To this a British officer coldly replied that it is "he who has the wind in his sails who wins." [51]

That evening the questions discussed in these conversations were drawn up by the Germans in the form of counterproposals which were chiefly concerned with such matters as more time to evacuate territory, the elimination of clauses about the bridgeheads and the neutral zone, the reduction in the amount of rolling stock demanded, the honorable retirement of German troops from East Africa, and the lifting of the blockade.[52]

50. Foch, *Mémoires,* II, 298–301; Weygand, *Le 11 Novembre,* pp. 63–65.
51. Erzberger, *Erlebnisse,* p. 333.
52. *Ibid.,* p. 333; Foch, *Mémoires,* II, 301.

XIV

The Kaiser Abdicates

NOVEMBER 8, the day on which Erzberger and Foch began their negotiations, was to be a nightmare for Germany. The armies were in full retreat from the Dutch frontier to the Côtes de Meuse. And on the home front the Government was in full retreat before the revolution.

Prince Max understood his precarious position. "On the morning of November 8," he writes, "the following reports of the revolution lay before us: Brunswick had gone Red at seven in the evening; during the night Munich had gone Red, and its War Ministry had been occupied by the Workers' and Soldiers' Council. A republic had been proclaimed and the abdication of the King was demanded by twelve noon. In Stuttgart the Workers' and Soldiers' Council had seized control of the Government. During the night a trainload of sailors had been derailed at Paulinenaue and the sailors had started for Berlin on foot." [1]

The Chancellor was especially distressed over the revolution in Bavaria; he saw it as a new center of revolt, independent of that at Kiel. King Ludwig was said to have abdicated and Kurt Eisner to be head of the new republic. Other cities were infected: Bremen, Coblenz, Mainz, Magdeburg, Halle, Leipzig, Frankfurt a.M., and Cologne. The revolutionaries were now in control of important rail centers and supply depots; the authorities felt great concern about food transport and supply for the Army and the civilian population.

The Government in Berlin took extensive precautions. Newspapers were instructed to restrict their reports on radical activities in other parts of the country. All Army officers in the city were ordered to report at noon, ready for emergency action.[2] The headquarters of the Independent Socialists were closed. Civilians were warned that they would be shot if they appeared on the streets between 6 P.M. and 7 A.M.[3]

It was impossible, however, to keep the rebellious spirit in

1. Max, *Erinnerungen,* p. 615.
2. According to *Vossische Zeitung,* November 8, 1918, No. 572.
3. *Vorwärts,* November 8, 1918, No. 308.

check. The ultimatum of the Socialists was being discussed openly in the newspapers. Everyone was wondering whether the Kaiser would abdicate or not. It was learned that the Chancellor had offered his resignation. At a meeting of the Inter-Party Committee the Centrists and the Progressives came out for immediate abdication.[4] The *Frankfurter Zeitung* called for the abdication of both the Kaiser and the Crown Prince.

The fear that the Social Democrats would withdraw from the Government and join the revolutionary movement in an effort to keep the extreme radicals from winning control of the masses, combined with the hope that they would oppose Bolshevism with all their might if the Kaiser should withdraw, led Chancellor Max to draft a second message for transmission by telephone to the Kaiser, pointing out that it was necessary to keep the Social Democrats in the Government and to keep the masses from going over to the extremist side. He informed the Kaiser that these goals could be achieved without accepting the ultimatum of the Socialists, who had yielded to Prince Max's threat to resign and promised to support the Government until the armistice had been concluded. To outmaneuver the Social Democrats, the Chancellor now asked the Kaiser to declare himself ready to abdicate as soon as armistice negotiations permitted the election of a constitutional convention, which would fix the form of Germany's future government as well as settle the legal problems involved in abdication. Until that time the Emperor should appoint a deputy. The Chancellor told the Kaiser there were many advantages in these proposals: the monarchical principle would score on the republican because the initiative for the elections would come from the Crown; the Crown would not be yielding to the Social Democrats but the latter would yield to the Crown; abdication by the Kaiser and renunciation by the Crown Prince and the appointment of a regency would be postponed; public opinion would be diverted from civil war to legal methods of settling these important matters. To give power to his recommendations, the Chancellor added a paragraph on revolutionary activities in Stuttgart and Munich.[5]

The Cabinet met at ten o'clock with von Payer in the chair. General Scheüch gave a favorable report on the military situation in Berlin: railway traffic had been resumed except for service to

4. Adolf Stutzenberger, *Die Abdankung Kaiser Wilhelms II,* pp. 178–179, 183–184.

5. Max, *Erinnerungen,* pp. 615–616.

Hanover and Hamburg; at the Lehrter station troops with machine guns were ready for any armed mutineers who might come to the city; some sailors who had arrived had been arrested and returned to their ships. During this Cabinet session Scheidemann appeared quite optimistic. Although his ultimatum to Prince Max had been temporarily withdrawn, its extensive publication throughout the city had achieved its prime purpose of winning support for the Majority Socialists among the working classes to keep them from going over to the Independents. "My party will see to it," he assured his colleagues, "that Germany is saved from Bolshevism." [6]

According to the Chancellor, hopes were high in the Imperial Chancellery on the morning of November 8, particularly because of the belief that the Social Democrats were becoming stronger and would be able to control the populace when the Kaiser abdicated. And his abdication was expected within a few hours. On this assumption Payer sought to persuade Max to remain as Chancellor, threatening otherwise to resign his own post. Others joined him in pointing out to Prince Max that his work would not be done until peace had been concluded.

The Kaiser, however, was not considering giving up the imperial crown. At Spa von Hintze, Foreign Office Representative, who had received Prince Max's message with its suggestion of abdication and of a constitutional convention to be elected by the people, had no wish to carry such proposals to the Kaiser. He thought that some responsible Cabinet minister should talk directly with the Emperor about so grave a matter. It was his belief and that of von Grünau, who attended the Kaiser as Representative of the Foreign Office, that the Emperor would reply to such suggestions with the question: "Is the Army willing and ready to stand by me and to suppress the revolutionary movement in Germany?" He had that very morning expressed the intention of restoring order at home at the head of the Army; he had even commanded General Groener to prepare the démarche.[7] Von Hintze and von Grünau asked Hindenburg and Groener whether the Army would support a move to oppose the revolution, but the Generals refused to take a position on the question. Only after this feeler did Hintze and Grünau deliver Prince

6. *Ibid.*, pp. 617–618.

7. According to an account of events in the memorandum of July 27, 1919, by Hindenburg, von Plessen, von Hintze, von Marschall, and Count Schulenburg, printed as document 523 in Lutz, *Fall of the German Empire,* II, 538.

Max's message to the Kaiser, who listened quietly and said, "Tell the Imperial Chancellor that the Kaiser is not thinking of abdicating." [8]

At noon telegrams from Spa informed Prince Max that the Kaiser would neither abandon his throne nor accept the proffered resignation of his Chancellor. Writing his memoirs as late as 1927, Prince Max was convinced that everything had been done to acquaint the Kaiser with the truth; and he was equally convinced that revolution would not have occurred in Germany if the Kaiser had done as he had requested.[9]

The Social Democrats met at noon in the Reichstag to hear from Scheidemann about his negotiations with the Chancellor regarding the Kaiser's abdication. They approved what their leader had done by passing the following resolution:

> Since the Imperial Chancellor has declared that he has informed the Kaiser of the ultimatum presented yesterday by the party, it [the Social Democratic party] does not ask for the resignation of the Chancellor because it seeks to avoid endangering the armistice negotiations and will not ask its members to withdraw from the Government until the armistice is concluded.[10]

The party did not know, of course, that the Chancellor was actually engaged in circumventing its purposes by suggesting to the Kaiser ways of strengthening the monarchy by making it the agent for Germany's democratization.

The Social Democrats now issued an appeal to the workers, urging them to be patient a few hours longer. It was explained that the time limit of the ultimatum had originally been fixed for that day in the belief that the armistice would be concluded by then. "The conclusion of the armistice," the appeal read, "would be endangered by our withdrawal from the Government." [11]

At a meeting that evening in party headquarters the Socialists heard how much factory workers had been aroused by recent events. It was known that the Independent Socialists had asked them to march out of the factories at nine o'clock the next morning in a general strike. If they did, there was no telling what the consequences would be—or how many workers would be killed in

8. Stutzenberger, *Die Abdankung Kaiser Wilhelms II,* pp. 176–177.
9. Max, *Erinnerungen,* pp. 618–619.
10. Scheidemann, *Memoiren,* II, 290–291.
11. Max, *Erinnerungen,* p. 621.

street fighting. Scheidemann saw that strong measures were needed to prevent bloodshed, and he got the representatives of the workers to promise to do all they could to keep the men in the factories, at least until nine Saturday morning. By that time he hoped the armistice would be signed and the Kaiser would have abdicated.[12]

During the afternoon of the 8th the fear that the Majority Socialists might go over to the opposition produced a feeling of terror in the Chancellery, and a number of proposals were considered to avert such a catastrophe. Events were pressing hard on the Chancellor. In the afternoon von Linsingen, who had charge of protecting Berlin against the rebels, had got into difficulties with the Minister of War and resigned. Army officers who had answered appeals to help defend the city found everything so disorganized that they returned home. It was apparent that few troops would be available in case rebels marched into the city. Reports kept coming in of other cities succumbing to the Red revolution. One of the leaders of the Independent Socialists in Berlin was arrested while occupied, according to a report, with preparations for revolution in the capital. Despite these developments the Minister of War, Scheüch, retained his confidence that the situation in Berlin could be kept in hand.[13]

Everything depended upon the Kaiser's decision; but nothing had been reported from Army Headquarters to indicate that the Emperor had changed his mind since noon. At 8 P.M. the Chancellor decided to talk to the Kaiser himself over the telephone, as von Hintze had suggested in the morning. Prince Max summoned his aide, von Prittwitz, and instructed him to write down what was said. Addressing the Emperor in the second person singular, Prince Max spoke for about twenty minutes as follows:

The advice I have sent your Majesty by Herr von Hintze I must repeat to you as a relative. Your abdication has become necessary to save Germany from civil war and to fulfill your mission as the peace-making Emperor to the end. The blood that is shed would be laid upon your head. The great majority of the people believe you to be responsible for the present situation. The belief is false, but there it is. If civil war and worse can now be prevented through your abdication, your name will be blessed by future generations. The Inter-Party Committee has spoken, but it has not informed me of

12. Scheidemann, *Memoiren,* II, 295–296.
13. Max, *Erinnerungen,* pp. 619–623.

the decision it took today. If nothing is done, the demand will now be made in the Reichstag and will go through. Since the time I took over the business of Government, I have always maintained my independence in the Cabinet. Today, now that the Social Democrats' ultimatum has been presented, an ultimatum which I had been able to avoid till now, my protecting hand can no longer shield the occupant of the throne. The demand contained in the ultimatum is now being made by very many others besides the Social Democrats. Disorders have already occurred. It might be possible perhaps to put them down by force in the beginning, but once blood has flowed the cry for vengeance will be heard everywhere. The troops are not to be depended on. [Here follows a list of towns which have gone Red.] Nowhere have the military been of any value. We are heading straight for civil war. I have struggled against that thought, but the situation is today untenable; the abdication would be received with universal gratitude and hailed as a liberating and healing act.

There are two possibilities: 1. Abdication, appointment of a deputy, and convocation of a national assembly. 2. Abdication, renunciation by the Crown Prince, and a regency for your grandson.

The latter is demanded by the Inter-Party Committee. The former course is in my opinion the better and gives the monarchy the best possible chance. But whatever step is decided on, it must be taken with the greatest possible speed. This sacrifice, if made after blood has once flowed, will have lost all its power for good. Up to now I have confined myself to merely giving information, but since yesterday, in view of the extreme gravity of the situation, I have had to speak frankly. Should the Kaiser take this step, with the help of the Social Democrats the situation can be saved. Otherwise republic and revolution are imminent. If the troops could be depended on, things would be different.

The abdication proposal does not originate either exclusively or primarily with the Social Democrats; they have taken it up only in order not to lose their leadership.

This is the last possible moment. It is even possible that the abdication might produce a decisive turn in the course of the peace negotiations and take the wind out of the sails of Entente jingoes.

Unless the abdication takes place today I can no longer coöperate; nor can the German Princes shield the Kaiser any more.

Such is the terrible situation in which I am bound to speak out and not gloss over things. I have heard that some persons have been denouncing me for intrigues against you. That is a lie, as any one of my colleagues can show you. But for my efforts to shield you the question would already have become acute a week ago.

I speak to you today as your relative and as a German Prince. This voluntary sacrifice is necessary to keep your good name in history.[14]

This painful effort was without success. "His Majesty," writes Prince Max, "announced his fixed determination not to yield. It was his desire to restore order in the country at the head of the Army; the necessary instructions had already been issued. Angrily and vehemently he rejected my proposals. I begged the Kaiser to dismiss me immediately and to name a new Chancellor since I no longer possessed his confidence. The Kaiser refused with the words: 'You sent out the armistice offer, you will also have to accept the conditions.' "[15]

Prince Max answered that he was willing to remain in office until the armistice was signed.

Immediately after this telephone conversation Prince Max sent the Kaiser a telegram reporting that the German Princes ruling in Bavaria, Brunswick, and Mecklenburg-Schwerin had renounced their thrones or had accepted the demands of Workers' and Soldiers' Councils; that the Cabinet, whose majority had opposed abdication the day before, was now convinced that it was the only way to avert a bloody civil war; that the Vice-Chancellor and the entire War Cabinet would go if the Chancellor should resign; and that, because of the difficulty of getting a working majority in the Reichstag, the German nation would be "without a Chancellor, without a Government, without a parliamentary majority" and thus incapable of negotiating an armistice.[16]

Undersecretary of State Wahnschaffe called from Berlin late that evening and asked Grünau to transmit this telegram to the Emperor, but he refused to do so since the Kaiser had already gone to bed. Furthermore, he felt that a message of such importance was not to be delivered to the Kaiser by telephone or by any third person; only responsible members of the Government in person should carry out a mission of that nature. The Chancellor yielded to the argument and got in touch with Solf, who prepared to go to Spa that night, late as it was. It was doubtful, however,

14. *Ibid.*, pp. 623–624.
15. *Ibid.*, pp. 624–625.
16. *Ibid.*, p. 625; Niemann, *Revolution von Oben*, p. 278.

whether such a mission could accomplish its purpose soon enough. Scheidemann was encouraging when asked about it; but Ebert said, "The decision of the Kaiser would produce an effect only if made by nine o'clock tomorrow morning." The Social Democrats had already decided, according to Ebert, that if the morning papers carried news of the Kaiser's abdication, the workers would remain in the factories; otherwise, they would walk out and participate in demonstrations throughout the city.

Because time was running short, the plan to send Solf to Spa was abandoned. Instead, Ebert's statement was forwarded that night, and also the following telegram from Solf:

> Most humbly do I inform Your Majesty that the participation of the Majority Socialists is the indispensable condition for carrying on the work of peace. If their ultimatum is disregarded, they will retire from the Government immediately. Then only a military dictatorship is possible. In any case, so far as the Entente is concerned, the Government would be no longer qualified to negotiate. In such circumstances hostilities would be continued by the Entente.
>
> Getting the Socialists to withdraw their resolution [that is, their ultimatum] was futile, simply impossible. The Majority Socialists cannot and will not let the Independents and the Spartacus group get control of the masses.
>
> Whether civil war is to be avoided depends exclusively on Your Majesty's immediate decision. In all humility, therefore, I beg Your Majesty to make the greatest sacrifice for the Empire and thus to bring about the peace which alone can save it.[17]

Pressure was put on the Chancellor late that evening for a *coup* that would compel the Kaiser to abdicate and at the same time would keep workers and soldiers in check. All he had to do, he was told, would be to issue a notice to the press: "I am convinced of the necessity of abdication. I have demanded it and will force it through. The people must be patient until the armistice is concluded." The Chancellor replied that he would make no move against the Kaiser.[18]

Explaining to himself why the Kaiser remained adamant the night of November 8, Prince Max says that the Kaiser still believed strongly that the troops at the front could be relied upon,

17. Max, *Erinnerungen,* pp. 627–628. Cf. Stutzenberger, *Die Abdankung Kaiser Wilhelms II,* pp. 187–188.
18. Max, *Erinnerungen,* p. 629.

even to fight the people at home in his behalf. At the time the Chancellor had no reason for believing that the Army Command did not share this optimism, particularly after von Payer had failed to gain Groener's support that evening in an effort to exert pressure on the Emperor. Almost a year later he was to learn that just one hour after his telephone conversation with the Emperor Hindenburg, Groener, and General von Plessen had conferred and had reached the conclusion that there was no prospect of success for the Kaiser's plan to lead his Armies against the revolution at home. They knew that Workers' and Soldiers' Councils had taken over in important cities, that supply depots and rail centers were under their control, that home garrisons had gone over to the revolution, that the Army in the field showed signs of disintegration. Of particular significance to the three generals was the fact that "the division regarded as particularly dependable and selected for the task of covering the rear of General Headquarters against the revolutionaries, who had got as far as Aix-la-Chapelle from Cologne, refused to obey their officers and, contrary to the commands of the latter, had started to march home." These conditions convinced General Groener that the plan for an offensive against the revolution on the home front was hopeless. With the enemy attacking hard in the west, it would be impossible to get enough reliable troops for such large-scale operations. With a heavy heart von Hindenburg accepted Groener's conclusions. General von Plessen alone still argued that it was unthinkable that the Kaiser and the Army should yield to a handful of rebels. Why the Army Command failed that night to inform the Kaiser of the hopelessness of his intent to suppress the revolution was a question to which the Chancellor never found the answer.[19]

November 9 dawned, a day of destiny. Before it closed, the Kaiser was to abdicate, Prince Max to resign, and the German republic to be proclaimed.

The Chancellor learned in the morning that the revolution had made gains during the night. But Berlin still seemed to be firmly under Government control. He was assured that "the three dependable Jäger battalions were in the city, one at the Palace, one in the Alexander barracks, and one at the bridges in the center of the city." During the night the Independent Socialists had issued the call for a general strike, finding justification for the

19. *Ibid.*, pp. 626–627 and note.

step in the arrest of one of their number the day before. The Chancellor felt convinced that the Social Democrats could defeat this appeal to the workers and could keep them at work provided the Kaiser should announce his abdication.[20]

Scheidemann had passed a sleepless night. He was up at six; before seven he telephoned to the Chancellery.

"Has the Kaiser abdicated?" he asked.

"Not yet, but we are expecting any moment the news of his abdication."

"I will wait only one hour longer," answered Scheidemann; "if he is not out by that time, then I go."

Toward nine o'clock he called the Chancellery again.

"Not yet," was the answer; "perhaps at noon."

"I don't need that much time to make up my mind," burst out Scheidemann. "Please inform the Chancellor that I am resigning. Within a quarter of an hour you will have my resignation in writing. . . . I shouldn't be in such a hurry? I beg your pardon; above all, one should never put off anything until it is too late." Shortly after nine his resignation was before the Cabinet.[21]

At 9.15 von Hintze telephoned the Chancellery from Spa that the Supreme Army Command had decided to tell the Kaiser immediately that the Army would not and could not support him in the effort to suppress the revolution. People in the Chancellery believed that this meant the Kaiser must abdicate, and preparations were made accordingly. In this not wholly justified conviction, Undersecretary Wahnschaffe telephoned to Ebert to demand that he hold up the street demonstrations.

"Too late!" answered Ebert; "the die is cast. One factory has already gone into the streets." [22]

About ten o'clock it was reported to the Chancellery that many thousands of unarmed workers were moving toward the center of the city. Women and children led the procession, and people carried placards reading, "Brothers, don't shoot!" Some efforts had already been made to persuade troops to go over to the cause of the Social Democrats.[23] Reports of other demonstrations in the city poured in. A telephone call to the Chief of Police brought the information that the revolutionaries had made an attack on

20. *Ibid.,* p. 630.
21. Scheidemann, *Memoiren,* II, 296–297; also Scheidemann, *Der Zusammenbruch,* p. 208.
22. Max, *Erinnerungen,* pp. 630–631.
23. Maurice Baumont, *The Fall of the Kaiser* (New York, 1931), p. 209.

one of the soldiers' barracks and that blood had already been spilled. Directly after that news came the report that destroyed the last basis of confidence: "The Naumbürger Jäger have gone over to the insurgents!" This information was sent to Spa together with the many reports coming in telling of troops in mutiny. The Chancellor accompanied these reports with reiterated demands that the Kaiser abdicate—it was no longer a question of hours, it was a question of minutes. These telephone calls went on until eleven o'clock, and the Chancellor was put off with such words as "The decision is about to be made" or "Events are taking their course."

At eleven o'clock the telephone calls from Spa became more definite. They stated that "the matter is now actually decided; people are engaged in putting it into words," that "the Kaiser has made up his mind in favor of abdication. In half an hour we should have the wording of it." Prince Max found these reports convincing and got in touch with Simons to express approval of his suggestion of the previous day that "in this situation Ebert is the only possible Chancellor." It was thought too risky to let the rebels name either Ebert or Liebknecht; better that the Kaiser should abdicate and name Ebert Chancellor. Then a constitutional convention should be called, to turn revolutionary energies into the normal channels of a regular election.

If reports from Spa were becoming clearer, so also were reports of revolutionary activities in Berlin. At many places the soldiers were in mutiny and refused to fire on the people. Some troop formations were said to be in negotiation with the Social Democrats, eager to place themselves at the disposal of the people. Soldiers were demonstrating on the streets with the workers. The Social Democratic leader, David, told Prince Max that his party colleagues were trying to calm the revolutionaries and warned that the use of force would simply make a bad situation worse, an opinion with which the Chancellor agreed.

Prince Max waited impatiently for news of the abdication of the Kaiser to come from Spa; but the minutes went by without bringing it. The danger was that the masses in the streets might at any moment simply proclaim the Kaiser dethroned. If he and his house were to derive any benefit from the abdication, it must be done immediately.

"We tried repeatedly," writes the Chancellor, "to reach the Kaiser. The receiver on one telephone at Villa Fraineuse [where the Kaiser was staying] had been removed, the other was engaged. I found myself confronted with the choice of either waiting and doing nothing, or acting on my own responsibility. I knew well that I had not been formally authorized to publish anything without the Kaiser's express consent. But I thought it my duty to make known, while it offered the hope of some advantage, the decision I was told the Kaiser had taken. Except for Simons I talked with nobody about my purpose. He urgently advised me to disregard any hesitation on the score of legal propriety at a time when it was still perhaps possible to preserve the monarchy." [24]

With these motives in mind the Chancellor gave the Wolff Telegraph Agency the following declaration, which became known to the people on the streets at noon:

The Kaiser and King has resolved to *renounce the throne*. The Imperial Chancellor will remain at his post until decisions have been made on questions connected with the Kaiser's abdication, the Crown Prince's renunciation of the Imperial and Prussian thrones, and the creation of a regency. He intends to propose to the regent that Reichstag representative Ebert be named Chancellor and that a bill be enacted for the immediate calling of general elections for a German constitutional national assembly, upon which would rest the responsibility for the final formation of a government for the German people, including those groups of people that might wish to be included within the boundaries of the German Empire.[25]

No sooner had this declaration reached the public than a delegation of Social Democrats was announced, headed by Ebert and Scheidemann. With the Chancellor during the interview that followed were von Payer, Solf, Count Roedern, Haussmann, the former Ambassador to the United States, Count Bernstorff, and Simons, who arrived after the conference had commenced. Ebert was spokesman for the delegation.

"To maintain peace and order," he said, "our party colleagues have authorized us to declare to the Imperial Chancellor that we believe it absolutely necessary, if bloodshed is to be avoided, for the Government to be in the hands of those who possess the complete confidence of the people. For that reason we deem it neces-

24. Max, *Erinnerungen,* pp. 632–634. In a note on p. 634 Simons explains why he gave this advice.

25. *Ibid.,* pp. 634–635. See also the Chancellor's account of the Kaiser's abdication in the *Berliner Tageblatt,* August 9, 1919, No. 367, which is translated and printed in Lutz, *Fall of the German Empire,* II, 529–537.

sary that the office of Imperial Chancellor and the post of highest military command in Prussia be taken over by members of our party. In this matter we have both our own party and also that of the Independent Socialists solidly behind us. Even the soldiers have been won over to our side. The Independent Socialists have not yet agreed whether to participate in the new Government; if they decide in favor of it, we must desire and demand that they be taken in. Nor do we have any objections to the entry of representatives of the bourgeois parties into the Government; only we must keep the decisive majority of the Government. We have to negotiate further on that matter." [26]

The Chancellor reminded Scheidemann that he was still a Secretary of State, but Scheidemann said he had already resigned. Max then asked Ebert whether the party leaders were possessed of the determination and the power to keep the revolutionary movement from becoming violent and whether they could give guarantees that peace and order would be maintained. Scheidemann answered that all the garrisons and regiments of Greater Berlin had gone over to the Social Democrats and had sent delegations to inform them of the fact. Doubting this assertion, Haussmann asked for evidence. Scheidemann suggested that they ride together to the various barracks in the city: the cheers of the troops would be evidence enough. The challenge was declined, for Haussmann had no desire to give the appearance of supporting the movement. Prince Max informed Ebert that he had proposed to the Kaiser the summoning of a constituent assembly to determine Germany's future government. Ebert said he approved the idea of such an assembly.

Max then withdrew with his ministers to consider what answer he should give Ebert. None of them objected when he made known his decision to relinquish the chancellorship to Ebert. After a brief consultation on this matter, and with little regard for constitutional propriety, the Chancellor called in Ebert and his colleagues to ask whether he was prepared to accept the office of Chancellor.

"It is a difficult post," answered Ebert, "but I will take it over."

"Are you ready," asked Solf, "to be head of a Government within the framework of the constitution?"

Ebert answered yes.

Solf amplified the question: "Even within a monarchical constitution?"

26. Max, *Erinnerungen,* p. 635.

"Yesterday," answered Ebert, "I would have answered, yes, absolutely; today I must first consult my friends."

"Now," said Prince Max, "we have to solve the question of the regency."

"It's too late," replied Ebert, and behind him his party comrades chorused: "Too late! Too late!"

The Chancellor was still without news of any decision by the Kaiser; he had, therefore, no authority to do what the situation demanded. He believed that matters would have developed very differently if he had been in a position to say to the Social Democrats that the Kaiser had already named a deputy.[27]

While still at the Chancellery, Ebert tried to arrange with the leaders of the Independent Socialists for their party to participate in the new Government. The conference of the two Socialist groups was said to be by no means a friendly one, and no agreement could be reached at that time.[28]

In the meantime Scheidemann had returned to the Reichstag, where he reported to party colleagues on the morning's events and where the party resolved to issue an appeal to the people for support. Later, while he was having a thin-soup luncheon in the Reichstag restaurant with Ebert, who had returned from the Chancellery, a crowd of workers and soldiers broke in. "People

27. *Ibid.*, pp. 635–639. Scheidemann (*Memoiren,* II, 300–309) has raised a very serious question about this scene in the Chancellery. He says that neither he nor others present at the time recall this interchange of words as recorded by Prince Max. What he and the others recall was that Prince Max asked Ebert, as head of the only political party deemed capable of coping with the revolutionary situation, to take over the chancellorship—there was no talk of the constitution, no talk of the Kaiser and his summoning a constituent assembly that would determine whether Germany would be a monarchy or a republic. Scheidemann says that everybody present had a definite feeling that this was the end of the monarchy. He suggests, however, that the dialogue given by Prince Max takes on unusual significance in the light of a disclosure made later that the Chancellor had had a private meeting earlier that morning with Ebert and had assured himself that Ebert was a safe man to be his successor as Chancellor because he was not opposed to the monarchy. Max's description of the transfer of power would belong more appropriately to that earlier scene; it does not describe what took place at this time. Scheidemann suggests that he and his colleagues would have objected most strenuously to anything like the talk reported by Prince Max. Simons had been one of the first men to recommend Ebert to the Chancellor (Max, *Erinnerungen,* pp. 618, 632). According to Scheidemann (p. 301), the Foreign Office Counselor knew "that Ebert was no opponent of monarchy on the basis of principle." Perhaps these views of Ebert caused Prince Max to think it possible (*Erinnerungen,* p. 632) that the Kaiser, when abdicating, might name Ebert the new Chancellor.

28. Max, *Erinnerungen,* p. 640; Scheidemann, *Memoiren,* II, 309.

by the tens of thousands are standing out there," they told him, "demanding that you speak to them." Scheidemann finally consented and went out to the balcony. On the way his companions told him that Liebknecht was speaking from the balcony of the palace and that he was going to proclaim a Soviet Republic for Germany. Scheidemann shuddered at the thought that Germany might thus become a part of Russia. He was warmly greeted when he appeared on the balcony and spoke briefly to the crowd assembled below. He said that the Kaiser "and his friends have disappeared," that the people had triumphed, that the Chancellor had handed over his post to Ebert, who was going to form a workers' government composed of all the Socialist parties. "The old and the rotten, the monarchy," he shouted in conclusion, "has collapsed. Long live the new! Long live the German Republic!" The crowd shouted its approval, and Scheidemann returned to his soup.[29]

A few minutes later, while Ebert and Scheidemann were finishing their luncheon, people rushed into the Reichstag and shouted that Scheidemann had proclaimed the republic. Ebert turned red with rage and shouted at his companion, as he banged the table with his fist, "Is that true?" Scheidemann answered that it was not only true—it was obvious. "You have no right," cried Ebert, "to proclaim a republic! What Germany is to be, a republic or anything else, is for the Constituent Assembly to decide." [30]

November 9 was to be a day of important decisions at Spa.[31] The morning was a bleak one, typical of the season of the year,

29. Scheidemann, *Memoiren,* II, 310–312. See also Max, *Erinnerungen,* pp. 640–641.

30. Scheidemann explains Ebert's bad temper in this matter by referring to the fact that he had committed himself to monarchy in a secret conference with Prince Max. Scheidemann, *Memoiren,* II, 313–314. See also note 27 in this chapter.

31. Many accounts have been given of Spa on November 9. The more important are the following: Niemann, *Der Weg Kaiser Wilhelms II. vom Thron in die Fremde* (Stuttgart, 1932), pp. 68 *et seq.; Memoirs of the Crown Prince of Germany,* pp. 285–322; Maurice Baumont, *The Fall of the Kaiser* (New York, 1931), pp. 81–160; S. Miles Bouton, *And the Kaiser Abdicates* (New Haven, 1921), pp. 178–182; Niemann, *Revolution von Oben,* pp. 282–312. An account by Schulenburg is to be found in the Berlin paper, *Die Freiheit,* Nos. 163 and 164, morning and evening editions respectively, April 5, 1919. The most important of all accounts is that in the memorandum of July 27, 1919, by Hindenburg, von Plessen, von Hintze, and Count Schulenburg. The German text, first published in the newspapers, is available in Niemann, *Revolution von Oben,* pp. 334–342. An English translation is given in R. H. Lutz, *Fall of the German Empire,* II, 537–548.

cold and foggy, with rain dripping from the almost leafless trees. In spite of the weather the Kaiser took his usual morning walk, his last in Germany.

At 10 A.M. von Hindenburg and General Groener reported to the Kaiser on the military situation in the presence of General von Plessen, General Baron von Marschall, General Count Schulenburg, and Major Niemann. Von Hintze came in whenever he had reports for the Emperor.

Before making his report, von Hindenburg asked to be dismissed; it would be easier for him then to say what he had to say. The Kaiser made no decision on this request but asked the men to speak. General Groener then described the military situation as it had looked to the conferees the preceding night and declared it would be impossible to lead the Army against the revolution. Hindenburg concurred. During the report and afterward Schulenburg and von Plessen expressed dissent. Schulenburg said that the situation was made to appear too dark; he believed that civil war could be avoided if reliable troops were at once energetically despatched against the revolutionaries. Recent battles on the front had shown clearly that the majority of the troops were still loyal to their leaders. With the coming of the armistice and the troops somewhat refreshed, morale would be so improved that the Army could be used against the revolutionaries in its rear at Verviers, Aix-la-Chapelle, and Cologne. General von Plessen supported these views. He believed the Kaiser should leave nothing untried to restore order at home. Hindenburg and Groener, while appreciating these sentiments, found it impossible to agree. They said that the Army had no provisions, that it was folly to talk of immediate action against the revolution and of the need of giving the Army a rest, which the enemy would not permit. They opposed every detail of the plan put forward by von Plessen and Count von Schulenburg.[32]

With these conflicting views before him the Kaiser had to make up his mind. In the words of the Crown Prince, he "stood resolutely by his original decision," but, "in face of the irreconcilable opposition between the two views of the situation and the logical conclusions involved, he had ultimately turned to General Groener and declared with great firmness that, in this exceedingly grave matter, he could not acquiesce in the opinion expressed by the general but must insist upon a written statement signed by the field-marshal general, von Hindenburg, and by General Groener

32. Memorandum of July 27, 1919.

—a statement based upon the judgments to be obtained from all the army leaders of the west front. The notion of waging a civil war lay outside the scope of his consideration; but he held firmly to his desire to lead the army back home in good order after the conclusion of the armistice."[33]

General Groener then adopted an attitude which seemed to indicate that he regarded all further discussion as a waste of time in face of the Kaiser's definitely fixed purpose; he remarked brusquely, "The army will march back home in good order under its leaders and commanding generals, but not under the leadership of Your Majesty, for it no longer stands behind Your Majesty." Schulenburg protested.

The Kaiser then asked General Groener, "How do you come to make such a report? Count Schulenburg reports the reverse!"

"I have different information," answered the Quartermaster General.

Hindenburg "had come to the practical conclusion of General Groener, namely, that, on the basis of the information received by the Higher Command from home and from the armies, it must be assumed that the revolution could no longer be suppressed. Like Groener, he too was unable to take upon himself responsibility for the trustworthiness of the troops."

The Kaiser ended the discussion by repeating his request that the Commanders-in-Chief be asked for their views. "If you report to me," he said, "that the army is no longer loyal to me, I shall be prepared to go—but not till then!"[34]

The question of abdication was not touched upon during the report about the military situation. Toward the end of this report the first demand for abdication arrived from the Imperial Chancellery at Berlin. The demands were repeated with ever-increasing insistence so that the military report had to be broken off. The Kaiser and the others went into the garden, where the consultations were continued as the Kaiser talked with one small group after the other and the various groups deliberated among themselves.

About noon the Crown Prince arrived, "stiff and frozen to the marrow." He entered the garden with Count Schulenburg, who had recounted the morning's happenings and had begged him to keep the Kaiser from making overhasty and irretrievable decisions. In his memoirs he has given an account of what he saw:

33. *Memoirs of the Crown Prince*, pp. 289–290.
34. *Ibid.*, pp. 290–291; Memorandum of July 27, 1919.

"He [the Kaiser] stood in the garden surrounded by a group of gentlemen. Never shall I forget the picture of that half-score of men in their gray uniforms, thrown into relief by the withered and faded flower-beds of ending autumn, and framed by the surrounding mist-mantled hills with their glorious foliage of vanishing green and every shade of brown, of yellow and of red.

"The Kaiser stood there as though he had suddenly halted in his agitated passing up and down. Passionately excited, he addressed himself to those near him with violently expressive gestures. His eyes were upon General Groener and His Excellency von Hintze; but a glance was cast now and then at the field-marshal general, who, with his gaze fixed on the distance, nodded silently; and an occasional look was also turned towards the white-haired General von Plessen. Somewhat aloof from the group, stood General von Marschall, the Legation Councillor von Grünau and Major von Hirschfeld.

"With their bowed attitudes, most of the men seemed oppressed by the thought that there was no egress from their entanglement—seemed, while the Kaiser alone spoke, to have been paralyzed into muteness.

"Catching sight of me, my father beckoned me to approach and, himself, came forward a few paces.

"And now, as I stood opposite him, I saw clearly how distraught were his features—how his emaciated and sallowed face twitched and winced.

"He left me scarcely time to greet the field-marshal general and the rest; hastily he addressed himself to me, and, while the others retired a little and General Groener returned to the house, he burst upon me with all he had to say." [35]

The Emperor told the Crown Prince that the troops were said to be untrustworthy, that the revolution made his return to Berlin impossible, that he would abdicate and give von Hindenburg the chief command of the Army. The Crown Prince tried to dissuade his father; he should not abdicate as King of Prussia, he must remain with the Army.

"I suggested," writes the Crown Prince, "his coming with me and marching back at the head of my troops." [36]

Toward one o'clock Colonel Heye appeared in the garden to report to the Kaiser the result of the discussion with the thirty-nine generals and regimental commanders of the three Army

35. *Memoirs of the Crown Prince,* pp. 293–294; Memorandum of July 27, 1919.
36. *Memoirs of the Crown Prince,* pp. 295–296.

groups under Crown Prince Rupprecht, the German Crown Prince, and Gallwitz. During the night these officers had been summoned to Spa by the Army Command to report on the prevailing sentiment in the Army. The Field Marshal had not been able to participate in this conference; he had to leave to make his report on the military situation to the Kaiser. Colonel Heye took a poll of the officers on two questions:

1. What is the attitude of the troops toward the Kaiser? Will it be possible for the Kaiser at the head of the troops to reconquer the country by force?
2. How do the troops stand toward Bolshevism? Will they fight Bolshevism in their own country?

Only one officer answered the first question with "Yes"; 15 left the answer more or less doubtful, and 23 said "No." On the loyalty of the Crown Prince's troops in particular the answers were 4 doubtful, 12 "No," and not a single "Yes"—an interesting contrast to his Chief of Staff's estimate. As to question two, 8 officers believed it impossible to get the troops to oppose Bolshevism, 12 held a protracted period of rest necessary in order to get them in hand again by appropriate enlightenment and training, and 19 were doubtful whether the men *en masse* or even a part of them would fight against Bolshevism.

"The troops are yet loyal to Your Majesty," reported Heye to the Kaiser, "but they are tired and indifferent, and wish only rest and peace. They will not march against the country at present, not even with Your Majesty at their head. Nor will they march against Bolshevism; they want simply and solely an armistice, and that soon; therefore, every hour is important."

The Kaiser asked whether or not the troops would march home without him.

Schulenburg believed that they would not. He said that the great majority of the Army, if faced with the question whether to break their oaths and desert their sovereign and Chief War Lord in his time of need, would certainly prove loyal to the Kaiser.

"At this," writes the Crown Prince, "General Groener merely shrugged his shoulders and sneered superciliously. 'Military oaths? War Lords? Those are, after all, only words; those are, when all is said, mere ideas.' "

Schulenburg retorted, according to the Crown Prince, "that such statements as his only showed that he did not know the heart and mind of the men at the front, that the army was true to its oath and that, at the end of those four years of war, it would not abandon its Kaiser." [37]

This minor debate was ended by the arrival of von Hintze. During the morning in the Kaiser's villa he had been receiving from Berlin the telegrams that insisted upon the Kaiser's abdication. He had been told that most of the troops had gone over to the revolution, that "Berlin was drenched in blood" as a result of fierce street fighting. Only abdication could avert civil war.[38] Only abdication could save the dynasty. "The decision was to be made at once; it was not a matter of hours, but of minutes." To the Kaiser von Hintze reported that the Chancellor had resigned and that the monarchy could no longer be saved unless the Kaiser resolved upon immediate abdication.

"When von Hintze had finished," reports the Crown Prince, "he [the Kaiser] gave a brief nod; and his eyes sought those of the field-marshal general as though searching them for strength and succor in his anguish. But he found nothing. Motionless, deeply touched, silenced by despair, the great old man stood paralyzed, while his King and lord, whom he had served so long and so faithfully as a soldier, moved on to the fulfilment of his destiny.

"The Kaiser was alone. Not one of all the men of the General Higher Command, not one of the men whom Ludendorff had once welded into a firm entity, hastened to his assistance. Here, as at home, disruption and decay. Here, where an iron will should have been busy enforcing itself in all the positions of authority and gathering all the reliable forces at the front to make itself effective, there was only one vast void. The spirit of General Groener was now dominant, and that spirit left the Kaiser to his fate.

"Hoarse, strange and unreal was my father's voice as he instructed Hintze, who was still waiting, to telephone the Imperial Chancellor that he was prepared to renounce the Imperial Crown, if thereby alone general civil war in Germany were to

37. Memorandum of July 27, 1919; *Memoirs of the Crown Prince,* pp. 297–298.

38. Efforts were made by an officer at Spa to learn the facts of the situation in Berlin from the Minister of War. It was found that the majority of the troops had gone over, but that the street fights were not of great magnitude; only twenty or thirty wounded had been reported. Von Hintze called attention to this discrepancy, only to be told once more that abdication was necessary. Memorandum of July 27, 1919.

be avoided, but that he remained King of Prussia and would not leave the army." [39]

The Kaiser had made it clear earlier that day that the most he would do was to abdicate the Imperial throne; to renounce the royal throne of Prussia was not to be considered under any circumstances. Groener had been skeptical, believing that the German people would no longer be satisfied with such a decision. Hindenburg and Schulenburg, on the other hand, had supported their Emperor; they had insisted that neither the Imperial Chancellor nor the Reichstag had the right to demand the Kaiser's abdication as King of Prussia.[40]

"The gentlemen were silent. The state secretary [the retired Secretary of State von Hintze] was about to depart, when Schulenburg pointed out that it was, in any case, essential first to make a written record of this highly significant decision of His Majesty. Not until such a document had been ratified and signed could it be communicated to the Imperial Chancellor.

"The Kaiser expressed his thanks. Yes, he said, that was true; and he instructed Lieutenant-General von Plessen, General von Marschall, His Excellency von Hintze and Count von der Schulenburg to draw up a declaration and submit it to him for signature." [41]

It was to be explained to the Imperial Chancellor that His Majesty, in order to avoid bloodshed, *was ready to abdicate as German Kaiser but not as King of Prussia.* His Majesty wished to remain King of Prussia for the sake of the Army; otherwise, the officers would leave and the Army without its leaders would dissolve. This must be prevented. His Majesty did not wish civil war. Abdicating as German Kaiser, he would order Field Marshal von Hindenburg to take over the Supreme Command of the German Army and he himself would remain with the Prussian troops.[42]

The committee set to work on this formal abdication while the Kaiser and others went to lunch, a "silent meal."

Just after two o'clock the Kaiser was called away from a talk with the Crown Prince and Schulenburg. Von Hintze desired to

39. *Memoirs of the Crown Prince,* pp. 298–299; also the Memorandum of July 27, 1919.

40. *Memoirs of the Crown Prince,* pp. 291–292; Memorandum of July 27, 1919; Niemann, *Der Weg Kaiser Wilhelms II. vom Thron in die Fremde,* p. 71.

41. *Memoirs of the Crown Prince,* p. 299.

42. Memorandum of July 27, 1919.

see him, to report what had happened while he was telephoning Berlin to give the Chancellery the wording of the formal abdication. As he had begun to read the declaration, Undersecretary of State Wahnschaffe at the Chancellery interrupted, "That is of no use, complete abdication is to be pronounced, and Herr von Hintze must listen to what is now being telephoned to him." Von Hintze objected and insisted upon reading the decision of the Kaiser first. This was done. But it was no sooner done than he was told that a complete abdication of the Kaiser *and Prussian King* had already been made public by the Wolff News Bureau. Von Hintze protested that there had been no authorization from the Kaiser for such action and made it clear that all he had said was that the Kaiser was going to make a decision on the matter. Prince Max came to the telephone and said he took the responsibility for publishing the abdication of the Kaiser and the King of Prussia as well as the renunciation of the Crown Prince, in spite of the fact that the latter question had never been discussed at Spa.

"I am and I remain King of Prussia and as such with my troops," the Kaiser exploded when von Hintze ceased speaking. He instructed von Hintze immediately to inform von Hindenburg and General Groener about the new turn of events.[43]

"Schulenburg and I," says the Crown Prince, "importuned His Majesty never, under any circumstances, to submit to this *coup d'état*, but to oppose the machinations of the Prince with every possible means and to abide unalterably by his previously formed resolution. The Count also emphasized the fact that this incident rendered it all the more essential for the Kaiser, as Chief War Lord, to remain with the Army."

The Crown Prince and his Chief of Staff "offered to undertake the subjection of the revolutionary elements at home, proposing first to restore order in Cologne. But this suggestion the Kaiser declined to entertain, as he would have no war of Germans against Germans." [44]

Toward 3.30 P.M. there was a meeting in Hindenburg's villa to discuss the new situation. General Groener, Count Schulenburg, Baron von Marschall, Secretary of State von Hintze, and Legation Councilor von Grünau participated. The generals declared that military means were not available to force Berlin to repudiate the published abdication. Von Hintze won support for

43. Memorandum of July 27, 1919.

44. *Memoirs of the Crown Prince,* pp. 304–305.

a proposal to draw up a formal protest against the unauthorized act; the Kaiser was to sign it and the document was to be kept in a safe place for later publication.

During this meeting there was discussion of providing for the Kaiser's safety. Hindenburg argued that the Kaiser should go to some neutral country. "I cannot assume," he said, "the responsibility of having Your Majesty taken by mutinous troops to Berlin and surrendered as prisoner to the revolutionary government." [45] But where should he go if Army Headquarters found it impossible to assure him of protection? Some suggested Switzerland. Hindenburg expressed a preference for Holland, because it was a monarchical country and only about 60 kilometers from Spa. This was the decision made at the meeting. Only Count von Schulenburg believed that it would be a grave mistake for the Kaiser to leave the Army.[46]

At four o'clock the participants in this meeting, with the exception of Count Schulenburg, who had returned to his military quarters, made their report to the Kaiser. General von Plessen and Admiral Scheer were also present. Hindenburg informed the Emperor that it was impossible to quell the revolution by military force. His Majesty agreed to the proposal for a formal written protest against the abdication announcement published in Berlin. He asked Hindenburg to take over the Supreme Command of the Army and to lead the troops home. Then it was pointed out to the Kaiser that for him "the road home was closed." The Emperor was told that Holland was the country best suited for asylum. This decision was not final, for the Kaiser could not persuade himself to accept it. Arms and ammunition were gathered for the purpose of defending the villa in case the rebels should make an attack, for it was learned that soldiers were forming revolutionary councils even at Spa.[47]

The Kaiser decided to spend the night on the imperial train, which stood at the station. Von Hintze pointed out that certain steps would have to be taken in case the journey to Holland should be decided upon. The Kaiser ordered him to take the necessary measures, and von Hintze got in touch with the representatives of Germany in Belgium and Holland.

The Field Marshal left the Kaiser at five o'clock, never think-

45. Niemann, *Der Weg Kaiser Wilhelms II. vom Thron in die Fremde,* p. 141.
46. *Memoirs of the Crown Prince,* pp. 306–307; Memorandum of July 27, 1919.
47. Memorandum of July 27, 1919; Niemann, *Der Weg Kaiser Wilhelms II. vom Thron in die Fremde,* pp. 82–86.

ing it was to be a final parting. He fully expected to see the Emperor the next day to learn what his decision was. At 7.30 in the evening he heard from General von Plessen that the Emperor had decided to leave for Holland. Back in the imperial train von Plessen suggested to the Kaiser that he abandon the proposed journey. And the Kaiser so decided. This change of mind disturbed von Hintze, who sent von Grünau at ten o'clock to point out that flight later on would not have the valuable element of surprise which leaving immediately would have. The Kaiser was persuaded and fixed his departure for five the next morning.[48]

During the evening the Kaiser sat in his quarters in the royal train and received officers who sought to resign their commissions. He asked them to remain with the Army. He wrote letters to various people, one to the Crown Prince, whom he had urged in the afternoon to remain with the Army. The letter is worth quoting since it shows what was in the Kaiser's mind when about to leave the land he had ruled for thirty years. It reads:

My dear boy,

As the Field-Marshal cannot guarantee my safety here and will not pledge himself for the reliability of the troops, I have decided, after a severe inward struggle, to leave the disorganized army. Berlin is totally lost; it is in the hands of the Socialists, and two governments have been formed there—one with Ebert as Chancellor and one by the Independents. Till the troops start their march home, I recommend your holding out at your post and keeping the troops together! God willing, I trust we shall meet again. General von Marschall will give you further information.

Your deeply-bowed father,

Wilhelm.[49]

He had said good-by to his son in the early afternoon. "As I held his hand in mine," says the Crown Prince, "I never imagined that I should not see him again for a year and that it would then be in Holland." [50]

On Sunday morning, at 5 A.M., the royal train left Spa. Those close to the Kaiser wondered whether it would be allowed to go

48. Memorandum of July 27, 1919.

49. Niemann, *Der Weg Kaiser Wilhelms II. vom Thron in die Fremde,* pp. 87–88; *Memoirs of the Crown Prince,* pp. 317–318.

50. *Memoirs of the Crown Prince,* pp. 304-305.

through; an armed officer sat in the cab near the engineer, ready to shoot anyone who might attempt to halt them. At a station not far from Spa the cars came to a stop to let the Kaiser and some of his escort get off and proceed the rest of the way to the Dutch frontier in automobiles that had been secretly sent ahead from Spa for the purpose. The Emperor took his seat with three officers in the second of four cars that now drove on in the early morning toward Holland. Shortly after seven they reached the Dutch border, not far from Eysden station. A telephone call to the local commandant brought him and some representatives of the Dutch Government who had been notified the evening before that the Kaiser would come. The Emperor walked over to the station, and Grünau telephoned to the German Minister at The Hague, who immediately got in touch with the Dutch Government. The Queen quickly summoned a session of her Cabinet and it was soon decided to offer asylum to the German ruler. In the evening Cabinet ministers, including the Foreign Minister, arrived at Eysden and welcomed the Kaiser to Dutch territory in the name of their Queen.

The Kaiser remained at Eysden until it was decided where he should go; his safety had to be provided for. The castle at Amerongen was finally selected and the Count who owned the place gave his consent. On the morning of November 11 the Kaiser started his trip to Maarn, the station for Amerongen. At some of the larger stations there were hostile demonstrations. At one the wife of the British Minister at The Hague tried to get into the coach where the Kaiser was; with difficulty she was taken away, repeating that she wanted to tell the Crown Prince to his face of her utter contempt for him.

The Kaiser stayed at Amerongen until May 15, 1920, when he moved to Doorn.[51]

51. Baumont, *The Fall of the Kaiser,* pp. 159–160; Niemann, *Der Weg Kaiser Wilhelms II. vom Thron in die Fremde,* pp. 87–90.

XV

Signing the Armistice

WHILE the German armistice delegates at Rethondes in the forest of Compiègne—for that was the rendezvous of the armistice commissions—worked through the morning of November 9 on their draft of counterproposals to the Allied terms, Foch returned for a few hours to his headquarters at Senlis, where he received Clemenceau and Mordacq. The Premier and his companion were disturbed by the reports of revolution coming from Germany and wondered, as did many others, whether the German delegation had authority to negotiate for the new Government in Germany. Clemenceau wished to tell Marshal Foch that he did not want the negotiations dragged out. Mordacq was not much worried about this; if the negotiations were broken off, the Allies could start their attack through Lorraine. Foch, as usual, was calm, but his face was alight with joy. Describing what had taken place in the interview the day before, he expressed surprise at the readiness with which the Germans accepted the drastic terms regarding bridgeheads, the surrender of the fleet, and the occupation of territory, whereas, on the other hand they turned pale and wilted at the mention of the surrender of artillery, machine guns, and locomotives. Erzberger had cried out, "Why, then we are lost! How shall we be able to defend ourselves against Bolshevism? . . . Do you not understand that, in taking from us the means of defense against Bolshevism, you will destroy us, and will also destroy yourselves? You will come into that situation in turn."

Foch showed Clemenceau the telegram being sent to the Commanders-in-Chief of the different Allied Armies, a message that expressed the Premier's own thoughts:

Disorganized by our repeated attacks, the enemy is yielding along the entire front. It is important to sustain and to intensify our efforts. I appeal to the energy and the initiative of the Commanders-in-chief and of their armies to make final the results thus far achieved.

With a laugh the Marshal added, "So far as the Germans are concerned one must be prepared for anything." [1]

Returning to Paris that evening, Clemenceau reported to Colonel House on his visit with Foch, and House relayed the information to Washington without delay. Mention was made of the German objections to the armistice terms, but Clemenceau felt certain that the enemy would sign. The revolutionary situation in Germany might mean that the Government signing the armistice could not make itself obeyed; the difficulties of the German courier in getting through his own lines with the draft of the armistice were cited as possibly signifying such a breakdown of authority. In that case assurance was given that "Foch will continue his march forward." [2] In a later telegram to President Wilson Colonel House reported that the delay experienced by the German courier might mean that "we will probably not receive any definite news until Sunday night or Monday morning." [3]

At 3.45 in the afternoon Count Oberndorff and General von Winterfeldt handed Weygand the text of the German counterproposals which Erzberger had discussed with his fellow delegates the night before and had drafted in the morning.[4] The document was entitled "Observations on the Conditions of an Armistice with Germany" and it was presented to Foch with words that, according to the latter, added nothing new to the arguments of the day before.[5] After discussing them by telephone with Clemenceau Foch informed the Germans that, except for details, he could give them no satisfaction.[6] The detailed written reply of the Allies was not given to Erzberger until late the next afternoon.[7]

Toward evening on the 9th it was learned in Paris that Max von Baden had resigned and that a new Government had been created. Clemenceau was somewhat disturbed by this news and continued to question whether the German delegation had any

1. Mordacq, *La Vérité,* pp. 28–33; Mordacq, *L'Armistice,* pp. 8–13.

2. House to Lansing, November 9, 1918, *Foreign Relations, 1918,* Supplement I, I, 489–490; Seymour, *House Papers,* IV, 139–140.

3. House to President Wilson, November 9, 1918, Seymour, *House Papers,* IV, 140.

4. Foch, *Mémoires,* II, 301; Erzberger, *Erlebnisse,* p. 333; Mordacq, *La Vérité,* p. 35.

5. The original armistice terms, the German "observations," and Foch's reply are all found in parallel columns in Kraus and Rödiger, *Urkunden zum Friedensvertrage von Versailles vom 28. Juni 1919* (Berlin, 1920), I, 23–59.

6. Mordacq, *La Vérité,* p. 35; Mordacq, *L'Armistice,* p. 15.

7. Foch, *Mémoires,* II, 301.

right to speak for the new regime. "It would appear that the plenipotentiaries have no longer any powers," wrote Admiral Wemyss, "and one would think that Erzberger at any rate has no longer any standing." [8] Clemenceau returned to his home in Paris and Mordacq went to bed at the Ministry of War, both convinced that, before the night ended, clearer information would arrive about Germany's internal situation. Toward 3 A.M. it was learned definitely that the Kaiser had abdicated, a new popular Government had been established, and the garrisons in the city of Berlin had placed themselves at the disposal of the new regime.[9]

Although November 10 was a Sunday, Clemenceau appeared early at the War Ministry, where a report was received at ten o'clock from Foch saying that the German delegates were "particularly conciliatory." To avoid useless bloodshed they desired to indicate to the Allies the location of delayed-action mines in territory recently conquered by the French.

"Too polite to be decent," exclaimed Clemenceau when Mordacq brought this news. "If they are getting conciliatory," he added, "it is because they have received reports on the internal situation in Germany and know that at home matters are going none too well. In my opinion that is a rather good sign for us. Whatever it is, it is absolutely necessary to be on guard against fellows like that."

Still worried about the chaos in Germany and the legal standing of the German delegation, Clemenceau had Mordacq telephone to Foch at eleven o'clock with regard to the signing of the armistice. The Marshal was to demand a written declaration from the German delegates stating that they were the representatives of the Government now functioning in Berlin and that they believed this Government capable of guaranteeing the execution of the armistice terms.

Foch reported at noon that it would be easy to get the first part of the declaration but he was not sure about the second part. As it turned out, he got that also.[10]

The Germans also were worried about their predicament. Early Saturday evening Erzberger learned that the Kaiser had abdicated and that the Crown Prince had renounced the throne.

8. Lady Wester Wemyss, *Life and Times of Admiral Wemyss*, pp. 392–393.
9. Mordacq, *La Vérité*, pp. 35–36; Mordacq, *L'Armistice*, p. 16.
10. Mordacq, *L'Armistice*, pp. 17–18; Mordacq, *La Vérité*, pp. 39–40.

But it was not until midnight that the French High Command communicated to him a press despatch stating that a new popular Government had been formed with Ebert at its head. Erzberger was now more than ever bewildered; he did not even know whether Germany was a monarchy or a republic. Three German officers who arrived at Rethondes the morning of November 10 from General Headquarters could not set his mind at ease.

When the British naval officers asked Captain Vanselow whether the new German Government would be in a position to fulfill the armistice conditions, he did not know what to say. The German delegation discussed their quandary at some length and reached the conclusion that, if the new Government authorized the signing of the armistice, it must be assumed that it had the power to carry out the obligations entered into. The English delegation announced that it reserved the right, in case the armistice conditions were not carried out, to impose them by force of arms and, if necessary, to occupy Helgoland.

Other conversations between the Germans and the Allies went on during the morning, with the former continually emphasizing the danger of Bolshevism and with the latter completely distrustful of all the Germans said.

French workers attached to the special trains approached Erzberger once and said that, although it was forbidden to give him any newspapers, they wished him to see the headline: "The Kaiser has abdicated." They were radiant with joy. While waiting for more official information from Germany, Erzberger and Oberndorff went for a walk through the forest, the weather being particularly pleasant. The wood had been fenced off in the neighborhood of the trains, but they were allowed to wander within a radius of two kilometers.

With the Allies' written reply to the "Observations," which the Germans received late in the afternoon, was a letter of warning from General Weygand:

According to the terms of the text given to Marshal Foch, the powers of the German plenipotentiaries for concluding an armistice depend on the Chancellor's approval.

As the time allowed for the coming to an agreement expires at 11 A.M. tomorrow, I have the honor to ask whether the German plenipotentiaries have received the German Chancellor's approval of the terms communicated to him, and, if not, whether it would not be advisable to solicit without delay an answer from him.

The Germans replied at 9.30 P.M. that "a decision of the Imperial Chancellor had not yet come to them," asserting that they were trying to have instructions transmitted as quickly as possible.[11]

There were good reasons why Erzberger had to wait so long for instructions from Germany. Responsible people in Berlin had much more to think of on Sunday, November 10, than about Erzberger in the quiet and solitude of Compiègne.[12] A Government had to be formed. Ebert's acceptance of the post of Chancellor and Scheidemann's proclamation of a republic on November 9 had not created a government. Approval by the people in some form was regarded as essential. The outlook at that time for an orderly solution of affairs was not a bright one. Soldiers in their barracks, even the special guards at the palaces in Potsdam, were forming councils on the Russian soviet model; workers were choosing their councils, and many went out on strike. Whoever could control the workers and soldiers would be likely to gain control of the Government; hence the Majority Socialists, the Independent Socialists, and the extreme Spartacus group of Rosa Luxemburg and Karl Liebknecht were all seeking the favor of these large revolutionary bodies. There was little violence during the day except for some firing that occurred near the royal palaces and near the University of Berlin.

On the afternoon of November 9 Ebert asked the people in a formal appeal to stay at home and keep off the street so that order could be maintained and food and health services could be kept functioning. He stated that he had been made Chancellor and promised that a new government would be formed on the basis of popular will. People in administrative positions in the Government were asked to remain at their posts.[13]

While Ebert was making this appeal for order, the more radical groups were maneuvering to get control of affairs. The Independents and the Spartacists addressed a proclamation to "Workers, Soldiers, Comrades," calling for the formation of a Socialist Republic on the Russian style, with Soldiers' and Workers' Councils in control. To that end soldiers and workers

11. Foch, *Mémoires*, II, 301–302; Erzberger, *Erlebnisse*, pp. 334–335.

12. For accounts of the happenings in Berlin on November 10 see Eduard Bernstein, *Die Deutsche Revolution* (Berlin, 1921), pp. 40–50; Hermann Müller, *Die November Revolution* (Berlin, 1928), pp. 62–72; Scheidemann, *Memoiren*, II, 316–322.

13. Bernstein, *Die Deutsche Revolution*, pp. 31–32; H. Müller, *Die November Revolution*, pp. 51–52.

were asked to hold elections on Sunday morning at ten in their separate factory and barrack organizations to choose delegates for a mass meeting at five that afternoon in the Zirkus Busch.

As he returned from the Chancellery Saturday afternoon after accepting the post of Chancellor from Prince Max, Ebert met two Independent Socialists and asked them for their party's coöperation in the formation of a new government. They expressed their personal willingness to participate in such an effort, but made it clear that they had no authority to speak for their party. Only a policy meeting of the whole group could render such a decision; and no session could be held until their leader, Hugo Haase, had returned from Kiel. To get a government that would be able to prevent civil war and sign an armistice, Ebert was willing to coöperate even with the Spartacist leader Karl Liebknecht, if it could be arranged.

In the evening the Social Democrats acquainted the Independents with the terms on which they would be willing to coöperate with a group whose political demands were so extreme. But a decision on the question had to be postponed to Sunday, a delay that irked the ever-impatient Scheidemann.

The same evening there was a meeting of Workers' and Soldiers' Councils at which the revolutionary Leftist Emil Barth presided. Arrangements were worked out for the Sunday morning elections of delegates to the conference scheduled to meet at the Zirkus Busch in the afternoon.

Sunday morning, November 10, brought some visible signs of the revolutionary changes taking place. Berliners must have rubbed their eyes in amazement at what they saw. The words of loyalty to monarchy, of devotion to the house of Hohenzollern, had disappeared from the masthead of papers that had been ardently royalist. There was no Kaiser! The Berlin *Lokal Anzeiger* had a new title and a new sponsor; it was now *Die Rote Fahne*, organ of the Spartacists. *Die Norddeutsche Allgemeine Zeitung* appeared as *Die Internationale*, representing the Independent Socialists. *Vorwärts* had undergone no change of control or policy. As the organ of the party trying to form the new Government, it may well have seemed more conservative than usual, particularly after the shift of some newspapers from Right to Left during the preceding twenty-four hours.

In the morning the Independent Socialists met to consider the matter of coöperation with the Majority Socialists, Haase having returned in the night from a revolutionary itinerary in the north. A strong minority, siding actually with the Spartacists, opposed collaboration with a man like Scheidemann, whom they looked upon as a traitor to the cause of socialism. When motions were made and carried, it was clear that this minority was only a minority, with more voice than votes. The outcome was an agreement that three members of the Independent Socialists could coöperate on terms of equality, although the far smaller party, with three Majority Socialists to form a Cabinet provided the arrangement met with the approval of the delegates at the Zirkus Busch in the afternoon.

At noon a group met at the Chancellery. It could not be called a legally constituted Cabinet—that had not yet been formed. But Ebert acted as Chancellor and called these people in, including a number of men from the outgoing regime. After a few introductory words he asked Secretary Solf to read the armistice terms and the accompanying request of the High Command that the conditions be accepted "without delay and without change." It was explained that the High Command was ready to issue a public statement on this policy if that were thought necessary to quiet the people. "There was no doubt," writes von Payer, "what had to be done." The Minister of War said that the Armies were not able to get better conditions by continuing to fight. Instructions were telegraphed to the High Command to inform Erzberger that the Government accepted the terms offered by Foch, even though the "Cabinet" expressed doubt as to its competency to do so.[14]

The terms were hard and Solf felt constrained to address the following appeal by wireless to President Wilson:

Convinced of the common aims and ideals of democracy the German Government has addressed itself to the President of the United States with the request to reestablish peace.

This peace was meant to correspond with the principles which the President has always maintained. Its aim was to be a just solution of all questions in dispute, followed by a permanent reconciliation of all nations.

Furthermore the President has declared that he did not wish to make war on the German people and that he did not wish to impede with its peaceful developments.

14. Payer, *Von Bethmann Hollweg,* p. 168; Haussmann, *Journal,* pp. 318–319; H. Müller, *Die November Revolution,* p. 63.

The German Government has received the conditions of the armistice.

After a blockade of 50 months these conditions, especially the surrender of the means of transport and the sustenance of the troops of occupation would make it impossible to provide Germany with food and would cause the starvation of millions of men, women and children, all the more as the blockade is to continue.

We had to accept the conditions.

But we feel it our duty to draw President Wilson's attention most solemnly and with all earnestness to the fact that the enforcement of these conditions must produce amongst the German people feelings contrary to those upon which alone the reconstruction of the community of nations can rest, guaranteeing a just and durable peace.

The German people therefore, in this fateful hour, address themselves again to the President with the request to use his influence with the Allied powers in order to mitigate those fearful conditions.[15]

Ebert needed the coöperation of the Independent Socialists and some kind of popular support for the new regime before it could properly function. The Spartacists were showing their open defiance of the Chancellor and his appeal for peace and order; they urged the people to stay on the streets, to keep their firearms, and to be on guard against Ebert, whose appointment was represented as a move on the part of the Kaiser to restore the old system of rule.

The Zirkus Busch meeting thus came to be a session of major importance, and the Majority Socialists, at first not a party to the plan for the conference, became convinced of the need of trying to influence that meeting in favor of their program. While the people were selecting their delegates Sunday morning, the Social Democrats sent automobiles through the city to distribute appeals to soldiers to meet at the *Vorwärts* building at two in the afternoon. At the appointed hour the soldiers gathered to hear Otto Wels warn them of the critical importance of the Zirkus Busch meeting, where it was feared the group in control would be hostile to the Social Democrats. The consequence was the working out of a careful plan of strategy to keep the extremists from upsetting the plans of the Socialists for an orderly government.[16]

15. Solf to Lansing, November 10, 1918, *Lansing Papers,* II, 173.
16. H. Müller, *Die November Revolution,* pp. 69–70.

At 4.15 these soldiers went to the Zirkus Busch, where about three thousand delegates had gathered. Such was the confusion that an inspection of credentials was impossible. The meeting opened at 5.30 and some time was spent in determining procedure before the representatives of the different political parties could be heard: Ebert for the Majority Socialists, Liebknecht for the Spartacists, and Haase for the Independents.

Great applause greeted Ebert when he informed the audience of the proposal to form a Cabinet in which both Socialist parties would be represented by three members each. Liebknecht and his followers sought to obstruct the meeting and to delay all action when the trend of opinion failed to move as they desired. Debate began and seemed to be leading to an *impasse* when a soldier stood up and shouted, "If you people cannot come to a final agreement about the Government, we soldiers will name one ourselves." [17] Nothing more was needed. The conference endorsed the bi-socialist Government that had been proposed; and something like a new order, for Berlin at any rate, had begun.

All this time Erzberger waited at Rethondes for word from Germany, not knowing what was happening to the nation for which he was to end more than four years of war. Between seven and eight in the evening two radio messages from the Government arrived for him, one directly, the other by way of the German High Command. The first said simply, "The German Government accepts the armistice conditions offered on November 9." It was signed "The Imperial Chancellor, 3084." [18]

The second message stated that Erzberger was "authorized to sign the armistice." It instructed him also to state that the execution of the terms would cause famine in Germany and to request permission to negotiate for better conditions to assure Germany adequate food supplies. The High Command asked that it be notified when the armistice terms were signed.[19]

These two telegrams were immediately transmitted to Paris, where Mordacq informed Clemenceau of them. The French Premier was critical; even though the situation at home and on the front made it necessary for the Germans to accept the armistice, he said, they still sought to evade the issue. "What are

17. Bernstein, *Die Deutsche Revolution,* p. 47.

18. Foch, *Mémoires,* II, 302–303.

19. *Ibid.,* pp. 303–304; documents 108 and 109, *Amtliche Urkunden;* see also House to Lansing, November 11, 1918, *Foreign Relations, 1918,* Supplement I, I, 493–494.

they waiting for before they sign?" he asked impatiently. He instructed Foch to ask for immediate signing; the matter must be brought to a conclusion. He asked Mordacq to keep him informed if "anything interesting" happened during the night, when, he hoped, the Germans might get some sense.[20]

Colonel House also was informed that the German Government had accepted but that the signing of the formal document had not yet taken place.[21]

Delivering the two radiograms to Erzberger, Weygand inquired whether they were a final acceptance of the armistice terms by the Chancellor. Erzberger said they were: the number 3084 attached to the signature of the first had been pre-arranged as the mark of authenticity.[22] The Germans were asked when they would be prepared for a conference to agree to and sign the final armistice terms. They replied that they wished first to have a message from Hindenburg, which was coming in code and would have to be deciphered.[23] When decoded, it read as follows:

An attempt must be made to get a modification of the following points in the armistice terms:

1. The extension to two months of the time for evacuation, the greater part of this time needed for the evacuation of the Rhine Provinces, the Palatinate and Hesse, otherwise the Army will collapse, as the technical execution of the terms is absolutely impossible.

2. The right wing of the Army must be allowed to march through the corner of Maastricht [Holland].

3. The abandonment of neutral zones for reasons of internal order, at least must be restricted to a depth of 10 kilometers.

4. Honorable capitulation of East Africa.

5. A considerable reduction must be effected in the railway material to be surrendered, otherwise [German] economy will be seriously

20. Mordacq, *L'Armistice*, pp. 18–19; Mordacq, *La Vérité*, pp. 41–42.

21. House to President Wilson, November 10, 1918, Seymour, *House Papers*, IV, 141.

22. Erzberger, who gives surprisingly few details of these conferences at Rethondes tells a different story. He was alarmed by the fact that the authorization to sign came in an open despatch and seemed to nullify his efforts to have the terms modified. In his account the telegram was signed "The Imperial Chancellor, Schluss." The French interpreter asked if "Schluss" was the name of the new Chancellor: nobody had ever heard of him. Erzberger had to explain that "Schluss" meant "stop," the end of the telegram. Erzberger, *Erlebnisse*, p. 335.

23. Foch, *Mémoires*, II, 304; Erzberger, *Erlebnisse*, p. 335; Mordacq, *L'Armistice*, p. 19.

endangered. With regard to paragraph 7, only a small number of personnel can be left; more detailed arrangements required on this point.

6. Army provided with only 18,000 motor lorries, 50 per cent usable; surrender of the number demanded would mean complete breakdown of Army supply system.

7. Only 1,700 pursuit and bombing airplanes in existence.

8. If there is to be a one-sided surrender of prisoners of war, at least the present agreements as to treatment of the latter must remain in force.

9. The blockade must be raised so far as food supplies are concerned. Commissioners to deal with regulation of food supplies are on the way.

If it is impossible to gain these points, it would nevertheless be advisable to conclude the agreement. In case of the refusal of points 1, 4, 5, 6, 8, 9 a fiery protest should be raised along with an appeal to Wilson.[24]

As soon as he knew he had authority to conclude the armistice negotiations, Erzberger sent the following message in cipher to the German High Command for transmission to the Imperial Chancellor:

Plenipotentiary powers have just arrived. As soon as the armistice is concluded, we recommend that you inform President Wilson of this immediately by wireless and request him to institute without delay negotiations for the conclusion of a preliminary peace so as to avoid famine and anarchy. We also ask that you make arrangements through Holland's mediation for the first meeting of plenipotentiaries to take place immediately at The Hague. Only by the immediate conclusion of the preliminary peace will it be possible to mitigate the disastrous effect of the execution of the armistice terms.

Up to the present our enemies are completely without any understanding of this danger.[25]

Having sent this telegram and having drafted his protest against the armistice terms, Erzberger informed Marshal Foch at 2.05 A.M, November 11, that he was ready for the final meeting. The session began at 2.15. It was not necessary to wait for

24. Document 107, *Amtliche Urkunden.* Also, Mordacq, *L'Armistice,* pp. 54–55. This message was telegraphed to the War Ministry in Berlin at the same time that it was wirelessed to Erzberger, but it did not arrive in the capital until the afternoon of November 11, after the actual signing of the armistice.

25. Document 106, *Amtliche Urkunden.*

Admiral Wemyss, who was ready, having been warned beforehand that the Germans might ask for a final session on armistice terms that night.[26]

Erzberger has described this final conference. "I tried," he writes, "with each separate article of the armistice to get even milder terms and mentioned particularly the advantages of a smaller number in the enemy's army of occupation; Foch had told me that he wanted fifty divisions in the region of the left bank of the Rhine. The most lively argument arose in connection with article 26, which provided for the continuation of the blockade. We struggled over that article for more than an hour. In detail I pointed out that by means of this article an essential part of the World War was being continued, namely, England's starvation policy, under which German women and children suffered the most. With Count Oberndorff I explained that this was 'not fair,' a remark that brought from the English Admiral [Wemyss] the excited retort, 'Not fair? Why, you sank our ships without discrimination.' Nevertheless, the English replied that they would inform their Government of our wish to have the blockade lifted. An important amelioration was gained in the promise of the Entente to supply Germany with food during the period of the armistice. Discussion of the separate articles continued until 5.12 in the morning. On the motion of Marshal Foch it was then decided to make it five o'clock so that the armistice could come into force six hours later, at eleven A.M., French time."

"The negotiations were now interrupted and immediately by wireless I reported the conclusion of the armistice to the German High Command. On the suggestion of Marshal Foch the last page of the agreement [actually, p. 13] was signed, since the drafting of the other pages and the copying would go on for some hours yet. The signing began at 5.20. Two copies were prepared. Marshal Foch and Admiral Wemyss signed first, then the German plenipotentiaries. Tears were in the eyes of our two brave officers, General von Winterfeldt and Captain Vanselow, when they forced themselves to sign."[27]

26. Foch, *Mémoires,* II, 304; Erzberger, *Erlebnisse,* p. 335; Lady Wester Wemyss, *Life and Times of Admiral Wemyss,* p. 393.

27. Erzberger, *Erlebnisse,* pp. 335–336. See also the brief account in Lady Wester Wemyss, *Life and Times of Admiral Wemyss,* pp. 393–394. Foch writes that the terms were agreed to at 5.05 and that the signing began at 5.10. Foch, *Mémoires,* II, 317. The last page of the armistice with the signatures is found reproduced in Foch, opposite p. 304. The full armistice terms in French are found *ibid.,* pp. 305–316. The final English text is in Appendix G.

The Allied High Command wished to add the following clause to the armistice text because of the political events taking place in Germany:

In case German ships are not handed over within the time limit indicated, the Governments of the Allies and of the United States shall have the right to occupy Helgoland to assure the delivery of such ships.

The German delegates declared themselves incompetent to sign this clause; but they agreed to urge the German Government to accept it. A special agreement covered the matter.[28]

Erzberger then asked permission to speak. He read the following declaration and gave Foch a copy, which was signed by the four members of the German delegation:

A DECLARATION OF THE GERMAN PLENIPOTENTIARIES ON THE OCCASION OF SIGNING THE ARMISTICE

The German Government will naturally endeavor with all its powers to see that the conditions imposed are executed.

The undersigned plenipotentiaries realize that in some points, at their suggestion, a certain good will has been shown. As a result they can consider that the observations they made November 9 with regard to the armistice terms with Germany and the reply given to them on November 10 constitute an integral part of the agreement as a whole.

But they can let no doubt remain concerning the fact that, specifically, the short period of time allowed for evacuation, as well as the surrender of essential means of transportation, threatens to create a situation making it impossible for them to bring about the execution of the conditions without its being the fault of either the German Government or the German people.

Calling attention to their repeated written and oral declaration, the undersigned plenipotentiaries regard it furthermore as their duty to insist strongly that the execution of this agreement can drive the German people into anarchy and famine.

28. Foch, *Mémoires,* II, 317. The supplementary agreements on evacuation, on communications and transportation, on Helgoland, as well as the list of ships to be surrendered, are all found in Kraus and Rödiger, *Urkunden zum Friedensvertrage,* I, 18–22.

Considering the discussions leading to the armistice, we might have hoped for conditions that would have brought an end to the sufferings of noncombatants, of women and children, at the same time that it assured the enemy full and complete military security.

The German people, which held off a world of enemies for fifty months, will preserve their liberty and their unity despite every kind of violence.

A nation of seventy millions of people suffers, but it does not die.[29]

"Très bien," said Marshal Foch. He thereupon declared the session at an end, and the German delegates withdrew. It was 5.30. There was no shaking of hands as the two delegations took leave of each other.[30]

Foch immediately sent the following message to the Commanders-in-Chief on all fronts by radio and by telephone:

1. Hostilities will cease on the entire front on November 11, at 11 A.M., French time.

2. Until further orders Allied troops will not go beyond the line reached on this day and at this hour.

Make a precise report on this line.

3. All communication with the enemy is forbidden until the receipt of instructions sent to the commanders of armies.[31]

At 5.45 Mordacq received word in Paris that the armistice was signed. He hurried to report to Clemenceau, arriving at six o'clock. The Premier had not slept well during the night; when he heard the good news, he was unable to speak. He held Mordacq in his arms, pressing him close, too deeply moved to say anything for several minutes. Mordacq went on to notify Poincaré, President of the Republic, whom he informed of Clemenceau's plan to keep the armistice a secret until he could reveal it to the Chamber of Deputies in the afternoon. He also called on Foreign Minister Pichon, Naval Minister Leygues, and Colonel House. All were still abed. Everyone was profoundly moved to realize that the war was ended. Colonel House said it was the greatest joy in his life. "In the history of mankind," he commented, "it was one more triumph of civilization over barbarism."

29. Foch, *Mémoires,* II, 318–319.
30. *Ibid.,* p. 319; Erzberger, *Erlebnisse,* p. 336.
31. Foch, *Mémoires,* II, 319.

And he concluded with the remark that "at last our dead on the *Lusitania* are avenged." [32]

At about 9.30 Clemenceau received Marshal Foch and Admiral Wemyss at the War Ministry, the Marshal carrying in his brief case the terms of armistice signed by the Germans that morning. "I drove back to Paris with the Marshal," writes Wemyss, "and went straight with him to the Ministry of War, where we were received by Clemenceau, whose joy and satisfaction he made no attempt to conceal, and taking my right hand in his left and the Marshal's left hand in his right, Foch and I joining hands equally, we all warmly congratulated one another." [33]

About 10.30 Foch called on Poincaré. He told the President that Clemenceau had abandoned his intention to keep the armistice a secret until the meeting of the Deputies in the afternoon, reserving for that occasion the publication of the actual terms of armistice. According to Poincaré Foch said "that the Germans accepted the conditions that he gave them, but that they did not declare themselves vanquished and the worst is that they do not believe that they are vanquished." It was not until 3.30 in the afternoon, at a meeting of the Council of Ministers, that Poincaré saw Clemenceau, whom he kissed warmly in gratitude for the work that had been accomplished. "Since this morning," said Clemenceau, "I have been kissed by more than five hundred girls." [34]

At four o'clock Clemenceau read the terms of the armistice to an enthusiastic and emotional Chamber of Deputies. He had no comment to make on the terms. "For me, after the reading of the armistice agreement," he said, "it seems that . . . my work is done." Then in the name of the Republic, "one and indivisible," he hailed the return of Alsace and Lorraine. He paid a lofty tribute to the *poilu* of France, who was, in his words, "yesterday the soldier of God, today is the soldier of humanity and will always be the soldier of the ideal." The Deputies voted their gratitude immediately to "Citizen Georges Clemenceau, the Armies of the Republic, and Marshal Foch."

A similar scene was enacted in the Senate when Clemenceau appeared to read the armistice terms there. He repeated his

32. Mordacq, *L'Armistice,* pp. 78–81; Mordacq, *La Vérité,* pp. 43–44. Colonel House knew at 5.30 that the armistice had been signed. Seymour, *House Papers,* IV, 142.

33. Lady Wester Wemyss, *Life and Letters of Admiral Wemyss,* p. 395. Cf. Weygand, *Le 11 Novembre,* pp. 75–78.

34. Poincaré, *Victoire et Armistice, 1918,* p. 413.

emotional welcome to Alsace and Lorraine. The real significance for France of the victory over Germany became manifest in the reading of the protest of the French National Assembly of 1871 against the incorporation of the two provinces into Germany. Clemenceau had signed that protest! The Senate voted that a bust of Clemenceau should be made and placed beside those of the great men of France.

At eleven o'clock that night General Pétain signed France's last war communiqué. There would be no more for the files. Underneath his signature of approval he scribbled the words, "Fermé pour cause de victoire." [35]

England, like France, was profoundly stirred by the early morning news that the war was over; but the Anglo-Saxon reaction differed from the French. In the morning there was a meeting of the Cabinet and fears were expressed on Bolshevism's taking control in Germany. In telegrams to Lloyd George the day before Clemenceau had expressed his fear "that Germany will break up and Bolshevism become rampant." After the Cabinet meeting the Army Council went to Buckingham Palace, to be received by the King and Queen. "The King made us the most charming little speech, and the Queen cried. A *delightful* little informal human ceremony," wrote Field Marshal Sir Henry Wilson in his diary.[36]

It had been agreed by Clemenceau and Lloyd George that the parliaments of England and of France should learn of the armistice terms at the same hour, at four in the afternoon. At the appointed hour Lloyd George read the terms in the House of Commons. There were no emotional outbursts like those that interrupted Clemenceau in the Chamber of Deputies. He ended his reading with these words:

> Those are the conditions of the Armistice. Thus at 11 o'clock this morning came to an end the cruellest and most terrible war that has ever scourged mankind. I hope we may say that thus, this fateful morning, came to an end all wars.
>
> This is no time for words. Our hearts are too full of a gratitude to which no tongue can give adequate expression. I will, therefore, move "That this House do immediately adjourn, until this time to-

35. Mordacq, *L'Armistice,* p. 214 note.
36. Callwell, *Field-Marshal Sir Henry Wilson,* II, 148–149.

morrow, and that we proceed, as a House of Commons, to St. Margaret's, to give humble and reverent thanks for the deliverance of the world from its greatest peril."

The motion was adopted and both Houses of Parliament "attended a Service of Thanksgiving to Almighty God, on the conclusion of the Armistice signed this day." [37]

Walking home after dinner that night at 10 Downing Street, Sir Henry Wilson found enthusiastic crowds everywhere. "As he made his way along Buckingham Palace Road he came upon an elderly well-dressed woman, a pathetic figure in deep mourning, alone and sobbing her heart out. Distressed at such a spectacle amid the tumultuous rejoicings on all sides, he went up to her, stopped and murmured, 'You are in trouble—is there anything that I can do for you?' She looked up bravely. 'Thank you. No,' she replied. 'I am crying, but I am happy, for now I know that all my three sons who have been killed in the war have not died in vain.' " [38]

In Washington President Wilson had sat up late waiting for reports that the armistice had been signed. But when the news arrived at 2.25 A.M. he had gone to bed and did not learn of it until breakfast. He then declared a holiday for government workers and prepared the following announcement for the people of the United States:

> The armistice was signed this morning. Everything for which America fought has been accomplished. It will now be our fortunate duty to assist by example, by sober, friendly counsel and by material aid in the establishment of just democracy throughout the world.[39]

At one o'clock the President addressed Congress in the House Chamber. After reading the armistice terms, which were cheered, he had these words to say, which were not cheered:

> The war thus comes to an end; for, having accepted these terms of armistice, it will be impossible for the German command to renew it.

37. *Parliamentary Debates, House of Commons,* November 11, 1918. Cf. *War Memoirs of David Lloyd George,* VI, 292–293.
38. Callwell, *Field-Marshal Sir Henry Wilson,* II, 149.
39. Baker, *Wilson,* VIII, 580. Cf. Edith Bolling Wilson, *My Memoir* (Indianapolis, 1938), p. 170.

It is not now possible to assess the consequences of this great consummation. . . . We know . . . that the object of the war is attained . . . and attained with a sweeping completeness which even now we do not realize. Armed imperialism . . . is at an end. . . . The great nations which associated themselves to destroy it have now definitely united in the common purpose to set up such a peace as will satisfy the longing of the whole world for disinterested justice, embodied in settlements which are based upon something much better and more lasting than the selfish competitive interests of powerful states. There is no longer any conjecture as to the objects the victors have in mind. They have a mind in the matter, not only, but a heart also. Their avowed and concerted purpose is to satisfy and protect the weak as well as to accord their just rights to the strong.

The humane temper and intention of the victorious Governments has already been manifested in a very practical way. Their representatives in the Supreme War Council at Versailles have by unanimous resolution assured the peoples of the Central Powers that everything that is possible in the circumstances will be done to supply them with food and relieve the distressing want that is in so many places threatening their very lives. . . . Hunger does not breed reform; it breeds madness and all the ugly distempers that make an ordered life impossible. . . .

To conquer with arms is to make only a temporary conquest; to conquer the world by earning its esteem is to make permanent conquest. I am confident that the nations that have learned the discipline of freedom and that have settled with self-possession to its ordered practice are now about to make conquest of the world by the sheer power of example and of friendly helpfulness.[40]

A sense of destiny possessed many Americans at this point in history, difficult to reconcile with the "normalcy" the nation was soon to restore. Comments on the armistice were in the grand manner of men given to viewing perspectives of history. "Surely, therefore," wrote the editor of the *New York Tribune* on the morning of November 12 about the war, "this was not for us the great adventure. Destiny must have reserved for us an errand that shall really try our strength."

President Wilson's Secretary of Agriculture, David F. Houston, expressed better than anybody else what the significance of the armistice was not to be:

40. *Congressional Record,* November 11, 1918, pp. 11538–11539.

This armistice marks the turning point in one of the world's great epochs. It may be thought of in comparison with the turning back of the Persians, the Fall of Rome, the breaking up of the Feudal System, and the French Revolution.[41]

Forced to wait until they had received their copies of the armistice documents, the German delegates could not leave Rethondes until after 11 A.M. on November 11. At their request the French gave every facility to Captain Geyer to leave by air for German Army Headquarters with a copy of the armistice and with maps needed for the evacuation of troops from occupied areas.[42]

Although doubtful that the German Government could carry out the terms of the armistice, Erzberger felt satisfied with the work he had done. He was most deeply troubled by the Allied occupation of the left bank of the Rhine and by the failure to return German war prisoners. He felt that he had moderated the Allied demands in important respects: Alsace-Lorraine was not to be regarded as occupied territory but was to be treated as a part of Germany; the number of machine guns to be handed over had been cut from 30,000 to 25,000; the number of airplanes cut down from 2,000 to 1,700; the neutral zone on the right bank of the Rhine narrowed in width from 30–40 kilometers to 10; the time limit for evacuating Rhenish territory had been increased from 25 to 31 days. It was gratifying to get a promise that "nobody [in evacuated territory] would be punished for participation in war measures prior to the signing of the armistice." The promise was also given that no policy would be adopted in occupied territories injurious to industrial establishments or reducing the number of workers. The number of lorries to be handed over had been reduced from 10,000 to 5,000, the transfer to take place in 36 days instead of the original 15. There was to be no interference with the repatriation of German prisoners in neutral countries. The Allies promised that the repatriation of Germans held as prisoners of war would be regulated when the preliminary peace was signed. There was no demand that German troops be immediately evacuated out of territory formerly belonging to Russia. At first the Allies had sought the surrender of 160 submarines—many more than Germany possessed; in the

41. Houston, *Eight Years with Wilson's Cabinet,* I, 326.
42. Foch, *Mémoires,* II, 319; Erzberger, *Erlebnisse,* p. 338.

end she was required to hand over merely all she had.[43] Erzberger was pleased that the Allies would "consider" the feeding of Germany, as found necessary, during the period of the armistice. And the armistice was extended from 30 to 36 days.[44]

About ten o'clock Monday morning other German officers arrived, but there was nothing for them to do. Their demands or desires had already been taken care of. Erzberger learned from them that the Kaiser and the Crown Prince had both fled to Holland. But more surprising, he learned that the telegram that had come the previous night with the signature of the Imperial Chancellor authorizing him to sign the armistice had not come from the Chancellor but had issued from the Army High Command instead. The Chancellor had agreed to it after the despatch had gone out.[45]

The coaches had drawn shades when they left Rethondes the morning of the 11th with the German armistice delegation. The stations they passed were crowded with people, who manifested great joy and sometimes uttered threats against the Germans. At 4 P.M. the Armistice Commission arrived at Tergnier; two hours later it left by automobile for Germany. At 2 A.M. on the 12th the delegates arrived at the French front; at 9 they were in Spa. Here Erzberger received the congratulations of the Representative of the Foreign Office, who said that everybody at headquarters had been surprised that he had achieved so much in his negotiations with the enemy. A meeting was held to set up the German branch of the International Armistice Commission at Spa, with General von Winterfeldt to be its head.

Erzberger now learned about the revolution in Germany. He had heard that the Soldiers' and Workers' Council at Spa had threatened to arrest both Groener and Hindenburg. He saw that the men refused to salute their officers and went about in cars flying Red flags. At one o'clock a special train arrived with delegates from a Soldiers' and Workers' Council in Hanover, on their way to Brussels, where they planned to proclaim the "world

43. It is interesting that both Erzberger and Wemyss should be pleased with this point. "On discussing the submarine situation," writes Wemyss in his account of the final drafting of the armistice terms, "he [Erzberger] told me, somewhat to my surprise, that there were not nearly a hundred and sixty to be had—this gave me the chance of getting what I had always wanted, viz. *all* the submarines." Lady Wester Wemyss, *Life and Letters of Admiral Wemyss,* p. 394.

44. Erzberger, *Erlebnisse,* pp. 336–337.

45. *Ibid.,* p. 338. Erzberger is in error regarding the Crown Prince, who did not leave Germany for Holland until the morning of November 12.

revolution." They wished to make Liebknecht President of Germany. Erzberger dissuaded them from going on to Brussels and even got them to take him to Berlin in the train they had commandeered. Everywhere they saw trains crowded with soldiers. Late Wednesday afternoon, November 13, Erzberger reached Berlin and made his report to the new Socialist Government. He found the officials nervous because there was no protection against the Independents and the Spartacists, who might at any moment seize power and form a radical government.[46]

The armistice led to no celebrations in Berlin, where the provisional Government was busily striving against great odds to strengthen its feeble foundations. Actually, the news that the war had ended was of minor significance by comparison with reports of princes abandoning their thrones, of cities falling under revolutionary control, of republics springing up everywhere. There was relief, to be sure, in the thought that the fighting was over "out there." But at home, it seemed, the fighting was about to begin. The bi-Socialist Government in Berlin knew that its days were numbered if it failed to win the support of the masses. The evils of the war had to be liquidated if civil war were to be averted. To that task the Government gave its first attention. Proclamations announced the end of martial law; the press and the theater were no longer subject to censorship; religious liberty was to be guaranteed; political prisoners were to be amnestied; the eight-hour day would be adopted with the beginning of the new year; and free elections would determine Germany's political future. But what was needed above all was food, and food would come when the blockade of the armistice came to an end in peace. Hence the Government's plea to Wilson:

> Now that the armistice has been concluded, the German Government begs the President of the United States to initiate negotiations for peace. Since haste is essential, the Government suggests consideration of the proposal to conclude a preliminary peace and asks to be informed of the time and place for the commencement of such negotiations. Because of the threatening food shortage the German Government attaches special importance to the immediate inception of such negotiations.[47]

At the same time the leaders of the two Socialist parties ap-

46. *Ibid.*, pp. 338–340.
47. *Vossische Zeitung*, November 12, 1918, No. 580.

pealed to the proletariat of other lands for help, to prevent the spoliation of Germany by the common capitalist enemy of all workers. There was a blind belief that the common man everywhere was in revolution or about to rebel, that a protest could be addressed to him against the armistice and the blockade. There was a faith that a new era—an international socialist era—had begun.

XVI

Conclusion

SINCE 1918 the armistice has been both misunderstood and regretted in Germany as well as in the countries that fought her. In both camps people have argued that the war ended too soon and that the peace that followed would have been a better one if the fighting had gone on to a decisive finish. Among themselves Germans have disputed the question of responsibility for ending the war more than they have argued with the victorious Allies over the question of responsibility for causing the war.

The German High Command, finding early that its request for peace and armistice brought with it some unpleasant consequences for Germany's future and for its own reputation, created a legend that shifted the responsibility from Ludendorff and Hindenburg to others—civilians, Socialists, Bolsheviks, Jews, Free Masons, and pacifists were eventually included in the treasonous group—who "stabbed in the back" an Army and a Navy eager to continue the fight and capable of achieving a complete victory. Even though it was apparent to many in October, 1918, that the High Command was trying to shift the blame to others when it failed to get the Government of Prince Max to break off the negotiations it had forced the Government to initiate, the myth became reality for millions of Germans. Even Prince Max more or less unwittingly contributed to the legend by criticizing Scheidemann and other Socialists, by attacking the mutineers in the Navy, and by shielding the High Command with his own name in early October, when it would have been most damaging to let the Entente Powers or Germans on the fighting front know that the Government's ranking military leaders had found the military outlook utterly hopeless and desired an immediate end to the war.

This "stab-in-the-back" explanation of Germany's collapse in 1918 is one of the boldest and most successful attempts in history to tamper with fact and to shift responsibility. It would be foolish to assert that discontent on the home front had nothing to do with the poor morale on the fighting front, that radical propaganda at home and from abroad—including the Fourteen Points—played no role whatsoever, that Majority Socialists, Independent Socialists, and even Russian agents did nothing to weaken Germany's political front. To make these factors, on the other hand, the sole cause or even the major cause of Germany's defeat is an equally untenable thesis. The truth lies between the two extremes and places a greater responsibility on the sponsors of the "stab-in-the-back" legend.

Whoever blames the Bolsheviks and makes the Russian Embassy in Berlin the center of revolutionary propaganda in 1918 places a good deal of responsibility on General Ludendorff, who had arranged in 1917 for the passage of Lenin across Germany to Russia. Ludendorff says that the move to bring about the collapse of Russia was justifiable from the military point of view; but he adds that the responsibility was a great one since the Government would have to take precautions lest Germany suffer harm from it.[1]

But Ludendorff has a greater responsibility than this. In fact, if one must choose between simple alternatives, it is possible to point an accusing finger at him and say that he stabbed the German Army in the back in 1918. When he came at the end of September to the conclusion that an immediate armistice was absolutely necessary, he reached that decision without consulting any of the generals on the fighting front although he claimed later he had done so. He did consult Hindenburg, who approved; but the latter was hardly more than a sounding board for the opinions that came from the First Quartermaster General. The fighting men, from the highest ranks down, did not know that Ludendorff had made this decision and had forced the Government of Prince Max to send the first note to Wilson. Officers of the Army and Navy believed that the peace move was wholly the voluntary act of the new regime, and they proceeded to blame the Chancellor for its damaging effect on morale. These officers were amazed to learn later that Ludendorff had been behind the move.

The first note to Wilson and Prince Max's speech to the Reichstag on October 5 marked the turning point in 1918. Germans never recovered from the shock produced by the revelation that further fighting was hopeless. Ludendorff professed his complete inability to understand why this should be so—he knew it was to his interest to put on the cloak of innocence.

To millions of war-weary Germans the prospect of ending the war in a peace based on Wilson's Fourteen Points brought great hope; they saw no reason for continuing a costly struggle for something far worse. Quite naturally, the masses of people acquired a vested interest in a Wilsonian peace, and the new Gov-

1. Ludendorff, *Kriegserinnerungen,* p. 407.

ernment—particularly the Socialists in it—could not betray that hope. This was the moment when Ludendorff changed his mind and argued that negotiations with Wilson should be broken off; suddenly, for reasons he could never get his critics to understand, he became convinced that Germany could fight on and get better terms than those offered by Wilson. In his mind these terms would be better only because none could be worse. The refusal of the civilian Government to comply with the demand of the Army and Navy Commands to cancel the negotiations with the American President tends to confer a measure of credibility on the "stab-in-the-back" legend. This is to omit, however, the responsibility of Ludendorff for what had led to this attitude in Berlin.

The Army and Navy now took matters into their own hands. In defiance of the Government Ludendorff and Hindenburg issued their proclamation to the Army on the 24th virtually calling for a break with Wilson because his third note was "a demand for unconditional surrender . . . unacceptable to us soldiers"; then they hurried off to Berlin to persuade the Kaiser to break with Wilson. All this was too much for Prince Max, who forced the Kaiser to dismiss Ludendorff. The Naval Command was more cautious. It made plans for a final battle with the British fleet in order to avoid surrender without a fight—sufficiently doubtful of the propriety of the plan to keep all knowledge of its intentions from civilian authorities in Berlin—and that led to the mutiny in the Navy.

Whatever else one can say, nothing can eliminate these facts from history: that Ludendorff was the first to insist upon an armistice, that he lied when he said he had consulted other generals about it, that he forced his decision on a civilian Government which opposed it and wanted to keep on fighting, that he later changed his mind and sought to make others responsible for the consequences of his own acts.

Although the first person to insist upon an armistice, Ludendorff was not the first to suggest that the Fourteen Points be made the basis of the coming peace. That suggestion came from three civilians in the Foreign Office and was made before the High Command had decided that the war must end. Ludendorff was too much concerned with avoiding defeat to consider anything but the urgency of ending the hostilities. His frequent use of the expressions "mass attacks" and "break-through" suggests what his fears were. His utter refusal to consider the consequences of the move to end the war, his forcing the new Government against its judgment to despatch the first note to Wilson, his later efforts to have negotiations broken off (possibly because the break-through he had feared did not occur), his impassioned disclaimers of all responsibility—all this gives the impression of a man obsessed by fear, fear of defeat and fear for his own reputation.

It was unfortunate that, for the sake of the symbol, Ludendorff could not have been made to approach Foch bearing the white flag of surrender. By that time, however, Ludendorff had been dismissed from his post. Even if he had continued in the High Command, he would not have been entrusted with that particular mission. Two reasons would have counseled against his appointment to the Armistice Commission: first, reports from abroad that the Allies would not negotiate with any member of the High Command; and, second, the certainty that Ludendorff would have been glad to have the opportunity to break off negotiations with President Wilson. Such a break was the last thing the Government wanted.

There is no evidence to support the assertion that the new Government was merely a front behind which the High Command and the Kaiser sought to hide in order to bring the war to an end in a way favorable to their interests. It was natural, however, for the Allies to think so in 1918, when relatively minor steps had been taken toward making Germany a democratic state. The Kaiser sought to get credit at home and abroad for this constitutional transformation, but he was thwarted in his efforts by Prince Max and others in the Cabinet. So opposed eventually were the interests of the Kaiser and Ludendorff to those of the new Government that collaboration between them became impossible. The parties in the Cabinet of Prince Max were democratic parties; and there is no small element of tragedy in the fact that wartime propaganda against Germany and the want of information about developments in that country kept the old democracies from giving much-needed assistance to the newest one.

The armistice of November, 1918, was not an unconditional surrender even though Germany accepted virtually all the terms that the Entente Powers had drafted. Erzberger would have denied that he accepted the Allies' terms without question or negotiation; in fact, he looked upon his work at Rethondes as very successful diplomacy and was proud of the ameliorations he effected in the original terms presented to him by Foch. In their first note to Wilson the Germans had not merely requested an armistice; they also asked him to summon a conference of all belligerents to establish peace on the basis of the program he had enunciated. In the pre-armistice agreement the Entente Powers declared themselves willing to make peace with Germany on the basis of Wilson's principles except for the two qualifications about the "freedom of the seas" and reparations. This binding promise and the belief that a conference would soon be summoned to make such a peace enabled the Germans to sign the armistice without feeling they were signing a blank check. The pre-armistice agreement deprived the Entente of the legal and moral right to do as they pleased with Germany, a right they could be presumed to have acquired under an unconditional surrender. This obligation was acknowledged by the Allied and Associated Powers on June 16, 1919, when they answered the charge of the German peace delegates that the treaty of peace violated the Wilsonian principles that were to be its foundation. "These are the principles upon which hostilities were abandoned in November, 1918," said the Allied note; "these are the principles upon which the Allied and Associated Powers agreed that peace might be based; these are the principles which have guided them in the deliberations which have led to the formulation of the conditions of peace."[2]

Would the Germans have asked for an armistice when they did if there had been no Fourteen Points? So far as Ludendorff goes, the question must be answered affirmatively; he had to have the war ended without much consideration of conditions. But could Ludendorff have forced the Government of Prince Max to send off a note to Wilson had there been no Fourteen Points? Although we have no evidence to make a definite answer to the question, it seems very likely that the Fourteen Points made it possible for the Government to accede to Ludendorff's demand, even though doubts were expressed about some of those points. When Prince Max's correspondence with Wilson revealed to the masses of Ger-

2. For the correspondence between the Germans and the Allied and Associated Powers on this point see Kraus and Rödiger, *Urkunden zum Friedensvertrage,* I, 433–549, 555–683. General Smuts also agreed "that we are under solemn obligation . . . to make a Wilson Peace," but he thought that "a number of provisions . . . seem to me to be both against the letter and the spirit of [the Fourteen] Points." Smuts to Wilson, May 30, 1919, R. S. Baker, *Woodrow Wilson and World Settlement* (three vols., New York, 1923), III, 466–468. Commenting on Wilson's second note in the middle of October, 1918, Winston Churchill said that the Allies "are not asking for the unconditional surrender of the German nation." He believed that "the terms of President Wilson clearly offer to the Germans the assurance of safety, of life and of freedom." Quoted in the London *Times,* October 16, 1918.

man people that a better peace could be had by negotiation than by fighting, public opinion in favor of such a peace became so strong that the Army, the Navy, and the Government had to yield to it. The Fourteen Points had done their work well. Had the Germans been confronted by a demand for unconditional surrender in 1918, the war would not have ended in that year.

In the course of time many Germans came to regret that they had placed any faith in Wilson, in his Fourteen Points, in talk of a peace of reconciliation and of understanding, in any promise of good in the creation of a league of nations. Von Tirpitz came to be regarded as a prophet for his warning to the Government in 1918 that the Fourteen Points were sharp barbs on a hook rather than a charter for a new world order. For most Germans the passing of time was to justify the varying degrees of doubt that many leaders had of the Fourteen Points in 1918—Prince Max, Walther Rathenau, Stresemann, and others.

Within the Entente the opinion has been often expressed that the armistice was premature, that Germany should have been invaded and forced to consume at home the type of violence hitherto made in Germany for consumption abroad, that the military machine could and should have been crushed, that the armistice should have been signed in Berlin, that the Fourteen Points should not have been allowed to obstruct that consummation of the war, that the armistice and peace treaty were too mild and generous. Between 1918 and his death in 1929 Marshal Foch had to defend himself against French critics who said that he agreed too soon to an armistice. In defense he argued that there was no sense in prolonging the war and killing some hundreds of thousands more men merely to get accepted in Berlin the very conditions the enemy was ready to accept elsewhere. Furthermore, Haig and Pétain had agreed with Foch; only Pershing dissented. Conditions in France and England made both Clemenceau and Lloyd George anxious to have the war over as soon as possible. After four years of fighting people in both countries were war weary; they thought that the Americans, with their relatively small losses, had no real understanding of what it meant to continue the war. In fact, both Haig and Pétain believed it difficult for the English and French Armies to carry the war into Germany; nobody seemed to think that the Americans were capable of doing it. Pershing's opposition to the armistice and his desire to keep on fighting were regarded as both naïve and theatrical. Clemenceau's anxiety lest Erzberger had been deprived by revolution of the authority to sign an armistice for Germany and his determination despite that fear to have Erzberger sign for his country signify much with regard to the French Premier's eagerness to have the war ended. In England, the lack of replacements for the Army, the numerous strikes, the growing coal shortage, the devastating influenza epidemic,[3] and the perennial Irish question had much to do with Lloyd George's wish to bring the war to an end. As we have seen, war-weariness was a strong force in 1918 in France and England; and each power feared that the other would make demands so harsh that Germany would not agree to an armistice. The fear of spreading Bolshevism was real even though it was often said that Germany was deceiving the Allies by using the argument to win favors for herself. Neither France nor England desired to see Germany possessed by that demonic spirit. Foch was sufficiently impressed by Erzberger's fears of Bolshevism to allow the Germans more machine guns to block the advancing terror.

President Wilson, too, had his reasons for speeding the end of the war. Once the opportunity offered itself to refashion the world on the framework of the Fourteen Points, he could only hasten to its consummation. His readiness to incur the wrath of his political enemies at home and of the Allies abroad in order to accomplish this act of creation is a tribute to his quixotic and optimistic idealism, whatever one may think or say about the practicability of his program or the methods used in getting the Allies to accept it. To get them into the proper frame of mind to accept his program he favored an armistice that, while making it impossible for Germany to renew the struggle, would leave her strong enough to produce that feeling of insecurity which would predispose England and France toward a genuine peace settlement. By exerting every pressure Colonel House and President Wilson got the Fourteen Points essentially accepted by Italy, France, and England only to find that the program, which had been made the major issue in the Congressional elections of November 5, was not acceptable to the American people, who rejected the President's plea for support by returning a Republican Congress. Wilson and the liberal Germans who had taken control of the Government in October had a great faith and a high stake in the Fourteen Points, and both made the venture of faith only to lose. A more tragic experience than Wilson's on November 5 is hard to come by—the day dawned as triumph, it ended as defeat. Those who would

3. For the last half of October and the early days of November over 7,000 deaths a week were being reported in Great Britain.

blame a cynical Clemenceau or a mercurial Lloyd George for that outcome should re-study the history of the United States in the fall of 1918.

The Allies have charged that Wilson forced them into a premature armistice. The fact is that he left it to them on October 23 to decide whether or not an armistice should be granted. Wilson's responsibility lies in his determination to commit the Allies to his peace program when they decided to grant an armistice. War-weariness abroad and the general popularity of his program among those who desired a peace of reconciliation came to his assistance. Some people have charged that Wilson gave the Allies too little time to consider armistice terms by waiting until October 23 before submitting to them the correspondence he had had with Germany. The fact is that Frenchmen and Englishmen actually began their consideration of specific terms before the United States did: Wemyss and Foch set to work in their respective countries immediately after the despatch of the first German note to America. They were better prepared than was General Pershing, who wanted to debate the question whether any armistice should be granted.

So weary of war had people everywhere become by the fall of 1918 that November 11 was greeted with a delirium of joy throughout the world. In their sense of relief men thought that a new era had begun; in fact, only a war had come to an end. The treaties that followed the war should have inaugurated that new era. The fact, however, that the signing of the armistice on November 11, 1918, should be more celebrated than the signing of the Treaty of Versailles on June 28, 1919, is a monument to the simple truth that men find it easier to end a war than to make a peace.

APPENDIX A

PRESIDENT WILSON'S PROGRAM

A. The Fourteen Points, January 8, 1918

1. Open covenants of peace, openly arrived at, after which there shall be no private international understandings of any kind but diplomacy shall proceed always frankly and in the public view.
2. Absolute freedom of navigation upon the seas, outside territorial waters, alike in peace and in war, except as the seas may be closed in whole or in part by international action for the enforcement of international covenants.
3. The removal, so far as possible, of all economic barriers and the establishment of an equality of trade conditions among all the nations consenting to the peace and associating themselves for its maintenance.
4. Adequate guarantees given and taken that national armaments will be reduced to the lowest point consistent with domestic safety.
5. A free, open-minded, and absolutely impartial adjustment of all colonial claims, based upon a strict observance of the principle that in determining all such questions of sovereignty the interests of the populations concerned must have equal weight with the equitable claims of the government whose title is to be determined.
6. The evacuation of all Russian territory and such a settlement of all questions affecting Russia as will secure the best and freest cooperation of the other nations of the world in obtaining for her an unhampered and unembarrassed opportunity for the independent determination of her own political development and national policy and assure her of a sincere welcome into the society of free nations under institutions of her own choosing; and, more than a welcome, assistance also of every kind that she may need and may herself desire. The treatment accorded Russia by her sister nations in the months to come will be the acid test of their good will, of their comprehension of her needs as distinguished from their own interests, and of their intelligent and unselfish sympathy.
7. Belgium, the whole world will agree, must be evacuated and restored, without any attempt to limit the sovereignty which she enjoys in common with all other free nations. No other single act will serve as this will serve to restore confidence among the nations in the laws which they have themselves set and determined for the

government of their relations with one another. Without this healing act the whole structure and validity of international law is forever impaired.

8. All French territory should be freed and the invaded portions restored, and the wrong done to France by Prussia in 1871 in the matter of Alsace-Lorraine, which has unsettled the peace of the world for nearly fifty years, should be righted, in order that peace may once more be made secure in the interest of all.

9. A readjustment of the frontiers of Italy should be effected along clearly recognizable lines of nationality.

10. The peoples of Austria-Hungary, whose place among the nations we wish to see safeguarded and assured, should be accorded the freest opportunity of autonomous development.

11. Rumania, Serbia, and Montenegro should be evacuated; occupied territories restored; Serbia accorded free and secure access to the sea; and the relations of the several Balkan states to one another determined by friendly counsel along historically established lines of allegiance and nationality; and international guarantees of the political and economic independence and territorial integrity of the several Balkan states should be entered into.

12. The Turkish portions of the present Ottoman Empire should be assured a secure sovereignty, but the other nationalities which are now under Turkish rule should be assured an undoubted security of life and an absolutely unmolested opportunity of autonomous development, and the Dardanelles should be permanently opened as a free passage to the ships and commerce of all nations under international guarantees.

13. An independent Polish state should be erected which should include the territories inhabited by indisputably Polish populations, which should be assured a free and secure access to the sea, and whose political and economic independence and territorial integrity should be guaranteed by international covenant.

14. A general association of nations must be formed under specific covenants for the purpose of affording mutual guarantees of political independence and territorial integrity to great and small states alike.

B. The Four Principles of February 11, 1918

1. That each part of the final settlement must be based upon the essential justice of that particular case and upon such adjustments as are most likely to bring a peace that will be permanent.

2. That peoples and provinces are not to be bartered about from sovereignty to sovereignty as if they were mere chattels and pawns in a game, even the great game, now forever discredited, of the balance of power, but that,
3. Every territorial settlement involved in this war must be made in the interest and for the benefit of the populations concerned, and not as a part of any mere adjustment or compromise of claims amongst rival states; and
4. That all well-defined national aspirations shall be accorded the utmost satisfaction that can be accorded them without introducing new or perpetuating old elements of discord and antagonism that would be likely in time to break the peace of Europe and consequently of the world.

C. The Four Points of July 4, 1918

1. The destruction of every arbitrary power anywhere that can separately, secretly, and of its single choice disturb the peace of the world; or, if it cannot be presently destroyed, at the least its reduction to virtual impotence.
2. The settlement of every question, whether of territory, of sovereignty, of economic arrangement, or of political relationship upon the basis of the free acceptance of that settlement by the people immediately concerned, and not upon the basis of the material interest or advantage of any other nation or people which may desire a different settlement for the sake of its own exterior influence or mastery.
3. The consent of all nations to be governed in their conduct toward each other by the same principles of honor and of respect for the common law of civilized society that govern the individual citizens of all modern States in their relations with one another; to the end that all promises and covenants may be sacredly observed, no private plots or conspiracies hatched, no selfish injuries wrought with impunity, and a mutual trust established upon the handsome foundation of a mutual respect for right.
4. The establishment of an organization of peace which shall make it certain that the combined power of free nations will check every invasion of right and serve to make peace and justice the more secure by affording a definite tribunal of opinion to which all must submit and by which every international readjustment that cannot be amicably agreed upon by the peoples directly concerned shall be sanctioned. These great objects can be put into a single sentence.

What we seek is the reign of law, based upon the consent of the governed and sustained by the organized opinion of mankind.

D. The five particulars of September 27, 1918

1. The impartial justice meted out must involve no discrimination between those to whom we wish to be just and those to whom we do not wish to be just. It must be a justice that plays no favourites, and knows no standards but the equal rights of the several peoples concerned.
2. No special or separate interest of any single nation or group of nations can be made the basis of any part of the settlement which is not consistent with the common interest of all.
3. There can be no leagues or alliances or special covenants and understandings within the general and common family of the League of Nations.
4. And more specifically, there can be no special, selfish, economic combinations within the League, and no employment of any form of economic boycott or exclusion except as the power of economic penalty by exclusion from the markets of the world may be vested in the League of Nations itself as a means of discipline and control.
5. All international agreements and treaties of every kind must be made known in their entirety to the rest of the world.

APPENDIX B

THE ARMISTICE CONVENTION WITH BULGARIA

Signed September 29, 1918

I. Immediate evacuation, in conformity with an arrangement to be concluded, of the territories still occupied in Greece and Serbia. There shall be removed from these territories neither cattle, grain, nor stores of any kind. No damage shall be done on departure. The Bulgarian Administration shall continue to exercise its functions in the parts of Bulgaria at present occupied by the Allies.

II. Immediate demobilization of all Bulgarian armies, save for the maintenance on a war footing of a group of all arms, comprising three divisions of sixteen battalions each and four regiments of cavalry, which shall be thus disposed: two divisions for the defence of the Eastern frontier of Bulgaria and of the Dobrudja, and the 148th Division for the protection of the railways.

III. Deposit, at points to be indicated by the High Command of the Armies of the East, of the arms, ammunition, and military vehicles belonging to the demobilized units which shall thereafter be stored by the Bulgarian authorities, under the control of the Allies.

The horses likewise will be handed over to the Allies.

IV. Restoration to Greece of the material of the IVth Greek Army Corps, which was taken from the Greek army at the time of the occupation of Eastern Macedonia, in so far as it has not been sent to Germany.

V. The units of the Bulgarian troops at the present time west of the meridian of Uskub, and belonging to the XIth German Army, shall lay down their arms and shall be considered until further notice to be prisoners of war. The officers shall retain their arms.

VI. Employment by the Allied Armies of Bulgarian prisoners of war in the East until the conclusion of peace, without reciprocity as regards Allied prisoners of war. These latter shall be handed over without delay to the Allied authorities, and deported civilians shall be entirely free to return to their homes.

VII. Germany and Austria-Hungary shall have a period of four weeks to withdraw their troops and military organizations. Within the same period the diplomatic and consular representatives of the

Central Powers, as also their nationals, must leave the territory of the Kingdom. Orders for the cessation of hostilities shall be given by the signatories of the present convention.

[Signed] General Franchet D'Esperey
André Liapchef
E. T. Loukof

General Headquarters,
September 29, 1918, 10.50 P.M.

APPENDIX C

THE ARMISTICE WITH AUSTRIA-HUNGARY

I. *Military Clauses*

1. The immediate cessation of hostilities by land, sea and air.

2. Total demobilization of the Austro-Hungarian Army and immediate withdrawal of all Austro-Hungarian forces operating on the front from the North Sea to Switzerland.

Within Austro-Hungarian territory, limited as in clause 3 below, there shall only be maintained as an organized military force a [maximum of 20 divisions], reduced to pre-war [peace] effectives.

Half the divisional, corps and army artillery and equipment shall be collected at points to be indicated by the Allies and United States of America for delivery to them, beginning with all such material as exists in the territories to be evacuated by the Austro-Hungarian forces.

3. Evacuation of all territories invaded by Austria-Hungary since the beginning of war. Withdrawal within such periods as shall be determined by the commander in chief of the Allied forces on each front of the Austro-Hungarian armies behind a line fixed as follows: From Piz Umbrail to the north of the Stelvio it will follow the crest of the Rhetian Alps up to the sources of the Adige and the Eisach, passing thence by Mounts Reschen and Brenner and the Heights of Ötz and Ziller. The line thence turns south crossing Mount Toblach and meeting the present frontier [of the] Carnic Alps. It follows this frontier up to Mount Tarvis and after Mount Tarvis the watershed of the Julian Alps by the Col of Predil, Mount Mangart, the Tricorno (Terglou) and the watershed of the Cols di Podberdo, Podlanischam and Idria. From this point the line turns southeast towards the Schneeberg, excluding the whole basin of the Save and its tributaries; from the Schneeberg it goes down towards the coast in such a way as to include Castua, Mattuglie and Volosca in the evacuated territories.

It will also follow the administrative limits of the present province of Dalmatia, including to the north Lisarica and Trivania and, to the south, territory limited by a line from the [shore] of Cape Planca to the summits of the watershed eastwards so as to include in the evacuated area all the valleys and water courses flowing towards Sebenico, such as the Cikola, Kerka, Butišníca and their tributaries. It will also include all the islands in the north and west of Dalmatia from Premuda, Selve, Ulbo, Scherda, Maon, Pago and Puntadura in the north up to Melida in the south, embracing Sant' Andrea, Busi, Lissa, Lesina, Torcola, Curzola, Cazza and Lagosta, as well as the neighboring rocks and islets and [Pelagosa], only excepting the islands of Great and Small Zirona, Bua, Solta and Brazza.

All territory thus evacuated [will be occupied by the troops] of the Allies and of the United States of America.

All military and railway equipment of all kinds, including coal, belonging to or within those territories, to be left *in situ* and surrendered to the Allies according to special orders given by the commanders in chief of the forces of the Associated Powers on the different fronts. No new destruction, pillage or requisition to be done by enemy troops in the territories to be evacuated by them and occupied by the forces of the Associated Powers.

4. The Allies shall have the right of free movement over all road and rail and waterways in Austro-Hungarian territory and of the use of the necessary Austrian and Hungarian means of transportation.

The armies of the Associated Powers shall occupy such strategic points in Austria-Hungary at such times as they may deem necessary to enable them to conduct military operations or to maintain order.

They shall have the right of requisition on payment for the troops of the Associated Powers wherever they may be.

5. Complete evacuation of all German troops within 15 days, not only from the Italian and Balkan fronts, but from all Austro-Hungarian territory.

Internment of all German troops which have not left Austria-Hungary within that date.

6. The administration of the evacuated territories of Austria-Hungary will be entrusted to the local authorities under the control of the Allied and Associated armies of occupation.

7. The immediate repatriation without reciprocity of all Allied prisoners of war and interned subjects and of civil populations evacuated from their homes on conditions to be laid down by the commanders in chief of the forces of the Associated Powers on the various fronts.

8. Sick and wounded who can not be removed from evacuated territory will be cared for by Austro-Hungarian personnel who will be left on the spot with the medical material required.

II. Naval Conditions

1. Immediate cessation of all hostilities at sea, and definite information to be given as to the location and movements of all Austro-Hungarian ships.

Notification to be made to neutrals that freedom of navigation in all territorial waters is given to the naval and mercantile marines of the Allied and Associated Powers, all questions of neutrality being waived.

2. Surrender to the Allies and the United States of America of 15 Austro-Hungarian submarines, completed between the years 1910 and 1918, and of all German submarines which are in or may hereafter enter Austro-Hungarian territorial waters. All other Austro-Hungarian submarines to be paid off and completely disarmed, and to remain under the supervision of the Allies and United States of America.

3. Surrender to the Allies and United States of America with their complete armament and equipment of 3 battleships, 3 light cruisers, 9 destroyers, 12 torpedo boats, 1 mine layer, 6 Danube monitors, to be designated by the Allies and United States of America. All other surface warships, including river craft, are to be concentrated in Austro-Hungarian naval bases to be designated by the Allies and United States of America and are to be paid off and completely disarmed and placed under the supervision of the Allies and United States of America.

4. Freedom of navigation to all warships and merchant ships of the Allied and Associated Powers to be given in the Adriatic and up the River Danube and its tributaries in the territorial waters and territory of Austria-Hungary.

The Allied and Associated Powers shall have the right to sweep up all mine fields and obstructions and the positions of these are to be indicated.

In order to insure the freedom of navigation on the Danube, the Allies and the United States of America shall be empowered to occupy or to dismantle all fortifications or defense works.

5. The existing blockade conditions set up by the Allied and Associated Powers are to remain unchanged and all Austro-Hungarian merchant ships found at sea are to remain liable to capture, save exceptions which may be made by a commission nominated by the Allies and United States of America.

6. All naval aircraft are to be concentrated and immobilized in

Austro-Hungarian bases to be designated by the Allies and United States of America.

7. Evacuation of all the Italian coasts and of all ports occupied by Austria-Hungary outside their national territory, and the abandonment of all floating craft, naval materials, equipment and materials for inland navigation of all kinds.

8. Occupation by the Allies and the United States of America of the land and sea fortifications and the islands which form the defenses and of the dockyards and arsenal at Pola.

9. All merchant vessels held by Austria-Hungary belonging to the Allied and Associated Powers to be returned.

10. No destruction of ships or of materials to be permitted before evacuation, surrender or restoration.

11. All naval and mercantile marine prisoners of war of the Allied and Associated Powers in Austro-Hungarian hands to be returned without reciprocity.

APPENDIX D

THE ARMISTICE WITH TURKEY

1. Opening of the Dardanelles and Bosphorus and access to the Black Sea. Allied occupation of the Dardanelles and Bosphorus forts.

2. Positions of all mine fields, torpedo tubes and other [obstructions] in Turkish waters to be indicated and assistance given to sweep or remove them as may be required.

3. All available information as to mines in Black Sea to be communicated.

4. All Allied prisoners of war and Armenian interned [persons] and prisoners to be collected at Constantinople and handed over unconditionally to Allies.

5. Immediate demobilization of the Turkish Army except for such troops as are required for surveillance of the frontiers and for maintenance of internal order. (Number of effectives and their disposition to be determined later by Allies after consultation with Turkish Government.)

6. Surrender of all war vessels in Turkish waters or in waters occupied by Turkey, these ships to be interned at such Turkish port or ports as may be directed, except such small vessels as required for police or similar purposes in Turkish territorial waters.

7. The Allies to have the right of occupation of any strategic points, in the event of situation arising which threatens the security of Allies.

8. Free use by Allied ships of all ports and anchorages now in Turkish occupation and denial of their use by [*to*] enemy. Similar conditions to apply to Turkish mercantile shipping in Turkish waters for purposes of trade and the demobilization of the army.

9. Use of all ship repair facilities at all Turkish ports and arsenals.

10. Allied occupation of the Taurus tunnel system.

11. Immediate withdrawal of Turkish troops from northwest Persia to behind the pre-war frontiers has already been ordered and will be carried out. Part of Trans-Caucasus has already been ordered to be evacuated by Turkish troops, the remainder to be evacuated if required by Allies after they have studied the situation there.

12. Wireless telegraph and cable stations to be controlled by Allies, Turkish Government messages excepted.

13. Prohibition to destroy any naval, military or commercial material.

14. Facilities to be given for purchase of coal, oil, fuel and naval material from Turkish sources after requirements of the country have been met. None of the above material to be exported.

15. Allied control officers to be placed on all railways including such portions of Trans-Caucasus railways now under Turkish control which must be placed at the free and complete disposal of the Allied authorities, due consideration being given to needs of population. This clause to include Allied occupation of Batoum. Turks will raise no objection to occupation of Baku by Allies.

16. Surrender of all garrisons in Hedjaz, Asir, Yemen, Syria and Mesopotamia to nearest Allied commander and the withdrawal of troops from Cilicia except those necessary to maintain order as will be determined under clause 5.

17. The surrender of all Turkish officers in Tripolitania and Cyrenaica to nearest Italian garrison. Turkey guarantees to stop supplies and communication with these officers if they do not obey the order to surrender.

18. The surrender of all ports occupied in Tripolitania and Cyrenaica, including Misurata, to nearest Allied garrisons.

19. All Germans and Austrians, naval, military and civilian, to be evacuated within one month from Turkish dominions; those in remote districts as soon after as may be possible.

20. Compliance with such orders as may be conveyed for disposal of the equipment, arms and ammunition, including transport of that portion of the Turkish Army which is demobilized under clause 5.

21. An Allied representative to be attached to Turkish Ministry in order to safeguard Allied interests. This representative to be furnished with all [aid] necessary for this purpose.

22. Turkish prisoners to be kept at the disposal of Allied Powers. The release of Turkish civilian prisoners and prisoners over military age to be considered.

23. Obligation on the part of Turkey to cease all relations with Central Powers.

24. In case of disorder in the six Armenian vilayets the Allies reserve the right to occupy any part of them.

25. Hostilities between the Allies and Turkey shall cease from noon, local time, Thursday, October 31, 1918.

APPENDIX E

MEMORANDUM OF COBB AND LIPPMANN ON THE FOURTEEN POINTS

1. Open covenants of peace, openly arrived at, after which there shall be no private international understandings of any kind, but diplomacy shall proceed always frankly and in the public view.

The purpose is clearly to prohibit treaties, sections of treaties or understandings that are secret, such as the [Triple Alliance], etc.

The phrase "openly arrived at" need not cause difficulty. In fact, the President explained to the Senate last winter that the phrase was not meant to exclude confidential diplomatic negotiations involving delicate matters. The intention is that nothing which occurs in the course of such confidential negotiations shall be binding unless it appears in the final covenant made public to the world.

The matter may perhaps be put this way: it is proposed that in future every treaty be part of the public law of the world, and that every nation assume a certain obligation in regard to its enforcement. Obviously, nations cannot assume obligations in matters of which they are ignorant; and therefore any secret treaty tends to undermine the solidity of the whole structure of international covenants which it is proposed to erect.

2. Absolute freedom of navigation upon the seas, outside territorial waters, alike in peace and in war, except as the seas may be closed in whole or in part by international action for the enforcement of international covenants.

This proposition must be read in connection with number 14 which proposes a league of nations. It refers to navigation under the three following conditions: (1) general peace; (2) a general war, entered into by the League of Nations for the purpose of enforcing international covenants; (3) limited war, involving no breach of international covenants.

Under "(1) General peace" no serious dispute exists. There is implied freedom to come and go [on the high seas].

No serious dispute exists as to the intention under "(2) A general war entered into by the League of Nations to enforce international covenants." Obviously such a war is conducted against an outlaw nation and complete non-intercourse with that nation is intended.

"(3) A limited war, involving no breach of international covenants" is the crux of the whole difficulty. The question is, what are to be the rights of neutral shipping and private property on the high seas during a war between a limited number of nations when that war involves no issue upon which the League of Nations cares to take sides. In other words, a war in which the League of Nations remains neutral. Clearly, it is the intention of the proposal that in such a war the rights of neutrals shall be maintained against the belligerents, the rights of both to be clearly and precisely defined in the law of nations.

3. The removal, so far as possible, of all economic barriers and the establishment of an equality of trade conditions among all the nations consenting to the peace and associating themselves for its maintenance.

The proposal applies only to those nations which accept the responsibilities of membership in the League of Nations. It means the destruction of all special commercial agreements, each putting the trade of every other nation in the League on the same basis, the most-favored-nation clause applying automatically to all members of the League of Nations. Thus a nation could legally maintain a tariff or a special railroad rate or a port restriction against the whole world, or against all the signatory powers. It could maintain any kind of restriction which it chose against a nation not in the League. But it could not discriminate as between its partners in the League.

This clause naturally contemplates fair and equitable understanding as to the distribution of raw materials.

4. Adequate guarantees given and taken that national armaments will be reduced to the lowest points consistent with domestic safety.

"Domestic safety" clearly implies not only internal policing, but the protection of territory against invasion. The accumulation of armaments above this level would be a violation of the intention of the proposal.

What guarantees should be given and taken, or what are to be the standards of judgment have never been determined. It will be necessary to adopt the general principle and then institute some kind [of international commission of investigation] to prepare detailed projects for its execution.

5. A free, open-minded and absolutely impartial adjustment of all colonial claims, based upon a strict observance of the principle that in determining all such questions of sovereignty, the interests of the populations concerned must have equal weight with the equitable claims of the government whose title is to be determined.

Some fear is expressed in France [and England] that this involves reopening of all colonial questions. Obviously it is not so intended. It applies clearly [to those] colonial claims which have been created by the war. That means the German colonies and any other colonies which may come under international consideration as a result of the war.

The stipulation is that in the case of the German colonies the title is to be determined after the conclusion of the war by "impartial adjustment" based on certain principles. These are of two kinds: (1) "equitable" claims; (2) the interests of the populations concerned.

What are the "equitable" claims put forth by Great Britain and Japan, the two chief heirs of the German colonial empire, that the colonies cannot be returned to Germany? Because she will use them as submarine bases, because she will arm the blacks, because she uses the colonies as bases of intrigue, because she oppresses the natives. What are the "equitable" claims put forth by Germany? That she needs access to tropical raw material, that she needs a field for the expansion of her population, that under the principles of the peace proposed, conquest gives her enemies no title to her colonies.

What are the "interests of the populations"? That they should not be militarized, that exploitation should be conducted on the principle of the "open door," and under the strictest regulation as to labor conditions, profits and taxes, that a sanitary regime be maintained, that permanent improvements in the way of roads, etc., be made, that native organization and custom be respected, that the protecting authority be stable and experienced enough to thwart intrigue and corruption, that the [protecting] power have adequate resources in money and competent administrators to act successfully.

It would seem as if the principle involved in this proposition is that a colonial power acts not as owner of its colonies, but as trustee for the natives and for the interests of the society of nations, that the terms on which the colonial administration is conducted are a matter of international concern and may legitimately be the subject of international inquiry, and that the peace conference may, therefore, write a code of colonial conduct binding upon [all] colonial powers.

6. The evacuation of all Russian territory and such a settlement of all questions affecting Russia as will secure the best and freest cooperation of the other nations of the world in obtaining for her an unhampered and unembarrassed opportunity for the independent determination of her own political development and national policy and assure her of a sincere welcome into the society of free nations under institutions of her own choosing; and, more than a welcome, assistance also of every kind that she may need and may herself desire. The treatment accorded Russia by her sister nations in the months to come will be the acid test of their good will, of their comprehension of her needs as distinguished from their own interests, and of their intelligent and unselfish sympathy.

The first question is whether Russian territory is synonymous with territory belonging to the former Russian Empire. This is clearly not so, because proposition 13 stipulates an independent Poland, a proposal which excludes the territorial reestablishment of the Empire. What is recognized as valid for the Poles will certainly have to be recognized for the Finns, the Lithuanians, the Letts, and perhaps also for the Ukrainians. Since the formulating of this condition these subject nationalities have emerged, and there can be no doubt that they will have to be granted an opportunity of free development.

The problem of these nationalities is complicated by two facts: (1) that they have conflicting claims; (2) that the evacuation called for in the proposal may be followed by Bolshevist revolutions in all of them.

The chief conflicts are: (*a*) between the Letts and Germans in Courland; (*b*) between the Poles and the Lithuanians on the northeast; (*c*) between the Poles and the White Ruthenians on the east; (*d*) between the Poles and the Ukrainians on the southeast (and in eastern Galicia).

In this whole borderland the relations of the German Poles [*sic*] to the other nationalities is roughly speaking that of landlord to peasant. Therefore the evacuating of the territory, if it resulted in class war, would very probably also take the form of a conflict of nationalities. It is clearly to the interests of a good settlement that the real nation in each territory should be consulted rather than the ruling and possessing class.

This can mean nothing less than the [recognition] by the peace conference of a series of [*de facto*] governments representing Finns, Esths, Lithuanians, Ukrainians. This primary [act] of recognition should be conditional upon the calling of national assemblies for the creation of *de facto* governments, as soon as the peace conference has drawn frontiers for these new states. The frontiers should be drawn so far as possible on ethnic lines, but in [every] case the right of unhampered economic [transit] should be reserved. No dynastic ties with German [or] Austrian or Romanoff princes should be permitted, and every inducement should be [given] to encourage federal [relations] between these new states. Under proposition 3 the economic sections of the treaty of Brest-Litovsk are obliterated, but this proposition should not be construed as forbidding a customs union, a monetary union, a railroad union, etc., of these states. Provision should also be made by which Great Russia can federate with these states on the same terms.

As for Great Russia and Siberia, the peace conference might well send a message asking for the creation of a government sufficiently [representative] to speak for these territories. It should be understood that economic rehabilitation is offered provided a government carrying sufficient credentials can appear at the peace conference.

The Allies should offer this provisional government any form of assistance it may need. The possibility of extending this will exist when the Dardanelles are opened.

The essence of the Russian problem then in the immediate future would seem to be: (1) the recognition of provisional governments; (2) assistance extended to and through these governments.

The Caucasus should probably be treated as part of the problem of the Turkish Empire. No information exists justifying an opinion on the proper policy in regard to Mohammedan Russia—that is, briefly, Central Asia. It may well be that some power will have to be given a limited mandate to act as protector.

In any case the treaties of Brest-Litovsk and Bucharest must be cancelled as palpably fraudulent. Provision must be made for the withdrawal of all German troops in Russia and the peace conference [will] have a clean slate on which to write a policy for all the Russian peoples.

7. Belgium, the whole world will agree, must be evacuated and restored without any attempt to limit the sovereignty which she en-

joys in common with all other free nations. No other single act will serve as this will serve to restore confidence among the nations in the laws which they have themselves set and determined for the government of their relations with one another. Without this healing act the whole structure and validity of international law is forever impaired.

The only problem raised here is in the word "restored." Whether restoration is to be in kind or how the amount of the indemnity is to be determined is a matter of detail, not of principle. The principle that should be established is that in the case of Belgium there exists no distinction between "legitimate" and "illegitimate" destruction. The initial act of invasion was illegitimate and therefore all the consequences of that act are of the same character. Among the consequences may be put the war debt of Belgium. The recognition of this principle would constitute "the healing act" of which the President speaks.

8. All French territory should be freed and the invaded portions restored, and the wrong done to France by Prussia in 1871 in the matter of Alsace-Lorraine, which has unsettled the peace of the world for nearly fifty years, should be righted in order that peace may once more be made secure in the interest of all.

In regard to the restoration of French territory it might well be argued that the invasion of northern France, being the result of the illegal act as regards Belgium, was in itself illegal. But the case is not perfect. As the world stood in 1914, war between France and Germany was not in itself a violation of international law, and great insistence should be put upon keeping the Belgian case distinct and symbolic. Thus Belgium might well, as indicated above, claim reimbursement not only for destruction but for the cost of carrying on the war. France could not claim payment, it would seem, for more than the damage done to her northeastern departments.

The status of Alsace-Lorraine was settled by the official statement issued a few days ago. It is to be restored completely to French sovereignty.

Attention is called to the strong current of French opinion which claims "the boundaries of 1914 [*1814*]" rather than of 1871. The territory claimed is the valley of the Saar with its coalfields. No claim on grounds of nationality can be established, but the argument leans on the possibility of taking this territory in lieu of indemnity;

it would seem to be a clear violation of the President's proposal.

Attention is called also to the fact that no reference is made to status of Luxemburg. The best solution would seem to be a free choice by the [people of] Luxemburg themselves.

9. A readjustment of the frontiers of Italy should be effected along clearly recognizable lines of nationality.

This proposal is less than the Italian claim; less, of course, than the territory allotted by the treaty of London; less than the arrangement made between the Italian Government and the Jugo-Slav state.

In the region of Trent the Italians claim a strategic rather than an ethnic frontier. It should be noted in this connection that [Italy] and Germany will become neighbors if German Austria joins the German Empire. And if Italy obtains the best geographical frontier she will assume sovereignty over a large number of Germans. This is a violation of principle. But it may be argued that by drawing a sharp line along the crest of the Alps, Italy's security will be enormously enhanced and the necessity of heavy armaments reduced. It might, therefore, be provided that Italy should have her claim in the Trentino, but that the northern part, inhabited by Germans, should be completely autonomous and that the population should not be liable to military service in the Italian Army. Italy could thus occupy the uninhabited Alpine peaks for military purposes, but would not govern the cultural life of the alien population to the south of her frontier.

The other problems of the frontier are questions between Italy and Jugo-Slavia, Italy and the Balkans, Italy and Greece.

The agreement reached with Jugo-Slavs may well be allowed to stand, although it should be insisted for [the protection of] the hinterland that both Trieste and Fiume be free ports. This is [essential] to Bohemia, German Austria, Hungary, as well as to prosperity of the cities themselves.

Italy appears in Balkan politics through her claim to a protectorate over Albania and the possession of Valona. There is no serious objection raised to this, [although the] terms of the protectorate need to be vigorously controlled. If Italy is protector of Albania, [the local] life of Albania should be guaranteed by the League of Nations.

A conflict with Greece appears through the Greek claim to northern Epirus, or what is now southern Albania. This would bring Greece closer to Valona than Italy desires. A second conflict with

Greece occurs over the Aegean Islands of the Dodekanese, but it is understood that a solution favorable to Greece is being worked out.

Italy's claims in Turkey belong to the problem of the Turkish Empire.

10. The peoples of Austria-Hungary, whose place among the nations we wish to see safeguarded and assured, should be accorded the freest opportunity of autonomous development.

This proposition no longer holds. Instead we have [to-day] the following elements:

(1). *Czecho-Slovakia.* Its territories include at least a million Germans for whom some provision must be made.

The independence of Slovakia means the dismemberment of the northwestern countries of Hungary.

(2). *Galicia.* Western Galicia is clearly Polish. Eastern Galicia is in large measure Ukrainian (or Ruthenian) and does not of right belong to Poland.

There also are several hundred thousand Ukrainians along the north and northeastern borders of Hungary and in parts of Bukowina (which belonged to Austria).

(3). *German Austria.* This territory should of right be permitted to join Germany, but there is strong objection in [France] because of the increase of [population] involved.

(4). *Jugo-Slavia.* It faces the following problems: (*a*) Frontier questions with Italy in Istria and the Dalmatian coast; with Roumania in the Banat. (*b*) An international problem arises out of the refusal of the Croats to accept the domination of the Serbs of the Servian Kingdom. (*c*) A problem of the Mohammedan Serbs of Bosnia who are said to be loyal to the Hapsburgs. They constitute a little less than one-third of the population.

(5). *Transylvania.* Will undoubtedly join Roumania, but provision must be made for the protection of the Magyars, Szeklers and Germans who constitute a large minority.

(6). *Hungary.* Now independent and very democratic in form, but governed by Magyars whose aim is to prevent the detachment of territory of nationalities on the fringe.

The United States is clearly committed to the program of national unity and independence. It must stipulate, however, for the protection of national minorities, for freedom of access to the Adriatic and the Black Sea, and it supports a program aiming at a confederation of southeastern Europe.

11. Roumania, [Serbia,] and Montenegro should be evacuated; occupied territories restored; Serbia accorded free and secure access to the sea; and the relations of the several Balkan states to one another determined by friendly counsel along historically established lines of allegiance and nationality; and international guarantees of the political and economic independence and territorial integrity of the several Balkan states should be entered into.

This proposal is also altered by events. Servia will appear as Jugo-Slavia with access to the Adriatic. Roumania will have acquired the Dobrudja, Bessarabia and probably Transylvania. These two states will have eleven or twelve million inhabitants and will be far greater and stronger than Bulgaria.

Bulgaria should clearly have her frontier in the southern Dobrudja as it stood before the second Balkan War. She should also have Thrace up to the Enos-Midia line and perhaps even to the Midia-Rodosto line.

Macedonia should be allotted after an impartial investigation. The line which might be taken as a basis of investigation is the southern line of the "contested zone" agreed upon by Serbia and Bulgaria before the first Balkan War.

Albania could be under a protectorate, no doubt of Italy, and its frontiers in the north might be essentially those of the London conference.

12. The Turkish portions of the present Ottoman Empire should be assured a secure sovereignty, but the other nationalities which are now under Turkish rule should be assured an undoubted security of life and an absolutely unmolested opportunity of autonomous development, and the Dardanelles should be permanently opened as a free passage to the ships and commerce of all nations under international guarantees.

The same difficulty arises here as in the case of Austria-Hungary concerning the word "autonomous."

It is clear that the Straits and Constantinople, while they may remain nominally Turkish, should be under international control. This control may be collective or be in the hands of one power as mandatory of the League.

Anatolia should be reserved for the Turks. The coast lands, where Greeks predominate, should be under special international control, perhaps with Greece as mandatory.

Armenia must be [given] a port on the Mediterranean, and a protecting power established. France may claim it, but the Armenians would prefer Great Britain.

Syria has already been allotted to France by agreement with Great Britain.

Great Britain is clearly the best mandatory for Palestine, Mesopotamia and Arabia.

A general code of guarantees binding upon all mandatories in Asia Minor should be written into the treaty of peace.

This should contain provisions for minorities and the "open door." The trunk railroad lines should be internationalized.

13. An independent Polish state should be erected which should include the territories inhabited by indisputably Polish populations, which should be assured a free and secure access to the sea, and whose political and economic independence and territorial integrity should be guaranteed by international covenants.

The chief problem is whether Poland is to obtain territory west of the Vistula, which would cut off the Germans of East Prussia from the Empire, or whether Danzig can be made a free port and the Vistula internationalized.

On the east, Poland should receive no territory in which Lithuanians or Ukrainians predominate.

If Posen and Silesia go to Poland, rigid protection must be afforded the minorities of Germans and Jews living there, as well as in other parts of the Polish state.

The principle on which frontiers will be [delimited] is contained in the President's word "indisputably." This may imply the taking of an impartial census before frontiers are marked.

14. A general association of nations must be formed under specific covenants for the purpose of affording mutual guarantees of political independence and territorial integrity to great and small [states] alike.

The principle of a league of nations as the primary essential of a permanent peace has been so clearly presented by President Wilson in his speech of September 27, 1918, that no further elucidation is required. It is the foundation of the whole diplomatic structure of a permanent peace.

APPENDIX F

MEMORANDUM NO. 65. UNITED STATES NAVAL INTERESTS IN THE ARMISTICE TERMS

Paris, France, 4 November, 1918.

I. All of the Great Powers now considering armistice terms and peace terms with the Central Powers have constantly in view postwar conditions and possibilities. It is perfectly legitimate, according to precedent, for each of those Powers to seek by the terms of armistice and by the terms of peace to strengthen to the maximum their position in the world. That they are following this policy astutely and consistently admits of no doubt.

II. There now appears to be an agreement between the representatives of Great Britain, France, and Italy by which Great Britain and France dictated the German armistice terms and Great Britain and Italy dictated the Austrian terms, Italy being accorded practically everything she asked for.

III. In view of the readiness with which France and Italy agreed to the taking over of German and Austrian vessels there can be little doubt that an understanding exists between France, Italy, and Great Britain as to the distribution of these vessels. In other words, there have been councils on this subject of vital importance to us from which we have been excluded.

IV. Table I gives the present strength of those Powers in dreadnoughts, battle cruisers, destroyers, and submarines:

TABLE I.—PRESENT BUILT

	Dreadnoughts	*Battle Cruisers*	*Destroyers*	*Submarines*
Great Britain	33	10	425	136
France	7	0	43	64
Italy	5	0	33	41
Japan	6	7	67	17
United States	17	0	172	55
Germany	21	6	218	177

V. Table II, which follows, gives a probable distribution of the German and Austrian vessels required by the armistice terms to be surrendered to the Allies, on the assumption that Great Britain gets two vessels for each one that is apportioned to France, Italy, and Japan, the United States not participating in the distribution. It is believed to be the correct policy for the United States not to participate in this distribution.

TABLE II.—ASSUMED DISTRIBUTION

	Dreadnoughts	*Battle Cruisers*	*Destroyers*	*Submarines*
Great Britain	2	6	24	70
France	4	0	12	35
Italy	4	0	12	35
Japan	3	0	11	35
United States	0	0	0	0

VI. By combining Tables I and II we get the probable postwar strength of the six greatest naval powers, as follows:

TABLE III.—PROBABLE POSTWAR STRENGTH

	Dreadnoughts	*Battle Cruisers*	*Destroyers*	*Submarines*
Great Britain	35	16	449	206
United States	17	0	172	55
France	11	0	55	99
Japan	9	7	78	52
Italy	9	0	45	76
Germany	11	0	168	17

VII. Table IV gives a comparison of strength of the principal naval Powers before and after the possible distribution of those German and Austrian vessels that are required by the armistice terms to be surrendered to the Allies and the United States:

TABLE IV.—TOTAL CAPITAL SHIPS BEFORE AND AFTER DISTRIBUTION

	Before	*After*		*Before*	*After*
Great Britain	43	51	Japan	13	16
United States	17	17	Italy	5	9
France	7	11	Germany	27	11

VIII. Assuming the distribution made as indicated, the United States with 17 modern capital ships would be faced at once with an alliance between Great Britain and Japan controlling a total of 67 capital ships. Even with Japan left out Great Britain would face us with three times the number of capital ships that we have. This in itself is an intolerable situation, but if we join to the mere recital of figures political considerations which we know has [*sic*] governed in the past, we shall see more clearly that our national interest demands that this distribution of vessels shall not take place.

IX. Four great Powers have arisen in the world to compete with Great Britain for commercial supremacy on the seas—Spain, Holland, France, Germany. Each one of those Powers in succession have [*sic*] been defeated by Great Britain and her fugitive Allies. A fifth commercial Power, the greatest one yet, is now arising to compete for at least commercial equality with Great Britain. Already the signs of jealousy are visible. Historical precedent warns us to watch closely the moves we make or permit to be made.

X. If the German and Austrian Fleets be reduced by those vessels designated in the armistice terms for surrender or internment, and if those vessels be destroyed—

(a) Other European nations will require no increase in their fleets, since French and Italian interests do not conflict and neither nation can compete with Great Britain at sea. Germany will be out of the running for many years because of the burdens of an imposed peace.

(b) The relative naval strengths of Great Britain, France, Italy, and Japan will remain unchanged, but the naval position of the United States will be greatly weakened, since there will remain in Europe no real balancing influence on the activities of the British Fleet.

(c) Japan will require no augmentation of her fleet unless her intentions are hostile to the interests of the United States.

(d) The alliance between Great Britain and Japan will still be strong in relation to the United States in the proportion of 56 capital ships to 17—a more than three to one preponderance.

XI. With these facts in view, we may be sure that if Great Britain demands, either directly or, as is more likely, indirectly through France or Italy, a distribution of surrendered and interned vessels that she has solely in view her future relations with the United States. A prominent British subject recently said to an American in Sweden: "If you want freedom of the seas you jolly well will have to fight for it."

XII. The distribution of German and Austrian submarines would be a special menace to all the merchant ships of the world, no matter into whose hands those submarines fell. Prominent officers in the British Admiralty have justified on military grounds the German use of submarines in unrestricted warfare.

XIII. Unless we leave in Europe some restraining influence on British naval power Great Britain will be able to exert throughout the world an influence unknown to her in time of peace in the recent past. It may be right and proper that she shall have a greater navy than any other European Power, since she must by the nature of her insular position assure to herself the opportunity to live by the importation of food. It is not, however, in the interest of humanity that she shall occupy so commanding a naval position that she may regulate the high seas through the world in accordance with her will.

CONCLUSIONS

1. All German and Austrian submarines should be destroyed.
2. No German or Austrian naval vessel should be used to increase the naval armament of any power whatsoever.[1]

1. Navy Department, Office of Naval Intelligence, Historical Section, Publication Number 7. *The American Naval Planning Section London* (Washington, Government Printing Office, 1923), pp. 457–460.

APPENDIX G

CONDITIONS OF AN ARMISTICE WITH GERMANY

A. On the western front

I. Cessation of hostilities on land and in the air six hours after the signature of the Armistice.

II. Immediate evacuation of the invaded countries: Belgium, France, Luxembourg, as well as Alsace-Lorraine, so ordered as to be completed within fifteen days from the signature of the Armistice. German troops which have not evacuated the above-mentioned territories within the period fixed will be made prisoners of war. Joint occupation by the Allied and United States forces shall keep pace with evacuation in these areas. All movements of evacuation or occupation shall be regulated in accordance with a note (annex No. 1), drawn up at the time of signature of the Armistice.

III. Repatriation, beginning at once, to be completed within fifteen days, of all inhabitants of the countries above enumerated (including hostages, persons under trial, or convicted).

IV. Surrender in good condition by the German Armies of the following war material:

- 5,000 guns (2,500 heavy, 2,500 field).
- 25,000 machine guns.
- 3,000 trench mortars.
- 1,700 fighting and bombing aeroplanes—in the first place, all D7's and all night-bombing aeroplanes.

The above to be delivered *in situ* to the Allied and United States troops in accordance with the detailed conditions laid down in the note (annex No. 1) determined at the time of the signing of the Armistice.

V. Evacuation by the German Armies of the districts on the left bank of the Rhine. These districts on the left bank of the Rhine shall be administered by the local authorities under the control of the Allied and United States Armies of Occupation.

The occupation of these territories by Allied and United States troops shall be assured by garrisons holding the principal crossings of the Rhine (Mainz, Coblenz, Cologne), together with bridgeheads at these points of a 30-kilometer radius on the right bank, and by garrisons similarly holding the strategic points of the area.

A neutral zone shall be reserved on the right bank of the Rhine, between the river and a line drawn parallel to the bridgeheads and to the river and 10 kilometers distant from them, between the Dutch frontier and the Swiss frontier.

The evacuation by the enemy of the Rhine districts (right and left banks) shall be so ordered as to be completed within a further period of 16 days, in all 31 days after the signing of the Armistice.

All movements of evacuation and occupation shall be regulated according to the note (annex No. 1) determined at the time of the signing of the Armistice.

VI. In all territories evacuated by the enemy, evacuation of the inhabitants shall be forbidden; no damage or harm shall be done to the persons or property of the inhabitants.

No person shall be prosecuted for having taken part in any military measures previous to the signing of the Armistice.

No destruction of any kind to be committed.

Military establishments of all kinds shall be delivered intact, as well as military stores, food, munitions and equipment, which shall not have been removed during the periods fixed for evacuation.

Stores of food of all kinds for the civil population, cattle, etc., shall be left *in situ.*

No measure of a general character shall be taken, and no official order shall be given which would have as a consequence the depreciation of industrial establishments or a reduction of their personnel.

VII. Roads and means of communications of every kind, railroads, waterways, roads, bridges, telegraphs, telephones, shall be in no manner impaired.

All civil and military personnel at present employed on them shall remain.

5,000 locomotives and 150,000 wagons, in good working order, with all necessary spare parts and fittings, shall be delivered to the Associated Powers within the period fixed in annex 2, not exceeding 31 days in all.

5,000 motor lorries are also to be delivered in good condition within 36 days.

The railways of Alsace-Lorraine shall be handed over within 31 days, together with all personnel and material belonging to the organization of this system.

Further, the necessary working material in the territories on the left bank of the Rhine shall be left *in situ.*

All stores of coal and material for the upkeep of permanent way, signals and repair shops shall be left *in situ* and kept in an efficient state by Germany, so far as the working of the means of communication on the left bank of the Rhine is concerned.

All lighters taken from the Allies shall be restored to them.

The note (annex 2) defines the details of these measures.

VIII. The German Command shall be responsible for revealing within 48 hours after the signing of the Armistice, all mines or delay-action fuses disposed on territories evacuated by the German troops, and shall assist in their discovery and destruction.

The German Command shall also reveal all destructive measures that may have been taken (such as poisoning or pollution of wells, springs, etc.).

Breaches of these clauses will involve reprisals.

IX. The right of requisition shall be exercised by the Allied and United States armies in all occupied territories save for settlement of accounts with authorized persons.

The upkeep of the troops of occupation in the Rhine districts (excluding Alsace-Lorraine) shall be charged to the German Government.

X. The immediate repatriation, without reciprocity, according to detailed conditions which shall be fixed, of all Allied and United States prisoners of war, including those under trial and condemned. The Allied Powers and the United States of America shall be able to dispose of these prisoners as they think fit. This condition annuls all other conventions regarding prisoners of war, including that of July 1918, now being ratified. However, the return of German prisoners of war interned in Holland and Switzerland shall continue as heretofore. The return of German prisoners of war shall be settled at the conclusion of the peace preliminaries.

XI. Sick and wounded who cannot be removed from territory evacuated by the German forces shall be cared for by German personnel, who shall be left on the spot with the material required.

B. *Dispositions relating to the eastern frontiers of Germany.*

XII. All German troops at present in any territory which before the war formed part of Austria-Hungary, Roumania, or Turkey, shall withdraw within the frontiers of Germany as they existed on August 1, 1914, and all German troops at present in territories which before the war formed part of Russia, must likewise return to within the frontiers of Germany as above defined, as soon as the Allies shall think the moment suitable, having regard to the internal situation of these territories.

XIII. Evacuation of German troops to begin at once, and all German instructors, prisoners and agents, civilian as well as military, now on the territory of Russia (as defined on August 1, 1914) to be recalled.

XIV. German troops to cease at once all requisitions and seizures and any other coercive measures with a view to obtaining supplies intended for Germany in Roumania and Russia (as defined on August 1, 1914).

XV. Annulment of the treaties of Bucharest and Brest-Litovsk and of the supplementary treaties.

XVI. The Allies shall have free access to the territories evacuated by the Germans on their eastern frontier, either through Danzig or by the Vistula, in order to convey supplies to the populations of these territories or for the purpose of maintaining order.

C. *Clause relating to East Africa.*

XVII. Evacuation of all German forces operating in East Africa within a period specified by the Allies.

D. *General clauses.*

XVIII. Repatriation without reciprocity, within a maximum period of one month, in accordance with detailed conditions hereafter to be fixed, of all interned civilians, including hostages and persons under trial and condemned, who may be subjects of Allied or Associated States other than those mentioned in Clause III.

Financial clauses.

XIX. With the reservation that any subsequent concessions and claims by the Allies and United States remain unaffected, the following financial conditions are imposed:

Reparation for damage done.

While the Armistice lasts, no public securities shall be removed by the enemy which can serve as a pledge to the Allies to cover reparation for war losses.

Immediate restitution of the cash deposit in the National Bank of Belgium and, in general, immediate return of all documents, specie, stocks, shares, paper money, together with plant for the issue thereof affecting public or private interests in the invaded countries.

Restitution of the Russian and Roumanian gold yielded to Germany or taken by that Power.

This gold to be delivered in trust to the Allies until peace is concluded.

E. *Naval clauses.*

XX. Immediate cessation of all hostilities at sea, and definite information to be given as to the position and movements of all German ships.

Notification to be given to neutrals that freedom of navigation in all territorial waters is given to the navies and mercantile marines of the Allied and Associated Powers, all questions of neutrality being waived.

XXI. All naval and mercantile marine prisoners of war of the Allied and Associated Powers in German hands to be returned without reciprocity.

XXII. To surrender at the ports specified by the Allies and the United States all submarines at present in existence (including all submarine cruisers and minelayers), with armament and equipment complete. Those that cannot put to sea shall be deprived of armament and equipment, and shall remain under the supervision of the Allies and the United States. Submarines ready to put to sea shall be prepared to leave German ports immediately on receipt of a wireless order to sail to the port of surrender, the remainder to follow as early as possible. The conditions of this article shall be completed within 14 days of the signing of the Armistice.

XXIII. The following German surface warships which shall be designated by the Allies and the United States of America, shall forthwith be disarmed and thereafter interned in neutral ports, or, failing them, Allied ports, to be designated by the Allies and the United States of America, and placed under the surveillance of the Allies and the United States of America, only caretakers being left on board, namely:

6 battle cruisers.
10 battleships.
8 light cruisers (including two minelayers).
50 destroyers of the most modern type.

All other surface warships (including river craft) are to be concentrated in German naval bases to be designated by the Allies and the United States of America, completely disarmed and placed under the supervision of the Allies and the United States of America. All vessels of the auxiliary fleet are to be disarmed. All vessels specified for internment shall be ready to leave German ports seven days after the signing of the Armistice. Directions for the voyage shall be given by wireless.

XXIV. The Allies and the United States of America shall have the right to sweep up all minefields and destroy all obstructions laid by Germany outside German territorial waters, and the positions of these are to be indicated.

XXV. Freedom of access to and from the Baltic to be given to the navies and mercantile marines of the Allied and Associated Powers. This to be secured by the occupation of all German forts, fortifications, batteries and defence works of all kinds in all the routes from the Cattegat into the Baltic, and by the sweeping up and destruction of all mines and obstructions within and without German territorial waters without any questions of neutrality being raised by Germany, and the positions of all such mines and obstructions to be indicated, and the plans relating thereto are to be supplied.

XXVI. The existing blockade conditions set up by the Allied and Associated Powers are to remain unchanged, and all German merchant ships found at sea are to remain liable to capture. The Allies and United States contemplate the provisioning of Germany during the Armistice as shall be found necessary.

XXVII. All aerial forces are to be concentrated and immobilized in German bases to be specified by the Allies and the United States of America.

XXVIII. In evacuating the Belgian coasts and ports, Germany shall abandon, *in situ* and intact, the port material and material for inland waterways, also all merchant ships, tugs and lighters, all naval aircraft and air materials and stores, all arms and armaments and all stores and apparatus of all kinds.

XXIX. All Black Sea ports are to be evacuated by Germany; all Russian warships of all descriptions seized by Germany in the Black Sea are to be handed over to the Allies and the United States of America; all neutral merchant ships seized in the Black Sea are to be released; all warlike and other materials of all kinds seized in those ports are to be returned, and German materials as specified in Clause XXVIII are to be abandoned.

XXX. All merchant ships at present in German hands belonging to the Allied and Associated Powers are to be restored to ports specified by the Allies and the United States of America without reciprocity.

XXXI. No destruction of ships or of materials to be permitted before evacuation, surrender or restoration.

XXXII. The German Government shall formally notify all the neutral Governments, and particularly the Governments of Norway, Sweden, Denmark and Holland, that all restrictions placed on the trading of their vessels with the Allied and Associated countries, whether by the German Government or by private German interests, and whether in return for specific concessions, such as the export of shipbuilding materials, or not, are immediately cancelled.

XXXIII. No transfers of German merchant shipping of any description to any neutral flag are to take place after signature of the Armistice.

F. Duration of the Armistice.

XXXIV. The duration of the Armistice is to be 36 days, with option to extend. During this period, on failure of execution of any of the above clauses, the Armistice may be repudiated by one of the contracting parties on 48 hours' previous notice. It is understood that failure to execute Articles III and XVIII completely in the periods specified is not to give reason for a repudiation of the Armistice, save where such failure is due to malice aforethought.

To assure the execution of the present convention under the most favorable conditions, the principle of a permanent International Armistice Commission is recognized. This Commission shall act under the supreme authority of the High Command, military and naval, of the Allied Armies.

The present Armistice was signed on the 11th day of November 1918, at 5 o'clock A.M. (French time).

F. Foch — Erzberger
R. E. Wemyss — A. Oberndorff
v. Winterfeldt
Vanselow

Index

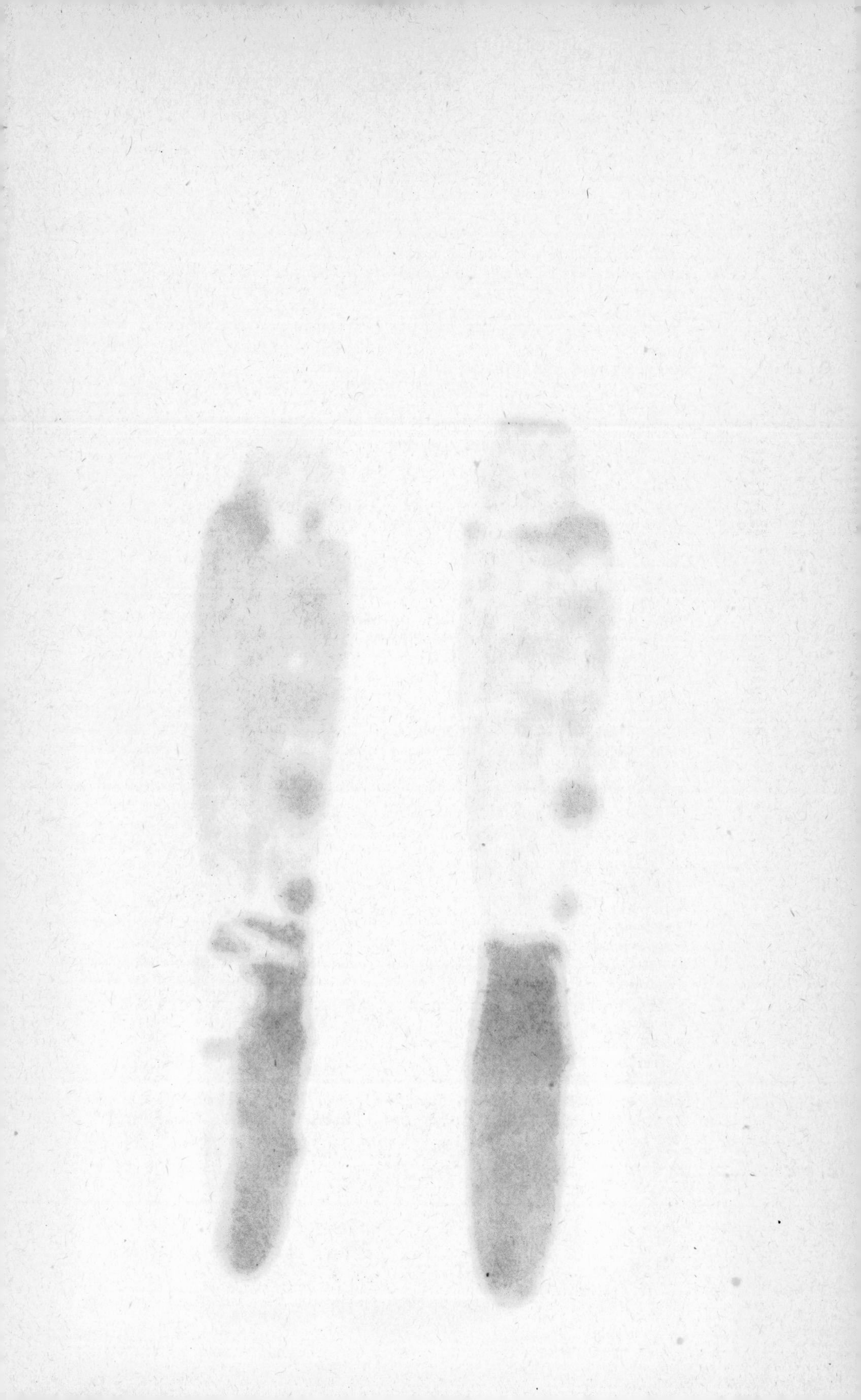

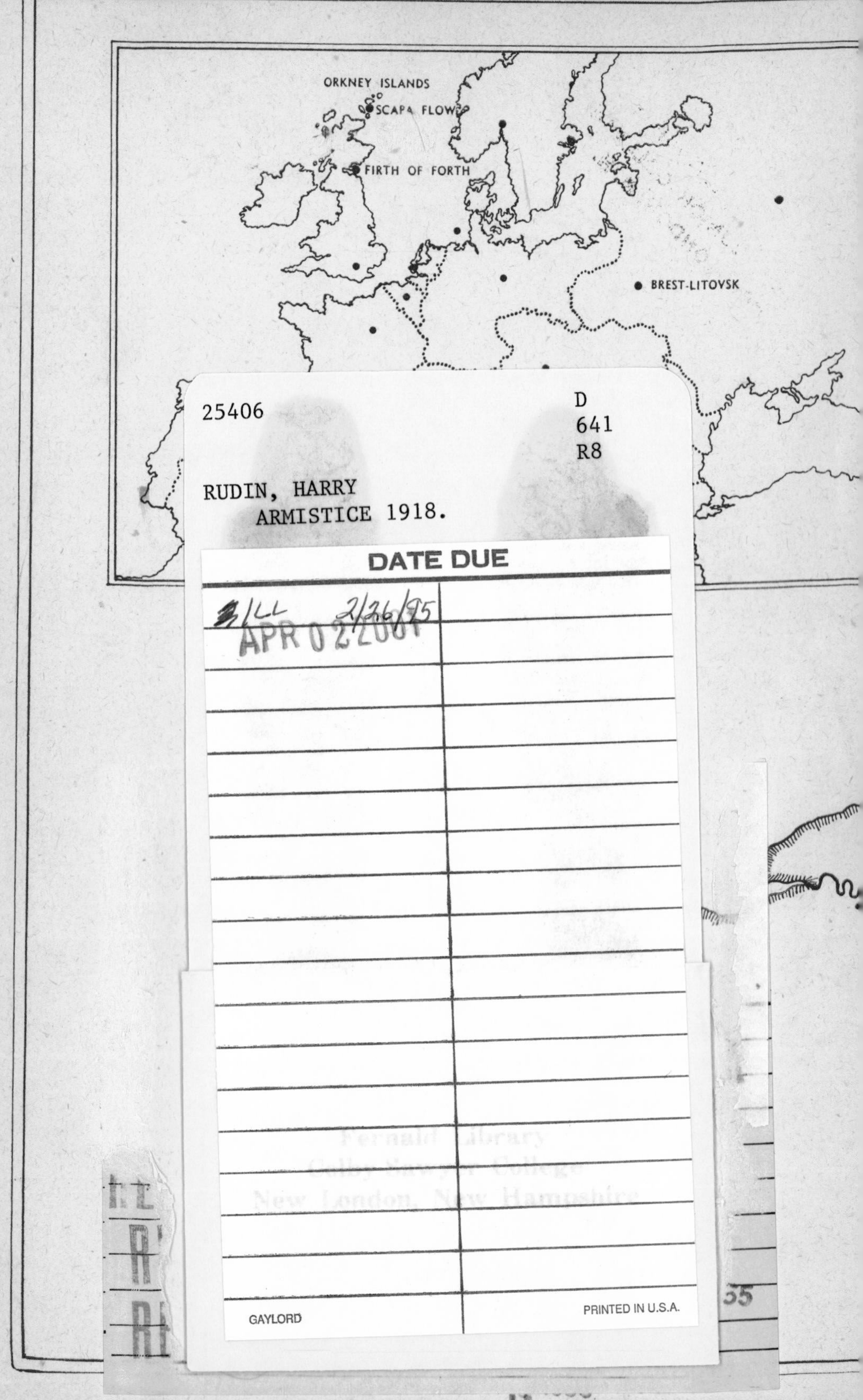
ORKNEY ISLANDS
SCAPA FLOW
FIRTH OF FORTH
BREST-LITOVSK